# MARXISM, COLONIALISM, AND CRICKET

|||||

**THE C. L. R. JAMES ARCHIVES** recovers and reproduces for a contemporary audience the work of one of the great intellectual figures of the twentieth century, in all their rich texture, and will present, over and above historical works, new and current scholarly explorations of James's oeuvre.

*Robert A. Hill, Series Editor*

# MARXISM, COLONIALISM, AND CRICKET

C. L. R. James's *Beyond a Boundary*

| | | | |

DAVID FEATHERSTONE,

CHRISTOPHER GAIR, CHRISTIAN HØGSBJERG,

AND ANDREW SMITH, EDITORS

DUKE UNIVERSITY PRESS   DURHAM AND LONDON   2018

© 2018 Duke University Press
All rights reserved
Printed in the United States of America on acid-free paper ∞
Designed by Amy Ruth Buchanan
Typeset in Arno Pro by Westchester Publishing Services

Library of Congress Cataloging-in-Publication Data
Names: Featherstone, David, [date] editor. | Gair, Christopher, [date] editor. | Høgsbjerg, Christian, [date] editor. | Smith, Andrew, [date] editor.
Title: Marxism, colonialism, and cricket : C. L. R. James's Beyond a Boundary / edited by David Featherstone, Christopher Gair, Christian Høgsbjerg, and Andrew Smith.
Description: Durham : Duke University Press, 2018. | Series: The C. L. R. James archives | Includes bibliographical references and index.
Identifiers: LCCN 2018008224 (print)
LCCN 2018009530 (ebook)
ISBN 9781478002550 (ebook)
ISBN 9781478001126 (hardcover : alk. paper)
ISBN 9781478001478 (pbk. : alk. paper)
Subjects: LCSH: James, C. L. R. (Cyril Lionel Robert), 1901–1989. Beyond a boundary. | Cricket—West Indies. | Sports and state—West Indies. | West Indies—Social conditions.
Classification: LCC GV928.W47 (ebook) | LCC GV928.W47 J3536 2018 (print) | DDC 796.35809729—dc23
LC record available at https://lccn.loc.gov/2018008224

Cover art: West Indies captain Frank Worrell leading his team onto the field, followed by fast bowler Wes Hall. The Saffrons, Eastbourne, England, 1963. Photo by Ken Kelly/Popperfoto/Getty Images.

# CONTENTS

FOREWORD | Opening Up
DAVID FEATHERSTONE, CHRISTOPHER GAIR,
CHRISTIAN HØGSBJERG, AND ANDREW SMITH  vii

INTRODUCTION | *Beyond a Boundary* at Fifty
DAVID FEATHERSTONE, CHRISTOPHER GAIR,
CHRISTIAN HØGSBJERG, AND ANDREW SMITH  1

## Part I: Cricket, Empire, and the Caribbean

1  C. L. R. James: Plumbing His Caribbean Roots
SELWYN R. CUDJOE  35

2  C. L. R. James's "British Civilization"? Exploring the "Dark Unfathomed Caves" of *Beyond a Boundary*
CHRISTIAN HØGSBJERG  51

3  The Boundaries of Publication: The Making of *Beyond a Boundary*
ROY MCCREE  72

4  "West Indian Through and Through, and Very British": C. L. R. James's *Beyond a Boundary*, Coloniality, and Theorizing Caribbean Independence
MINKAH MAKALANI  88

5  Looking Beyond the Boundary, or Bondman without the Bat: Modernism and Culture in the Worldview of C. L. R. James
DAVID AUSTIN  103

## Part II: The Politics of Representation in Beyond a Boundary

6  "Periodically I Pondered over It": Reading the Absence/Presence of Women in *Beyond a Boundary*
ANIMA ADJEPONG  123

7   C. L. R. James, W. G. Grace, and the Representative Claim
    NEIL WASHBOURNE   137

8   Shannonism: Learie Constantine and the Origins of
    C. L. R. James's Worrell Captaincy Campaign of 1959–60:
    A Preliminary Assessment
    CLEM SEECHARAN   153

## Part III: Art, History, and Culture in C. L. R. James

9   C. L. R. James and the Arts of *Beyond a Boundary*: Literary
    Lessons, Cricketing Aesthetics, and World-Historical Heroes
    CLAIRE WESTALL   173

10  The Very Stuff of Human Life: C. L. R. James on Cricket,
    History, and Human Nature
    ANDREW SMITH   191

11  C. L. R. James: Beyond the Boundaries of Culture
    PAGET HENRY   204

## Part IV: Reflections

12  Socrates and C. L. R. James
    MICHAEL BREARLEY   223

13  My Journey to James: Cricket, Caribbean Identity,
    and Cricket Writing
    HILARY MCD. BECKLES   240

14  Confronting Imperial Boundaries
    SELMA JAMES   254

APPENDIX | What Do They Know of England?
C. L. R. JAMES   263

REFERENCES   267

CONTRIBUTORS   283

INDEX   287

FOREWORD | Opening Up

DAVID FEATHERSTONE, CHRISTOPHER GAIR,
CHRISTIAN HØGSBJERG, AND ANDREW SMITH

*Beyond a Boundary* is that rarest of things: a serious book about popular culture, a book that reckons with the ways in which sporting practices can express political meanings and can act as the "muster points" of political struggle while also being shaped in themselves by the passions and divisions of the historical contexts in which people play and watch sports. Rarer still, perhaps, it is a serious book that has become profoundly popular, taken up not just by scholars or by the cricket cognoscenti but by audiences across the world. (The first translated version, to the best of our knowledge, has just been completed in Japan by Ted Motohashi, under the title *Kyokai wo Koete* [境界を越えて].) The enduring popularity of James's book is, in that respect, both a testament to the lucidity of his writing and a vindication of his lifelong defense of the capacity for astute critical awareness on the part of ordinary readers. This volume brings together a collection of new essays and reflections on *Beyond a Boundary* by writers from the United Kingdom, the United States, and the Caribbean. In the wake of the fiftieth anniversary of the publication of the text, it provides the first collection of critical studies dedicated to James's masterpiece. These essays acknowledge and celebrate James's achievement, but they also recognize the truth of Stuart Hall's injunction that to honor James means taking his ideas "seriously and debating them, extending them, quarrelling with them and making them live again" (Hall 1992: 3). In that respect they include critical questioning of—among other things—James's treatment of gender, his historical analysis of cricketing development, the representative qualities that he ascribed to leading players of the game, and the effects of James's own background on his ideas and presumptions. We hope, in this respect, that they open up new ways to engage with and make use of *Beyond a Boundary* for the future.

This volume has its roots in a conference held at the University of Glasgow in 2013, timed to coincide with, and celebrate, the fiftieth anniversary of the publication of *Beyond a Boundary*. We received considerable financial support from a range of sources, which made the conference possible. In particular, we acknowledge the support of the Economic and Social Research Council (ESRC)'s Centre on Dynamics of Ethnicity (ESRC Grant ES/K002198/1) and, at the University of Glasgow, the School of Critical Studies, the School of Social and Political Sciences, and the Human Geography Research Group. All sessions at the conference were filmed by the cooperative filmmaking group World Write, whose feature-length documentary on James, *Every Cook Can Govern: The Life, Impact and Works of C. L. R. James*, was released in 2016. Footage from the conference is available via World Write's online portal dedicated to James and his work (www.clrjames.uk). The site also includes the video record of a keynote address by Robert A. Hill that compellingly situates *Beyond a Boundary* in its historical and political context, as well as further keynote addresses by Wai Chee Dimock and Mike Brearley and a closing plenary discussion involving Selwyn Cudjoe, Clem Seecharan, and Selma James. The presence of the filmmakers at the conference was enabled by the support of the Glasgow University Knowledge Exchange Fund.

During the course of the writing of this volume a number of significant scholars and activists who contributed to our understanding of *Beyond a Boundary* and the wider politics of sporting and cultural practices in our world, died. By way of tribute we would just like to record their names here: Lionel Cliffe, both a pioneering political economist of Africa and an antiracist campaigner in Yorkshire cricket; Stuart Hall, whose work engaged so persistently and originally with conjectures and intersections which were of interest to James; Darcus Howe, James's great-nephew and himself a theorist, activist, and West Indian cricket fan; Mike Marqusee, whose penetrating readings of the politics of contemporary cricket are so much in the spirit of James himself; Frank Rosengarten, whose critical study of James remains necessary reading for anyone interested in understanding his work. Finally, we owe a debt of thanks to all of those who attended the conference in Glasgow and whose papers and other contributions made it such a stimulating event, as well as to the many students and administrative staff who worked very hard, behind the scenes, to make sure that things ran smoothly.

INTRODUCTION | *Beyond a Boundary* at Fifty

DAVID FEATHERSTONE, CHRIST(
GAIR, CHRISTIAN HØGSBJERG, AND
ANDREW SMITH

This book is neither cricket reminiscence nor autobiography. It poses the question *What do they know of cricket who only cricket know?* To answer involves ideas as well as facts.
—C. L. R. James, *Beyond a Boundary* (1963)

Sexual intercourse began
In nineteen sixty-three
(which was rather late for me)—
Between the end of the *Chatterley* ban
And the Beatles' first LP.
—Philip Larkin, "Annus Mirabilis" (1967)

*Beyond a Boundary* was published at a pivotal moment in world history, making it, in some ways, a key harbinger of the events that would transform the world in the 1960s. At that point, C. L. R. James was at the vanguard of the struggle for West Indian self-government that was matched by independence movements in Africa and by civil rights in the United States. He had campaigned tirelessly—and successfully—for the appointment of Frank Worrell as captain of the West Indian cricket team at a time when the role had almost always been held by white men and recorded, with joy, the reception accorded Worrell's team in Australia in 1960–61. He was one of the first cultural historians to listen to the voices of the people and recognize the significance of sports as a marker of wider transformative patterns, and he was perhaps the first writer to proffer a sustained case for sports to be appreciated as art.

In other ways, however, there is a danger that the book appears to be little more than a historical relic: self-government was achieved for Trinidad and Tobago and for Jamaica in August 1962 and for Barbados in 1966, while in the United States, President Lyndon B. Johnson signed the Civil Rights Act in July 1964. At the other extreme, the assassinations of John F. and Bobby Kennedy, Malcolm X, and Martin Luther King signified a shift that, while far from unprecedented (with, for example, Leon Trotsky's assassination coming the year after James had visited him in Mexico in 1939), represented a sinister side of the 1960s. In other ways, the decade of the Beatles, Jimi Hendrix, the Black Power and women's liberation movements, free love, and Woodstock seemed far removed from the "security-minded age" (James 2013 [1963]: 216) of men in gray-flannel suits that James describes as the context for the dull cricket that he watched in England after his return from the United States.[1] While James wrote much of *Beyond a Boundary* during the 1950s—an era that tends to be remembered in terms of drab standardization—it is notable that in redrafting the manuscript in 1962, he felt that he "had no need to change a word" about "the rut into which [cricket] had sunk" (213).

In "Annus Mirabilis," Philip Larkin identifies 1963 as the year in which the swinging '60s really began and a moment when, in Britain, the drab austerity of the postwar years was finally cast off. While he did not have cricket in mind, 1963 was also something of an annus mirabilis for the game and the moment in which the transformation from the dull, ensure-the-draw-first mentality to the modern version of the sport began. Unexpectedly, perhaps, one marker of this occurred at Lord's during the Test between England and the West Indies, where Brian Close repeatedly ran down the wicket to Wes Hall and Charlie Griffith in an attempt to score quick runs and win the match. This could have been seen as an isolated incident, and the game is best remembered now for the grainy black-and-white television images of David Allen blocking out the final balls to ensure a draw rather than attempting to secure victory, while Colin Cowdrey looked on from the other end, having heroically returned with his arm in plaster after it was broken by Hall. Nevertheless, the year also witnessed the first staging of the Gillette Cup, initially a sixty-five overs per side competition, designed to save the county game in England from bankruptcy. Of course, the introduction of corporate-sponsored one-day cricket—seen at the time as a second string to the County Championship—revolutionized the game that James had known up to the publication of *Beyond a Boundary* and, ultimately, has also had a pronounced effect on how Test cricket is played. Given the success of its most recent descendants—the Indian Premier League (IPL), the Australian KFC Twenty20 Big Bash League, and other, similar tournaments—it could be argued that Learie Constantine's prediction (made to James) that ' of cricket lies along the road of the league" (134) has been real ironically, in a format entirely alien to Constantine and James. these developments later, but they serve to make clear the ext· cricket might be taken to have strayed far from the hope, expressed by J... at the end of *Beyond a Boundary*, that Worrell's batting in Australia in 1960–61 heralded a return to a cherished Golden Age (259).

While *Beyond a Boundary* is most frequently discussed in terms of cricket and postcolonial and transnational studies, it also returns repeatedly to James's other "obsession" (17)—with Thackeray's *Vanity Fair* (1847–48) in particular, and more generally with nineteenth-century English literature and its role in the transformation of English society. James's reading of the centrality of W. G. Grace as a seminal figure in the emergence of "organized sport" at a moment in which "this same public that wanted sports and games so eagerly wanted popular democracy too" (153) is twinned with his appreciation of the place of Charles Dickens in the Victorian imagination. Thus, for example, "In 1854 *Hard Times* showed labour rebellious and despairing against the conditions imposed upon it by the new industrial processes" (161) in a manner that was understood by large numbers of readers and whose significance extended far beyond the realms of "high" culture.

Unsurprisingly, given his fifteen-year residence in the United States and encyclopedic knowledge of American literary culture—as illustrated in *Mariners, Renegades and Castaways* (1953) and the posthumously published *American Civilization* (1992)—James is also well versed in nineteenth-century American fiction and references it in *Beyond a Boundary*. Thus, among many pertinent allusions to the United States and its culture, James devotes an important passage to Harriet Beecher Stowe's antislavery novel *Uncle Tom's Cabin* (1852), the best-selling work of fiction in the United States in the nineteenth century, and to the immensely popular stage adaptations that continued to pack theaters for the next fifty years. The reference to Stowe is indicative of James's willingness to illustrate his argument with allusions to popular literary-political culture that extend well beyond the Caribbean and British settings and provide the framework for his own book. Moreover, it serves as an exemplary instance of his ability to extrapolate across cultures to bolster his core argument. In this case, rather than limiting his argument to the specifics of the struggle against racism, he suggests that Eliza's pursuers (as she flees across the icy river to freedom) were "shot down to the cheers and tears of thousands [of theatergoers] who in real life would have nothing whatever to do with such violent disturbances of the established order" in a manner that marked largely white audiences' awareness of their own plight at a time when industrialization brought "furies vague but pursuing" (181). In itself, the moment in *Beyond a Boundary* resonates with James's recent immersion in Herman Melville's *Moby-Dick* (1851) and desire to construct class-based revolutionary narratives that were able to transcend racial boundaries. Of equal importance, however, in terms of his methodology in *Beyond a Boundary* is how James uses his allusion to Stowe elliptically, to help explain what made Grace "one of the greatest of popular heroes" because of "what he signified . . . in the lives [of the English people] that they themselves lived from day to day" (182). Like E. P. Thompson, whose *The Making of the English Working Class* was also published in 1963, James challenges conventional (for the time) writings of history in his pursuit of an understanding of how and why people lived and of what they feared and desired. As the earlier example illustrates, however, James goes further than Thompson in his ability to draw on a broad transatlantic economy of ideas to situate local and national events within transnational patterns.

It is unsurprising that the adult James should have retained his early acquired affection for the Victorian novel, since as a genre it played a preeminent role in the reformist movements of its age and could also serve as a model for the kinds of "popular democracy" that James advocated for West Indian self-government. While there are limits to the extent to which *Beyond a Boundary* can be read straightforwardly as autobiography (which we discuss in more detail later), the Dickensian version of the *bildungsroman* does leave its mark on the structure of *Beyond a Boundary*. Novels such as *The Life and Adventures of Martin Chuzzlewit* (1843–44) and *David Copperfield* (1850), for example, feature protagonists who, after early demonstrations of talent, manifest a hubristic unwillingness to heed the advice of others and must experience chastening, yet ultimately redemptive, journeys (geographical, internal, or both) before returning home fully formed and able to act as exemplary members of a particular new moral order—in Dickens's case, the English reformist middle class. James's self-representation constructs an almost quintessentially Dickensian hero: as a child, he displays talent and is rewarded with success in the form of the free exhibition to the Queen's Royal College. As he recollects near the start of *Beyond a Boundary*, however, this success was short-lived, and he quickly became a "catastrophe . . . for all . . . who were so interested in me." He continues, "My scholastic career was one long nightmare to me, my teachers and my family. My scholastic shortcomings were accompanied by breaches of discipline which I blush to think of even today" (23). The "temptation," of course, was cricket, to which James "succumbed without a struggle" (24), and he recounts how his "distracted father lectured me, punished me, flogged me," imposed curfews, and ordered him to stop playing. In time, James finds himself "entangled in such a web of lies, forged letters, borrowed clothes and borrowed money that it was no wonder that the family looked on me as a sort of trial from heaven sent to test them as Job was tested" (27–28).

While there is certainly an element of hyperbole to James's witty and self-deprecating reflections, they are important to an understanding of how *Beyond a Boundary* is structured. Toward the end of his narrative, James poses the oft-cited question, "What do they know of cricket who only cricket know?" (233). While he never says as much, it seems reasonable to suggest that this is a question that he directs in part at his own, youthful self. While the young James evidently, in one way, does know about other things, such as literature, he is unable to relate his knowledge of cricket to other elements of his life. At one level, this is simply a matter of the contrast between behavior on and off the cricket field. On the field, he writes, "We learned to obey the umpire's decision without question.... We learned to play with the team, which meant subordinating your personal inclinations, and even interests" and "never cheated" (25–26). In contrast, inside the classroom "we lied and cheated without any sense of shame.... We submitted, or did not submit, to moral discipline, according to upbringing and temperament" (25). There is, however, a much more significant structural logic to James's imperative: it is only once he has lived in England and the United States and spent many years both in the contemplation of cricketers such as Grace, Constantine, Worrell, and George Headley and in the study of political philosophy, American culture, and many other disciplines that James is able to draw the analogies that enable him to *know* cricket and to understand, for example—as he does at the book's conclusion—the relationship between his advocacy of West Indian self-government and his campaign to have Worrell made captain of the West Indian team.

It is this appreciation that enables the James who writes *Beyond a Boundary* to cast a retrospective glance on his life and draw patterns that were not apparent to his younger self. James starts his narrative with anecdotes about two local cricketers: Matthew Bondman, a "ne'er-do-well, in fact vicious character" who became "all grace and style" (4) when he had a bat in his hand, and Arthur Jones, a "medium-sized man" who "talked quickly and even stammered a little" (5), but who could play the square cut in a manner that James only rarely witnessed in Test or county cricket. As James explains, "It is only within very recent years that Matthew Bondman and the cutting of Arthur Jones ceased to be merely isolated memories and fell into place as starting points of a connected pattern. They only appear as starting points. In reality they were the end, the last stones put into place, of a pyramid whose base constantly widened, until it embraced those aspects of social relations, politics and art laid bare when the veil of the temple has been rent in twain as ours has been" (7).

James repeats the point soon after in his account of Cousin Cudjoe, a blacksmith who was "quite black, with a professional chest and shoulders." A wicketkeeper and "hitter," he had been "the only black man in a team of white men" (8) who, according to Cudjoe, took him "everywhere they went" (9). Again, James stresses that "at the time I did not understand the significance of Cudjoe . . . being the only coloured man in a white team," and even the James who reminisces on this childhood memory does not specifically seem to understand "what skill it was, or charm of manner, or both, which gave him that unique position" (9). Nevertheless, the incident offers an ironic reflection on the final chapters of the book in which the campaign to have Worrell appointed captain of the West Indian team to tour Australia depends on his replacing Gerry Alexander, who was often the only white man on the team that he captained.

| | | | |

In part, then, *Beyond a Boundary* is a book that takes shape around James's own experiences and his subsequent recognition of the ways in which those experiences formed part of a "wider pattern." Part of that pattern, however, is born of James's growing awareness of the injustices of British imperial rule in Trinidad as they manifested themselves while he was playing, watching, and reporting cricket and growing to intellectual maturity as a black colonial subject of the British Empire. "Cricket," James famously noted, "had plunged me into politics long before I was aware of it. When I did turn to politics I did not have much to learn" (65). Given that all sections of Trinidadian society had cricket clubs that regularly played one another, from the "white and often wealthy" Queen's Park to the "totally black and with no social status whatever" plebeian Stingo (49–50), it was easy to compare all the top players at close range. James never failed to be shocked and outraged at continually seeing high-quality black cricketers, such as the Stingo player and docker Telemaque, who deserved inclusion in the West Indian national side but was left out by openly ignorant and racist white selectors (71). Moreover, the simple fact that "white and wealthy" and "totally black" played cricket regularly against each other cast light on the totality of society. One moment both teams would be on the pitch, "playing with a straight bat," treating the other as equals and offering each other consolation ("bad luck"), only to then return to all the old deference and racism in the pavilion. Given this, together with the colonial state's repression of overtly political activism—particularly after the mass dockworkers strike that shook Port of Spain in late 1919—it is not surprising that some cricket matches took on immensely powerful symbolic significance, not least when the island's best "black" team, that of Shannon (with cricketers such as Constantine and Wilton St. Hill), played Queen's Park.

James himself—as a former student turned schoolmaster at the elite Queen's Royal College, to which he had won a scholarship—played not for Shannon but used to open with Clifford Roach for the more middle-class Maple. He later noted that his decision not to join Shannon delayed his intellectual and political identification with the cause of West Indian nationalism. Yet the fact that the social antagonisms of race, class, and power in this small Caribbean island implicitly played themselves out on the cricket pitch weekly meant that James always naturally felt he had the sense of seeing things whole. He would argue later that a fully comprehensive and undivided vision was something that had been lost in the modern world and was last truly seen in the great English writer William Hazlitt, who wrote wonderfully about games and sports in early nineteenth-century England, before the class conflicts of the industrial age became central to popular consciousness. James felt that early twentieth-century Caribbean society in some ways mirrored English society in the age of Hazlitt—the society that saw the creation of, among other things, the game of cricket (159–60).

In 1932, ostensibly to help his friend and compatriot Learie Constantine (who had voyaged into imperial Britain in the 1920s to play professionally for Nelson in the Lancashire League) write his autobiography *Cricket and I* (1933), James himself made the "voyage in" to the "mother country." Ross McKibbin (1998: 332) notes that "sport was one of the most powerful of England's civil cultures," and James witnessed first-hand cricket's popularity in the working-class cotton textile town of Nelson, where thousands would turn out to watch league games. James's outstandingly detailed knowledge of the game meant he soon secured a post as "the first West Indian, the first man of colour, to serve as cricket reporter for the [*Manchester*] *Guardian*" and, indeed, possibly the first black professional sports reporter in British history (Buhle 1993: 42). "It was a great feeling," James later recalled in an interview, "to sit beside *The Times* in the Number One seat allowed to the *Manchester Guardian* at Old Trafford," Lancashire's home cricket ground.[2] More crucially, this position also allowed him an opportunity to cast his gaze over a custom and practice that was not only claimed as the "national game" in the imperial metropolis itself but, since its "golden age," had become the game of English-speaking peoples across the empire. A dozen of some of James's finest articles, first for the *Manchester Guardian* (1933–35), working with Neville Cardus, and then for the *Glasgow Herald* (1937–38), have been republished as part of a wider collection of his writing on his beloved game (James 2006).[3]

As has been noted elsewhere, many of James's "central arguments" in *Beyond a Boundary* "are already discernible" in his early cricket writing, not least "his sense of the relationship between cricketing technique and a wider historical zeitgeist . . . and his passionate defense of the sport as art" (Smith 2006b: 95). James's provocative and thought-provoking comparison of the dramatic spectacle of cricket with "high art" was in keeping with the emerging tradition of cricket literature and aligned closely to Cardus's own philosophy. Yet what always also distinguished James's analysis of cricket was "the fact that he understands it to be serious and significant *because of*, and not despite, its status as a popular activity" (Smith 2006a: 49). Here the Marxism that James had embraced during the Great Depression as a result of his witnessing the rising threat of fascism in continental Europe firsthand and his experience of reading Leon Trotsky's *History of the Russian Revolution* amid the struggles of the English working class in Lancashire was arguably critical.

Yet James's writing of *Beyond a Boundary* has to be located as an attempt to make not only an intervention in the field of Marxist cultural theory but also a political intervention within the greater tumult of decolonization. James stressed the wider, implicitly political significance and symbolism of the rise of the great West Indies cricket team of the Three Ws: Worrell, Clyde Walcott, and Everton Weekes. As Stuart Hall (1992: 13–15) reminds us, "James often remarked that the British said that the Empire was won on the playing fields of Eton and would be lost on the playing fields of Lord's cricket ground. Just as the British had trained themselves to create the Empire on the playing fields, so on the playing fields they would symbolically lose the Empire." Moreover, because (as James punned), "It was the new drawing together of the energies of the Caribbean people that created the cricket team of the 1950s and allowed Worrell to play with grace," *Beyond a Boundary* "had a profound and imaginative anti-imperialist message."

Indeed, the draft manuscript of what became *Beyond a Boundary* was, for a long period, titled *Who Only Cricket Know*, inspired by the question Rudyard Kipling posed in "The English Flag": "What should they know of England who only England know?" (James 1986: 70). Although James tells us in *Beyond a Boundary* how impressed he had been as a schoolboy with Kipling's *Plain Tales from the Hills*, the fact that a veteran anti-colonialist like James could have been inspired by such a figure as Kipling—traditionally regarded as "the high priest" of the "Imperial gospel," as George Padmore (1972: 1964) described him (c.f. Westall 2010)—might seem surprising.[4] Kipling's relationship with empire was always complex, of course, although as James (1969: 23) himself would later note, he represented "the new attitude" in Britain in favor of colonialism at the zenith of British imperial power that "was signalised by the Boer War." In 1902 in "The Islanders," and after observing the mess the British had made fighting the Boers, Kipling railed against "flannelled fools at the wicket and muddied oafs in goal," urging public schools to teach boys not cricket or football but how to ride and shoot so they were better prepared in future for the real "great game" of colonial warfare (Thornton 1959: 91; c.f. Major 2008: 296). However, in the 1950s Kipling's question "What do they know of England?"—itself being leveled by racists at the black migrant workers arriving on British shores from the Caribbean—went to the crux of the matter: the crisis of national identity now posed by decolonization and mass migration. What indeed could be known of England if Britain was now without her overseas colonies? James thought a serious study of those "flannelled fools at the wicket" and the public school code connected with cricket might go some way toward coming up with an answer—and, in the process, demonstrate that black West Indians had a far deeper understanding of "British civilization" than those racists rallying to the banner "Keep Britain White." Moreover, for James, the end of empire meant it was surely time that people turned the tables and started asking questions about imperial figures such as Kipling: "What do they know of cricket who only cricket know?"

If in one sense James's work was about "British civilization," *Beyond a Boundary* was also about Caribbean civilization; as David Scott (2004: 145) suggests, "As he seeks to do with the United States in *American Civilization*, so in *Beyond a Boundary* James is sketching an outline of the *civilizational* structure of the Caribbean, the constitutive relations between culture, society and politics."

et the question of how to categorize *Beyond a Boundary* remains contentious. Some scholars have preferred to situate the work less as a *civilizational* macro-history than as a personal intervention in life writing. The late, great historian Manning Marable (1985: 38), for example, once suggested that "*Beyond a Boundary* is technically a book about West Indian cricket in the twentieth century, but it is first and foremost an autobiography of a living legend—probably the greatest social theorist of our times." Although in his preface to *Beyond a Boundary* James himself famously stressed that it "is neither cricket reminiscences nor autobiography," he did note that there was an "autobiographical framework" to the book (xxvii), a fact that we have considered.

In the important essay "'What Do Men Live By?' Autobiography and Intention in C. L. R. James's *Beyond a Boundary*" (1989), published in *Caribbean Quarterly*, Consuelo Lopez Springfield suggested that James's desire to utilize the form of autobiography flowed in part from a vindicationist urge to challenge the racist discourse epitomized by the English biographer of Thomas Carlyle, J. A. Froude, and his famous comment on the West Indies: "There are no people there, with a purpose and character of their own." As Froude (1888: 347) had put it in *The English in the West Indies*, "There has been no saint in the West Indies since Las Casas, no hero unless philonegro enthusiasm can make one out of Toussaint." Just as Toussaint Louverture, leader of the Haitian Revolution, found it necessary to write up his life story in the form of "memoirs" while in captivity to try to justify his work to the new French Emperor Napoleon Bonaparte (Girard 2014), so James was implicitly challenging racism in itself by utilizing the form of autobiography to write about himself and the lives of other West Indians.

Another possible source of inspiration for James, aside from Toussaint, may well have been Trotsky, who, in exile in Turkey from the Soviet Union in the late 1920s, wrote his masterly *My Life: An Attempt at an Autobiography* (1930). Trotsky's concerns in writing *My Life* were first and foremost to defend his political work as a revolutionary Marxist from a growing chorus of slander and denigration of "Trotskyism" as something alien and opposed to "Leninism." This grew to a crescendo in the Soviet Union after Lenin's death as part of what Trotsky (1937) declared "the Stalin school of falsification." Trotsky's *My Life* was also an outstanding demonstration of how Marxist theory and, in particular, the linked theories relating to the law of uneven and combined development and permanent revolution that Trotsky himself had done so much to develop, could illuminate and help make sense of an individual life—in this case, Trotsky's own early life growing up in what is now the rural Ukraine but then was part of the tsarist Russian empire. (For further discussion, including consideration of James's apparent use of these theories in his own account of his early life in *Beyond a Boundary*, see Høgsbjerg 2014: 76–79.)

Yet with respect to the "autobiographical framework" of *Beyond a Boundary*, James's own Marxism is in general somewhat muted, even consciously downplayed at times. "Thackeray, not Marx, bears the heaviest responsibility for me" (39), James insists early on, which most likely would have come as something of a surprise to most readers of *Beyond a Boundary* who knew the author. In *My Life*, Trotsky details his own political and intellectual evolution toward Marxism and his activism in the Marxist movement in both tsarist Russia and in exile among various émigré communities, with the narrative climaxing as Russia underwent revolution in 1905 and then 1917, giving readers a firsthand account of what it is like to be a revolutionary who plays a critical role in a social revolution. James's approach in *Beyond a Boundary* is somewhat different. Indeed, the moment James's account moves closer to the years in which he actually joins the tiny Trotskyist movement and becomes an organized revolutionary in 1934, the narrative breaks suddenly from the "autobiographical framework" that provides the chronology in parts 1–4, and moves back to the nineteenth century for a historical analysis of W. G. Grace. Indeed, the years of James's life after 1933–34 (during which he became a Marxist and was most active as an organized revolutionary, in and then outside the official Trotskyist movement in Britain and America) are covered in a solitary paragraph:

> Fiction-writing drained out of me and was replaced by politics. I became a Marxist, a Trotskyist. I published large books and small articles on these and kindred subjects. I wrote and spoke. Like many others, I expected war, and during or after war social revolution. In 1938 a lecture tour took me to the United States and I stayed there fifteen years. The war came. It did not bring soviets and proletarian power. Instead the bureaucratic-totalitarian monster grew stronger and spread. As early as 1941 I had begun to question the premises of Trotskyism. It took nearly a decade of incessant labour and collaboration to break with it and reorganise my Marxist ideas to cope with the post-war world. That was a matter of doctrine, of history, or economics and politics. These pursuits I shared with collaborators, rivals, enemies and our public. We covered the ground thoroughly. (151)

James does, of course, allude in *Beyond a Boundary* to aspects and incidents relating to his life and work as a revolutionary socialist from the mid-1930s to the mid-1950s, but it is telling that the "autobiographical framework" remerges in a fundamental sense with his return to Trinidad in 1958, and his involvement in the transition to independence in the final section of the work, part 7. Yet James's life and work from 1958 to 1962 was a period when, as Frank Rosengarten (2008) puts it, the "national-popular" tended to come before his revolutionary Marxism. Indeed, James explicitly makes the link to his pre-Marxist days in the Trinidad of his youth clear, noting that immediately on his return to the Caribbean, he "was immersed up to the eyes in 'The Case for West Indian Self-Government'" (225), a reference to the title of his earlier pamphlet from 1933.

It is unclear whether James's downplaying of his revolutionary Marxist politics throughout *Beyond a Boundary* was a conscious decision, perhaps related to the parlous state of his finances and the urgent need to find a degree of commercial success with the book. Alternatively, the decision could be understood as unconscious. It may have been dictated by James's sense of the work's form first and foremost as a meditation on cricket rather than an attempt to write an autobiography in the manner of Toussaint and Trotsky. Nonetheless, James's subtle occlusion of his political activism in *Beyond a Boundary* stands as a critical reason why Marable's suggestion that the work is "first and foremost an autobiography" remains problematic; read exclusively in this way, the book would provide us with a distinctly partial vision of James and his politics (c.f. Moore-Gilbert 2009: 19–25).

| | | | |

In a review of *Beyond a Boundary* published in *Encounter* in 1963, V. S. Naipaul notes that contemporary responses to the book failed to grasp both the full complexity of James's account and the complexity of the relationships he was seeking to understand. "With one or two exceptions," Naipaul (1972: 19) writes, "a journalistic reaction to his material—cricket—has obscured the originality of Mr. James's purpose and method." James's concern, he notes, is precisely to get beyond an understanding of West Indian cricket that situates it within a safely "picturesque" imagining of the islands: all sunshine, Carnival, and calypso. Naipaul must have had in mind reviews such as the brief notice the book received in *The Times*, the condescending conclusion of which is that "[James] manages in *Beyond a Boundary* to give in a rambling way an impression of himself and his background which is at once easy reading and useful to an understanding of the island way of life."[5] Rather more considered reviews, such as that by the poet Alan Ross in *The Observer*, praised James's "rewardingly close scrutiny of technique" and his concern to understand the game's relationship to "social history," although Ross nevertheless suggested that the book was "marred here and there by a disfiguring militancy."[6] Clearly, *Beyond a Boundary*'s insistent focus on cricket's political expressiveness was unsettling to many of James's initial readers. As George MacDonald Fraser noted in a review for one of James's former papers, the *Glasgow Herald*, "Not many Englishmen could even think of [politics] in the same thought with cover drives.... It takes a West Indian to do that, and to relate both to art, sociology, and literature."[7] Fraser's response to the book was extremely positive, but he, too, confesses that "the reader coming fresh to it may wonder how on earth a man could be a Marxist and at the same be imbued with a love amounting to worship for ... the spirit of cricket ... with all its reactionary associations." Neville Cardus's review of the book comments equally sardonically on the political lessons that James insists on drawing from the game. Despite his somewhat pointed references to James's intellectual debts ("I have sometimes had the impression that I was 'briefing' Mr. James's forensic performances" [1963: 7]), Cardus is careful to distance himself from James's prediction that cricketing values will find their way into a newly and differently arranged society.

Early reviews of *Beyond a Boundary* thus point toward one persistent and frequently skeptical line of response to the text, the first of a number of critical responses that will be considered here. This is the suggestion that James's love of cricket and his avowed politics are in contradiction. For many of his early reviewers, clearly, it was the politics that were the "disfiguring" aspect of this conjunction, although some more recent readers, such as the former cricketer Ed Smith (2008: chap. 15), have also questioned whether James's commitment to Marxism can be reconciled with his account. For many other readers, however, the problem is contrariwise: it is James's love of cricket that seems politically "disfiguring"—a "mutation," Cedric Robinson (1995: 245) has called it—and is taken to be where his otherwise critical and anti-imperial sensibility lets him down.

According to this criticism, James's defense of the cricketing "code" of conduct in *Beyond a Boundary* fails to acknowledge the ways in which that code served as a form of moral discipline in the context of empire, helping to create pliant colonial subjects (see, e.g., discussions by Alleyne 2006; Hartmann 2003; Tiffin 1995). We might question whether the historical evidence supports this view of cricket as straightforwardly a weapon of cultural imperialism. It is arguable that in both the Caribbean and other contexts such as India, the spread of the game was at least as much a result of popular appropriation as it was of its introduction to a relatively small number of elite schools (Beckles 1995b; Majumdar 2002; Stoddart 1995). Nevertheless, there is a broader point here with regard to the politics of the sport. In his superb discussion of crowd riots at West Indian grounds in the immediate context of decolonization, Orlando Patterson (1995 [1969]: 144) insisted on a much more ambivalent reading of cricket than James, arguing that the sports symbolized "the English culture we have been forced to love, for it is the only one we have, but the culture we must despise for what it has done to us." Moreover, Patterson argued, the symbolic solidarity that cricket established meant very different things before and after decolonization. In the aftermath of empire, the "we" established by West Indian cricket binds the ordinary spectator to a nationalism from which they do not benefit and against which they periodically rebel. More recently, Robert Gregg has repeated and extended these criticisms, insisting that the universalism that James wants to defend as the redemptive promise of cricket simply fails to reckon with the way in which the game is structured around exclusions. "Cricket claims but it cannot represent universal truths," Gregg (2000: 110) insists. Thus, James's defense of the "proper" boundaries of the game not only reveals a "vestigial imperialism" nestling at the heart of his text; it ties him "to a projection of a new nationalist elite" (Gregg 2000: 110).

These criticisms, which recall in some respects the skeptical response to mass culture associated with thinkers of the Frankfurt School, are reflected on in a number of the contributions that make up this volume. We might offer an initial and qualified defense of James, however, by noting that he is quite explicit in *Beyond a Boundary* that a willingness to defer to the symbolic rules governing practice on the cricket pitch does not, in any necessary sense, inculcate political or social deference. James's account of his own access to the game, won through a sustained rebellion against parental, family, and school discipline, makes this quite clear at an autobiographical level. It was also, of course, cricketing experience that informed Constantine's repudiation of colonial racism, a lesson that he presses on James (112). If James says relatively little in *Beyond a Boundary* about the sport's entailment in the construction of forms of hegemony, this is not because he is oblivious to that possibility, but because his central concern in the text is to consider the counter-hegemonic possibilities that emerge in the same moment. That counter-hegemonic potential rested on a respect for the symbolic autonomy of the cricket field; it was the rules of practice that governed cricket as a meaningful activity that allowed it to become a distinct kind of social space in and on which forms of rebellion could be enacted that were not easily enacted elsewhere in the everyday life of the colonial Caribbean (see Farred 1996a; Kingwell 2002; Smith 2006b). Having described the highly racialized and classed structure of domestic cricket in Trinidad, we might remember, James insists, against those readers who might presume to read his account as a longing for some form of historical catharsis, "I do not wish to be liberated from that past" (59). He says this, of course, *not* because he thinks nostalgically of the forms of exclusion and inequality that were expressed on the cricket fields of the Caribbean, but because he recognizes that it was—in part, at least—on those very fields that such exclusions could be called into question. Thus it is that he famously finishes his statement: "Above all, I do not wish to be liberated from its future." This is the crucial point: we would do well not to forget the emphatically dialectical approach that James brings to an understanding of the politics of sports. James was certainly guilty of ignoring the exclusions that structured cricket as it was played, especially the heavily gendered nature of the sport, and it is also the case—as is explored in contributions to this volume (see also Diawara 1990)—that his account in *Beyond a Boundary* seems at points oddly inattentive to class (or attentive to class in odd ways). But this does not in itself invalidate James's claim that, read dialectically, sports offer one context in which we might seek out the glimpses of a future that struggles to emerge from within an unequal and antagonistic present.

Kenneth Surin is among a number of the readers of *Beyond a Boundary* who have emphasized the extent to which James's whole interpretative account is oriented futureward, toward that "something yet to come" that may be discerned in the game's symbolic encounters. In two elegant essays, Surin (1995, 1996) also raises a further series of critical questions regarding *Beyond a Boundary* that merit attention. Surin takes issue, in particular, with James's willingness to celebrate, in Hegelian terms, "world historical" figures such as Garry Sobers or W. G. Grace, whose play is read as a consummation of currents of wider social and political history. Such a reading, Surin argues, not only places an impossible symbolic load on the shoulders of these individuals but also (as Gregg also notes) risks complicity with a deeply elitist view of the struggle for independence and its aftermath: "If one assumes that myriad forces and experiences constitute West Indian history, then it is hard to see how a single individual ... can 'express' even a fraction of these many impulses and dispositions" (318).

The issue of the "representative figure" in James is also addressed in some of the chapters that follow, but it is worth noting that his claim about the way in which particular players come to have representative status is not one that rests simply on a presumption about those players as individuals and their ability to compress a diverse history within themselves. Rather, James emphasizes the way in which specific players may come to be constituted as representative in and through the acclaim of the popular audience for how they play the game in a given context. "Representativeness" should thus be understood as something profoundly relational and born in part of a popular—rather than elite—search for expressions of togetherness and united purpose. The historical meaningfulness of a given player of the game in this regard is a function of the way in which audiences *find* meaning in their play rather than something that springs from within them: a gift of the crowd as much as of the gifted player.

A third and related criticism, which we touched on earlier, concerns the extent to which James's approach to making sense of the game is called into question by the way in which the sport has evolved in the fifty years since the book was published. The emergence of an increasingly cosmopolitan, professional elite whose sporting lives are played out in growing detachment from the game at any local level has, according to this argument, not only revealed the profound limitations of James's reading of the "representative" figure, but has also cast an unflattering light on a lingering romanticism in his account of the game. Without mentioning James specifically, Paul Gilroy is indicative in arguing that changes in cricketing practice make it an increasingly unlikely vehicle for progressive or popular politics: "Its old imperial logics are lost, and its civilizing codes are increasingly anachronistic and unmoving in a world sharply and permanently divided into the two great camps—a select group of winners and an ever-expanding legion of losers whose plight is more accurately represented by the TV-friendly tempo of baseball than the languor of cricket" (Gilroy 2004: 122; see also Stoddart 2006).

The game, of course, *has* changed in many ways since the publication of *Beyond a Boundary*, but we should note that an account of this kind, which interprets Test cricket as increasingly out of sync with the rhythms of globalization, is itself a profoundly Jamesian reading. A "reading" of the Indian Premier League or the Big Bash that relates those emerging forms of the game—with their compression of time, engineering of batting pyrotechnics, commodification of talent—to the changes in the wider sociopol[itical con]text of twenty-first-century capitalism would owe a profound debt [to his] pioneering efforts to understand the ways in which cricket is sha[ped by the] economic and political structures of the world in which it is playe[d.]

In this regard, the details of James's specific reading of crick[eting prac]tice in the historical moment before decolonization needs to be separated out from the wider method that he proposes for understanding the political meaningfulness of sports in general. His own consistent reinterpretation of the game at different historical conjunctures makes this amply clear. While James's focus on the interaction between audience and players would seem to imply that some form of symbolically representative relationship is always a likely outcome of spectator sport, his reading of Worrell, for example, as a player invested with the popular hopes for decolonization is clearly a view that belongs to its time. And this is indeed the point for James: all readings of the game need to be *of their time*. This does not mean, of course, that everything about the game may be explicable and discernible in any given moment. As noted earlier, James is clear that he comes to understand the significance of a figure such as Matthew Bondman many years *after* he watched him play. What it does mean is that for James, it is possible to make proper sense of the game only historically, in terms of the social and political relations out of which it emerges, relations that it cannot but refract in its own particular forms.

Where Gilroy and Surin differ markedly from James is in their implication that recent shifts in the game, or in the way in which the game is socially situated, might represent its quashing as a space of symbolic resistance. One hears here echoes of assessments, not only from Theodor Adorno's account of mass culture, but also from a writer such as Pierre Bourdieu, who has described the core trajectory of sports in capitalist society in terms of an increasingly complete commodification and a corresponding and increasingly total displacement of active popular participation into merely passive consumption: "Games produced by the people, return to the people, like 'folk music,' in the form of spectacles produced for the populace" (Bourdieu 1993: 123). James, by contrast, never lost sight of the extent to which the antagonisms of a capitalist society continually made themselves felt and were discernible on the terrain of what he called the "popular arts." His consistent defense of this dialectical reading of the popular is not simply a result of his Marxism. Not all Marxists, after all, have shared even his qualified optimism in this regard. It is a position that is also informed to an important extent by his awareness of the long history of ways in which popular cultural traditions formed a part of resistance to empire, discussions of which feature in *The Black Jacobins*; in his early survey, *A History of Negro Revolt*; and in his writings on black struggle in America. It is telling, in this respect, that James's critical attentiveness to the politics of popular culture is reflected in the work of many other writers concerned with resistance to colonialism and to racism. W. E. B. Du Bois, Ngũgĩ wa Thiong'o, Chinua Achebe, and Frantz Fanon all come to mind.

James might have despaired at much of what newer, shorter versions of cricket involve or imply for the game. He might well have seen in so-called "T20" cricket, with its repetitive clobbering, a kind of synthetic, lifeless cloning of those moments of transcendence that he looked for in the studied rhythms of a Test match. In its way, the compressed version of the game is no less destructive of cricket's expressive freedom than the dull defensiveness he so hated in English cricket of the 1950s. At the same time, though, James would not have lost sight of how these new forms of the sport still refract the *unresolved* antagonisms of a globalized world. One might "read" the IPL, for example, as the final triumph of capitalism over cricket. But a more Jamesian question would be to ask, How do those mass-mediated performances, in their frenzy *and* in their astonishing skillfulness, speak to the longing for "something yet to come" among popular audiences in India and in diaspora around the world, who face the growing inequalities of unfettered capitalism, on the one hand, and various forms of racism and exclusion, on the other?

We can conclude this brief assessment of the critical responses to James's text by noting that in many ways the nonacademic influence of *Beyond a Boundary* has been more obvious and more thoroughgoing than its academic influence. This, of course, would have been exactly how James would have wished things to be, rejecting as he did the confinements of discipline and specialism and concerned as he always was to engage with a wide public audience. Among lovers of cricket, and of sports more generally, *Beyond a Boundary* is securely established as a classic, helped in no small part by the effusive review by John Arlott (1964: 993), which claimed, succinctly, that it was "the finest book written about the game of cricket," before adding, "There may be a better book about any sport than *Beyond a Boundary*: if so, the present reviewer has not seen it." Since then its position in the canon of sporting literature has been consistently reaffirmed: the inclusion of the text in *Sports Illustrated* magazine's Top One Hundred Sports Books of All Time, and—at number 3—in the *Observer Sports Monthly*'s Top Fifty Sports Books, suggests that Arlott's verdict continues to command agreement across a broad audience. More important, perhaps, the book has been profoundly influential in shaping how cricket, and sports more generally, are written about and understood. When James addressed a debate, hosted by the Cricket Society in 1957, arguing, "Neither Toss, Weather nor Wicket Were Decisive Elements in the Defeat of Australia Last Season," one can sense his own hesitant awareness that the historical materialist interpretation of cricketing performance that he was pursuing might seem outlandish to his audience. "There is a certain point of view I am putting forward," he reiterates in his peroration; "a certain proposition that I am opening up" (James 1986: 86). James won the debate in 1957, and ever since the publication of *Beyond a Boundary* that proposition has continued to win ground. It is discernible in any number of subsequent and popular accounts of the game from different contexts, such as Derek Birley's *A Social History of English Cricket* (1999); Ramachandra Guha's *A Corner of a Foreign Field: The Indian History of a British Sport* (2002); and, recently, Peter Oborne's *Wounded Tiger: A History of Cricket in Pakistan* (2014). Oborne's book might be taken as indicative, not simply because of its explicit references to James, but also in that the study itself repeatedly seeks to relate Pakistani cricket to the passions of decolonization and to the crises and frustrated longings of postcolonial nationalism. Even for a cricket writer whose politics are markedly different from James's, the core proposition of *Beyond a Boundary* has clearly opened up a compelling way to make sense of sports.

In academic circles, however, James's reception has been more scattered and partial. Predictably, *Beyond a Boundary* is a pivotal reference point in the burgeoning field of sports studies, especially for those concerned with understanding sports sociologically (e.g., Carrington 2013). James's work has also been influential on those concerned with understanding the politics of culture in the Caribbean (e.g., Edmondson 1994; Kamugisha 2013; Wynter 1992); in postcolonial Britain, especially through his influence on the work of Stuart Hall (1992) and of the *Race Today* Collective (see Bunce and Field 2014); and in the ever expanding field of postcolonial studies. In this last respect, we might recall that James was a significant influence on Edward Said (2000: 373), so it is no surprise that one of the first issues of the flagship postcolonial studies journal *Interventions* would dedicate a series of essays to James or that he would be a central point of reference in recent cultural and literary studies more generally, alongside other critically minded analysts of popular culture such as Raymond Williams, Fredric Jameson, Cornel

West, and bell hooks. It is arguable, though, that these uses have created a rather lopsided James, whose Marxism and wider corpus of writing on the history of anti-imperialism, antiracism, and state capitalism seem to have been subject to a kind of amputation (see Cudjoe 1992b; Larsen 1996). This risks distorting not only the way in which James is remembered, but also our understanding of his writings on cultural practices specifically, which have to be treated as inextricable from his socialist and antiracist politics more generally (Smith 2011b).

There is one further respect in which James, even as he opens a path to a critical reading of culture in colonial and postcolonial contexts, seems very distant from the kinds of analyses that dominate academic cultural and postcolonial studies, and this lies in his writing itself. As Derek Walcott (1995: 36) has noted, James was "not only a polemic person but also ... someone who believed in elegance." A great deal of contemporary academic criticism seems to be the stylistic equivalent of T20 cricket: technocratic, jargon-heavy, and full of empty pyrotechnics. All of this is in complete contrast to the "grace" of James's writing, as Walcott rightly calls it, which has all the elegance one might expect of the onetime novelist and longtime public speaker. It is not an uncommon experience to read academic expositions of *Beyond a Boundary* whose stylistic extravagances are cast in a deeply unflattering light whenever they come to quote from James's original text, with all of its clarity and poise.

Finally, it should be noted that some of the most pioneering aspects of *Beyond a Boundary* seem simply to have been under-recognized, even where James's account preempts later developments and topics of discussion across various academic fields. We might point, for example, to the fact that James's focus on sports allowed him to broach questions of embodied experience, and of the politics of such experience, long before they became fashionable in the arts and humanities (Appadurai 1996; St. Louis 2007: chap. 5). Or we might note James's emphasis on the constitutive role of the audience in establishing the historical meanings of sport. The significance and originality of this claim remains, likewise, largely underappreciated, even though a concern with audience, readership, and reception has proliferated in cultural and media studies in recent years. Perhaps this is because James's account, while it recognizes the capacity of audiences to shape the meanings of culture, remains rooted in the materiality of a game in which there is no disputing success and failure. In that regard, James insisted that evaluative judgments—judgments about the relative quality of different players—were an unavoidable part of any properly historical materialist understanding of cricket. He would have had no more time for the "anything goes" interpretive turn that dominates some branches of cultural studies than he did for the "determinist" reading of culture that dominated some forms of Marxism and that made the opposite but corresponding error of presuming that cultural outcomes were simply pre-scripted by class or by economic forces.

In a similar way, James's pivotal defense of cricket as a form of art has been almost completely overlooked by contemporary discussions of aesthetics (although see Todd 2007). As recently as 2005, the philosopher Wolfgang Welsch could mount a defense of "Sport Viewed Aesthetically, and Even as Art?" that is presented as being without precedent. Welsch argues that sports share many of the symbolic qualities of art, emphasizing their characteristic conjunction of rule-governed action and contingent event and considering their ability to provoke a sense of *mea res agitur* on the part of the audience. "Sport is drama without a script," Welsch (2005: 146) argues. "It creates its own drama." All of this looks new because its reference points are limited to the West European—and especially German—philosophical tradition of aesthetics. But it is, of course, not new at all: it is an argument that was preempted in almost all of its central claims nearly five decades earlier by a writer from the Caribbean who knew the German philosophical tradition well enough, but knew other traditions as well.

It is telling, in this respect, that the famous English art critic, novelist, and painter John Berger regarded *Beyond a Boundary*, on first reading, as "a marvellous book. . . . I read every page with discovery or admiration."[8] James had sent Berger (then based in Switzerland) a copy of the work in early 1969, soon after their first meeting. He wrote, "I have sent you *Beyond a Boundary*. Your wife need only read the first three chapters for they tell what Vidia Naipaul found very important—the early life of a West Indian writer. *The* important chapter in that book so far as art is concerned is the chapter called 'What is art?' The rest is cricket and is to be read or rejected, or read and taken to heart, according to one's liking for games or for that particular game: I am an addict."[9] Berger responded to James on 11 February 1969, "You write with an ease and mastery that is exemplary. You wonder whether I am interested in cricket. Not particularly, but equally, intensely. You only have to understand the quality of style in any human activity to appreciate its value in all others. I can appreciate it in the cricket or the long-jumping or the poker that I have witnessed. Although your arguments for cricket as a synthetic art form are entirely convincing which can't be said for the average European theater."[10]

If, as Naipaul said, the first readers of *Beyond a Boundary* failed to grasp the complexity and originality of James's approach, it may be that this complexity and originality is still out of reach of intellectual methodologies bound by discipline and by a still resilient cultural nationalism. *Beyond a Boundary*, in its reaching across historical and social contexts, in its bringing together of popular and high culture, and in its profoundly political concern for the wholeness of human experience, is the enduring and still provocative expression of what Caryl Phillips (2001: 171) describes as James's "discursive, restless, curious and ultimately annealing intellect."

| | | | | |
|---|---|---|---|---|

The contributions to this book engage with *Beyond a Boundary* through approaches that seek to gain the measure of this restless, curious intellect. The chapters assess both the historical and contemporary relevance of this text in diverse ways and from a range of contrasting positions.

The first, substantive part of the book, "Cricket, Empire, and the Caribbean," opens with Selwyn R. Cudjoe's essay "C. L. R. James: Plumbing His Caribbean Roots." Cudjoe insists on the importance of locating James within the context of the vibrant intellectual, political, and literary traditions of Trinidad and Tobago. Thus, he argues that we can "better understand James's *Beyond a Boundary*, if we locate him in a tradition that made him who he was." He positions the text in relation to the important migrations of Africans from Barbados to the Tacarigua, Tunapuna, and Arouca areas of Trinidad, especially the sugar estates that characterized the area. The chapter stresses that these Barbadians brought with them "particularly strong forms of Anglican tradition" and argues that "James's Barbadian origins, his Anglicanism, and his knowledge of the Bible were important in shaping his literary and intellectual life." Despite drawing attention to this placed character of his formation, however, Cudjoe positions *Beyond a Boundary* as a diasporic text, arguing that it was a work that James "needed to write to reconcile what and who he was when he left the island in 1932 with the man he had become as a result of his long sojourn abroad." This dynamic reading of the text in relation to James's trajectories makes a significant contribution to Cudjoe's broader project to locate James within the contours and context of significant Trinidadian radical political intellectual cultures (Cudjoe 2003: 304–6).

Christian Høgsbjerg's chapter, "C. L. R. James's 'British Civilization'? Exploring the 'Dark Unfathomed Caves' of *Beyond a Boundary*," offers a different emphasis on the influence of the intellectual political and literary culture of Trinidad on James. Høgsbjerg engages with what Bill Schwarz (2003b: 12) has called the "unusually deep penetration of the institutions of Victorian civic life in the cultural organisation of the colonial Caribbean." Paradoxically, however, this position allowed figures such as James to have significant insights into the nature of "British civilization." In this regard, Høgsbjerg argues that "a fundamental aim of *Beyond a Boundary* was to historically situate the rise of English cricket alongside the Industrial Revolution for the first time in order to say something new about 'English civilization.'" Noting how James positions cricket as a game decisively shaped by the agency of artisans, the chapter probes the terms on which the text addresses the connections among sports, games, and struggles for popular democracy. While the chapter signals the importance of James's framing of these relations, it also unsettles the manner in which he engages with these, focusing particularly on his characterization of the reform movements of the nineteenth century. Høgsbjerg develops some insightful critical discussion of the influence of T. S. Eliot and Raymond Williams on James. This influence, Høgsbjerg argues, is particularly discernible in James's articulation of the concept of national cultures. The chapter draws attention, simultaneously, to some of the limits of such a conception. In this regard, Høgsbjerg closes with an important reminder of the importance of situating *Beyond a Boundary* in relation to the "cultural concerns of the 'first New Left' in Britain, born in the aftermath of the Hungarian Revolution and 'Suez Crisis' of 1956."

In chapter 3, "The Boundaries of Publication: The Making of *Beyond a Boundary*," Roy McCree makes a distinctive contribution to the scholarship on *Beyond a Boundary* by providing a detailed reading of correspondence among James, publishers, and the Barbadian novelist George Lamming. McCree draws attention to the struggles that James had, not only to secure a publisher, but also over the timing and naming of the book. He also notes that James's original title was *Who Only Cricket Know*, which was later changed to the enigmatic *W. G., A West Indian Grace* and *West Indian Progeny of W. G.* In January and February 1960, James published the drafts of what would become chapters 13 ("Prolegomena to W. G.") and 14 ("W. G.") of *Beyond a Boundary* in the newspaper that he edited, *The Nation*, in the form of three linked articles.[11] Their publication, across three issues of the paper in January and February 1960, was timed to coincide with the English tour of the West Indies. James closed the series in the last of these issues by noting, there I had intended to end these three articles.... However, their reception has been most encouraging. Dr. Williams said on reading the second: "Oh, boy! Oh, boy!"; Mr. Manley calls the articles a "tour de force," such I say has been the reception that I have been encouraged to bring the analysis up to date by showing what has happened to cricket since Grace's career came to an end. That, however, will wait until the [Marylebone Cricket Club (MCC)] return. This series was conceived in honour of them, and recent events have made the articles all the more timely.[12]

The "recent events" mentioned by James were the controversies over the captaincy of the West Indies team and his campaign to ensure that Worrell replaced Alexander in this capacity. Indeed, that issue of *The Nation* had carried the famous headline and article "Alexander Must Go: Make Worrell Captain." In a subsequent letter written later that year to Eric Williams and eventually republished in *Party Politics in the West Indies* (1962: 69), James had given his former student a summary of his past and future plans: "My wife and I are members of a political organization. This organization has been at work for 19 years preparing a revaluation of the theory and practice of Marxism. We have worked at philosophy, political economy, the arts, and practical activity. In 1957 with the Hungarian Revolution we felt we were ready and planned a series of books *intended now for the general public*, which should embody our ideas in terms easily grasped."

The future book projects James outlined included a reference to his *Nation* article "The Revaluation of Dr. W. G. Grace in English History," which he called "a small part of a whole volume which sees cricket and popular games in terms of a philosophy of art which abolishes the division between the fine arts and the games loved by the populace" (James 1962: 69; see also Strauther 1963).

In McCree's chapter, which explores James's attempts to publish what would emerge as *Beyond a Boundary* from 1960 onward, Lamming emerges as a key intermediary in getting Hutchinson, which had published *In the Castle of My Skin*, to accept the work. Further, he demonstrates that Lamming played a key role in the naming of the text, titling it "Beyond" because the word "implies that there were social and historical issues which went further than the game of cricket." This stress on James's links with Lamming situates the work in relation to the "political trans-national field force" of the black Atlantic which "was peculiarly over-determined, each site of political struggle interconnecting with the next, each disparate struggle taking on the complexions of something larger" (Schwarz 2007: 13).

The ways in which such a political context shaped struggles to form a West Indian federation in the postindependence era are shown to be central to *Beyond a Boundary* in Minkah Makalani's chapter, "'West Indian Through and Through, and Very British': C. L. R. James's *Beyond a Boundary*, Coloniality, and Theorizing Caribbean Independence." We see James traveling through the Caribbean attempting to shore up "the support of local political leaders for a strong federal government that worked in the interests of the Caribbean masses." Makalani suggests the importance of James's role in struggles to "shape a new national life through the Federation, lest the Caribbean 'have the flag and ... the national anthem' but 'remain essentially colonial.'" It is notable, in this regard, that Learie Constantine wrote to Eric Williams in 1963—the year in which the book was published, of course—reporting on James's "very precarious" position, politically and financially, in the United Kingdom. Constantine adds, tellingly, "Several meetings he has held since I last wrote you and his theme is mainly that Colonialism continues in Trinidad under a different guise."[13] It is against this backdrop that Makalani perceptively locates *Beyond a Boundary* as both part of the imaginative processes of decoloniality and a neglected contribution in relation to debates on postcolonial state formation, especially through problematizing postcolonial "modes of governance." For Makalani, these concerns become figured in *Beyond a Boundary* through the discussion of Matthew Bondman, since the "appeal of his artistry stemmed from his social position." Bondman serves "not primarily [as] a bridge between the colonial black elite and the poor" but, rather, as "a marker of a key constitutive element of democracy."

Chapter 5, "Looking Beyond the Boundary, or Bondman without the Bat: Modernism and Culture in the Worldview of C. L. R. James," by David Austin, pushes an engagement with the tensions in James's depiction of Bondman further. Austin engages with the "imbalanced contrapuntalism" that structures James's oeuvre, noting "the hegemony of Euro-Western modernity ... and its embedded assumptions in James's work," particularly through his assessment of Matthew Bondman. He observes the paradox that despite James's "preoccupation with the creative capacities of 'ordinary people,'" he actually "wrote very little about the social history of the Caribbean's underclass." In particular, Austin uses a critical discussion of James's depiction of Bondman to probe some of the ambivalence in relation to the articulation of subalternity in the text. Thus, Austin notes not just the troubling representation of Bondman, particularly in reference to his dirtiness and his curled-back lips, but also the silence of previous critics on these elements. Further, he observes that the characterization of Bondman is shorn of context and "denies us the curiosity and sense of history that we have come to expect from James." Austin, however, relates Bondman to broader contexts, drawing on Sylvia Wynter's comparison of Bondman with Rastafari: "Like the Bondmans of the Caribbean, Rastafarians represented the outcasted and the dispossessed." He concludes by drawing on Richard Iton's assessment of the possibilities of an "aesthetic-political narrative" of the black fantastic, which includes the creative capacities of Bondman even without—or especially without—the bat.

While Austin's chapter engages critically with the ways in which forms of masculinity uncritically structure the text, in chapter 6, "'Periodically I Pondered over It': Reading the Absence/Presence of Women in *Beyond a Boundary*," Anima Adjepong develops a "decolonial feminist reading" that explores the contested absence/presence of women in *Beyond a Boundary*. Locating her chapter—the first in part II, "The Politics of Representation in *Beyond a Boundary*"—in a broader critique of the ways in which "ideologies of masculinity" organized James's politics, Adjepong demonstrates the importance of challenging James's occlusion of the "gendered implications of centering cricket as a site where 'social and political passions [could express] themselves so fiercely.'" To unsettle the gendered politics of *Beyond a Boundary*, Adjepong skillfully draws out the dynamics of the absence and presence of women in the text. She uses a particular focus on James's representation of Aunt Judith, arguing that while he does not necessarily acknowledge it, her "emotional and physical support of cricket" can be foregrounded through a subtle reading of *Beyond a Boundary*. For Adjepong, this has important political implications. Thus, she notes that "when Judith's labor in the domestic sphere is rightly recognized as supporting anticolonial efforts and invested in the politics played out within the boundary, she can be acknowledged as a martyr for the cause." She demonstrates how a "decolonial feminist reading of this text" can contribute in significant ways "to reorienting how we think about black women's historical engagement in antiracist and other political struggles."

The dynamics of representation are further problematized in Neil Washbourne's chapter, "C. L. R. James, W. G. Grace and the Representative Claim." For Washbourne, James adopts a "creolized and culturalized model of [the concept of] general will," and he notes that Rousseau's framing of this concept is an important, if unacknowledged, influence on *Beyond a Boundary*. He argues, however, that James's account of how representative claims are made and understood is marred by a lack of engagement with practices of mediation. The implications of this are developed through a critical interrogation of James's reading of Grace's role. Washbourne argues that James's uncritical acceptance of Grace's public acclaim as a representative hero in 1895 is "a very significant misreading of Grace and contains the core of a misleading account." Further, he argues that James misses the way that "Grace used his power to *reinforce, intensify*, and *extend* the divide" between amateurs and professionals.

Clem Seecharan's contribution, "Shannonism: Learie Constantine and the Origins of C. L. R. James's Worrell Captaincy Campaign of 1959–60: A Preliminary Assessment," explores in depth James's positioning in relation to the *different* cricketing clubs of Trinidad, constituted as they were, on the basis of "race, color, or class." He notes, in particular, the significance of James's decision to join Maple rather than Shannon—the club of the "black lower middle class, of the Constantines . . . , [and of] Wilton St. Hill." For Seecharan, this decision was a profound rupture that "severely undermined [James's] relationship with many lower-middle-class black Trinidadians, particularly Learie Constantine." Seecharan sees this choice as an ongoing fault line in James's relationship with Constantine, but he nonetheless signals the importance of this relationship, built in Nelson, Lancashire. Thus, Seecharan argues that James's brief campaign to make Worrell the first captain of the West Indian team in 1960 ("to have a black man, selected on merit, captain the West Indies team") was a culmination of what Constantine had expressed in *Cricket and I* in 1933, ghostwritten by James. He argues that this campaign represented James's "exorcising of the gnawing guilt of going fair or light" and notes the significance of James's view that Worrell's belated elevation to the captaincy was "an exemplification of Shannonism."

Chapter 9, "C. L. R. James and the Arts of *Beyond a Boundary*: Literary Lessons, Cricketing Aesthetics, and World-Historical Heroes," by Claire Westall—the first in part III, "Art, History and Culture"—critically engages with constructions of heroism in *Beyond a Boundary*. Drawing on David Scott, Westall notes that James "was preoccupied by hero-worship" that was shaped in part by his intellectual journeys "through the traditions of German Romanticism (that stood behind Marxism) as reframed by Britain's imperial literary culture." She traces how James's "aesthetics of heroic endeavor" and his "commitment to masculine heroics" shape his engagement with cricket. While she draws on critical interrogations of the politics that emerge from such a focus on male world-historical figures by theorists such as Hazel Carby, Westall nuances such critiques with a sense of some of the ambiguities of James's work. She notes, for example, that it is difficult "to determine whether the revolutionary weight of a world-historical figure is to be desired, admired, or passed by on the way to a new world order." Developing a productive comparison between Fanonian and Jamesian discussions of heroics, she notes how James, in contrast to Fanon, "positions the people as being the 'uplift' that brings life to, and is expressed in, exceptional action, cricketing and revolutionary."

Westall provides an illuminating set of reflections on James's articulations of universality, arguing that he "blows apart colonial claims to universality without abandoning universal ambition itself." In chapter 10, "The Very Stuff of Human Life: C. L. R. James on Cricket, History, and Human Nature," Andrew Smith provides a different lens through which to assess James's account of universality. He engages with the relations between specificity and broader claims in James's text. Smith draws attention to the ways in which this articulation of universality shapes James's distinctive theorization of art, culture, and sports. In particular, Smith is alive to the ways in which James's account of cricket is sensitive to different forms of agency in shaping the game. In this regard, he argues, James proposes an idea of "universality as becoming" rather than as given. The attention to the creative potential of human action and practices locates James's work in relation to a broader transnational terrain of humanist Marxism in the postwar period. This links James's intellectual project to figures such as Agnes Heller and Henri Lefebvre, as well as to Raya Dunayevskaya and Grace Lee, who were James's close political comrades in the United States and who sought to "make the question of 'concrete' human struggles central to their account of *why* political struggle occurs."

Paget Henry's chapter, "C. L. R. James: Beyond the Boundaries of Culture," resonates with Smith's approach to *Beyond a Boundary* by articulating a "comprehensive account of . . . James's theory of culture." Henry positions James's work at the intersection of "civilizational sociology" and a "Caribbean ontology of creative realism." He uses this approach to locate *Beyond a Boundary* as part of a broader attempt to link creative expression and the formation of collective identities in James's work. Thus, he argues that the narrative strategy that James adopts in *Beyond a Boundary*, as in his novel *Minty Alley*, is "one that takes an open-ended, incomplete, and implicit approach to the expressive structures of human subjectivity." Through a dialogue with Tim Hector's writings on cricket, Henry explores how James's civilizational sociology has been extended by other writers on West Indian cricket, in particular those who have engaged with its decline as well as its ascent, and with the subsequent destabilization of cricket as a "centre-piece of Caribbean civilization." Finally, Henry explores how James's "poetic sociohistoricism" went "beyond the binary contradictions of analytic thinking to include crossing disciplinary boundaries, multiplying the centers of revolutionary discourse to embrace race, gender, culture, and sports." In particular, he notes Sylvia Wynter's argument that James adopted a "pluri-conceptual framework" in which "such factors as gender, color, class and education are non-dogmatically integrated" (Wynter 1992: 63).

Part IV, "Reflections," brings together three figures central to cricket, to the Caribbean, and to political struggles who offer different, personal reflections on the importance of *Beyond a Boundary*. Chapter 12, "Socrates and C. L. R. James," by Michael Brearley, erstwhile captain of Cambridge University, Middlesex, and England, emphasizes the extent to which the book had an impact on players of cricket, as well as on political activists and academic commentators. Brearley focuses on what it is to "know cricket," and he engages with the different forms of knowledge of players, captains, and coaches. His chapter reflects on his own experiences as the captain of Middlesex and explores how he would draw on the different contributions and understandings of the game provided by different players. As his important role in supporting antiapartheid struggles attests, he has long been keenly aware of the broader social context of sports. Brearley, for example, seconded David Sheppard's motion of no confidence in the MCC during the "D'Oliveira affair," part of the pressure that led to the cancellation of the tour of South Africa in 1968.[14] In this regard, his chapter draws inspiration from James's critique of the ways in which "most accounts of social history ignore sports and its place in people's lives."

Hilary McD. Beckles, currently vice-chancellor of the University of the West Indies and one of the leading social historians of the contemporary Caribbean, offers moving personal reflections on James, Caribbean identity, and cricket in chapter 13, "My Journey to James: Cricket, Caribbean Identity, and Cricket Writing." Central to the chapter is his account of attending Worrell's funeral with his grandmother. He recalls standing with her "beyond the boundary" of the official space of the funeral gathering: "on the outside, scattered among the bushes, [we] buried our fears and shed no tears." He follows this memory with a powerful discussion of his own grandmother's funeral, noting how he spoke "from the pulpit of her love of cricket and her awareness of the politics of social justice and moral outrage it had spawned across the Caribbean." Beckles recalls asking, "How was it that a barely literate, barefooted peasant woman could read so complex a cultural practice with precision and stand up for the principles that produced cricketers who represented the game's finest values?" He ends with some thoughtful reflections on the state of West Indian cricket in "post-nationalist" times. In particular, he speculates that James would have theorized Chris Gayle's clash with the West Indian Cricket Board as "indicative of the general youth revolt against the oppressiveness of post-nationalist Caribbean society."

Beckles observes that James's "campaign for Frank Worrell as captain was a metaphor for the rise of democracy in a dying colonialism." This political project of *Beyond a Boundary* is central to Selma James's closing contribution to the volume, "Confronting Imperial Boundaries." In line with her internationally acclaimed role as a political activist who has been at the forefront of attempts to analyze race, class, and gender inequality, she insists on the importance of locating *Beyond a Boundary* within the context of C. L. R. James's political trajectories. In particular, she notes how the text is animated by the "interconnection between cricket and divisions of race and class." She also signals the importance of James's return to Trinidad near the completion of the manuscript and the way he used his role as editor of *The Nation* to spearhead the struggle to make Worrell captain. In this regard, Selma James positions the book as part of a broader constellation of forces that politicized sports in radical ways in the 1960s and 1970s, noting the antiapartheid boycott and the Black Power salute of Tommie Smith and John Carlos at the 1968 Olympics. She speaks, moreover, to ongoing struggles over discrimination in sports. As she concluded, in a recent reflection on *Beyond a Boundary*: "Everywhere we are confined by boundaries, but we struggle to break out."[15]

**Notes**

*Epigraphs:* James 2013 [1963]: n.p.; Larkin 1988: 167.

1. Hereafter, page numbers in parentheses refer to this edition of *Beyond a Boundary*.
2. Alex Hamilton, "Profile: An Interview with C. L. R. James," *The Guardian*, 25 June 1980.
3. This collection was first published in 1986 by Allison and Busby and was entitled, simply, *Cricket*. On James's early cricket writings, see Høgsbjerg 2016 and Smith 2006a.

4. For further discussion of the naming of the text, see chapter 3 in this volume.
5. "Quick Guide to New Reading," *The Times*, 23 May 1963.
6. "A Broad View of Cricket," *The Observer*, 2 June 1963.
7. George MacDonald Fraser, "Straight-Batting Marxist," *Glasgow Herald*, 20 June 1963.
8. John Berger to C. L. R. James, 27 February 1969, C. L. R. James Papers, Rare Book and Manuscript Library Collections, Columbia University, New York (hereafter, James Papers), box 2, folder 1.
9. C. L. R. James to John Berger, 7 February 1969, James Papers, box 2, folder 1.
10. John Berger to C. L. R. James, 11 February 1969, James Papers, box 2, folder 1.
11. C. L. R. James, "Homage to English Cricket (In Honour of MCC): W. G. Grace and His Place in English History; A Revaluation," *The Nation*, 15 January, 22 January, 5 February 1960.
12. James, "Homage to English Cricket," 5 February 1960.
13. Learie Constantine to Eric Williams, 7 March 1963, letter, in Constantine Collection, Special Collections, National Library of Trinidad and Tobago, Port of Spain.
14. The D'Oliveira affair followed the attempt by English cricket's governing body to exclude Basil D'Oliveira from selection in the English touring party bound for South Africa in 1968. D'Oliveira, who had been born and raised in South Africa, was designated "coloured" by the apartheid regime, and his omission from the touring party was widely seen as an attempt to conciliate the regime on the part of the MCC (see Oborne 2004).
15. Selma James, "How *Beyond a Boundary* Broke Down the Barriers of Race, Class and Empire," *The Guardian*, 2 April 2013, 32.

# PART I.
# CRICKET, EMPIRE, AND THE CARIBBEAN

1 | C. L. R. James: Plumbing His Caribbean Roots
SELWYN R. CUDJOE

There are no people without a history or who can be understood without it. Their history, like ours, is incomprehensible outside its setting in a wider world (which has become coterminous with the inhabited globe) and, certainly, in the past half-millennium it cannot be understood except through the interactions of different types of social organization, each modified by interaction with others.
—Eric Hobsbawm, *On History*

During the twentieth century, Trinidad and Tobago produced many outstanding scholars and political activists. They include Sylvester Williams, usually called the father of Pan-Africanism; George Padmore, activist and author of *Pan-Africanism or Communism*; Eugene Chen, twice minister of foreign affairs in the nationalist government of China under Sun Yat-sen; Oliver Cromwell Cox, author of *Race, Caste and Class*; C. L. R. James, Marxist scholar and author of *The Black Jacobins* and *Beyond a Boundary*; and Eric Williams, author of *Capitalism and Slavery* and prime minister of Trinidad and Tobago. In 1975, J. R. Hooker (1975: 3) observed, "That Trinidad has produced a disproportionate number of unusual men is a truism; that so many of them have been forgotten is a scandal. Any small island capable of producing an Eric Williams, a C. L. R. James, a George Padmore, a Vidia Naipaul, to mention a few whose reputations are secure, requires attention." We can better understand James's *Beyond a Boundary* if we locate him in a tradition that made him who he was.

When James arrived in London in 1932, given the pressures of his time and perhaps the anxieties that he felt in a new land—in spite of his bravado—he sought to underplay the importance of the African ideas and West Indian practices that informed his life. He sought to emphasize his familiarity with English culture and ways of life to make himself more acceptable in the political and social circles of Europe. Reflecting on his high school education at Queen's Royal College (QRC), James noted:

> It was only long years after that I understood the limitation on spirit, vision, and self-respect which was imposed on us by the fact that our masters, our curriculum, our code of morals, *everything* began from the basis that Britain was the source of all light and leading, and our business was to admire, wonder, imitate, learn; our criterion of success was to have succeeded in approaching that distant ideal—to attain it was, of course impossible. The masters and boys accepted it as the very nature of things. The masters could not be offensive about it because they thought it was their function to do this, if they thought about it at all; and, as for me, it was the beacon that beckoned me on. (James 2013 [1963]: 29–30)[1]

That is the monkey that James wanted to get off his back when he began to write *Beyond a Boundary*.

Once James arrived in London, he could not possibly have been aware of how much he would have had to display his knowledge of European literature and culture at the expense of any exploration and knowledge of his own Trinidadian and West Indian culture. While it is true that James published *Minty Alley*, a novel set in Trinidad, he would not return to that subject—or to what one might call the "island sensibility"—until he undertook to examine his earlier life and beginnings in his memoir, *Beyond a Boundary*.

In writing *Beyond a Boundary*, James adopted the autobiographical turn that allowed him to bring himself to life through *graphie*, or writing. Such processes allowed him to affirm in his preface that although these ideas "originated in the West Indies it was only in England and in English life and history that I was able to track them down and test them" (n.p.). Thus, it may be that in some of the silences in the text—silences that James himself might not have known—we are able to get a better understanding of where James was coming from. Precisely because James was offering one way to see the world, he certainly needed the reader, a perceptive reader, to tease out what we in literature call "the unsaid of the text," or the "unconscious of the text," to get a better picture of what he was trying to say. (For a discussion of this approach, see Macherey 1978.)

James was born in the Tacarigua-Tunapuna-Arouca ward, a location in which there was a high concentration of Africans. Today we call it the East-West Corridor, where a large slice of the African and African-descended population still lives and many African practices still survive. Most of the

African population came to Trinidad between 1783 and 1833. Some came directly from Africa and some from Africa via the Americas, while others came from other West Indian islands. In 1800, Governor Thomas Picton reported the arrival of four royalist planters from Saint-Domingue, by way of Jamaica, accompanied by their families and about three hundred enslaved Africans. Jean Charles, Baron de Montalembert and Charles Joseph de Loppinot, who purchased a plantation in the Tacarigua ward, were among the royalist evacuees from Saint-Domingue who brought their slaves with them. Picton also acknowledged the landing in Trinidad of "'an uniformed corps of San Domingo Negroes amounting to nearly three hundred under the command of Count de Rouvray' whom General Trigge thought too dangerous to introduce to Martinique" (Epstein 2012: 224).

By 1802, when the island was ceded to Britain, about two-thirds of the slave population in Trinidad was African-born (Epstein 2012: 222). The 1851 census lists 6,035 native-born Africans—about 7 percent of the population—but by 1861 few native-born Africans were on the island. In 1889, J. J. Thomas listed about sixteen different African ethnic groups in Trinidad. The Yoruba, Mandingoes, and Congoes were the most populous groups among the Africans.

During the nineteenth century, many more Africans came in from Barbados to work in the Tacarigua, Tunapuna, and Arouca area, especially on the sugar estates that dominated the area. This provided an important intellectual connection for James. For reasons that are explained later, these Barbadians brought with them particularly strong forms of Anglican tradition, including the use the Book of Common Prayer and the Bible. Although primary school education did not become free until 1900, many of these immigrants and their offspring became acquainted with "the Word" through these sources. Owen Mathurin (1976: 16) notes, "It was almost legendary that Barbadian parents were always firm with their children, religious, church-going, and observant of the Sabbath, filling their children with stories of colored men in Barbados who had risen to important positions in spite of the handicap of color in a white-dominated society." James's maternal grandfather, Josh Rudder, came from Barbados around 1868. He was also a Protestant. In *Beyond a Boundary*, James admitted, "We were Anglicans" (25). In James's case, the love of the Word, the cadences of the King James Version of the Bible, and the practices of Anglicanism were important assets in his advancement in the new society.

Though James never actually noted it, his Barbadian origins, his Anglicanism, and knowledge of the Bible were important in shaping his literary and intellectual life. Andrew O'Shaughnessy (2000: 6) notes, "Barbados contained the largest proportion of small and middling planters, numbering some four thousand resident landowners in 1765. It had a better infrastructure with the oldest assembly in the British Caribbean, the first printing press, schools in every parish, the first newspaper, and a well-supported Anglican Church." In one of his footnotes, O'Shaughnessy (2000: 255) states, "Barbados alone resisted the attempts to disestablish and disendow the Anglican Church in the late nineteenth century by voting a local subsidy." If one listens attentively to the silences in James's text, one will hear these echoes coming through. In a remarkable passage in *Beyond a Boundary,* James alludes to this influence:

> As I dig into my memory I recall that the earliest books I could reach from the window-sill when I had nothing to do, or rain stopped the cricket or there was no cricket, were biblical. There was a series of large brightly colored religious pamphlets telling the story of Jacob and the Ladder, Ruth and Naomi and so forth. There was a large book called *The Throne of the House of David.* One day somebody must have told me, or I may have discovered it from listening to the lessons being read in church, that these stories could be found in the many Bibles that lay about the house, including the large one with the family births and deaths. Detective-like, I tracked down the originals and must have warmed the souls of my aunts and grandmother as they saw me poring over the Bible. That, I had heard often enough, was a good book. It fascinated me. When the parson read the lessons I strove to remember the names and numbers, second chapter of the Second Book of Kings, the Gospel according to St. Matthew, and so on, every Sunday morning. Rev. Allen had a fine voice and was a beautiful reader. I would go home and search and read half aloud to myself. (In school I was still fooling about with Standards 1 or 2: "Johnny's father had a gun and went shooting in the forest.") Somewhere along the way I must have caught the basic rhythms of English prose. My reading was chiefly in the Old Testament and I may have caught, too, some of the stern advice to life which was all around me, tempered, but only tempered, by family kindness. (17–18)

If James's parents had been Roman Catholics, James would not have been the heir to such a literary influence. Although he would eventually learn Latin and Greek when he went to QRC, at that time lay members of the Roman Catholic Church were forbidden to read the Bible. In fact, the parson kept the Word. James puts it this way in *Beyond a Boundary*: "My inheritance (you have already seen two, Puritanism and cricket) came from both sides of the family and a good case could be made out for predestination, including the position of the house in front of the recreation ground and the window exactly behind the wicket" (7).

When James's paternal grandfather arrived in Trinidad from Barbados, he possessed little by way of financial fortune. Through hard work and determination, he made his way up the employment ladder to become a pan boiler on a sugar estate. His work involved "the critical transition of the boiling cane-juice from liquid to sugar. It was a post in those days usually held by white men" (7). One day, James's grandfather felt grievously ill. After his death the family fortunes declined, and his son, Robert Alexander, had to pick up the slack. James says, "My father [Robert] took the obvious way out—teaching. He did well and gained a place as a student in the Government Training College, his course comprising history, literature, geometry, algebra and education. Yet Cousin Nancy, who lived a few yards away, told many stories of her early days as a house-slave. She must have been in her twenties when slavery was abolished in 1834. My father got his diploma, but he soon married" (8).

James's father turned out to be a teacher of note. After leaving the Government Training College, he taught at several primary schools throughout the island, including Arouca, Arima, Sans Souci, and Eastern Boys' Government. He took special pride in his job. Cyril Austin, the son of Richard and Judith Austin, the sister whom James celebrates in *Beyond a Boundary*, lived with James's family in Tunapuna and St. Joseph after Cyril's father died. James (1984: 204) noted that his "aunt's husband, Richard Austin, was a teacher too; my sister's godfather, he was a teacher; we were a teaching fraternity." This is why Robert was fond of the initials "I. S. M.—Imperial Service Medal[—]that was bestowed upon him by the king of England [George V]. James was a teacher and got this initial for the contribution that he made towards teaching."[2] He carried these initials with him wherever he went.

Robert was good at producing college exhibition winners, a feat he accomplished at most of the schools at which he taught. At Eastern Boys' Government School, Robert piloted his son through the college exhibition, which James won at age nine. Jean Besson, a childhood friend who was eventually trained in medicine at the University of Edinburgh, attests that James's father "had a good reputation as an excellent teacher in Arima and everyone knew of Mr. James and his son, who had won the Exhibition Examination so brilliantly at such an early age" (Besson 1989: 49).

James's father was responsible for encouraging other aspects of James's intellectual life. Cyril Austin noted that Robert reveled in everything that lifted the human spirit and dabbled in the liberal arts, music, and dancing. He loved classical composers such as Chopin, Tchaikovsky, and Schubert. He also led several choirs and was a member of the Arouca Debating Association, which conducted debates on the first and second Mondays of the month. On 2 April 1902, *The Mirror*, a Trinidadian newspaper, carried a report of the missionary meeting that took place at Arouca at the end of March: "The choir, under Mr. Robert James, here sang the anthem, 'Praise the Lord O-Jerusalem.' . . . The Rev. Dr. Whitter referred to the Arab slave trade in Africa and stated that its last stronghold had been destroyed during Lord Kitchener's Soudan campaign."[3] During that period, debating societies were an important part of the Trinidadian landscape. They contributed much to the literary education of a generation. James's father participated in the association's first debate, "Is the British Occupation of the Transvaal Justifiable?" Speaking from the affirmative position, he "referred to the compound system and the disgraceful manner in which the English in the Transvaal were treated by the Boers before the war."[4] Papers such as "The Life of Sir Walter Scott" were delivered on the days that the association set for the reading of papers.

Robert also wrote reports of events that took place in the village and sent them to the *Trinidad Chronicle*, the *Port of Spain Gazette*, and the *Trinidad Guardian* for publication. Cyril Austin recalls that he went to various lectures and "spent the day typing up his notes and sent these dispatches to the newspapers which they published. He became the appointed reporter of the district."[5] He infused his home life with music and literature. Most nights he would sit with his wife, Elizabeth (James refers to her as Bessie), and their two sons (Eric and C. L. R.) and read the classics aloud to them. Austin recalls, "Everybody would listen because there was nothing else to do at nights. And he played the piano. Winifred Atwell who later became a world-famous pianist, was a product of Robert James."[6] He spent his final days teaching music and shorthand. C. L. R. James notes that when he returned to Trinidad in 1958 at the invitation of Eric Williams and the People's National Movement (PNM), his father was already eighty but still active in intellect, his memory unimpaired to the day he died.

From his earliest school days, James's literary and political path was set. Besson (1989: 49–51), a classmate at QRC, captures the C. L. R. James that we would come to know, writing:

> I realized how much Nello [a pet name for James] knew because when he ought to have been doing his homework he was reading history and literature, that is, in the classroom. I mean instead of doing the class work he would actually be reading! I remember his reading Green's *English History* which the ordinary run of students like myself did not read; but he would read the masters' textbooks and he used to read Shakespeare and books which were entirely out of the curriculum. I used to lend him my text books and he used to make marginal notes, and in later days when I studied more into English Literature, I likened him to Samuel Taylor Coleridge.... So it was in those days, then, that Nello used to come up to our house and we used to study by candlelight or lamplight, because in those days there was no electricity, and for privacy we used to go into my little room to study.

At eighteen, James knew that he wanted to go abroad. At thirty, he wanted to devote himself to writing. He says:

> Intellectually, I lived abroad, chiefly in England. What ultimately vitiated all this was that it involved me with the people around me only in the most abstract way. I spoke. My audience listened and thought it was fine and that I was a learned man. In politics I took little interest. I taught at schools, but there were no controversies on education.... What now stands out a mile is that I was publicly involved only in cricket and soccer.... I was a sports journalist. The conflicts and rivalries which arose out of the conditions I have described gripped me. My Puritan soul burnt with indignation at injustice in the sphere of sport. I had to be careful: papers, even sporting papers, live by advertisements. Our community was small. I fought the good fight with all my might. I was in the toils of greater forces than I knew. Cricket had plunged me into politics long before I was aware of it. When I did turn to politics I did not have too much to learn. (65)

After James left QRC, he spent almost a decade in Trinidad participating in the intellectual, social, and political life of the country. First he started his own high school, Pamphilian High School, and produced his own dramas, including Shakespeare's *Merchant of Venice*. He also worked with the Beacon

Group and contributed several articles to their magazine. In it, he analyzed the life and times of Michel Maxwell Philip, who wrote *Emmanuel Appadocca* (1854), the first novel by a Trinidadian and undoubtedly one of the earliest novels in the Caribbean literary canon. In 1931, James also wrote "The Intelligence of the Negro," a scathing attack on the racism practiced in the West Indies. As a young man he admired Captain Arthur Cipriani, one of the most progressive politicians in the West Indies at the time, who led the fight to empower the "barefoot man." In 1932, he completed *The Life of Captain Cipriani*, three chapters of which were published a year later as *The Case for West Indian Self-Government*. While in Trinidad, he also completed *Minty Alley*, a novel set in a Port of Spain tenement yard that was published in England in 1936.

I will not recapitulate James's publishing career and history from this point on. In 1938, he published his seminal work, *The Black Jacobins*, which argued that the constant struggles that were waged in the colonies were related to the revolutionary activities that were taking place in the metropolitan countries and thereby helped to restructure the empire and, ultimately, the world. According to Robin Blackburn (1988: 28), *The Black Jacobins* "illuminated the essential workings of capitalism, racialism, colonialism and slavery—and the complex struggle to which they gave rise in St. Domingo."

In a way, *The Black Jacobins* represents a later expression of the intellectual work started by Canon Philip Douglin and J. J. Thomas in the second half of the nineteenth century, when both of them demonstrated how white racism and colonialism had deformed human relations. Douglin, a Barbadian Anglican pastor, was trained at Codrington College in Barbados. Later in his career, he spent several years in Rio Pongas, West Africa, as a missionary and as a chaplain at Sierra Leone's major Anglican Church before returning to Trinidad in 1887 to take up pastoral duties at St. Clements Anglican Church in the south of Trinidad. Thomas, like James's grandfather the son of a slave, had learned linguistics on his own, published *The Theory and Practice of Creole Grammar* (1869) and, later, *Froudacity* (1889) before he died suddenly at Kings Hospital in London in 1889. He was inducted into the London Philological Society. Mathurin (1976: 12) observed, "These Pan African and back-to-African thoughts of Jacob Thomas were to find expression in the words and deeds of Henry Sylvester Williams."

Thus, even in the greatness and originality of *The Black Jacobins*, James was continuing a conversation that was started by Philip, Douglin, Thomas, and Williams. Each in his own way sought to demonstrate the centrality of

Africa in the Caribbean liberation project (Philip), the ravages of slavery on the black psyche (Douglin), the illogicality of the entire colonial process (Thomas), and the need for Pan-African unity (Williams). (On these thinkers, see Cudjoe 2003; Harris 2008.) Each of these authors touched on the importance of Africa in the memory of the Caribbean person, the reclamation of self, and a working through of the question of Caribbean identity. In *Beyond a Boundary* and *The Black Jacobins*, James was engaged in a similar process. He noted in *Beyond a Boundary*, "We know nothing, nothing at all, of the results of what we do to children. My father had given me a bat and ball, I had learnt to play and at eighteen was a good cricketer. What a fiction! In reality my life up to ten had laid the powder for a war that lasted without respite for eight years, and intermittently for some time afterwards—a war between English Puritanism, English literature and cricket, and the realism of West Indian life" (21).

James, an apt reader of his own history, was aware of the dichotomy between the suppressed aspects of West Indian life and the English culture that was imposed on West Indian people. Like Sylvester Williams, James grew up in an atmosphere in which African religions and culture were prevalent. The Tunapuna-Tacarigua-Arouca area in which James and Williams grew up was the most intensely African-populated district/ward in the island.[7] Each of them was immensely aware of the pervasiveness of that culture on them, which is why James emphasizes these slave connections in *Beyond a Boundary*. Thus could Mathurin (1976: 4–5) report:

> During Williams's early manhood, and even at the turn of the century, the descendants of the slaves were still being called Africans. Their adoption of Christianity notwithstanding, some of them organized or participated in African ceremonies, dances, and feasts. Tribal differences of language and custom and consciousness of place of origin had largely faded where they had not disappeared under the policy of cultural genocide applied by the colonial rulers. It is remarkable, however, that to this day African values persist, most notably among people who claim descent from the Yoruba of western Nigeria—or "Yaraba," as an 1891 newspaper described one of them charged with "practicing obeah." They identified their African gods with the saints of the Roman Catholic Church and were thus able to envisage them as emanating out of the everyday world about them.

Needless to say, James was thinking of African religious practices (Shango or orisha religion in Trinidad), mating practices, and cultural, linguistic, and musical practices when he spoke about the dichotomies between West Indian and English life.[8] To take but one example, a new conception of marriage arose among enslaved Africans on the West Indian plantations. Dom Basil Matthews (1953: 20) notes, "The West Indian slave, with few exceptions, bluntly refused to be bound by any matrimonial tie. All but two slaves on a Trinidad estate preferred death to marriage.... They alleged that Negroes had lost in the New World all stability and restraint. If 'Massa King George' ordered them to marry white wives they would marry as many of them as he wished. Meanwhile the utmost they were willing to do was to 'try to live wid 'em first a little bit for trial.'"

After writing *The Black Jacobins*, James devoted a lot of time to discussing the "Negro Question" and the relation of the black liberation struggle in the United States to the resistance of colonial peoples worldwide (see James 2012). After spending several years in the United States, he was sent back to England by the US Immigration Services because he had little desire to return to Trinidad, his home. Once he left the island, he hardly wrote to his parents. Besson (1989: 97) related a visit that he made to Tunapuna in 1939: "I remember at this time receiving a visit from Mrs. James, the mother of my old school friend Nello. By this time Nello had emigrated to Britain and was becoming internationally known as the author C. L. R. James.... Mrs. James asked me to send word to her if I saw her son while I was in England, but in fact at around this time Nello left Britain for America." Cyril Austin, James's first cousin, confirmed this lack of correspondence with his parents.[9]

Once he returned to London, James began to work on *Beyond a Boundary*. In 1957, he went to Ghana to work for Kwame Nkrumah and to participate in the Ghanaian liberation struggle. In 1958, he returned to Trinidad at the request of Eric Williams to edit the *PNM Weekly* (renamed *The Nation*) and became the secretary of the West Indian Federal Labour Party. In 1961, James and Williams split. James gives an account of this split in his book *Party Politics in the West Indies* (1962). In 1965, James formed the Workers' and Farmers' Party, which was not successful in the general election of 1965. From that point on, he effectively ended his active association with Trinidadian politics, although he would be celebrated, and his theoretical works continued to be used by progressive political groups in the West Indies. (For discussion of James's influence on these groups, see Cudjoe and Cain 1995.) During those three years he spent in Trinidad, James continued to work on *Beyond a Boundary*, which he concluded in Spain in 1962 (Springfield 1989: 74).

*Beyond a Boundary* was a work that James needed to write to reconcile what and who he was when he left the island in 1932 with the man he had become as a result of his long sojourn abroad. Shaped and made primarily by Trinidad, James had to look within himself—and, by definition, his culture—to see what he had become. In reconciling himself to his past, James must have taken great pride in his people: in 1849, eleven years after apprenticeship had ended, two hundred and fifty of the most distinguished black and colored citizens came together in Port of Spain to celebrate the anniversary of Emancipation. Only three white persons attended: the registrar of the Supreme Court; the clerk of the Petty Civil Court of Port of Spain, and the inspector-general.

At the anniversary dinner, Michel Maxwell Philip, the author of *Emmanuel Appadocca* and later the solicitor-general of the island, spoke of the horrors of the Middle Passage. John O'Brien, another leading light of the day, affirmed the equality of all men and women. He saw the principal task of black men as combatting the error "of those descendant of the African race who disclaim all sympathy with the slaves, upon the simple ground that they, or their immediate ancestors, were not slaves (Loud cheers). If they want an example, I would point to them to that great man, Alexandre Dumas (Cheers). Does he deny that he is a descendant of a son or daughter of still degraded Africa? No. He prides himself upon it; and lest he should be mistaken, he nobly and exultingly points to his curly hair, and says, 'here are my credentials!' (Loud cheers)."[10] These proto-nationalists were aware that Alex Dumas, Alexandre's father and a famous general during the French Revolution, was one of "the most imposing as well possibly the most respected of Napoleon's officers" (Reiss 2013: 248–49) when he invaded Egypt in 1798. When James addressed students at Federal City College in 1969, five years after he wrote *Beyond a Boundary*, he described the disconcerting tendency among West Indian university students in London of the period who were studying and writing theses on authors such as T. S. Eliot, D. H. Lawrence, and Joseph Conrad rather than on Dumas, "one of the most remarkable figures of the nineteenth century" (James 1992: 398). After speaking of the contributions of the Romantic poets and novelists of whom Dumas was one of the most important, James wrote, "He was translated into every language. *The Count of Monte Cristo* and *The Three Musketeers* and the collected novels are European and universal novels. What I am saying is, not only did the black people contribute, not only did they fight in the ranks, but forging the kind of lives which people lived afterwards, one of the foremost men is a man from the Caribbean" (James 1992: 398–99).

James did not suggest that these West Indian students read Matthew Arnold's *Culture and Anarchy*.[11] Instead, he pointed them to the works of Dumas, someone his countrymen had discovered more than a century earlier; someone from whom they drew much inspiration; someone they had adopted since 1849. Moreover, the seminal importance that James ascribed to Dumas and his work suggested the shaping influence Caribbean culture had on the making of James and so many distinguished Caribbean thinkers. Thus could James say of the Nurses, his family, and the other black families who grew up around him in that area, "These West Indian black people were a remarkable set of people. They are the ancestors of what West Indian people are today, and what they will be tomorrow. I bring this up because it took me some time to realize the kind of people that I had grown up with, who were my relations, who were my friends, what were their ancestors and what they represented" (James 1984: 204). James offered this evaluation—in a speech given at Ladbroke Grove in London—eight years after he wrote *Beyond a Boundary*.

After making this observation, James named some of the distinguished writers and thinkers who came out of the West Indian social milieu. He started with René Maran, author of *Batoaula*, which won the Prix Goncourt in 1921. He continued, "After Rene Maran came Marcus Garvey, after Marcus Garvey came George Padmore. . . . After Padmore came Aimé Césaire, the man of Negritude and one of the great writers of our day. Then came Frantz Fanon, and mixed up with them is C. L. R. James. That is a notable list. You cannot under any circumstances write the history of Western civilization without listing these West Indians. People have often asked me why it is they played the role they have so far. I have been working at it and I think I have some answer" (205).

I am not too sure what James's answer would have been, but I have read enough of James to know that he would have located the source of these authors' tremendous intellectual power in the Caribbean soil out of which they came. In fact, he made this point with especial vigor in 1969 when he sought to demonstrate Thomas's analytical superiority over James Anthony Froude and his fables about the Caribbean. James (1969: 47) noted:

In the early years (which it seems established the logical premises of maturity), he [Thomas] could see that a white skin conferred no mental superiority. If he thought at all in historical or political terms he was impelled to historical laws which saw the relationship of races in a historical progression. On such an instinctual premise, reading and study abroad or at home would add fortitude and develop flexibility. Thomas did it in 1890 [*sic*]. Experience of advanced civilizations with their immense accumulations of knowledge, and their highly organized social institutions, these made of our native Thomases, a Garvey, a Padmore, a Fanon.

James reiterated this point in 1971 at a gathering that was organized to celebrate his seventieth birthday. Although he and his West Indian companions possessed a conception of European society after reading Arnold, Thackeray, Dickens, Shakespeare, Hazlitt, and others, when they arrived in Europe "and saw that the society did not correspond to what we had read, without exception we revolted against it.... I think we had lived a certain kind of life, had been educated in a certain way, had read certain books; we came abroad and found that neither the life we lived nor the things that we saw were in harmony with the things we had read, and we automatically were and remained *against*" (James 1984: 205).

This is not to suggest that these writers whom James and his companions read while they were in the West Indies had no effect on their ways of seeing the world. They did. James and his fellow writers—the ones he named—ought not, however, be seen in a narrow and restricting light. They should be seen as responding to an intellectual legacy by materials their ancestors handed down to them and from which they created "anew out of the future" (Marx 1926 [1852]: 26).

One only has to look at the similarities, in both cadence and sentiments, between James's "Michel Maxwell Philip: 1829–1888" (1978 [1931]) and L. B. Tronchin's "A Lecture: On the Political and Literary State of the Colony during the Administration of Lord Harris" (1888) to begin to understand the source from which James derived his style and approach to historical analysis. James and Tronchin compare Charles Warner's extraordinary intellectual gifts, respectively, with those of two native sons: Philip and William George Knox, the chief justice of the island during Lord Harris's governorship. James described Philip's brilliance by writing, "Mr. Philip was all his life an educated and scholarly man. There [at the Jesuit College at St. Mary's in Scotland] he learnt Latin and Greek, French, Spanish and Italian, and a master of those languages he remained until the end. Like his great rival for intellectual primacy, Mr. Charles Warner, he read a few lines of the classics every morning of his life and so kept his knowledge fresh" (James 1978 [1931]: 254–55). Tronchin (1888b: n.p.) contrasted the intellectual gifts of Judge Knox and Warner this way:

> The influence these two men exercised, for good or for evil, over the destiny of this colony is one of those remarkable particulars which proclaim loudly, the irresistible power of the intellect, even when that power is not controlled by virtue and patriotism. . . . [Knox's] immense erudition as a lawyer, and a classical scholar, was calculated to increase his natural vanity, and nothing was more pleasing to him than an occasion to display knowledge that was stored in his vast mind. . . . The Attorney-General [Warner] was the reverse of the Judge. With equal erudition, he surpassed his colleague by the richness of his imagination, the eloquence of his diction, and the diversity of his attainments. His proficiency in ancient literature was really wonderful, and his intimate acquaintance with the Greek and Latin authors enabled him to translate them with a facility and accuracy that would excite the jealousy of a professor.

Such eloquence was becoming of Tronchin. He was one of Trinidad's most learned men of his time, a member of the Trinidad Literary Society and the superintendent of the Normal and Model Schools in Woodbrook. He was the author of *Inez: The Last of the Aroucas* and several illuminating essays on the leading national and international figures of the day. Thomas, another leading intellectual of the day and a member of the Trinidad Literary Association, acknowledged Tronchin's assistance in his writing of *The Theory and Practice of Creole Grammar* when he wrote, "It remains now for me to record my obligations to Mr. L. B. Tronchin . . . for the courteous patience with which he revised such of my proof-sheets as I had an opportunity of submitting to him" (Thomas 1869: vi).

That was the circle from which James received his inspiration and his early literary training. When he criticized Froude for not understanding the history of the Caribbean and thereby tangling himself up, James (1969: 39) pointed out, "One would expect that in studying the English in the West Indies, a serious historian would have studied the history of the West Indies in general in order to seek what are the inherent movements and motives that are expressed in the West Indian development." A similar principle should hold when one attempts to analyze James's emergence as a literary, cultural, and political figure in the twentieth century. There can be no serious understanding of James's work if there is no understanding of where James came from and the factors that shaped the first thirty-one years of his life.

James had to write *Beyond a Boundary* to complete his Caribbean odyssey and to understand who he was. He notes in his preface, "To establish his own identity, Caliban, after three centuries, must himself pioneer into regions Caesar never knew" (n.p.). But to understand himself, after sixty-three years of living, James had to return to his early life to understand what those sixty-three years meant to him. James had come from far. He took pride in the fact that his family had lived in the same place for more than 150 years, which, in the Caribbean, was a long time. However, the searing question, "Who am I?" remained in his mind.

James had traveled much. He had seen many places, done many things, and received many accolades in relation to his scholarship. At the end of *Beyond a Boundary*, he confesses, "We have travelled, but only the outlines of character are changed. I have changed little. I know that more than ever now" (255). It is a position he would repeat thirteen years later when he sought to explain Padmore's origins to an English audience: "I am going to begin with the material circumstances in which he grew up and the social relations that shaped him: the longer I live the more I see that people are shaped to a degree they that they do not yet understand by the social relations and family and other groups in which they grew up" (James 1984: 251).

James had to tell his story if he wished to challenge the limitation of spirit, vision, and self-respect that British colonialism had imposed on West Indian people through their education, their religion, and their games, which were profound forms of politics. To do so, James had to go back into the 150 years of history that followed from the arrival of his people on the island to truly understand who he was and what he had become in a process that was shaped by slavery and colonial rule.

### Notes

*Epigraph:* Hobsbawm 1997: 227–28.

1. Hereafter, page numbers in parentheses refer to this edition of *Beyond a Boundary*.
2. Cyril Austin, interview by the author, Trinidad, 23 April 2009.
3. "Arouca," *The Mirror*, 2 April 1902.
4. "Arouca Debating Association," *The Mirror*, 13 March, 1902.
5. Austin interview.

**6.** Winifred Atwell (ca. 1910–83) continued her musical training in the United States in 1945 before going to London in 1946, to the Royal Academy of Music, to become a concert pianist. During the 1950s she enjoyed great popularity in the United Kingdom and Australia, selling twenty million records before rock-and-roll eclipsed her career (see Hurbert 2007). Atwell was "the first black person to have a number one hit in Britain, and still the only female instrumentalist to hit the top" (Rice et al. 1982: 17). The Jameses, Atwells and Warners were among the prominent families of Tunapuna during the first half of the twentieth century.

**7.** In 1802, the Tacarigua-Arouca area had the fourth largest population in the island. Close to 76 percent of the population were African. With the exception of the Naparimas, Tacarigua-Arouca had the largest concentration of Africans in the island. Tunapuna, as a village, came into being only in the 1850s; it was settled by former slaves after the end of apprenticeship in 1838 (see Cudjoe 1983, esp. chap. 5). James notes that at the beginning of the twentieth century, only three thousand people lived in Tunapuna.

**8.** On religious practices, see Henry 2001; Thomas 1988. On mating practices, see Matthews 1953. On cultural, linguistic, and musical practices, see, respectively, Herskovits and Herskovits 1947; Thomas 1869; Cowley 1996.

**9.** Austin interview.

**10.** John O'Brien, "Anniversary of Freedom, First of August Dinner," *The Trinidadian* 8 August 1849.

**11.** In his interesting book *C. L. R. James in Imperial Britain* (2014), Christian Høgsbjerg argues that James was made or influenced in his Trinidad years (1901–32) by Matthew Arnold's *Culture and Anarchy*. Consuelo Lopez Springfield offers a more persuasive rendering of the impact that English writers (such as William Thackeray and William Hazlitt) had on James's character. She argues, "If any British intellectual were his creative mentor, it certainly would be William Hazlitt. Throughout his long, productive life, James like Hazlitt before him, maintains his convictions, even when unpopular, and makes them comprehensible, even palpable, to diverse audiences" (Springfield 1989: 81).

2 | C. L. R. James's "British Civilization"?: Exploring the "Dark Unfathomed Caves" of *Beyond a Boundary*

CHRISTIAN HØGSBJERG

It seems to me that a book like this which delves so deep and shows cricket to have been a part of every period of the history of England and the colonial territories makes one thing clear, that cricket is an integral part of the British civilization. I believe that whatever road that civilization takes, it will take cricket with it.
—C. L. R. James, "'Introduction' to *Cricket*"

Cricket is a game at the very foundation of British civilization.
—C. L. R. James, "C. L. R. James's First Cricket XI"

In 1963, in a letter written to his friend and fellow Trinidadian writer V. S. Naipaul, C. L. R. James confided, "I believe that, originating as we are within the British structure, but living under such different social conditions, we have a lot to say about the British civilization itself which we see more sharply than they themselves" (James 1986: 117). As many writers have noted, James was a profoundly "civilizational thinker," particularly concerned throughout his long life with the historical relationship of black people—particularly black West Indians—to "Western civilization," and with the multitude of ways in which they were "in but not of the West" (see Hill 1999).[1] In 1963, James had arguably more than justified his statement about British West Indians' insight into "British civilization" with the publication of his cultural history of cricket, *Beyond a Boundary*. Here, James, the veteran anti-colonialist, mused that "it has taken me a long time," but he now felt he could finally "begin to understand" the relationship between "Britain" and "her colonies," and "the British people" and "the colonial peoples" (James 2013 [1963]: 24).[2]

Like other colonial subjects of Britain, West Indians such as James were officially "British" and indeed identified themselves as such. At one point in one of his draft manuscripts of *Beyond a Boundary*, in a section that did not make it into the final work, James wrote that West Indians were "different from any other coloured colonials. Language, religion, outlook, aims are cast in the British mould. I could not imagine any future in which we would not revere Milton and Shakespeare, Hazlitt and Shelley, W. G. Grace and Sidney Barnes, Jack Hobbs and Denis Compton."[3] West Indians had to contend with what Bill Schwarz calls "the unusually deep penetration of the institutions of Victorian civic life into the cultural organisation of the colonial Caribbean" (Schwarz 2003b: 12; see also Rush 2011). In no small part as a result of their "colonial Victorianism," James recalled, the West Indians living in London during the 1930s formed a distinctive group among other colonial subjects in the metropolis and were described by their African friends as the "Black Englishmen" or the "black white men" (see James 1984: 263; Schwarz 2003c: 148; see also Høgsbjerg 2014: 17–21). James himself, at the time a cricket reporter with the *Manchester Guardian* and then the *Glasgow Herald*, always stood out in particular as a very "British" West Indian, to the extent that his second wife, Constance Webb (2003: 171), noted that "in London, among friends, he was often called *the last of the Victorians.*" Yet, during the 1950s, as Schwarz (2002: 82) notes, "In the intellectual *disorder* of decolonization entire systems of thought were breached." The transnational meanings of "Britishness" as an imperial identity steadily dissolved in the face of victorious national independence movements, while the great postwar migration from the Caribbean brought the "colonial frontier" home, throwing not just Britishness but also Englishness as a national identity into flux (see Schwarz 1996).[4]

In this context, as Schwarz has persuasively shown through a study of the Trinidadian activist Claudia Jones, founder of the *West Indian Gazette* in 1958 and the Notting Hill Carnival in 1959, West Indians in Britain were not idle spectators as the kaleidoscope of "Britishness" and "Englishness" was being turned upside down during decolonization. They played their part in reordering these national identities as the fragmented pieces began to settle. As Schwarz (2003a: 268) notes, "The West Indian emigrant—or immigrant, as he or she became the moment they disembarked—became an important, if often reluctant, agent in imagining a future for Britain after colonialism." If the Windrush Generation as a whole, then, were forced to become "conscripts of postcoloniality" on arriving in Britain, it is clear that James, who had long since acclimatized to British civilization, was one of those leading the conscription.[5]

James's model anti-colonialist, as he wrote in his classic history of the Haitian Revolution, *The Black Jacobins* (1938: 288), was one "who could combine within their single selves the unrelenting suspicion and ruthless ferocity necessary to deal with imperialism and yet retain undimmed their creative impulse and their respect for the attainments of the very culture they fought so fiercely." With British imperialism in retreat by the 1950s, James tells us that when he was writing *Beyond a Boundary* he wanted to undertake what he called a "respectful re-examination" of British cultural history (25). After James had completed the draft of what was to become *Beyond a Boundary*, he wrote to his American comrades on 31 March 1957, outlining the essential themes of what he simply called "the cricket book." An extract from this letter gives a flavor:

> The first two or three chapters deal with my early childhood. . . . My theme is my upbringing with English literature, cricket and puritanism. These are the three fundamental characteristics of English middle-class society. I shall show first of all that, precisely because they were not native to the West Indies, they assumed a reality for me that placed me in violent contrast with the people among whom I lived. . . . I show the interconnections between these three to show how British the literature, the cricket and puritanism are. By cricket I mean not only the game but the code connected with it. . . . Behind it all is the question of what constitutes an education. The British code as an education for the British upper classes. (James 1986: 87–88)

James's concern with respectfully re-examining British imperial metropolitan cultural codes in *Beyond a Boundary*, however, has meant that many postcolonial critics have found the book somewhat frustrating. As Helen Tiffin (1995: 367) has noted, "In *Minty Alley* and *The Black Jacobins*, the periphery was magically metamorphosed into the centre—an extraordinary feat of psychic decolonization. But, in *Beyond a Boundary*, the centre remains in England. . . . [I]n cricket the colonial simply proves he can abide by the rules and the morality of the British game. He does not and has not in any significant sense altered the assumptions behind it."

Yet as James noted in a speech in 1963, he felt the process by which colonial peoples could begin to reshape the game anew was only now becoming a reality with decolonization: "The West Indies have reached where they are because certain of them have had the opportunity to absorb to a large degree, and to adapt to their own uses, a certain definite tradition. But they have to bring something of their own now to the life that they have to live, and I believe in the cricket that they have been playing over the last two or three years they have found something of their own" (1986 [1963]: 147).

James scholars have tended to resist attempting to understand *Beyond a Boundary* through the prism of James's "Notes on British Civilization." For Frank Rosengarten, *Beyond a Boundary* is not about "civilization" at all, and he sees the work as "a form of 'breakaway' from previous writing projects and areas of inquiry that had satisfied [James] up to the mid-1950s" (Rosengarten 2008: 235). Stephen Howe (2003: 154) once sounded a note of regret that a work by James explicitly called *British Civilization* never appeared: "Although most of his later life, from 1953 onwards, was spent in London, he never investigated Britain in anything like the way that, in the hugely ambitious, uncompleted *American Civilization*, he did the USA. The suggestive but brief comments about Britishness in *Beyond a Boundary* . . . were never expanded upon by a man who, in his later British years, had neither energy nor inclination for new, large-scale projects."

Yet we should perhaps instead follow Schwarz in seeing *Beyond a Boundary* as the logical culmination of James's "civilizational" thinking, and as a deeper and more finished work than *American Civilization*. "In both," Schwarz (2006: 131) writes, "we can witness James explicitly interrogating the precepts of a civilization. And in both we can see a historical method peculiarly his own coming into effect. In this respect, *American Civilization* served James as a preparatory, experimental exercise—his *Grundrisse*, to draw an analogy from Marx scholarship—which made *Beyond a Boundary* possible."

The allusion to Marx's *Capital* is well placed in this reading, for as James (1993: 286) had once noted, "*Capital* is not only a study of abstract capitalism. It is the history of English capitalist development and there is no finer introduction to the history of Great Britain." In *Beyond a Boundary*, James stresses that, in making his specific arguments about cricket style and the connection to wider society, "my weapons . . . will be majestic and, I hope, imposing: the history of modern Britain and scientific method [Marxism]" (38). As Kenneth Surin (1995: 333) rightly noted of *Beyond a Boundary*,

> [James's] great achievement is to have been the first writer on cricket to have told us . . . that cricket is inextricably bound up with this thing, capitalism, and that we cannot therefore narrate the history of the game in isolation from the history of capitalism itself. His even greater achieve-

ment is to have theorised this relationship between cricket and capitalism from a standpoint which, for all its problems, is nonetheless remarkable for the judgement it delivered on previous phases of capitalist and cricketing development.

This chapter will, then, seek to demonstrate that a fundamental aim of *Beyond a Boundary* was to historically situate the rise of English cricket alongside the Industrial Revolution for the first time in order to say something new about "English civilization." After all, as Schwarz put it, "What could represent more profoundly the civilization of the English than cricket?" Even when James was not directly writing about cricket but about his early life in Trinidad, Schwarz (2006: 128) notes that James's "lyrical memories of a lost colonial order carry within them a devastating critique of England and its civilization." This essay will draw on, among other material, the draft manuscripts of what became *Beyond a Boundary*, one of which had as a working title *Who Only Cricket Know*, inspired by Rudyard Kipling, who according to James (speaking to West Indian students in Edinburgh in 1964) was "the finest and most emphatically English writer of the late nineteenth and early twentieth centuries" (James 1984: 147). The provisional chapter titles of *Who Only Cricket Know*, some of which made it into the final manuscript of *Beyond a Boundary*, make clear that James was drawing for inspiration on a far wider number of English cultural thinkers than simply Kipling. There are references and allusions to the writings of, among others, William Shakespeare ("All the World's a Stage," "Patient Merit," "The Most Unkindest Cut," "Wherefore Are These Things Hid?" "The Art and Practice Part"), John Milton ("To Interpose a Little Ease"), Thomas Hardy ("Return of the Native"), Rupert Brooke ("In That Rich Earth"), and C. P. Snow ("The Light and the Dark"). For example, one draft chapter in the section on Learie Constantine in the draft manuscript was headed "The Dark Unfathomed Caves," a reference to Thomas Gray's poem *Elegy Written in a Country Churchyard* (1751).[6] In the end, this title did not make it into *Beyond a Boundary*, although James did write in passing of how, while "swimming in the caves of league cricket between the wars, to this day dark and unfathomed, Constantine strengthened and flexed his strategic muscles" (132). It is my argument, then, that to this day there are a great many "dark and unfathomed caves" within the overall text of *Beyond a Boundary* that deserve greater archaeological excavation by James scholars. Indeed, as James himself suggested to his long-standing comrade Martin Glaberman, in comments dated 11 July 1963, and made in

Glaberman's personal copy of *Beyond a Boundary*, "I cannot prevent myself saying that within these covers, there is everything. I shall in time go into detail and will surprise even you" (Glaberman 1999: xxvii).

**William Gilbert Grace**

In his letter to Naipaul of 1963 about how British colonial subjects have the capacity to see "British civilization" more "sharply" than the British themselves, James (1986: 117) added, "I believe I have made that clear in the treatment of W. G. Grace." James's "treatment of W. G. Grace" in many ways forms the conceptual heart of the book—indeed part 5 of the work, "W. G.: Pre-Eminent Victorian," could almost stand as a complete piece of writing in its own right.[7] It is in this section, which begins with one of the two most critical methodological chapters of the work, "What Do Men Live By?" (the other is "What Is Art?"—both chapter titles inspired by Leo Tolstoy), that James reveals how and why Grace stands as such a central figure in his rethinking of "British civilization," someone James had begun to research in depth in 1953, right after his forced return from America to Britain.[8] As James wrote in a draft manuscript, "These chapters give a revaluation of the place of W. G. in English history and show that Thomas Arnold of Rugby, Thomas Hughes, the author of *Tom Brown's Schooldays*, and W. G. were three of the greatest cultural and educational influences in the shaping of the manners and morals of Victorian England."[9]

One important consequence of the domination of the British Empire in the late nineteenth century and early twentieth century was the spread of many organized sports—including cricket—that had their initial roots in Britain. As James noted in *Beyond a Boundary*,

> The organizational drive for sport had come from Britain. It was from Britain that cricket, and soccer more than cricket, had spread as nothing international had ever spread for centuries before.... I read and thought and read and unearthed a grievous scandal. This was that not a single English scholar, historian or social analyst of repute had deemed it worth his while to pay even the most cursory attention to these remarkable events in which his own country played so central, in fact the central, role.... Over the second half of the nineteenth century, sparking the great international movement, drawing all eyes to it, startling millions who otherwise would have paid no notice, creating the myth

and the legend, there began to loom the gigantic black-bearded figure of W. G. Grace. (153–54)

He goes on to say that Grace "still stands high in the historical memory of the British people and all who have been brought into close relations with their branch of Western civilization" (159). Yet Grace was noticeably absent from both *English Social History* (1942), by G. M. Trevelyan, whom James described as "a famous Liberal historian" writing "the social history of England in the nineteenth century," and *The Common People* (1938), by Raymond Postgate and G. D. H. Cole, "two famous socialists" who wrote "what they declared to be the history of the common people of England, and between them never once mention the man who was the best known Englishman of his time" (159).[10]

The person James felt had "got closest" to recognizing Grace's historical and social importance was the famous cricket writer and cultural critic Neville Cardus, whom James thought "deserves a critical study. . . . All his work is eloquent with the aesthetic appeal of cricket" (195). In 1930, Cardus had written a famous essay on Grace, "The Champion," which appeared as a chapter in his book *Cricket*. In 1932, Cardus had appointed James to work covering cricket matches alongside him on the *Manchester Guardian*, and the same year Cardus also contributed an article on Grace for *The Great Victorians*, edited by Hugh and H. J. Massingham. This volume had high-profile contributors such as G. K. Chesterton, J. L. Hammond, H. J. Laski, J. Middleton Murry, Herbert Read, Vita Sackville-West, and Rebecca West and discussed forty "great Victorian" figures, including Matthew Arnold, Thomas Carlyle, Charles Darwin, Charles Dickens, George Eliot, Lord Macaulay, Cecil Rhodes, Lord Tennyson, and William Makepeace Thackeray. That Cardus contributed an entry on Grace for such a prestigious volume as this suggests that Grace perhaps was not so neglected a cultural figure as James's reading in *Beyond a Boundary* asserts. Cardus was a quite original and remarkable cultural critic in his own right, and taking his cue from Lytton Strachey's famous *Eminent Victorians* (1918), which had included a biographical portrait of Thomas Arnold, he declared Grace to be "amongst the eminent Victorians." Indeed, "there would have been no Hobbs if Grace had not extended the machinery of batsmanship and achieved a revolution in bowling, by his great synthesis of offensive and defensive stroke play" (Cardus 1987: 94).

As Cardus (1987: 94) put it, "I am trying to get Grace into the Victorian scene, to see him as a Representative Man, and also to see him in relation to the crowd that invented his legend." Unlike so many others, Cardus had recognized and emphasized the mass appeal of Grace, who "stood for so much in the history of cricket at a time when hardly any other game challenged it as the national out-of-door sport and spectacle." Cardus (1987: 91–92) thought it

> astonishing that by means of a game of bat and ball, a man should have been able to stamp his shape and spirit on the imagination of thousands.... When I was a boy I lived in a family that did not interest itself in games. Yet often at breakfast W. G. Grace's name was mentioned. Everybody understood exactly who he was and what he signified in the diet of the day's news. From time to time, *Punch* used him as the subject for a cartoon; the Royal Family occasionally inquired after his health. When he was reported not out at Lord's at lunch, the London clubs emptied, and the road to St John's Wood all afternoon was tinkling with the old happy noise of the hansom cab. Sometimes he would play, at the height of his fame, in a country cricket match in some village in the West of England. And from far and wide the folk would come, on foot, in carriages, and homely gigs.

Although "W. G. himself, of course, did not know what he stood for in the national consciousness," Cardus (1987: 94) attempted to analyze sociologically and historically why Grace had made such an impact:

> When Grace began to stamp his personality on English sport, cricket was scarcely established, save as a rough-and-ready pastime on the village green.... A spectacular interest was wanting to attract the crowds; and the money was required to make a national game. W. G. came forward, at the ripe moment; the technique of cricket stood ready for expansion and masterly summary; the period was also ready for a game which everybody could watch, the gentry as well as the increasing population of the town workers. Grace's skill as a batsman may be said to have orchestrated the simple folk-song of the game; his personality placed it on the country's stage.

As Cardus concluded, "The fact of posterity remains to this moment: he is still the most widely known of all cricketers amongst folk who have seldom, if ever, seen a match.... [H]e really did transcend the game.... I cannot, and nobody possibly could, contain the stature of Grace in terms of the statistics recorded of his skill" (Cardus 1987: 95).

Such passages suggest that James owed much to Cardus's sociological insight and interrogation of the game, yet James insisted in *Beyond a Boundary* that an even deeper understanding of Grace's significance was possible:

> As usual, it is Mr. Neville Cardus, in his vivid darting style, who has got closest to W. G.: "The plain, lusty humours of his first practices in a Gloucestershire orchard were to be savoured throughout the man's gigantic rise to a national renown." Only it was not the plain, lusty humours of an orchard, but of a whole way of life. "He rendered rusticity cosmopolitan whenever he returned to it. And always did he cause to blow over the fashionable pleasances of St John's." . . . There they needed it least. It was to bleak Sheffield, to dusty Kennington and to grim Manchester that W. G. brought the life they had left behind. The breezes stirred by his bat had blown in their faces, north, south and east, as well as in the west. (181)[11]

Rather than seeing Grace as a "Representative Man" of the Victorian age, for James, Grace, though "his personality was sufficiently wide and firm to include a strong Victorian streak without being inhibited," was "in every respect that mattered a typical representative of the pre–Victorian Age" (177, 174). Cardus (1987: 92) had noted, "I have always been amused that W. G. Grace became famous while the Victorians were endowing cricket with moral unction, changing the lusty game that Squire Osbaldeston knew into the most priggish of the lot, and stealing rigour, temper, and character from it." For James, this contradiction was less a matter of "amusement" than absolutely critical to making sense of Grace. As he put it, "The man usually held as representative is never quite typical, is more subtly compounded. . . . Grace gives a more complex impression than is usually attributed to him. . . . [H]e was pre-Victorian in the Victorian Age but a pre-Victorian militant . . . a pre-Victorian who made a pre-Victorian game a part of the Victorian era" (177–78).

James described how Grace, born in 1848, was "a Victorian, but the game he transformed into a national institution was not Victorian either in origin or essence." Instead, it was a creation of "an England still unconquered by the Industrial Revolution" (159), the preindustrial emerging capitalist England of William Hazlitt (1778–1830). For Cardus (1987: 96), "Cricket is without a rival amongst open-air pastimes for the exhibition of native characteristics in Englishmen. It is a leisurely game on the whole, and its slow movement enables the cricketers to display themselves." James agreed that cricket "had been formed by rural and artisan Englishmen who had aimed at nothing but the creation of an activity which would disinterestedly express their native artistic instincts," but thought that "the Age of Hazlitt" was worthy of greater appreciation and attention. "In prose, in poetry, in criticism, in painting, [Hazlitt's] age was more creative than the country had been for two centuries before and would be for a century after. This was the age that among its other creations produced the game of cricket." For James, thus, the modern game of cricket evolved out of traditional rural and popular games through the creative labor of "the yeoman farmer, the gamekeeper, the potter, the tinker, the Nottingham coal-miner, the Yorkshire factory hand. These artisans made it, men of hand and eye" (160). Indeed, "If the Industrial Revolution organised into a concerted whole the particular movements of the artisans who practiced a trade, cricket organised into a whole the elementary tensions and stresses of back-swording, wrestling, racing and the other games of the 'veast'" (168; see also Surin 1995: 330).

Hazlitt himself, James noted, was "not a divided man, he has no acute consciousness either of class or of divided culture." Rather, he was a man who "writes as freely and as publicly of a most degrading love affair as of Elizabethan literature. The possibility of such completeness of expression ended with him and has not returned" (160). As James demonstrated so powerfully in *Beyond a Boundary*, the appeal of Grace for the new English working class forged in the towns and cities of Britain by the time Grace first came to make his impact as a first-class cricketer in the mid-1860s was the glimpse he gave his fellow countrymen of this past "completeness of expression." Cardus himself had said of Grace, "If a man is going to give his whole life to a game, let him play it like a full man, with no half-measures and no repressions" (Cardus 1987: 93). For James, Grace "brought and made secure a place for pre-industrial England in the iron and steel of the Victorian age. . . . Through W. G. Grace, cricket, the most complete expression of popular life in pre-industrial England, was incorporated into the life of the nation" (171, 182).

Cardus stressed that he was trying to see Grace "in relation to the crowd that invented his legend," although once again James thought there was a need to go further. As James noted in *Beyond a Boundary*, "We have peered below the surface at what W. G. did for the people. When we try to find what the people did for him we begin with a blank sheet." Grace, James wrote, was "strong with the strength of men who are filling a social need. . . . Except for commonplaces . . . we know as yet very little of the nourishment given to the hero by the crowd. Here it must have been very great—Grace's career was exceptionally long.... Burly as the figure was, it was sustained and lifted higher than ever before by what has been and always will be the most potent of all forces in our universe—the spontaneous, unqualified, disinterested enthusiasm and goodwill of a whole community" (182–83).

Thus, James recounted, for example, the mass enthusiasm when Grace, in his forty-eighth year, finally reached his one-hundredth first-class century and scored one thousand runs in a month—"the first player in the game ever to do so"—in May 1895:

> Never since the days of the Olympic champions of Greece has the sporting world known such enthusiasm and never since.... [O]n what other occasion, sporting or non-sporting, was there ever such enthusiasm, such an unforced sense of community, of the universal merged in an individual? At the end of a war? A victorious election? With its fears, its hatreds, its violent passions? Scrutinize the list of popular celebrations, the unofficial ones; that is to say, those not organised from above. I have heard of no other that approached this celebration of W. G.'s hundredth century. If this is not social history what is? It finds no place in the history of the people because the historians do not begin from what people seem to want but from what they think the people ought to want. (184–85)

### Capitalism, Class Struggle, and Cricket

"*Beyond a Boundary* is one of the finest and most finished books to come out of the West Indies, important to England, important to the West Indies." So wrote Naipaul (1974 [1963]: 106) in his review of the work in September 1963, paying explicit tribute to the importance of the book to England, given James's discussion of W. G. Grace, as well as the West Indies. James recalled the review the work received in the *Times Literary Supplement*, noting that

> where the reviewer expressed most clearly his astonishment that I had opened up perspectives about British social history of which he had not dreamt: if I remember rightly, he said that they were fantastic and improbable but had a rightness about them.... As a result of my deepest studies and feelings on the situation of the West Indian writer that I believe we have an immense amount to say about Western civilization which we

more than all other writers from the underdeveloped peoples can say. We not only open up ourselves but we open them too. (James 1986: 133)[12]

It is worth briefly registering some of the "fantastic and improbable" perspectives on British social history suggested in *Beyond a Boundary* that the reviewer for the *Times Literary Supplement* was possibly alluding to here. After noting how "organised games had been part and parcel of the civilization of Ancient Greece," James focused on the 1860s and 1870s, when "games and sports, organized as the Greeks had organised them ... all seemed to have returned within about a decade of each other, in frantic haste, as if there were only limited space and those who did not get in early would be permanently shut out." James noted that in Britain, for example, there was the founding of the Football Association in 1863, the first athletic championship held in England in 1866, and the invention of lawn tennis in 1873, and "the public flocked to these sports and games." He then wrote, "In that very decade this same public were occupied with other organizations of a very different type," noting, for example, the founding of the International Working Men's Association (the First International) in London in 1864, and the democratic agitation around the Second Reform Act of 1867. James famously concluded, "This same public that wanted sports and games so eagerly wanted popular democracy too. . . . Both groups were stirred at the same time. The conjunction hit me as it would have hit few of the students of society and culture in the international organization to which I [had] belonged"—that is, Trotsky's Fourth International (152–53).[13]

Yet in retrospect, the precise conjunction between "sport and politics in nineteenth-century Britain" suggested by James would have hit few other Marxist "students of society and culture" because it represents a rather problematic reading of the level of agitation for "popular democracy."[14] Despite the political significance of the 1867 Reform Act, the great movement of agitation for "popular democracy" in nineteenth-century Britain did not come in the 1860s or 1870s, despite a slight rise in class struggle in the 1860s compared with the 1850s. Rather, it came with the Chartist movement of the 1830s and 1840s.[15] Indeed, as James himself noted a little later in *Beyond a Boundary*, by the time Thomas Hughes was writing *Tom Brown's Schooldays* in 1857, "Chartism had died down, and with it the fear of social revolution. If the upper classes were acquiring stability and perspective, the working classes, or at least organised labour, were doing the same." James's reasons for wanting to make so much of the 1860s relate to his understanding of the important battles over the length of the working day that had been previously won—for example, in the Ten Hours Bill finally passed after years of radical campaigning in 1847—and analyzed by Marx in *Capital*. "In the ten years that followed the Factory Act of 1847 there had come into existence an enormous urban public, proletarian and clerical lower middle class. They had won for themselves one great victory, freedom on Saturday afternoons. They were 'waiting to be amused.' ... The decade of the sixties, with its rush to organise sports associations of every kind, was just round the corner" (170).

Yet while rightly situating the important changes that followed the Factory Act of 1847, which led to falling working hours and increased leisure time, the gain of Saturday afternoons off work did not come for skilled workers until 1874, and the idea of the "weekend" for all workers did not come until the 1890s (Collins 2013: 53). The changes James describes in the lives of working people in Victorian Britain—the rise and growth of trade unions as a form of mass democratic politics in their own right, as well as their struggles for popular suffrage (which did not advance for working-class men in a meaningful sense until 1884), and how these developments coincided with a mass popular enthusiasm for sports—need then to be extended over a much longer period from the 1860s to the 1900s rather than condensed and concentrated in the manner James tries to do with respect to the 1860s and early 1870s.[16]

These changes in sports also need to be integrated and understood with other social, economic, and cultural changes then under way, which James does not always fully register in *Beyond a Boundary*, despite their importance to understanding the material reality of life for the Victorian working class. As Tony Collins (2013: 53) notes in his superb and authoritative study *Sport in Capitalist Society*, "Three key elements had to be present for this sporting revolution to take place: an industrial working class, a unified national culture and a mass popular press."

Collins also writes that "the rise in real wages for the British working class in the last third of the nineteenth century and the dense urbanisation of the population made possible the creation of such a mass market with the spending power to support regular, continuous sporting events throughout a season." Cricket matches, for example, could now attract large crowds regularly, which they had not been able to do before, enabling a more profound commercialization as "a permanent market for sport was being created." The new popular enthusiasm for sports also has to be understood with respect to the new development of "home grounds," meaning that "the sports teams of the 1880s were symbols of locality, vehicles for civic pride, that placed huge importance on having a home ground of which other clubs would be envious." By giving expression to economic and municipal rivalries, sports allowed "a way for working class communities to express a sense of belonging, or identity" that "dovetailed neatly with the business needs of clubs and their financial backers, such as breweries and newspapers . . . being a supporter of a local team was a unique form of 'brand loyalty' to a business" (Collins 2013: 50–51).

More critically, noting James's elite education at Queen's Royal College in Trinidad, Collins (2013: 64) alleges that he "was so profoundly shaped by the education he received there that he remained in thrall to the sentimental cant of amateurism" and so said little about the division between the aristocratic gentlemen amateurs and the middle- and working-class professional players that socially segregated and scarred cricket in the nineteenth century and for most of the twentieth century. Francis Wheen has also puzzled over why James seemed to be so "in thrall to the Victorian public-school ideology." For Wheen, James was "a romantic traditionalist," as well as a Marxist. He notes that "the heroes of *Beyond a Boundary* were Thomas Arnold, the 19th century headmaster of Rugby, Thomas Hughes, the author of *Tom Brown's Schooldays*, and W. G. Grace," an amateur gentleman cricketer. "James was dazzled by the 'grandeur' and 'moral elevation' of Arnold's ideas, apparently happy to overlook the fact these ideas included a contempt for the working class and a terror of universal suffrage. What mattered, in C. L. R.'s view, was that Arnold introduced compulsory games for his pupils—'the only contribution of the English educational system of the 19th century to the general educational ideas of Western civilization'" (Wheen 1998: 10).

James's argument flowed from what he saw as the historical significance of how the Victorian middle class—through public schools such as Rugby and the ideology of muscular Christianity espoused by Thomas Arnold and propagandized by Thomas Hughes—had made cricket "the basis of what can only be described as a national culture. 'A straight bat' and 'It isn't cricket' became the watchwords of manners and virtue and the guardians of freedom and power," a way to morally organize their class, in many respects the new ruling class of Great Britain, through the public school code and ultimately helping maintain bourgeois hegemony (165; see also Lazarus 1995). As James explicitly noted himself back in 1957 in a letter to his American comrades, "The British bourgeoisie, who were just pushing the aristocracy out of power, needed an ideology. They took over the game of cricket and in the public schools established the rigorous code as a means of uniting and disciplining their class. This they exported to all the British colonies. That is what I learnt in the West Indies" (James 1986: 88).

Cardus (1987: 92) had noted, with no small degree of disgust, how "cricket was approved at the private schools for the sons of gentlemen, the detestable phrase 'It isn't cricket,' was heard in the land. The game acquired a cant of its own." Yet for James, "All sneering at these as cant and hypocrisy is ignorance or stupidity" (165):

> The system as finally adopted was not an invention but a discovery, or rather a rediscovery. Arnold might give a grudging recognition to Dissent. Yet every renewal of English life so far has gone back to the Puritan past, and his system was Puritan or it was nothing. Cricket and football provided a meeting place for the moral outlook of the dissenting middle classes and the athletic instincts of the aristocracy.... [T]he proof of its validity is its success, first of all at home and then almost as rapidly abroad, in the most diverse places and among peoples living lives which were poles removed from that whence it originally came. This signifies, as so often in any deeply national movement, that it contained elements of universality that went beyond the bounds of the originating nation. (166)

James's defense of Grace, despite what Collins called "the middle-class invention of amateurism"—or what in Grace's case has been called "shamateurism," given that he "earned far more as an amateur than any professional player of the late Victorian era"—also stands because of Grace's critical role in helping this newly refashioned game of cricket, with its amateurism and bourgeois ideological underpinning, become genuinely popular among the English working classes and so truly "hegemonic" (Collins 2013: 36; see also Flett 2013: 121–22). Given the way in which the British Empire then exported cricket and Grace's heroic exploits internationally, it is not surprising that, as Surin (1995: 315) notes, "James regards W. G. Grace as the one cricketer who comes nearest to being a world-historical individual (understanding this term in its full Hegelian sense, albeit as filtered, for James, through Marx)."

Following Cardus, James's Grace was a very "English" cricketer, albeit "typical of an England that was being superseded," whose blemishes were merely "the rubs and knots of an oak that was sound through and through" (176–77). Indeed, James's insistence that "what Arnold, Hughes and W. G. brought is now indelibly a part of the national life and character" (192), together with his wider discussion of cricket as a "national culture," defined as a "way of life" and "the national characteristics of great nations" (42; see also 192) in *Beyond a Boundary*, takes us to another problematic area of discussion. Rosengarten (2008: 238, 240) thought the "portraits of several top English and West Indian cricketers" in *Beyond a Boundary* and "the commentary that accompanies them are fed by impulses in James that are difficult to reconcile with a socialist egalitarian ethos," detecting a "falling back on the concept of the 'national-popular' rather than that of socialist internationalism."

The definition of "national culture" as "a way of life of a particular people living together in one place" was introduced by the brilliant but reactionary poet and critic T. S. Eliot in his *Notes towards the Definition of Culture* (1948: 40, 124–25). Eliot's definition was taken up by the socialist writer Raymond Williams, the author of *Culture and Society, 1780–1950* (1958). In *The Long Revolution*, Williams (1973 [1961]: 57) had declared the "social" definition of culture to be "a description of a particular way of life, which expresses certain meanings and values not only in art and learning but also in institutions and ordinary behavior." E. P. Thompson (1961: 9) famously challenged Williams's definition of "culture" here, counterpoising instead the idea of culture as "a way of *struggle*." In *Beyond a Boundary*, however, James was clearly inspired by Eliot and Williams, and in 1961 he declared Williams "the most remarkable writer that the socialist movement in England has produced for ten years or perhaps twenty," though he felt Williams still needed fully to master the Marxist method. Williams, James (1980: 114) suggested, "has developed the idea of culture from an exclusive possession of the educated and intellectuals and shown that the only meaning the word has for today is *a total way of life of the whole people*." Yet while the anti-elitism of Williams's position was certainly an advance, such a definition is rather problematic, given the heterogeneity of cultural formations and the impossibility of any purely "national cultures." As Terry Eagleton (1976: 95) noted, Williams's approach was surely closer to "romantic populism" and "idealism" than historical materialism, for how under capitalism is any form of "common culture" possible?

Eliot (1948: 17) had also argued that "we can assert with some confidence that our own period is one of decline; that the standards of culture are lower than they were fifty years ago; and that the evidences of this decline are visible in every department of human activity." The stress on "decline" was also to be a theme of *Beyond a Boundary*—hence, the chapter "Decline of the West," which James, with a nod to Oswald Spengler, saw in the batsmen's tendency to play the forward defensive in cricket after World War II. James understood this development as a stifling of cricket's aesthetic and as corresponding to the rise of what he called the "Welfare State of Mind," which he defined in 1957 to his comrades as the "security first, no risks" culture "characteristic of modern bureaucracy" (James 1986: 88). "The cricketers of today play the cricket of a specialized stratum, that of functionaries in the Welfare State," James wrote publicly that year.[17] James's critique here arguably had as much in common with New Right thinking about the welfare state in Britain—indeed, the phrase the "Welfare State of Mind" was coined by Sir Geoffrey Vickers—as it did with an anti-statist Marxist critique of a form of bureaucratic state capitalism (Vickers 1952).

## Conclusion

Although this needs further investigation, such comments remind us that James's *Beyond a Boundary* also needs to be located in relation to the cultural concerns of the "first New Left" in Britain, born in the aftermath of the Hungarian Revolution and the so-called Suez Crisis of 1956 (see Høgsbjerg 2007). James's analyses of the "modern bureaucracy" relate to his theory of state capitalism as a global system that had emerged by the 1950s and remind us once more of his Marxism.[18] Indeed, as Martin Glaberman (1999: xxi) suggested, *Beyond a Boundary* was written to "illustrate Marxist methodology." Neil Lazarus (1995: 342) has gone as far as to suggest that, "in his writings about cricket, James reveals himself to be one of the truly decisive Marxist cultural theorists" of the twentieth century, a figure comparable with Georg Lukács. Robert Hill notes, moreover, that James himself once described *Beyond a Boundary* as being explicitly about the relationship between "the proletariat and sport" (Hill 2013).

Such an explicit Marxist underpinning to the work has yet to be fully teased out and examined. James's pioneering analysis of the class forces at play in the formation of cricket as a game was one of the first to question the dominant mythological narratives about the game's origins, centered on what Collins (2013: 25–26) calls "the 'Merrie England' myth in which feudal England was viewed as bucolic idyll of deferential social harmony" and that are evident from Wordsworth's praise for the "boys who in yon meadow-ground in white-sleeved shirts are playing" in 1802, John Nyren's writing about the Hambledon men in the 1830s, and a multitude of other writers on cricket since (including Trevelyan). As Surin (1995: 329) noted, James's "materialist aesthetic" posed a challenge to the "old, 'idealist' ways, with their banalities about the 'stylishness' of Woolley, Graveney, Vengsarkar, et al. in that

James so amply demonstrated that any attempt to characterise cricketing 'style' must analyse the constitutive rhythms of the game, and that this analysis must necessarily take the form of an engagement with the history of wider political economy and culture." *Beyond a Boundary* brilliantly illuminated the evolution of cricket and the process by which, in the words of Collins (2013: 13), "The relationship between old and new was one of combined and uneven development, in which examples of continuity coexisted alongside instances of rapid change." Yet James's "materialist aesthetic" of cricket arguably failed to fully take register of the class divisions between amateurs and professionals and the masculine ethos around ideas of "muscular Christianity" as the game developed in Victorian Britain. More critically, James might be accused of not fully examining—as one might have expected in a Marxist analysis of cricket—the extent to which cricket is fundamentally linked to a competitive ethos of "winners" and "losers," the alienation resulting from the lack of control workers have over their lives, and the numerous other ways in which in general, to quote Collins, "modern sport was capitalism at play" (Collins 2013: 15). As Paul Blackledge (2014: 390) has noted, "Commercialisation preceded the emergence of most cricket clubs, which were largely formed to capitalise on this new phenomenon. James's alternative vision of cricket as an emergent artistic expression of artisan life obscures this process in a way that masks modern cricket's essence as a capitalist form."

Yet if *Beyond a Boundary* cannot then stand as the definitive Marxist analysis of cricket, James's analysis of Grace still represents a path-breaking contribution to our understanding of the relationship between "the proletariat and sport" in Victorian Britain. In *Capital*, Marx (1976: 928) described how, in any exploitative and alienating historical mode of production, "new forces and new passions spring up in the bosom of society, forces and passions which feel themselves to be fettered by that society."[19] In 1925, in "Where Is Britain Going?" Trotsky (1973: 148) had suggested that any future "British Revolution" will "inevitably awaken in the English working class the most unusual passions, which have hitherto been so artificially held down and turned aside, with the aid of social training, the Church, and the press, in the artificial channels of boxing, football, racing, and other sports." Such an analysis, stressing how the popularity of a sport such as football or cricket was ultimately an expression of the intense alienation created by modern capitalist society both in and outside the workplace, was an important advance for Marxist thinking on sports. Yet for James, who had discussed cricket with Trotsky in Coyoacán, Mexico, in 1939, cricket was not merely a diverting dramatic spectacle but part of the popular culture of society, and in *Beyond a Boundary*, James made his disagreement with Trotsky on the "sport question" explicit: "Trotsky had said that the workers were deflected from politics by sports. With my past I simply could not accept that. I was British" (153).

As James so eloquently insisted in *Beyond a Boundary*,

> What was in the minds and hearts of the people of Victorian England which made them see W. G. [Grace] as they did I cannot say for certain. But the passions and the forces which are embodied in great popular heroes—and W. G. was one of the greatest of popular heroes—these passions and forces do not yield their secrets to the antiquated instruments which the historians still cling to. Wilton St. Hill and Learie Constantine were more than makers of runs and takers of wickets to the people of Trinidad and Tobago. Who will write a biography of Sir Donald Bradman must be able to write a history of Australia in the same period. I have indicated what I think W. G. signified in the lives of the English people, not in what politicians did for them or poets wrote of them or what Carlyle and Ruskin preached to them, but in the lives that they themselves lived from day to day. We shall know more what men want and what they live by when we begin with what they do. They worshipped W. G. That is the fact. And I believe that we have never given this fact the attention it deserves. Some day we shall. Of that I have no doubt. (181–82)

## Notes

I thank Andrew Burgin for generously allowing me access to the draft manuscripts of *Beyond a Boundary* while they were in his possession and Ian Birchall, Paul Blackledge, Chris Gair, David Goodway, Bill Schwarz, and Andy Smith for their comments on this chapter in draft.

*Epigraphs:* James 1986 [1970]: 276; "C. L. R. James's First Cricket XI," *Daily Mail*, 17 June 1986, 21.

1. See also David Lambert, "'In but Not of the West': Caribbean Histories and Geographies," David Nicholls Memorial Trust Lecture, Oxford, 2011, http://www.dnmt.org.uk/app/images/Lambert-David-Nicholls-2012-lecture.pdf; chap. 11 in this volume.
2. Hereafter, page numbers in parentheses refer to this edition of *Beyond a Boundary*.
3. See C. L. R. James, "Who Only Cricket Know," *Beyond a Boundary* Papers, "File H." In 1968, James donated his *Beyond a Boundary* manuscripts to the British

Anti-Apartheid Movement for fundraising. See the relevant correspondence between C. L. R. James and the Manuscript Exhibition Appeal Committee in C. L. R. James Collection, Alma Jordan Library, University of the West Indies, St. Augustine, Trinidad and Tobago, box 10, file 241 in. After they came up for sale at auction again in 2001, they were purchased by the radical London bookseller Andrew Burgin. I am indebted to Burgin for allowing me to examine these papers in 2006 while they were in his possession. The papers are now housed in the archives of the C. L. R. James Cricket Research Centre Library, University of the West Indies, Cave Hill, Barbados.

4. Other national identities related to Britishness such as Scottishness would, of course, also be shaped by these forces, but the initial waves of migration from the Caribbean tended to settle in English cities such as London first.

5. I use the phrase "conscripts of postcoloniality" as passing acknowledgment of David Scott's *Conscripts of Modernity: The Tragedy of Colonial Enlightenment* (2004), a study of James's *The Black Jacobins*.

6. James, *Beyond a Boundary* Papers. Other allusions in chapter titles were to Edmund Burke ("Magnanimity in Politics"), Oswald Spengler ("Decline of the West"), Leo Tolstoy ("What Is Art?" "What Do Men Live By?"), and Mark Twain ("Prince and Pauper").

7. It is possible James was inspired with his title here by Joanna Richardson's *Preeminent Victorian: A Study of Tennyson* (1962).

8. James, *Beyond a Boundary* Papers, "File E."

9. James, *Beyond a Boundary* Papers.

10. G. D. H. Cole and Raymond Postgate's *The Common People* (1949) and the communist historian A. L. Morton's *A People's History of England* (1938), which incidentally also made no mention of W. G. Grace, were among the last books James read before he left Britain in 1938 (see Young 1999: 66).

11. The quotes from James cited here are from Cardus's essay on Grace, "The Champion" (1949 [1930]).

12. The reviewer for the *Times Literary Supplement* had declared of James's discussion of Thomas Hughes, Thomas Arnold and W. G. Grace that "the whole story has a kind of fantastic, improbable rightness about it": see Carew 1963: 459.

13. Although it did widen the franchise to include many in the great cities, the Second Reform Act of 1867 did not "introduce popular democracy in England" as James states. As Paul Adelman (1989: 13) notes, "The year 1867 did not inaugurate an age of Democracy; did not in fact give the working classes direct political power; no workingman, for example, was to be returned at the general election of 1868."

14. I thank David Goodway for directing me to this issue.

15. While the relationship between Chartism and cricket in Britain remains underexplored, Malcolm Chase has altered me to an intriguing connection between the Chartists and West Indian cricket through the famous Trinidadian family the Stollmeyers. In 1845, Conrad Stollmeyer moved from Britain to Trinidad in partnership

with the American inventor Johannes Etzler as moving spirits in the Tropical Emigration Society, which emerged amid the Chartist and socialist agitation in Britain (see Chase 2011: 209). For a recent novel about the Tropical Emigration Society, see Antoni 2015. Descendants of Conrad Stollmeyer include Hugh Stollmeyer, an artist in the Beacon Group in 1920s Trinidad around C. L. R. James; Jeffrey Stollmeyer, who would later captain the West Indies cricket team; and Victor Stollmeyer, who was taught by C. L. R. James when he was ten. Jeffrey and Victor Stollmeyer feature in *Beyond a Boundary*.

16. Even after 1884, only about 60 percent of adult men were entitled to vote until 1918 (see Belcham 1991: 8).

17. C. L. R. James, "Cricket and Contemporary Life," *Cricketer*, 22 June 1957, reprinted in James 2013 [1963]: 217.

18. For more on James's Marxism in Britain in this period, see Høgsbjerg 2006. James's collaboration with Cornelius Castoriadis during the 1950s also perhaps lies behind James's critique of "modern bureaucracy."

19. The relevant chapter is chapter 32, "The Historical Tendency of Capitalist Accumulation."

3 | The Boundaries of Publication:
The Making of *Beyond a Boundary*
ROY MCCREE

Since the publication of C. L. R. James's *Beyond a Boundary* in 1963, the evaluation and appreciation of the book has focused primarily on its value in showing the deep dialectical link between sports and broader sociopolitical processes within society. Indeed, the phenomenal and global acclaim for this text has rested primarily on the penetrative insights that it has provided into the links between sports and the issues of class, race, color, culture, politics, and identity formation generally in human society, together with its autobiographical approach (Bateman 2009; Beckles and Stoddart 1995; Carrington 2013; Cudjoe and Cain 1995; Farred 1996a; Hartmann 2003; Manley 1988; MacLean 2010; Rosengarten 2008; Smith 2010; Stoddart 1990). Jennifer Hargreaves and Ian McDonald (2000: 58) may have summed it up when they described the book as "one of the best examples of good cultural studies writing on sport . . . intertwining autobiography, political prose and penetrating portraits of the greats of West Indian cricket."

In this chapter, however, I do not provide yet another of these appraisals. Instead, the essay focuses not so much on the finished product as on the actual publication process through which the book was produced and its particular significance, vagaries, and contradictions in relation to two basic relationships: author-publisher and metropole-colony. In pursuing this objective, the chapter is divided into six parts, which relate to: (1) its methodology; (2) its analytical framework; (3) the early failed efforts at publication; (4) the final securing of a publisher; (5) the peculiarities or boundaries of the publication process as they relate particularly to the naming of the text and the date and timing of its publication; and (6) its broader socioeconomic and political significance as part of metropole-colony relations.

## Methodology

As a result of the upsurge in qualitative research over the past twenty-five years, there has been increasing interest in the study of documents (Denzin and Lincoln 1994; Silverman 1993, 2004), including letters (Chawansky 2010; Denzin 2012). Consistent with this trend, this chapter is based on an analysis of a series of letters exchanged by C. L. R. James, the publisher of *Beyond a Boundary* (i.e., Hutchinson), and a range of individuals who included journalists, cricket writers, and friends in the period leading up to the publication of the book between 1960 and 1963. These original letters, which have never been studied until now, are in the C. L. R. James Collection at the Alma Jordan Library, University of the West Indies, St. Augustine, Trinidad and Tobago. The examination of the letters, however, was constrained by several related limitations.

First, the available record of these letters starts in August 1960. As a result, it is impossible to tell whether James began the search for a publisher before he returned to Trinidad in 1958. No relevant letters were found from the time of his return to the island up to August 1960. This is curious, since most of the book had been completed before he returned to the West Indies: "I had finished it up to the end of Chapter 17 in Europe not having seen the West Indies for 26 years" (James, 1 May 1963).[1] Second, the collection did not contain all of the possible letters that were exchanged about the book during the period for which letters were available (1960–63); in several instances, references were made to letters or replies to letters that themselves were not found. In addition, we do not know whether there were other letters to which no secondary reference was made and of which there is no existing record. These gaps limit the interpretation or understanding of the publication process and the experiences that James endured and, furthermore, mean that it is important to recognize the tentative nature of the analysis that follows.

## Analytical Framework

In examining the process of publishing the book, it is suggested that it can be seen as representing a particular "figuration" of social relations. The term "figuration" was used by the German sociologist Norbert Elias to capture the interdependent or reciprocal nature of relations between people, although he recognized that such relations may also be characterized by inequalities in power and resources (Elias 1978, 1994 [1939]; Maguire 1999). In addition, in this figuration the ways in which people interact with one another as individuals or as representatives of groups, organizations, or even nations can have the effect of facilitating, as well as constraining, their actions and interests or capacity to act on their own. Relatedly, social relations or social interaction can be a very dynamic, open-ended, long-term, and unplanned process that may have unintended as well as intended effects. In short, social relations or "human figurations" can be interactive, processual, unequal, and dynamic.

In its application here, "figuration" refers to the nature of the relations or interaction that James had with the eventual publisher, with other potential publishers, and with certain friends who formed part of the publication process, which was facilitating, constraining, and characterized by both interdependence and dependence. In addition, another distinguishing feature of this publication figuration was that it formed part of a much broader figuration that consisted of the relationship between the metropole or imperial power at the time (i.e., Britain) and one of its former colonies (i.e., Trinidad). While James was able to exercise some measure of agency, initiative, or free will in this publication figuration, it is argued, he was also constrained by certain boundaries inherent in the author-publisher relationship, which were particularly evident in decisions relating to the date and title of the publication. Such agency was reflected in James's early attempts to get the book published and the reaction to his failure to do so.

### Early Publication Efforts and Rejection

As part of an attempt to promote the book internationally, James first tried to get excerpts of it serialized in the Australian press and the Caribbean but was met with rejection. Based on the available letters, these efforts appeared to have started in August 1960 when he wrote to the Australian journalist and cricket author (and former Australian Test cricketer) J. H. Fingleton in an attempt to get excerpts published in an Australian newspaper. This was timed to coincide with the West Indian tour of Australia, which was to start in October of that year (James, 31 August 1960). This effort, however, bore no fruit, for in a subsequent reply to one of Fingleton's (unavailable) letters to him on the matter, James wrote, "Thank you for your letter of the 9th November, and all the work you have done for my ms. It is unfortunate that the editors have not seen the light. But one is hardened to that now" (James, 18 November 1960).

Undeterred by rejection, however, James subsequently approached the renowned British cricket writer and commentator John Arlott to have the book published but was again turned down. It appears that this was due to doubts about the book's potential market value or profitability, given what was described as the "struggling" nature of "cricket book sales" at the time. In a letter to James dated 7 December 1960, Arlott wrote:

> My Dear CLRJ,
>
> Alas, I am sorry to have to return your typescript. Now, both John St. John and I enjoyed it immensely—it seems to me a very good book indeed. Cricket book sales, however—apart from [star] reminiscences and the occasional Neville Cardus are struggling nowadays, unless the writer has a fairly firm public. Thus, to break even, this book would have to do well in the West Indies. Our export manager has been there very recently and he cannot see sales of 500. There is a point at which a book "breaks even" and our experts in this matter cannot see your book achieving it. Both John St. John and I are extremely sorry. On pre-war costs we could—and would—have published it.
>
> I do hope you may have better luck with it elsewhere. I wonder if <u>printed</u> [underline in original] and published in the West Indies it might be a worthwhile proposition? (Arlott, 7 December 1960)

In response, James stated, among other things, that "it is to some degree a disappointment that the book is not immediately accepted, even with your recommendation. But I assure you that the only thing which would compensate for it is your generous appreciation of it. That means a great deal to me. Thanks very much" (James, 10 December 1960).

In the West Indies, James also tried to get local newspapers to promote the book but met with a mixed response. In this regard, while he had some luck with the *Daily Gleaner* of Jamaica, which paid him 480 British West Indian dollars for the "lifting rights on book dealing with cricket" (Burke, 18 January 1961), he was not so fortunate with the *Barbados Advocate*, which in 1961 rejected his offer for "the serialization rights" of the book because it was deemed "not suitable for publication in the *Advocate*" (Smith, 20 February 1961). However, these failed efforts to promote the book or obtain a publisher did not deter an indomitable James, and his perseverance was soon to pay off.

### Securing a Publisher

If the failed efforts of James to secure a publisher can serve to demonstrate his personal initiative and determination to get his book published, his fortitude and resilience were demonstrated even further after securing one, for he now had to deal with the preferences of the publisher, as well as with personal adversity following a serious car accident.

The decisive turn in James's luck and efforts to secure a publisher occurred in 1961 and came with the intervention of the famed West Indian author George Lamming, with whom he shared a close relationship. Lamming (1989: 196) noted that he had had "very close and frequent contact" with James ever since they first met accidentally at Charing Cross Road in London in 1954. What Lamming did was present James's book to the British publisher, Hutchinson, whose chairman (Robert Lusty) had played a decisive role in getting Lamming's own seminal book, *In the Castle of My Skin*, published some eight years earlier, in 1953 (Lamming, 27 June 1961).[2] Lusty wrote to Lamming on 29 May 1961:

> My dear Lamming,
>
> A brief note to say that we are much taken with James's book and have today written to him putting up a proposition for his manuscript. He has, I think rare qualities, although as I have told James I have some doubts whether this is the kind of book where we can anticipate large sales. I am most grateful to you for this introduction.

In a subsequent letter to James, also dated 29 May 1961, Lusty communicated his company's decision to publish the book, the apparently modest financial terms and conditions of publication, and their early dissatisfaction with the title of the manuscript, *Who Only Cricket Know* and need for "a rather better title":

> Dear Mr. James,
>
> I have been delighted to consider the manuscript of your book WHO ONLY CRICKET KNOW which has been submitted through the kind services of George Lamming.
>
> I would like most warmly to congratulate you on the achievement of your book for it is a memorable one and our only doubt is whether

it could expect to achieve the widespread circulation which it certainly merits. This doubt arise[s] from the possibility that cricketers might find in it too much "real life" and those interested in social and political problems might find too much cricket, but I think this is a risk which we would take in the interest of getting the book into print.

I am afraid that we cannot offer particularly attractive terms and I would suggest an advance payable on publication of £100 against royalties of 10% to 3,000 and 15% thereafter. It is a book which in my view requires a few illustrations or decorations—preferably line decorations—and I think that it certainly needs a rather better title than "Who Only Cricket Know".... I shall much look forward to your response and meeting you with a view to talking about various points, if you should be in London.

Understandably, after a period of rejection and after many years of literary toil, James expressed his delight over this offer of publication. In a letter to Lusty dated 12 June 1961, he wrote:

Dear Mr. Lusty,

I am delighted to read your view of my book and your offer of publication.... You can imagine after all these years how delighted I am at the turn of events and your acceptance of my book. I shall do nothing to defer publication and everything to expedite it. After an absence of thirty years,[3] I have been living for three years in the West Indies. There is a great deal of interest and excitement about the book and I sincerely hope, in fact I am fairly certain, that the book will do all that can be expected as a commercial publication.

Unfortunately, as fate would have it, his publication breakthrough came as James was recovering from a serious car accident that occurred in April 1961 while he was in Jamaica for a series of lectures. The accident would have taken place, therefore, mere weeks before he received formal notice of the publication offer in May 1961. The accident reportedly left him and the driver of the car "in an unconscious condition," and several days after, both were described as "still very ill."[4] This accident, however, was not going to deter James from seizing this publication opportunity, which he had long sought. While still in recuperation, therefore, he made it clear to Lusty that despite his condition and calls for him to "rest," he was "ready to look at proofs" and even promised to send him the last chapter "in a few days" (James, 12 June 1961).

The publication deal with Hutchinson seems to have given James a new lease on life, for although the accident had clearly left him "quite weak," he appears to have used the time offered by his convalescence to continue working feverishly on the book—so much so that, by the end of 1961, James had revised and sent the final chapters of the manuscript to the publisher. In a letter from Lusty dated 12 December 1961, we read, "Dear Mr. James, We received your letter and the concluding chapters of the manuscript today. Thank you so much."

James's decision to continue work on the book during his recovery after a nearly fatal accident is consistent with Lamming's (1989: 196) description of him as having "stamina" and as "a miracle of perseverance" in the context of his release from Ellis Island. However, after formal submission of the revised manuscript in 1961, three major decisions remained to be made relating to the date, the timing, and the title of the publication.

### The Boundaries of Publication: Date, Timing, and Title

The decisions surrounding the date, timing, and title, which can be seen as the boundaries of publication, serve to highlight the constraining nature of the publisher-author relationship, or the figuration in which James was located, since it was the publisher who had the final say on these issues, which went against the author's preferences. In dealing with these boundaries, however, James exercised what can be considered openness, compromise, and the capacity to be accommodating to safeguard the publication of the book.

The date and timing of the publication were first determined in April 1962, while the title was determined some six months later, in November 1962. When he was embarking on his search for a publisher, James had stated in a letter to Fingleton, "I expect [the book] to be published early in the new year" (James, 31 August 1960), which meant 1961. In 1961, however, as we have seen, James was lucky enough to find a publisher, due in no small measure to the influence of fellow West Indian George Lamming and his connections with the would-be publisher. As a result of the problems he had encountered in finding a publisher, combined with his nearly fatal accident, also in 1961, James was forced to change his publication plans to 1962, a year before the West Indian cricket tour of England of 1963. In a letter to Lusty dated 6 December 1961, and while he was still in recovery, James wrote in part:

> Dear Mr. Lusty,
>
> May I tell you what my plans are. I am slowly recovering my health, very slowly. I plan to be in England in the summer of 1963 when the West Indians play in England. I hope to persuade one of the big newspapers to let me do if only a weekly column on the matches. I am hoping that publication of the book as early as possible in 1962 will open the way to a paper edition <u>on sale</u> [underline in original] when the West Indians are playing and I am writing. If this should be compatible with your business necessities, I shall be very pleased.

It is suggested that James's preference for 1962 after the initial date of 1961 was dashed, possibly due to his car accident, may have been influenced by the fact that it was the year in which both Jamaica and Trinidad became the first West Indian islands to gain independence from Britain. The possible influence of this political factor on James's preference is suggested in a letter to Lusty dated 23 June 1961, in which James wrote in part:

> May I say that the book comes out at a particularly opportune time. There is an immense excitement among the people of the West Indies at the present time about everything, particularly in print, that deals with their past. The conference in England which fixed [*sic*] the independence has created amongst other things a great intellectual excitement.

In this context, therefore, the publication of the book in 1962 would have assumed symbolic importance, although it was as much a celebration of an English colonial legacy in sports as it was a critique of cricket as a symbol of empire.

James's preference for publication in 1962, however, was dashed when the publisher suggested that it would be more opportune to publish the book in 1963, to coincide with the West Indian cricket tour of England during that year. A major consideration for the publisher in determining the date and timing of the publication was economic, since it was reasoned that James's own publication or marketing plan would have "interfered with sales of the hard cover edition." Lusty wrote to James in a letter dated 27 April 1962:

> Dear Mr. James,
>
> It has been decided that it will be far better both from your point of view and ours to publish it to coincide with the arrival of the West Indian team next year, and not this year and follow on with a paperback edition so soon after. This would certainly interfere with sales of the hard cover edition. I am sure that you will appreciate that this is the right decision.

It turns out, therefore, that James's suggested publication date was not "compatible with [the] business necessities" of the publisher. Commercialism, therefore, appears to have trumped political symbolism and James's exercise of agency in suggesting the date of publication. Unfortunately, no letter was found in which James might have replied to this decision.

In relation to the title, the naming of the text might be considered one of the more intriguing or significant aspects of the publication process that produced *Beyond a Boundary*. It is significant because, while James had suggested several possible options, the final title was suggested by Lamming and found favor with the publisher.

The first title that had appeared on the original manuscript was *Who Only Cricket Know*. From the time that the publisher decided to publish the text, however, the suitability or appropriateness of the title had been questioned: "I think that it certainly needs a better title than 'Who Only Cricket Know'" (Lusty, 29 May 1961). In response, James was quick to express his openness to considering the possibility of changing the title, for he told Lusty:

> Your views about illustrations and a different name I shall be glad to learn more about. I have no special views on the matter, and from long experience I know that on those [sic] publishers know much more than authors. (James, 12 June 1961)

In December of that same year, James again raised the issue of the book's title but only to say that he was still "undecided" about it, although he suggested in the interim two seemingly strange options: *W. G., A West Indian Grace* and *West Indian Progeny of W. G.* (James, 6 December 1961). We can speculate as to what James could have meant by these apparently odd titles.

However, they serve to underline further the iconic status of Grace in James's imagination as a symbol of the game, batsmanship, cricketing greatness, Englishness itself, and cricket's transformation into a "national institution" from its humble origins in pre-Victorian and preindustrial England (James 2013 [1963]: 159–187). In the book itself, of course, James had devoted four chapters to Grace, and Grace was one of three cricketers to whom the book was personally dedicated, the other two being the West Indians Sir Learie Constantine and Sir Frank Worrell. Nevertheless, whatever the title chosen, James expressed a clear desire to have his adapted version of Rudyard Kipling's famous aphorism placed "below it." James wrote to Lusty on 6 December 1961:

Dear Mr. Lusty,

I am still undecided about the title. I believe that whatever title is decided upon, below it should be printed: "What do they know of cricket who only cricket know" (with apologies to Rudyard Kipling). . . . For the time being I suggest:
WG, A WEST INDIAN GRACE
WEST INDIAN PROGENY OF WG.

Sometime after, however, it appeared that James had abandoned these titles, preferring instead *The Cricket Crusaders* (Anderson, 13 November 1962). This option, however, was also rejected by the publisher, who expressed a preference instead for the title *Beyond a Boundary*, based on what appeared to be two related considerations—one of them economic; and the other, literary or sociological. First, there was an apparent concern that an explicitly cricketing title would have been too narrow, which could have limited the book's "appeal" to a broader public and, by extension presumably, a larger market. Second, it was felt that since the book dealt with broad sociopolitical issues of race, color, class, and nationalism that transcended the specificity of cricket or sports, *Beyond a Boundary* was more appropriate. In a letter dated 23 November 1962, James was notified thus:

Dear Mr. James,

I am sorry to bother you again about the title of your book, but we are having second thoughts on your decision to call it the CRICKET CRUSADERS.

The point is that this book is being published under the Hutchinson imprint, and it is felt that we should try to avoid any reference to cricket particularly as your work has a more important theme than cricket. Our Editorial Committee felt that the title should have an ambiguous reference to cricket rather than a direct one. In the circumstances, it has been decided that "BEYOND A BOUNDARY" would now be the most appropriate title to give to the book.

I do hope you agree with this and appreciate that our decision has taken in the interests of the appeal which the book will have for readers.

The available record of letters suggests that James did not respond to this letter (written in November 1962) until February 1963. In his reply, he seems to have agreed with the new suggested title of the book while expressing "personal astonishment" over the way the book "extended beyond a boundary," as noted by the publisher:

Dear Mr. Lusty,

I have read your letter with very great interest and I am able to tell you pretty much what I think practically at once. As I have been reading the proofs and rereading the book I confess frankly that I am personally astonished at the way in which what I have written has extended beyond a boundary. Therefore your statement that the book should not look like another volume of cricketing reminiscences I find very sympathetic. (James, 12 February 1963)

The title of the book, therefore, much like the date of publication itself, was significantly influenced by commercial considerations, although these "relations of production" did not undermine or compromise in any way its literary content or quality.

It must be noted, however, that it was not the publisher who had come up with the title of the book in the first instance, although it was Hutchinson's preferred option. Rather, this honor went to Lamming, who had first helped James secure the publisher. When I asked Lamming, "How did the book get its name or who named it?" Lamming replied:

The answer is quite straightforward—I chose the title which was originally *Beyond The Boundary*—and this may have appeared in the earliest edition. I was surprised to see the definite article, "the" replaced by an indefinite "A." Boundary in relation to cricket is very specific and just not any enclosure as for football, tennis, etc. I don't know who made the change or when. . . .

PS. Beyond implies that there were social and historical issues which went further than the game, cricket.[5]

In her recollection of Lamming's role in naming the book and the unexplained change in the definite article, Selma James wrote in 2013, "Years later I learned that it was Lamming who had named it—almost. He had proposed *Beyond the Boundary*, which the publisher changed to 'a' for no reason we could agree with. 'The' challenges all boundaries, not just cricket's—a true description of the book."[6]

Unfortunately, no letter was found in the available collection in which Lamming had suggested this title or in which the change from "the boundary" to "a boundary" was explained. However, in a letter to James dated 27 June 1961, written about two months after his accident in Jamaica and more than a year before Lusty's editorial decision in November 1962, Lamming revealed that he had spoken with Lusty over lunch about the title of the book, as well as the date of publication. But all the letter in question states in relation to the title of the book is, "The title of the 'cricket' book won't do; but there is no need to bother about that for the time being" (Lamming, 27 June 1961). Although Lamming played a decisive role in helping James secure a publisher and giving the book its name, he noted, "I played no part in the writing of the book beyond occasional discussion of the [manuscript]."[7]

However, while Lamming played "no part" in the actual writing of the book, he had played a formidable role, together with James, in the postwar flowering of West Indian literature that was intertwined with the deeper currents of West Indian decolonization, nationalism, and integration for which London, ironically, had served as the epicenter. Their close association, therefore, might be seen as a symbolic representation of this integration, which was a major theme or thread that connected their works and their Caribbeanist political outlook. It is within this broader sociopolitical context that the publication of *Beyond a Boundary* assumed even more significance.

Although James had played little or no role in setting the date for and the title of the publication, both of which were influenced by commercial considerations, he demonstrated a certain measure of openness, accommodation, and astuteness since, at the end of the day, he achieved what he had long sought: the publication of the book. This had translated into a win-win situation for him and the publisher. In any event, in accepting the publication offer, as noted earlier, James had clearly stated, "I shall do nothing to defer publication and everything to expedite it." His approach to these two issues was therefore consistent with this position, although it may have impinged on his agency. Nevertheless, in the same way that people may make history, but not on their own terms, they may also publish, but not on their own terms. In view of this, despite the concessions James had to make in relation to the date and title of the publication, he still made history.

The examination of this publisher-author figuration, however, has to be located within a broader metropole-colony figuration of which it was an integral part and that also proved contradictory: facilitating as well as constraining.

**Beyond the Publication**

The process of publishing *Beyond a Boundary* reveals something about the socioeconomic and political relations explored in the book that relate particularly to the metropole-colony figuration in which James and the publisher were located. This figuration was marked by three major related, contextual factors: (1) the colonial period in which James was writing; (2) the geographical and social origins of the author and publisher; and (3) the undeveloped nature of book publishing in the West Indies.

In these respects, it is worth reminding ourselves that at the time James was writing, the West Indian territories were still colonies of Britain, although the process of decolonization and the end of empire were well on the way following the end of World War II and signaled by the independence of India in 1947. During this colonial period, there was no local or West Indian book publishing company of any repute to which James might have turned to have his book published and marketed on an international scale. Consequently, James had to depend on a foreign publisher who, in this instance, was British.[8] In such a context, the production or publication of the book was clearly shaped by the general process of socioeconomic dependence of the West Indian islands on Great Britain at the time. In other words, the interaction between James and Hutchinson (author-publisher figuration) was part of a broader relationship or figuration between colony and metropole characterized by both dependence and interdependence.

It is ironic, therefore, that while James and many others in Jamaica and Trinidad were looking forward to celebrating political independence from Britain, which had been granted in 1962, James was looking forward to the publication of a book that depended on the commercial acumen and resources of a British publisher. Relatedly, with regard to the title, the phrase "Beyond a Boundary" has become a sort of discursive code to signify the function that cricket has come to serve in the West Indies as a symbol of West Indian anti-British imperialism, the struggle for decolonization, democratization, independence, nationalism, and even regionalism. However, at the same time, the book's publication still depended on a British publisher.

Yet this reading of the publication needs to be balanced by several other important considerations. First, we must admit that, notwithstanding its unequal nature, it is within this same figuration—or metropole-colony or publisher-author relationship—that James got the opportunity and support to publish his work that was not forthcoming in the West Indies itself. In this sense, therefore, we can say that the figuration was facilitating at the same time as it was constraining (e.g., in relation to determining the date of publication and the title). Second, though it depended on a British publisher and a British book market, a book written by a black West Indian, or "colonial," was able to set a new benchmark of literary brilliance in the study and writing about sports in general, and about cricket in particular. John Arlott, the same person who had turned the book down, commented, "It is the finest book written about the game of cricket" (Arlott 1964: 993). James, however, may have seen this tension or contradiction as merely consistent with our multiple identities as part British and part West Indian. This dual identity was also expressed in one of his letters about the book, in which he wrote, "The book is West Indian through and through, particularly in the early chapters on my family, my education and the portraits of West Indian cricketers of the previous generation, some of them unknown. But the book is very British. Not only the language but on page after page the (often unconscious) literary references, the turn of phrase, the mental and moral outlook. That is what we are, and we shall never know ourselves until we recognize that fully and freely and without strain" (James, 1 May 1963).

But this dualism notwithstanding (part West Indian and part British), the contradictory literary impact of James's work on the popular culture of the dominant imperial power can serve further to illustrate not just the general and reciprocal tendency within human relations. More specifically, it serves to demonstrate that the relationship between metropole and colony or dominant and subordinate was not always one-way traffic, or unidirectional, since they influenced each other, though in differing degrees. Therefore, this metropole-colony relationship or figuration, in which both James and Lusty were located, reflected the workings of a process that did not just contain contradictory elements. It also was interactive, reciprocal yet also unequal: (inter)dependent, dynamic, open-ended, and facilitating, as well as constraining.

**Conclusion**

With James battling against rejection, pessimism, and ill health after his nearly fatal car accident, *Beyond a Boundary* is a book that almost did not see the light of day. However, due to James's resilience, his unwavering commitment to his work and the game of cricket, and the forging of a West Indian nation, the injured author still played as straight as he could, never taking his eye off his objective. In the process, he produced a literary innings and record that, arguably, are yet to be surpassed.

While the publishers were generally pessimistic, the optimism shown by James was eventually vindicated as the book went on to become a classic sporting text—so much so, indeed, that in 2002 it was ranked thirty-sixth among the Top 100 Sports Books of All Time by, of all ironies, the American magazine *Sports Illustrated*.[9] For sure, Caliban's pioneering masterpiece had borne fruit, though aided in part by Caesar. So much for Arlott's "experts," who did not see the book even breaking even, and for the publisher's own "doubts whether this is the kind of book where we can anticipate large sales." Compare this with James, who, after receiving the offer of publication, wrote to Lusty in June 1961: "I am fairly certain, that the book will do all that can be expected as a commercial publication."

However, while much praise has been rightly heaped on James, less has been forthcoming for Lusty and the Hutchinson Editorial Committee, who should be commended for seeing the brilliance of both text and author, notwithstanding their understandable doubts, and taking the risk to publish the book at a time that such writing, particularly by a person of color and, more so, about sports, was not fashionable. Lamming's monumental role also has not been previously acknowledged as fully as it ought to have been; it was due in no small measure to the commercially driven boldness of the former and the literary support of the latter that the text has now become part not just of sporting history, but of social and political history more widely.

**Notes**

1. *Beyond a Boundary* has nineteen chapters, which suggests that James wrote the last two chapters during his stay in the West Indies. Letters in the C. L. R. James Collection consulted for this essay are cited in parentheses in the text by surname of writer and date.
2. George Lamming, email to the author, 26 February 2014.
3. James's recollection here is not accurate, for he left the Caribbean in 1932 and returned for the first time only in 1958. Depending on how we do the calculating, then, James was absent from the Caribbean for about twenty-six years, not thirty, as he suggests. James, in a subsequent letter to one H. S. Altham, refers to not "having seen the West Indies for 26 years" (James, 1 May 1963).
4. *Daily Gleaner,* 1 May 1961, 2 May 1961; *Trinidad Guardian,* 1 May 1961.
5. Lamming, email to the author.
6. Selma James, "How *Beyond a Boundary* Broke Down the Barriers of Race, Class and Empire," *The Guardian,* 2 April 2013. It is of interest to note that while Lamming understands "the" in "the Boundary" to have a specific meaning in the context of cricket, Selma James interprets it in a more general sense to refer to "all boundaries, not just cricket's."
7. Lamming, email to the author.
8. In this chapter, use of the terms "English" and "British" does not imply that Britain consists only of England.
9. See http://sportsillustrated.cnn.com/si_online/features/2002/top_sports_books/2.

# 4 | "West Indian Through and Through, and Very British": C. L. R. James's *Beyond a Boundary*, Coloniality, and Theorizing Caribbean Independence

MINKAH MAKALANI

In May 1963, just as *Beyond a Boundary* first appeared in print, C. L. R. James wrote to several prominent Caribbean intellectuals to relay his thinking about what would become possibly his most important work of political thought. Of its early chapters on his family, education, and early Caribbean cricketers, he explained, "The book is West Indian through and through," an otherwise unremarkable observation had he not, rather provocatively, also called it "very British, not only the language but . . . the mental and moral outlook," a commentary on the book's structure that he applied equally to Caribbean people and society. "That is what we are," he implored Grantley Adams, "and we shall never know ourselves until we recognize that fully and freely and without strain."[1] James never explained what it meant to be "West Indian through and through" and "very British," leaving it open whether he considered these identical or distinct, yet interrelated, identities. It may well be, as Simon Gikandi (2000: 159, 167) suggests, that James sought to appropriate and reformulate "a belated Victorianism" into a foundational mode of "black self-determination and rights" (see also Høgsbjerg 2014: 17–31), though I worry that such a framing risks confining James's vision of Caribbean independence to already available modes of governance.

When James alighted from the plane in Trinidad on 19 April 1958, after twenty-six years abroad and with the manuscript for *Beyond a Boundary* virtually finished, he returned with a sense of the uncharted possibilities for the Caribbean. The West Indies Federation was a foregone conclusion. Yet his decision to remain and work in Eric Williams's ruling People's National Movement (PNM) grew out of a concern for what he considered the "undoubted crisis" facing federation: whether Caribbean peoples would shape independence themselves or receive a form handed down by Britain's Colonial Office. Indeed, as his correspondence with Jamaica's Norman Manley reveals, James's first several months traveling throughout the Caribbean were preoccupied with shoring up the support of local political leaders for a strong federal government that worked in the interests of the Caribbean masses.[2]

Given these concerns, it is noteworthy that many of James's earliest public lectures focused on art. In the most celebrated of these, "The Artist in the Caribbean," which he delivered at the University of the West Indies (UWI), Jamaica, in the fall of 1959, James contemplated the role of the artist in developing national consciousness, focusing in particular on the great artist who through "a combination of learning . . . observation, imagination and creative logic" is able to "construct the personalities and relations of the future." The Caribbean could certainly produce such genius as long as there existed a "medium so native to the Caribbean . . . from which the artist can draw that strength which makes him a supreme practitioner." As far as James could see, at least in terms of what one might call "high" art, "There is nothing of the kind in the Caribbean." Although he routinely praised the literary talents of George Lamming, James nonetheless believed that working in the literary form, a foreign medium for a foreign audience, had "objectively circumscribed" Lamming. For the Barbadian cricketer Garfield Sobers, by contrast, James saw "no limits" to what he might achieve, having been "born into a tradition, into a medium which though transported was so well established that it has created a Caribbean tradition of its own" (James 1980 [1959]: 184–85, 187).

If the arts could play so central a role in shaping a Caribbean future, Sobers represented a model for such an artist. The suggestion in this lecture that cricket was not "high" art was rhetorical rather than a deeply held assessment, as James would elsewhere locate Sobers in a train of Caribbean intellectuals and artists, even calling him "an unprecedented, unimaginable practitioner of his particular art."[3] Sobers's imaginative powers and artistic genius grew from the fact that he was "the first genuine native son . . . born in the West Indies, educated in the West Indies, learning the foundations of his cricket there without benefit of secondary school, or British university" (James 1980 [1969]: 219–20). Writing a decade after his UWI lecture, he imagined that "as a small boy Sobers most certainly played cricket barefooted in the streets with a sour orange for a ball, and . . . a coconut branch hacked into an approximation of a bat." Although James had owned a bat ever since he was four and never went without shoes, he could remark nonetheless,

"All of *us* in the West Indies did that" (James 1980 [1969]: 221).[4] It was through imagining him playing barefoot in the streets, without the benefit of a British education, that James grounds Sobers in a cricketing tradition established by the colonial masses who transformed a British form into something uniquely Caribbean.

James's thinking about Caribbean independence, as several scholars have pointed out, involves the interaction among his Marxist historicism, anticolonial poetics, and modernist sensibilities. For James, these coalesced into a narrative in which the enslaved Africans in Saint-Domingue appeared "closer to a modern proletariat than any group of workers in existence at the time," a description that rendered them intelligible to a Marxist frame but failed to consider an African worldview guiding the revolution and leaves in place a modern-premodern divide. Still, we should not overstate James's veneration for British culture and art and Western philosophy. Paget Henry (2000: 48–49) reminds us that James's enmeshment in European thought both was productive of his anticolonial politics and Pan-Africanism and left "embarrassing traces" or Eurocentric values that, as with many other thinkers, tended to "limit the effectiveness of their critiques" (see also Bogues 2003: 80–81; James 2000: 99–100; Makalani 2011: 220–22).

The embarrassing traces in James's thinking should not, I would suggest, foreclose our consideration of how, within such a complex frame of thought, he also turned toward Africa in ways that were possibly unintended. It was in *The Black Jacobins* that, while detailing the planning of the slave uprising that would become a revolution, James (2001 [1938]: 69) declared, "Voodoo was the medium of the conspiracy," a point he seemingly returned to decades later when, while discussing how he might narrate that story differently, he said he would give greater weight to the thinking of the enslaved masses rather than simply to Toussaint Louverture. Indeed, the contemplation of colonial Trinidad's color, class, and social hierarchies forced James to grapple with complexities that lay outside the forensics of Marxist political economy. In her discussion of what she calls a Jamesian poiesis, Sylvia Wynter registers his seemingly contradictory makeup as a Caribbean radical who was "a Negro yet British, a colonial native yet culturally a part of the public school code[,] . . . of African descent yet Western." Wynter views these diverse qualities as guiding James toward a theory that sought neither to reconcile these apparent contradictions nor to tamp them down into a universal subject. "The quest for a frame to contain them all," she alerts us, "came to constitute the Jamesian poiesis"—a conceptual frame to unravel the full complexity of Caribbean political life (Wynter 1992: 69).

We might thus consider that when James describes the Caribbean as "backward" compared with Europe and America, a veneration of Western capitalism common (though not singularly so) to Marxist thought more generally, James is also offering a commentary on the Caribbean's politics and practices of governance. In that same letter to Adams, James offered possibly his most important insight into *Beyond a Boundary*: "Originating as we are within the British structure, but living under such different social conditions, we have a lot to say about the British civilization itself which we see more sharply than they themselves."[5] If boys playing barefoot in the streets had established a distinctly (albeit masculine) Caribbean tradition, it would seem they had not established for the practice of democratic rule similarly deep roots. Speaking in Kingston shortly after his "The Artist in the Caribbean" lecture, James explained the need to shape a new national life through federation, lest the Caribbean "have the flag and . . . the national anthem" but "remain essentially colonial . . . because the social, geographical, economic and even the historical surroundings of colonialism remain with us on every side."[6] As this suggests, James's concern with Federation was the mode of governance it would implement. Put differently, how might the Caribbean establish a democratic tradition when it had only known colonial rule? It was this question that in no small part informed his paradox of being "West Indian through and through" and "very British." James does not present democracy and colonial rule as distinct modes of governance, where the exigencies of colonial rule requires suspending (or subtending) democracy until such time as the pre-modern other develops into a modern subject suited to democratic rule. Rather, the two are deeply braided realities that, as Anthony Bogues puts it, demand an inquiry into how "the regimes of racial and colonial domination . . . are themselves constitutive [of liberal practice as] both historical and contemporary rule" (Bogues 2010: 32).

Attention to James's colonial Victorianism, while not unwarranted, threatens to obscure his sense of the Caribbean's unique position within Western civilization. The region's origins at the dawn of modernity and the sharpened vision that Caribbean peoples gained from these experiences reflect its emergence as what Michel-Rolph Trouillot has more recently called "Otherwise Modern"—entirely within modernity. The temporal break that modernity signals in a narrative of progress, Trouillot explains, means that "Caribbean history as we know it starts with an abrupt rupture between past and present—for Europeans, for Native Americans, and for enslaved Africans." The Caribbean represents neither the premodern nor modernity's untouched exteriority. The practices, knowledge regimes, and forms of governance ordering the colonial as a constitutive element of modernity does not identify the Caribbean as one among a series of alternative modernities (Asian, African, Latin American, etc.); the Caribbean is "modern from day one" (Trouillot 2003: 41, 44). As Walter Mignolo explains, extending Enrique Dussel's notion of coloniality as the underside of modernity, "Coloniality names the underlying logic of the foundation and unfolding of Western civilization . . . of which historical colonialisms have been a constitutive, although downplayed, dimension." Modernity appears "as a rhetoric of salvation" celebrating the achievements of Western civilization "while hiding at the same time its darker side, 'coloniality.'" Coloniality as a concept thus addresses more than the political structure of colonialism. It keeps in view genocide, plantation slavery, and colonial rule as practices and orientations foundational to modernity and offers an analytics for understanding the problems confronted after the end of formal colonial rule—the postcolony. Coloniality registers "the logic of oppression and exploitation" constitutive of modernity: "There is no modernity without coloniality" (Mignolo 2011: 2–3, 2007: 162).

I foreground my discussion of *Beyond a Boundary* with James's thinking about the artist, democracy, and what I read as his concern with Caribbean coloniality to argue that we can read James in this text as engaged in a practice of decolonial thought. Nelson Maldonado-Torres (2008: 7) describes the decolonial turn as a practice that draws on colonized and delegitimized knowledges and "highlights the epistemic relevance of the enslaved and colonized search for humanity," which in turn begins to "open up the sources for thinking and to break up the apartheid of theoretical domains through renewed forms of critique and epistemic creolization." Such a turn by James was indeed incomplete, as his thinking retained its core Marxist framing of uneven and combined development that led to his repeated descriptions of the Caribbean as "backward" (see Høgsbjerg 2014: 76–79, 177–78). Still, his imagining of and identification with a young, barefoot Sobers ("All of us in the West Indies did that") is helpful for unraveling a key aspect of his political thought—specifically, the possibility he saw in art and, equally important, the place of Africa in his thinking. It bears mentioning that Sobers did not recognize himself in James's imaginative rendering of his childhood; he would recall that after his father's death, his mother made sure he and his siblings were clean, went to school, and "had shoes on our feet and food in our bellies" (Sobers 2002: 1).[7] When James identifies himself with his imaginative portraiture of Sobers, he is announcing a shift toward those Caribbean masses who gave cricket its local traditions. It therefore hardly seems coincidental that James's portrait of a barefoot Sobers brings to mind the figure who loomed so large in his mind as he first sat to write *Beyond a Boundary*, whom James often watched as a young boy from his bedroom window: Matthew Bondman.

## Matthew Bondman and the Bound

James opens *Beyond a Boundary* with a compelling portrait of Matthew Bondman that bears quoting at length:

> He was a young man already when I first remember him, medium height and size, and an awful character. He was generally dirty. He would not work. His eyes were fierce, his language was violent and his voice loud. His lips curled back naturally and he intensified it by an almost perpetual snarl. My grandmother and aunts detested him. He would often without shame walk up the main street barefooted, "with his planks on the ground," as my grandmother would report.... The whole Bondman family, except for the father, was unsatisfactory. It was from his mother that Matthew had inherited or absorbed his flair for language and invective. His sister Marie was quiet but bad, and despite all the circumlocutions, or perhaps because of them, which my aunts employed, I knew it had something to do with "men." But the two families were linked. They rented from us, they had lived there for a long time, and their irregularity of life exercised its fascination for my puritanical aunts. But that is not why I remember Matthew. For ne'er-do-well, in fact vicious character, as he was, Matthew had one saving grace—Matthew could bat. More than that, Matthew, so crude and vulgar in every aspect of his life, with a bat in his hand was all grace and style.... He had one particular stroke that he played by going down low on one knee. It may have been a slash through the covers or a sweep to leg. But, whatever it was, whenever Matthew sank down and made it, a long, low "Ah!" came from many a spectator, and my own little soul thrilled with recognition and delight.... He was my first acquaintance with that *genus Britannicus*, a fine batsman. (James 2013 [1963]: 3–4)[8]

For James, the batsman was the central figure in the cricketing drama, his style, innovation, stroke making, his very approach to the crease possessing the ability of any "high" art to captivate an audience. He recognized this capacity in W. G. Grace, the nineteenth-century cricketer who transformed the game from an elite pastime into a popular English sport. In a formulation that became central to his thinking, James described Grace's achievements as possible not because he had mastered the cricket he inherited so much as he "took what he found and re-created it" (171). Announcing Matthew Bondman as his "first acquaintance with that *genus Britannicus*," James suggests a similarly transformative possibility in someone at the margins of colonial Trinidad's respectable, racialized society.

By beginning *Beyond a Boundary* with Bondman, James subtly announces his preoccupation with race and class, although Sylvia Wynter warns against viewing James as working out a sense of race as simply a manifestation of class struggle. Bondman the ne'er-do-well, walking on the main road barefoot, marks a particular location within a colonial Caribbean social hierarchy. In Trinidad, as elsewhere in the colonial world, whether or not one wore shoes involved, as Maureen Turim (2001: 62) notes, "significations of wealth, public space, and civilization itself." The African American poet Langston Hughes recognized this on his trip to Haiti in 1931, when he observed, "To be in the streets barefooted marks one as a low-caste person of no standing" (Hughes 1931: 12; see also Hughes 1932: 157). Bondman's artistry, his ability to enthrall the masses and colonial black elite alike, issued from his grounding in a Caribbean tradition established by a social group on the margins of colonial respectability.

James's well-known discussion of his choice of cricket clubs in Trinidad demonstrates the deeply braided nature of race and class in colonial Trinidad. James, black but middle class, had to choose whether he would play for "Maple, the club of the brown-skinned middle class," for whom "class did not matter so much . . . as colour," or the much better Shannon, "the club of the black lower-middle class." Maple did not welcome black players, but James knew many of its members well, which made his choice an agonizing one. "My social and political instincts, nursed on Dickens and Thackeray, were beginning to clarify themselves," and regardless of how appealing he found "the brilliant cricket Shannon played," he joined Maple. Socially, James remembers that he "was not bothered by my dark skin" yet admits "the principle on which the Maple Club was founded . . . stuck in my throat."

Interestingly, he recounts his dismissal of Stingo almost in passing: "They were plebeians: the butcher, the tailor, the candlestick maker, the casual labourer, with a sprinkling of unemployed. Totally black and no social status whatsoever" (50–51). For a young James, Stingo was "too low," or, as Grant Farred (1996a: 166) puts it, "beyond [his] most radical political imaginary." The James writing *Beyond a Boundary* was quite a different person politically.

Stingo figures prominently in James's thinking about cricket and the Caribbean. While it is reasonable to assume, as both Wynter and Farred suggest, that James seeks a bridge between his socially elite black middle-class background and Bondman, his discussion of Stingo's fast bowler George John suggests something unique. James introduces John through the story of the Caribbean bowler Joseph "Float" Woods, who once famously pleaded, albeit unsuccessfully, with his captain, Aucher Warner, to be allowed to bowl barefoot at the Bristol cricket ground. James saw in the tale a Caribbean reality for "West Indians [who] recall the origin of many a fine bowler" who "came to the nets, often without shoes" (73). It is clear that James locates George John in this tradition of barefoot boys who hone the cricket they learned playing in the streets and at the nets. It can easily go unnoticed that James came to understand John only through politics: "It is only recent political events in the West Indies which taught me that John incarnated the plebs of his time, their complete independence from the values and aspirations that competed in the spheres above" (73). John played in a tradition that had little regard for the brilliant cricket Shannon played, his "utter rejection of all standards and interests except his own" revealing a "fast bowling ... stoked by more dynamite than there was in all the Shannon eleven put together" (80).

When James locates Bondman in colonial Trinidad's social hierarchy, he tethers his first acquaintance with a *genus Britannicus* to a group that—in rejecting the cricket of Shannon, not to mention that of Maple, and possibly never having seriously considered either—transformed an English medium into a Caribbean tradition. Unlike with Sobers, James's portraiture of Bondman (loud, perpetual snarl, curled lips, barefoot) summoned modernist stereotypes of the primitive, premodern African carried into Trinidad's colonial present by its socially lagging lower classes. James refuses to decouple a shoeless Bondman or Sobers or George John from what he considered the cricket of Wilton St. Hill and Frank Worrell. Wynter, in her masterly treatment of a Jamesian poiesis, suggests that James's treatment of Bondman reflected a "struggle against a conception that had accorded the elite, and he among them, a place of privilege," that could guard "against the existential brutalization to which a Matthew Bondsman was condemned" (Wynter 1992: 71, 73). Yet that effort seems less concerned with bridging the gap between himself and Bondman than with reckoning with the basis of a Caribbean cricketing tradition. Indeed, James would note that, possibly as with John, "It is only within very recent years that Matthew Bondman and the cutting of Arthur Jones ... fell into place" in his thinking about the Caribbean. These were "the last stones ... of a pyramid whose base constantly widened, until it embraced those aspects of social relations, politics and art laid bare when the veil of the temple had been rent in train as ours has been" (7).

### Bondman, Africa, and Naming

Matthew Bondman's location as a cornerstone in the base of the ever widening pyramid of James's political thinking stemmed in part from his ability to enthrall "all around him, non-cricketers and cricketers alike," Trinidad's black colonial elite and its masses equally moved by his batting. It was, however, the difference between his status, and how people reacted to him on the pitch that, for James, "filled my growing mind and has occupied me to this day" (4). For James, at least in part, the appeal of his artistry stemmed from his social position. But rather than express this by describing the social standing of a single person, James broadens his scope to the Caribbean masses more generally.

The person whose batting so enthralled a young James was not, in fact, named Matthew Bondman. "Bondman" is a pseudonym chosen by James for the person whose batting continued to inform his worldview.[9] Although James was prompted to use a pseudonym by his publisher, choosing "Bondman" seems purposeful, an invocation of bondage and slavery, the very conditions under which Africans arrived in the West Indies and built their lives; a primitive other and colonial subject located in the Caribbean's socially black lower classes. James would have known the etymological root of the word "bondman" in the word "bond," a term that designated a rank below a town resident or citizen. Bondman is not, then—or, at least, not primarily—a bridge between the colonial black elite and the poor, between James and Bondman, but, rather, a marker of a key constitutive element of democracy (see also chapter 5 in this volume). Using the name and figure of Bondman works to subvert the very modernity on which many assumed a

Caribbean future must be built. That a British kind could appear in such a "vicious character" is neither mimicry nor an attempt to render Bondman intelligible, even if only momentarily. Rather, Bondman reflected the boundless possibilities of an artist who re-created what he inherited through an idiom tethered to the lifeworlds of Caribbean peoples. Bondman thus represents the artist and the African as the possibility of a Caribbean political future after formal colonialism and, more important, after coloniality.

It is undeniable that James seemed never to have considered Africa a source of thought or culture for the Caribbean (see Henry 2000: 48–67; Kamugisha 2006: 135). By the time *Beyond a Boundary* appeared in print, he would repeatedly insist (although not in this text) on Africa's importance to a Caribbean future. Through the person and the pseudonym Bondman, James is able to introduce, if only in muffled tones, Africa into Caribbean life and politics, not as racial lineage or romanticized premodern past, but as an index of the social and cultural worldviews enslaved Africans brought to the Caribbean. In a line from "From Toussaint L'Ouverture to Fidel Castro," the now famous appendix to the 1963 edition of *The Black Jacobins*, which has largely gone unremarked, James urges those in the British West Indies to "clear from [their] minds the stigma that anything African was inherently inferior and degraded" and insists that "the road to West Indian national identity lay through Africa" (James 1992 [1963]: 304). This was not an isolated remark. Speaking to the Caribbean Conference Committee in Montreal in 1966, he would insist on the importance of "the African heritage of West Indians" to a Caribbean political future (see also Austin 2009a: 15–18),[10] and he called Africans "a highly civilized body of people in Africa" who, when brought as slaves to the West Indies, "brought themselves"—their worldviews, knowledges, social practices—to the islands.[11] In possibly his most profound formulation, if woefully underdeveloped and never seriously pursued in any detail, he declared while talking with Caribbean students in a Marxist study group he and Selma James ran in London in the 1960s, "The origins of our nation are the Maroons who ran away from the plantations and hid in the mountains. Those are the real originators of the Haitian nation. Believe me!"[12]

The figure of Matthew Bondman thus serves to identify the artist and the African as the very possibility for a Caribbean political future—not merely after formal colonialism (postcolonial), but after coloniality (post-coloniality).[13] Bondman, like the youthful Sobers of James's imagination, exists in a line of

Caribbean artists who engaged in a practice of giving a foreign medium a Caribbean tradition. Central to this practice is how art taps into and expands on a popular consciousness—the virtuoso's ability to shape national consciousness and convey popular desires. The cricket of a Bondman, a John, or a Sobers thus subverts the very social hierarchies attendant to coloniality. These artists—the ne'er-do-well, the African Maroons who originated the Caribbean nation—have pioneered into the regions Caesar never knew: coloniality as the very condition of possibility for modernity. Upon arriving in England, the British intellectual does not, as James would have it, come home; rather, in turning on its head Kipling's phrase, "What should they know of England who only England know," James announces Caliban as pioneering into Africa, coming to see from the underside of modernity.

**Coloniality and Postcolonial Governance**

When James agreed to stay on in Trinidad and work with Williams's PNM, his interest was West Indies Federation, not just an independent Trinidadian nation-state. As he would make clear in his lectures at Port-of-Spain's public library in August 1960, "The national state today, despite all its power and despite all the degradation to which it reduces the men who try to run it, never achieves its purpose" (James 1973 [1960]: 84). Interestingly, we find a glimpse into what James saw as the problem of an independent Caribbean nation-state in a four-paragraph "Foreword" to the Carnival issue of the *Humming Bird*:

> Carnival is well established as a feature of our national life. The rhythms and ballads of Calypso have conquered the world. The singers in the Tents have demonstrated their art possessed more vitality and compulsive power than the feeble attempts of the better educated in their imitations of Chopin and Chaminad or Keats and Shelley, of John Ruskin and Robert Louis Stevenson... The more we clarify our past and analyse what is taking place around us, the more we prepare the ground from which the individual artist may spring.[14]

Where Bondman's batting could express a decolonial response to British Empire, calypso represented a mode of decoloniality in its very form and structure. Unlike the inherent limitations Lamming encountered with literature, a Bondman, a Sobers, or a calypsonian like the Mighty Sparrow had shown an ability to "master a medium, whatever it is, that had developed in a foreign territory," but then "seek and find out what is native, and build on that" (James 1962: 175). If the Caribbean was to realize a political existence beyond the cartography of the nation-state, the challenge remained how to realize an alternative form of democratic governance. Seeking out and building on what is native became a central frame for James.

Rather than the West Indies' origins at the beginning of British civilization marking their modernity and inherent democratic impulses, James cautioned against the "false and dangerous conception that we have been so educated by the British that the instinct for democracy is established among us" (James 1962: 123). Indeed, he even abandoned his earlier suggestion that India and Africa were hindered by tribalism and caste (see James 2014 [1932]: 50). Pointing to the colonial mode of governance the Caribbean had inherited from Britain, James argued that what issued from colonialism was less a new democratic society than one rooted in what Achille Mbembe has more recently called a *régime d'exception*, a form of rule that renders indistinct means and ends, ruling and civilizing—"a regime that depart[s] from the common law" as its basis for rule (Mbembe 2001: 26–35). It was this model that, James argued, left no trace of democracy in the Caribbean, for "when you are ruled by an imperialist power, armed force decides. When you have slavery, you live with armed force every hour of the day. There is established not democracy, but subordination to power either actual or in reserve." This was a Caribbean problem, or rather, a problem of coloniality. "I see every sign that the tendency to naked power and naked brutality, the result of West Indian historical development, is here all around us," James added. Unlike what so many have assumed about him in this period, James was concerned with more than simply Williams: "This has nothing to do with the supposed dictatorial plans of Dr. Williams." Caribbean political leaders more generally know, he explained, that they must win elections, "but after that the only type of government and social concept of government, their practice of government, is that of the old colonialist governors" (James 1962: 123–24).

It is undeniable that James viewed such problems in the Caribbean postcolony as inherent in any newly independent "backward" territory. His decolonial turn sat in tension with a continued commitment to notions of progressive social and historical development. Yet he could nonetheless explain to V. S. Naipaul in 1963, "I don't believe that there is any profound difference or rather fundamental difference between the stage of civilization in which India finds itself and the stage in which the Britain and the Europe of Hitler and Stalin find themselves."[15] Still, it is impossible to negate that James saw in cultural practices such as Rastafari, calypso, and cricket a rejection of the modern and Western civilization necessary for a mode of thought capable of pursuing a future beyond the already available—through what Arturo Escobar (2007: 186) calls modernity's exteriority, those colonized and delegitimized knowledges that make possible moving "beyond or outside modernity" to pursue a new world.

When he wrote to Naipaul in the summer of 1963, in response to a review of *Beyond a Boundary* that Naipaul had written for Trinidad's *Sunday Times*, James might have clarified not so much what he meant by being "West Indian through and through" and "very British" as what he felt concerned the question of the artist in his political thought. He directed Naipaul to the close of his appendix to *The Black Jacobins*, where he laments, "The West Indian had made a fool of himself imitating American journalism, Shakespeare, T. S. Eliot, Lorca" (James 2001 [1938]: 325). It might seem a curious charge for someone like James to make, when we consider his unabashed declaration that "Thackeray, not Marx, bears the heaviest responsibility for me" and his praise of Shakespeare, though the obvious retort is that he never urged the imitation of either. This is where he saw the greatest value in "West Indian writers hav[ing] discovered the West Indies and West Indians, a people in the middle of our disturbed century, concerned with the discovery of themselves." If the Caribbean were to become a new nation, it had to "bring something new. Otherwise it is a mere administrative convenience" (James 1992 [1963]: 314). It would seem this was the impulse behind *Beyond a Boundary* that he had hoped Naipaul would grasp. A batsman like Bondman elaborating a uniquely Caribbean art form that captured and conveyed the desires and motivations of Caribbean people was not following available maps or codes. The practice of innovating on a given form and creating something previously unimagined was, for James, a model for the Caribbean. "After immense labours I have at last arrived at something West Indian which will be ours, which can be ours," he explained to Naipaul. "I made the transition from the Olympic Games of Greece to Greek democracy. I believe that we in the West Indies will make the transition from Thomas Arnold, Thomas Hughes and W. G. to the concepts with which I conclude the appendix [to *The Black Jacobins*]." Rather than imitating liberal democracy like those colonial elites who imitated European classical art, the Caribbean was poised to create a new democratic form "to strip... the wrappings from Western civilization itself."[16] A form capacious enough to change—indeed, to conquer—the world.

**Notes**

1. C. L. R. James to Grantley Adams, n.d., C. L. R. James Papers, Rare Book and Manuscript Library, Columbia University, New York (hereafter, James Papers), box 1, folder 1; C. L. R. James to V. S. Naipaul, n.d., C. L. R. James Collection, Alma Jordan Library, University of the West Indies, St. Augustine, Trinidad and Tobago (hereafter, James Collection), box 3, folder 75.
2. *Trinidad Sunday Guardian*, 20 April 1958; C. L. R. James to George Padmore, 17 March 1958, James Collection, box 5, folder 105; C. L. R. James to Grantley Adams, 17 December 1957, James Papers, box 1, folder 1; C. L. R. James to Norman Manley, 22 September 1958, ICS40 A/3/2, 26 October 1958, ICS40 A/3/6, 8 May 1959, all in ICS40 A/3/13, C. L. R. James Papers, Institute of Commonwealth Studies, Archives and Manuscripts, University of London (hereafter, James ICS).
3. C. L. R. James, *The Making of the Caribbean Peoples*, 18, in James Papers, box 10, folder 8.
4. See also Minkah Makalani, "A Very Unusual People: An Interview with Erica James and Henry James," 2014, *sx Salon*, http://smallaxe.net/wordpress3/interviews/2014/07/09/a-very-unusual-people/#more-133.
5. C. L. R. James to Grantley Adams, n.d., James Papers, box 1, folder 1.
6. This appears in C. L. R. James's lecture "Federation—What Now," which was delivered to the Caribbean Society, Kingston, Jamaica, November 1959, and can be found in a pamphlet entitled *Federation: "We Failed Miserably," How and Why*, 28, James Papers, box 19, folder 15.
7. At the conference "*Beyond a Boundary* 50 Years On," held at the University of Glasgow in 2013, Michael Brearley noted that Sobers rejected the view that James held of his importance.
8. Hereafter, page numbers in parentheses refer to this edition of *Beyond a Boundary*.
9. C. L. R. James to Robert Anderson, February 1963, James Collection, box 3, folder 75. Presumably, the pseudonym was used to protect the Hutchinson publishing group from a possible lawsuit.
10. See the foreword in James, *The Making of the Caribbean Peoples*. See also *Marxism and the Caribbean*, pamphlet, James Collection, box 20, folder 377. On the speech to the Caribbean Conference Committee, see Austin 2009a: 15–18.
11. C. L. R. James, "Marxism and the Caribbean," 1, in James Collection, box 20, folder 377.

12. Clairmont Chung, dir., *W. A. R. Stories: Walter Anthony Rodney*, film, Roots and Culture Film, 2010, 10:01. On the Marxist study group in London, see Rodney 1990: 16.

13. I follow Richard Iton in distinguishing "post-colonial" ("that which occurs after or works against coloniality") from "postcolonial" ("that which occurs after or operates more narrowly against colonialism"): see Iton 2008: 301, n. 47.

14. C. L. R. James, "Foreword," *Humming Bird*, Carnival Number, December 1959, ICS40 1/2, James ICS.

15. C. L. R. James to Vidia [Naipaul], Summer 1963, James Collection, box 5, folder 106.

16. James to Naipaul, Summer 1963.

5 | Looking Beyond the Boundary, or Bondman without the Bat: Modernism and Culture in the Worldview of C. L. R. James

DAVID AUSTIN

In the value code of the hegemonic system, most of the dwellers of the yard are condemned like Bondsman [sic] to accept their inculcated zero value of identity, their own nothingness. In the frame of the later code, those like Bondsman and the ghetto shanty-town archipelago stand condemned, stigmatized as the lumpen, as "nonproductive labor" that is not really exploited.
—Sylvia Wynter, "Beyond the Categories of the Master Conception"

If modernity, that bundle of cultural, political, philosophical, and technological iterations and reiterations of the Renaissance, the Enlightenment, and the Industrial Revolution, "requires an alterity," as Michel-Rolph Trouillot suggests, if it implies and requires antonymic and problematic others—if it, to put it bluntly, needs "the nigger"—can those others constituted and marginalized in this manner viably challenge their circumstances without questioning the logic and language of their exclusion? —Richard Iton, *In Search of the Black Fantastic*

Let us waste no time in sterile litanies and nauseating mimicry. Leave this Europe where they are never done talking of Man, yet murder men everywhere they find them, at the corner of everyone one of their own streets, in all the corners of the globe. —Frantz Fanon, *The Wretched of the Earth*

In *The Tao of Cricket: On Games of Destiny and the Destiny of Games,* Ashis Nandy (2000: 6) argues that "the growth and spread of cricket was coeval with the high noon of the British empire and derived part of its legitimacy from its association with *Pax Britannica.*" Cricket, he argues, promoted "certain norms and virtues ... which ensured the political and economic success of Britain [in its colonies]." Nandy's slim volume captures the global, worldly, and even universal assumptions embedded in the practice of the sport. Beyond sports as leisure, the raison d'être of "importing" this quintessentially English pastime to the colonies was entirely wrapped up in the legitimization and entrenchment of colonialism. This process involved the passing on through the sport's codes of ethics and etiquette a particularly elusive conception of Britishness that, in the words of Bob Marley (though in reference to an entirely different but not unrelated context), was "a fleeting illusion, to be pursued/But never attained."[1] But despite its imperial connections, for Nandy it is obvious that cricket did not simply help to facilitate British imperialism. It was also a defining feature of nationalism. (He is speaking specifically about Indian and South Asian nationalism.) For Nandy (2000: 7), the sport "allowed Indians to assess their colonial rulers by western values reflected in the philosophy of cricket, and to find the rulers wanting." This is why he can make the unfettered statement that cricket is an Indian game (Nandy 2000: 122). To suggest otherwise would be to reduce the sport's popularity to a paternalistic assumption of "false consciousness" that does no justice to how, to invert Audre Lorde's famous dictum, the master's tools[2]—whether in the form of language, ideas, or, in this case, sport—are often used to disrupt the master's house, or how the adoption of "the master's God and reshaping the deity in one's own image" (Nettleford 1998: 82) might be subversive. If a game in which the British invested so much could be used as a tool to out-master the master on the cricket pitch, what were the potential implications of this prowess in the political arena? This is precisely the question that began, both consciously and unconsciously, to occupy increasing numbers of Caribbean women and men as West Indian cricket stoked the fires of Caribbean nationalism and Caribbean nationalism stoked the fires of West Indian cricket. By the time the British West Indies embarked on its many paths toward independence, the culture of cricket and its attendant codes had long ceased to be the master's tool and were increasingly an expression of West Indian autonomy.

While the popularity of other sports in the Caribbean, including the almost religious enthusiasm for soccer and the rising popularity of track and field (particularly the sprint events) rival cricket's popularity today, arguably none of these sports has captured the Pan-Caribbean imagination in the same way or carried the weight of Caribbean nationalism and identity as cricket has. The theater of the cricket pitch has been the home of intense drama whose implications—and this is particularly true of the 1950s and 1960s through to the 1970s and 1980s—has reverberated well beyond the cricket pitch, across the Caribbean, into the heart of the fallen but not dead empire in England and across the Indian Ocean to the Indian subcontinent and Africa.

Nettleford (1998: 82) has argued that cricket "served as a social protest for a long subjugated people, as strategy of demarginalization, or as defiant celebration of self in the face of persistent denigration." In his introduction to Michael Manley's volume on cricket, the former West Indian cricket captain Clive Lloyd (1998: v) puts it another way: "Cricket is the ethos around which West Indian society revolves [and] the instrument of Caribbean cohesion—the remover of arid insularity and nationalistic prejudice." But while the relationship between cricket and nationalism in the Caribbean has been largely taken for granted, there is dissension within the ranks of the game's critics. Natasha Barnes (2006: 29–30) has not only underscored the imperial premises on which cricket's codes were based but questions the credibility of the association of "a man's game" with genuine nationalism when women are limited to spectatorship, even if they are expert spectators, and seen as outside the sport's attendant codes of sportsmanship, character, universalism, and heroism (Barnes 2006: 38; see also Nettleford 1998: 89). In other words, if cricket was a symbol of Caribbean nationalism and its possibilities, then those possibilities were flawed and partial from the outset as a result of the limited role afforded women in the sport. Moreover, she asks, what are we to make of the West Indies' less than dominant performances on the cricket pitch in more recent times in relation to the fate of the Caribbean since formal independence? (Barnes 2006: 36). These are no doubt crucial queries that deserve considerable attention in terms of appreciating the eclipsed possibilities of formal postcolonialism at its very dawn, and Barnes is clearly suggesting that analyses of cricket and nationalism in the Caribbean have been wanting in this respect.

While recognizing Barnes's important critique, there is no doubt that the sport was a formative part of an (admittedly masculine) conception of Caribbean national identity on the eve of independence for the British Caribbean, yet it was still an instrumental and formative part of the Caribbean's political and aesthetic consciousness and awakening. Perhaps no one has given the sport a more sensitive appreciation, and particularly in relation to the Caribbean, than C. L. R. James. *Beyond a Boundary* is arguably the most critically acclaimed book ever written about cricket. But more than a great book about the sport, *Beyond a Boundary* is a philosophy of sports, a window into sports as art and politics, and into art and politics as sports. On the cricket pitch,

Caribbean possibilities were performed on the world stage in much the same way that Haitians took center stage during the Haitian Revolution or, for that brief but not fleeting moment, the Grenadian Revolution.³ Yet, as Michel-Rolph Trouillot's polite caution suggests, James's choice of title, *The Black Jacobins*, for his classic study of the Haitian Revolution is revealing. Trouillot (1995: 104) does not elaborate beyond encouraging the reader to "note the title," but he appears to be querying the degree to which James ties the Haitian Revolution to the historical trajectory of its French counterpart as part of a modernizing process that brought the aristocratic order to an abrupt and violent end. For James, both the ideals and the ideologues of the French Revolution were considered crucial to the challenges, successes, and failures of Toussaint Louverture, and it is impossible to understand Toussaint and the Haitian Revolution outside these parameters. It is the revolution's association with its French counterpart that makes it progressive for James. We might describe this as the consanguinity of revolution, or an imbalanced contrapuntalism in which the Haitian Revolution is framed, in part, not as an equal or a revolution that surpasses the ideals of the French Revolution but as a product, or even a byproduct, of Jacobinism and the French revolutionary spirit. Of course, this description does not do justice to James's magisterial book, but it does suggest something about how Toussaint, the revolution's chief protagonist in James's account, is framed as a modern in relation to other, more "Africanist" slaves, including the "barbarian" Dessalines, as James (1980 [1938]: 393) calls him, who ultimately led Saint-Domingue toward Haitian independence. My intention here is not to probe James's analysis of the Haitian Revolution specifically, but to make a larger point about the hegemony of Euro-Western modernity—"that bundle of cultural, political, philosophical, and technological iterations and reiterations of the Renaissance, the Enlightenment, and the Industrial Revolution" (Iton 2008: 13)—and its embedded assumptions in James's work, particularly in relation to his appreciation of cricket in the Caribbean as it is embodied in his assessment of Matthew Bondman. James's assessment of Bondman highlights the challenges associated with imagining a world beyond the boundaries of colonialism and coloniality while at the same time drawing on the master's tools to dismantle the master's house. As West Indian and Indian mastery of the game clearly demonstrates, cricket, for some time now, no longer belongs solely to the former master. As James has demonstrated perhaps more than anyone, cricket has been a crucial part of the Caribbean's emancipatory designs. But as I suggest, in the case of Bondman, James's appreciation of his creative potential is limited to his achievements on the cricket pitch; in so doing, he fails to appreciate the creative potential that Bondman represents as a symbol of the "barefoot man" who rebels against the constraints that the rules and attendant codes of cricket imposed on him and the significance of his rejection of these limitations.

**The Boy at the Window**

Peering through a bedroom window in his home in Tunapuna (James 2013 [1963]: 3),[4] cricket became a laboratory, a prism (might we also say a kind of prison?) through which James assessed the world around him. He played cricket for Queen's Royal College, the prestigious Trinidadian secondary boys' school where he mastered "the code," Victorian rules of conduct and social mores by which, at the time, he believed, the British in Britain lived. The code reigned supreme and sublime among British subjects who attended elite colonial schools, governing their understanding of truth, justice, and fair play. Yet part of James rejected the standards that were imposed by the code. As Sylvia Wynter (1992: 64–65) argues, there was the young rebel James, the intellectual who played the game of cricket, the boy who also forsook his formal education as a scholarship recipient for his love of reading and learning for its own sake, all of which put him at variance with the expectations of his parents and educators and went against the grain of the established social norms of the elite. As James himself put it, two people lived within him, "One, the rebel against all family and school discipline and order; the other a Puritan who would have cut off a finger sooner than do anything contrary to the ethics of the game" (28). The rebel and the code would struggle in James to reconcile the presumed binaries, part of which might be described as the Afro- versus Euro-Western division, both of which have been a crucial part of the Caribbean's formation.

Selwyn Cudjoe (note the fact that James had an uncle Cuffee and a cousin Cudjoe, Ghanaian names that hint at the haunting presence of Africa in Trinidad) suggests that while James emphasizes the presence of English periodicals and his fascination with English literature in his home, he ignores the impact of African-derived religions and culture, perhaps, as Cudjoe suggests, "to demonstrate that he hadn't learned about European literature under 'a mango tree'" (Cudjoe 1992a: 41). This was likely a strategic move on James's part, orchestrated to demonstrate the influence of Western European thought on his work. But if this is true, we perhaps need to query why James would feel the need to make such a move. Cudjoe's quote implies that the weight of colonialism and its legacy necessitated that he vindicate himself and the people of the Caribbean and demonstrate their humanity on British terms. But human personality and personal aesthetic tastes also play a role, and there is little doubt that James was drawn like a magnet to Europe and canonical European literature as a child, and this attraction, nurtured primarily by his mother, remained with him and sustained his ethical and aesthetic values and sensibilities as an adult. As Cudjoe suggests, regardless of whether James felt the need to acknowledge them, the impact of the local idioms and mores of the island's lower classes or underclass on James has to be accounted for. In other words, to rephrase or slightly modify Cudjoe's remarks in the form of a question, by way of the spiritual dimension of Trinidadian life: where is Shango in James's Caribbean?[5] The answer, I think, is that Shango is present in absentia, and James's elisions speak volumes.

James's relationship to African politics and African-derived cultural practices both in Africa and the Caribbean and the importance of ancient Greece to his vision of Caribbean nationalism have been discussed elsewhere (see Austin 2009b, 2010, 2013a). What is intriguing here is the fact that, given his preoccupation with the creative capacities of "ordinary people" and the capacity of the ordinary to produce the extraordinary, he wrote very little about the social history of the Caribbean's underclass. This said, it is not surprising that Matthew Bondman was important, and in some ways crucial, to James's nascent understanding not only of personality, but also of form, grace, and style. As James wrote in a now famous passage, "When I tired of playing in the yard I perched myself on the chair by the window. I doubt for some years I knew what I was looking at in detail. But this watching from the window shaped one of my strongest early impressions of personality in society. His name was Matthew Bondman and he lived next door to us" (3).

Here is how James goes on to describe Bondman:

> He was a young man already when I first remember him, medium height and size, and an awful character. He was generally dirty. He would not work. His eyes were fierce, his language was violent and his voice was loud. His lips curled back naturally and he intensified it by an almost perpetual snarl. My grandmother and my aunts detested him. He would often without shame walk up the main street barefooted, "with his planks on the ground," as my grandmother would report. He did it often and my grandmother must have seen it hundreds of times, but never failed to

report it, as if she had suddenly seen the parson walking down the street barefooted. The whole Bondman family, except for the father, was unsatisfactory. It was from his mother that Matthew had inherited or absorbed his flair for language and invective. His sister Marie was quiet but bad, and despite all the circumlocutions, or perhaps because of them, which my aunt employed, I knew it had something to do with "men." But the two families were linked. They rented from us, they had lived there for a long time, and their irregularity of life exercised its fascination for my puritanical aunts. (3–4)

The reference to Bondman's curled-back lips in this passage is particularly troubling, as it suggests an aesthetic sensibility in relation to physical attributes derived from Euro-Western standards of beauty—in this case, presumably, thin, uncurled lips. Even if we grant some allowance for literary license or device in which James establishes, or perhaps exaggerates, Bondman's flaws to recast him and elevate him to the level of an artist, his depiction of Bondman as "an awful character" who was "generally dirty" and who essentially lived a pitiful existence is, to say the least, hardly flattering. And yet, since these lines were first published, so many of us have read them, perhaps with varied degrees of discomfort, but failed to comment on them. Why? Out of fear that James's stature was not sufficiently secure as to withstand criticism? (Despite the rise in James's stature since his death in 1989, his oeuvre is still a long way from becoming the consistent and integral part of the academic establishment that it deserves to be.) Or perhaps because such descriptions, however troubling, are easily normalized because the dominant aesthetic values permit us to turn a blind eye to them? Whatever the reasons, James's recollection of Bondman should give us pause for thought.

James does, however, remember Bondman for other reasons:

For ne'er-do-well, in fact vicious character, as he was, Matthew had one saving grace—Matthew could bat. More than that, Matthew, so crude and vulgar in every aspect of his life, with a bat in his hand was all grace and style. When he practiced on an afternoon with the local club people stayed to watch and walked away when he was finished. He had one particular stroke that he played by going down low on one knee. It may have been a slash to the covers or a sweep to leg. But, whatever it was, whenever Matthew sank down and made it, a long, low "Ah!" came from many spectators, and my own little soul thrilled with recognition and delight. (4)

James's description of Bondman elevates him to the level of a fine artist. Perhaps nowhere else does James describe a batsman in such vivid and glowing language. Bondman is the batsman *par excellence,* and not because he could score run after run. It is quality, not quantity, that defines him as a batsman in James's eyes, apparently one of the finest James ever witnessed at the crease. It is to James's infinite credit that he rescued Bondman and, through him, the Bondmans of the world from history's dustbin, yet this is the kind of description and analysis that we might expect from someone who spent much of his life exploring human possibilities and the ability of the seemingly ordinary to achieve the extraordinary. Bondman represents these extraordinary qualities and through James becomes a symbol of all that is possible and remarkable "from below." But while James's description of Bondman's batting grace does wonders for Bondman and our imaginations, his description of him without the bat leaves much to be desired. In fact, his description is not only wanting but painfully inadequate.

**In Search of Bondman**

Who was Bondman? From James's description of him, he was the quintessential representative of a kind of Caribbean subclass, or the underclass. He is not quite a vagrant. He does not neatly fit within the category of a worker or member of the working class. We have no real sense of his educational background and attainment, his tastes or desires, his social context—that is to say, the social and economic circumstances that produced him. His characterization of Bondman denies us the curiosity and sense of history that we have come to expect from James. What social forces brought Bondman and his family into being? What did his parents do for a living? Did the family inherit their station from one generation to the next, part of the manumitted but disenfranchised caste that failed to make it into the ranks of respectability, in essence remaining "bonded," as his pseudonym implies? (See also chapter 4 in this volume.) Why did the Bondman family have to rent from the Jameses? Was Bondman's a family in decline? How did Bondman become, to use James's grandmother's words, "Good for nothing except to play cricket"? Based on James's description, Bondman and his family simply exist, or just are, but we have no real sense of Bondman's being and how he came to be. As Natasha Barnes remarks, Bondman is remarkably different from the heroic Hegelian figures that James portrays in *Beyond a Boundary* such as Learie Constantine, Everton Weekes, Frank Worrell, and Clyde Walcott, among others. Bondman both embraces and ultimately rejects the game, and James (2006: 34) struggles and fails to "read anything familiar in the cognitive map of Bondman's sportsmanship." Bondman was precisely the kind of figure whose social significance James would usually appreciate. But in this case, James failed to historicize him. Why? Again, this question poses a challenge that is perhaps beyond the realm of the strict humanities and enters the area of personal taste and aesthetic.

Cedric Robinson (2000 [1983]: 252) has argued that the sexual mores and morality "of the Black lower classes, for all their vitality and attractiveness, amounted to a rejection of English bourgeois sensibility" and represented "an affront to the morality of the colonial model set before the natives." This fear was not only biopolitical but also what I have described elsewhere as biosexual—that is, a fear of the spread of the contagion of blackness, defined as baseness through political, cultural, and sexual encounters (Austin 2013b). In this sense, the codes of conduct and the rules of progress meant that there was no place for the Bondmans of the Caribbean under colonialism and under the colonizer or, for that matter, the colonized Creole elite who had inherited the codes and values of the power elite and their pervasive color-coding. The bat-less Bondman, along with his culture and social mores, is homeless, outside the historical narrative of progress and displaced by what the theorist Richard Iton (2008: 16) refers to as the "hidden imperialisms that underwrite too many of our notions of progress, cosmopolitanism, the human and the universal." In other words, James does not have a full narrative for Bondman because Bondman does not, in many ways, fit his somewhat teleological narrative of progress as defined by Hegelianism, Marxism, and the exigencies of colonialism and capitalism. If *Beyond a Boundary* is Caliban's story, then it provides only a partial account of Caliban's castaway cousin. It is true that James "has long pricked our consciousness into structured appreciation of the cultural role of the game [of cricket] in the history of West Indian liberation and decolonization" (Nettleford 1998: 83), but in his account of Bondman we are deprived of a well-rounded appreciation of the batsman as a representative of his class.

James laments that Bondman's batting potential was never fully realized because "he would not practise regularly" and "he would not pay his subscription to the club" that he played for. (Could he afford it?) Nonetheless, he represented the *"genus Britannicus"* in James's eyes, "a fine batsman" (4). (It is worth noting here that, despite James's depiction of the marvels of West Indian batsmen, fine batting is equated to Britannia.) Wynter (1992: 85–86) suggests that James was among the first to salute Bondman's agency as a heretical (though not heroic, as Barnes suggests) figure who, like Rastafari, rejected the absurdities of Babylon and symbolized the latent potential of the underclass or the dispossessed, expressed through the medium of cricket. The connection that Wynter makes between Bondman and Rastafari is not an unreasonable leap. Like the Bondmans of the Caribbean, Rastafarians represented the outcast and the dispossessed. True to his appreciation of the "lower classes," James published a review in 1964 of Orlando Patterson's novel *The Children of Sisyphus* in which he acknowledged the emergence of Rastafari as a response to Babylon—that is, the global-cum-local system of oppression that has burdened black sufferers in Jamaica and across the Caribbean since the onset of slavery in the region. But while he acknowledged Rastafari as a rejection of Jamaica as a "bastardized version of British society which official and educated Jamaica seeks to foist upon them," he nonetheless emphasized what he described as Rastafari's "colossal stupidities," "inanities," and "absurd[ities]" (James 1964: 74). The review was written before Rastafari's rise as a global religion closely allied with reggae music, and James could not possibly have anticipated this phenomenon. But there is a bias in his analysis at this stage in his life that is worthy of investigation. As a religion grounded in a syncretic cosmology of Africanisms and Judeo-Christianity, how is Rastafari any more or less absurd than any other religion that calls for repatriation, anticipates messianic returns, and predicts apocalyptic cataclysms? The Rasta-cum-Bondman is the condemned, downtrodden, despised, disposed of, and dispossessed, or what Wynter (1992: 72) refers to as "Caliban niggerdom" or the "absolute zero of social and metaphysical value," modernity's underbelly or grotesque alter ego. But given James's description of both Bondman and Rastafari, can it really be said that they are saluted in James's work?

To appreciate the social and historical significance of the outcast Bondman, Wynter (1992: 66–67) argues that within the schema of bourgeois value that replaced the "fantasy of blood" that legitimated the aristocracy and the old feudal order, the Negro was the absence or lack of reason, associated with primates and pejorative views of African cultures. In this sense, and despite the small number of actual whites in Trinidad, whiteness was associated with value in the Marxian sense, and blackness was associated with "original sin" (Wynter 1992: 67–68). The Bondmans of the Caribbean became the necessary evil that was constitutive of capitalism, not only in terms of their value as laborers, but also as the negative value of Europe as a continental and transtlantic metaphor of civilization. Bondman is thus the antithesis of the civilized. He is the primitive. In *Beyond a Boundary*, James attempts to situate Bondman within what Wynter describes as his "pluri-consciousness," which incorporated the multiple dimensions of Marxism and Puritanism, African ("Negro") and Westerner, Marxist and onetime Trotskyist, and Pan-Africanism. For James, this meant that the particular category of Negro that Bondman came to embody could not be resolved or understood by simple binaries. While Wynter (1992: 68–69) suggests that James developed a poiesis, a counterdoctrine or worldview to frame the dimensions of race and nationalism and politics as he experienced them in Trinidad, I am suggesting that Bondman, for James, appears to be outside even the category of Negro. And if to be human means, in part, to have a historical context that explains who one is and a future that suggests what one can be—then Bondman is also outside the category of the human when he is not batting. There is no complementary binary within which Bondman can fit.

For the boyhood James, the code was everything, and while James later arrived at the conclusion that the code and Britain were not the source of light, as he once believed, he was never entirely free from the code as an adult—nor did he necessarily find it desirable to be so—and as his characterization of Bondman shows, he still struggled to place this wayward figure who did not fit neatly within the order of things. He did, later, shed those elements of the code that reinforced the "master conception" that separated Trinidad's local elite from the "masses" by binding them with loyalty to the colonizer, according to Wynter (1992: 71). There was the code, on the one hand, and "the existential brutalization to which Bondsman [sic] was condemned" (Wynter 1992: 72), on the other. Without a doubt, the code's association with the British colonial elite was at odds with James's lived experience and his image of Bondman at the crease. But rather than reconciling this gap by situating Bondman within the historical context of slavery and colonial Trinidad, he leaves Bondman to fend for himself.

Wynter suggests that Bondman and Sir Donald Bradman, the famous Australian batsman, can be juxtaposed in *Beyond a Boundary*, the latter having successfully realized his talent as a cricketer on the world stage while the former languished in obscurity, only to be resurrected in James's memoir. But we can take Bradman's context for granted in a way that we cannot with Bondman. In her essay, "In Quest of Matthew Bondman: Some Cultural Notes on a Jamesian Journey" (1986), Wynter goes further, arguing that while Bradman, the proficient batsman was "subordinated to the code of technological rationality," Bondman was "immersed in the imperatives of the popular underground counter-culture of Trinidad, a culture derived from Africa, yet toughened." The juxtaposition between these two players, Wynter (1986: 139) argues, thus "reveals a culture clash of *Reasons*." While Bradman embodies the Euro-Western hegemonic, mechanical and scientific reason, Bondman is part of the "counter-reason" of the "Afro-American archipelago" that produced calypso's Mighty Sparrow, jazz, reggae, and Rastafari, what Wynter (1986: 140) calls an "underground popular aesthetic imperative" that animated the institution of West Indian cricket, even if Bondman sat outside its gates.

There is, argues Wynter (1986: 75), a further comparison to be made between Bondman and the yard dwellers in James's novel *Minty Alley* (1936), who are condemned to "accept their inculcated zero value of identity, their own nothingness." But the characters of *Minty Alley* are afforded some dignity and even a sense of place in the order of things, while James's description of the bat-less Bondman leaves nothing worth redeeming. He simply is. Bondman is representative of former slaves whose surplus labor was essential, even constitutive of modern capitalism, but whose labor was then rendered superfluous in the post-slavery period. Here we have to break with Marx's category of labor and even the term "lumpen," as it does not suffice as a category to explain Bondman's status on the periphery of the so-called periphery. Selma James has remarked that Bondman is a renegade and castaway.[6] Perhaps he is the equivalent of Poor Tom of Shakespeare's *King Lear*, or even Rousseau's mythical Noble Savage (see, e.g., James 1985 [1953], 2009c). But while we can be thankful to James for bringing the once obscure Bondman to our attention, Bondman's background nonetheless remains shrouded in obscurity. Unlike the castaways on the *Pequod* whose stature James does so much to revive in his study of Herman Melville, or the wretchedness of Poor Tom for whom James provides historical context and hence a framework for understanding his social status during the early stages of the decline of the feudal order and the dawn of capitalism and modernism, Bondman and his wretchedness are taken for granted in *Beyond a Boundary*. He is outside the boundaries of humanity and makes the transition from *man* to *human*, to borrow from Wynter, only on the cricket pitch. In this sense he is both inside and outside the modernity-aesthetic paradigm. With bat in hand, he represents the pinnacle of grace, finesse, and style. The bat is his instrument, and with each stroke he swings himself into a potential new future, although this potential ultimately goes unrealized. Without this instrument of progress in his hands, Bondman symbolizes the wild and untamed, the crude and backward—the uncivilized and savage. For all intents and purposes, Bondman is the stereotypical primitive, or backward African, an ignoble savage; he is Quashee or the lazy, lackluster Sambo who, even when full of creative potential, lacks the discipline and culture, or the "stiff upper-lip," that would otherwise permit him to nurture his craft. And because he lacks this wherewithal and discipline, he is punished by history and confined to "niggerdom." The irony again is that—however ill-conceived and flawed the notion of modernity might be—Bondman is both constitutive and a constituent part of it—that is, the labor of his slave ancestors throughout the Caribbean, as James makes abundantly clear for us in *The Black Jacobins* in relation to Haiti, was crucial to the development and sustenance of modern capitalism (see James 1980 [1938]: 47–48, 86, 2009a). Wynter makes this very point by drawing on a lecture that James delivered in Montreal in 1966 (entitled "The Making of the Caribbean Peoples"). The Bondmans of the world, Wynter argues, were both "capital value and skilled labour value"; they were "coerced, yet trained in the necessary skills" that contributed to the development of modern capitalism in the interest of Europe and North America. To realize their own potential and exercise a humanity that had been denied them, they had to "live in an alternative cosmology, an underground culture which they reconstituted for themselves," and *"to desire as that by which alone they can live*, not the liberation of the productive forces (Liberalism and Marxism-Leninism) but the 'liberation of man'" (Wynter 1986: 137).

The point here is not to dismiss the seminal importance of James's profound and poignant analysis of cricket and his appreciation of Bondman's creative capacities. Nor am I suggesting that cricket does not belong to Bondman, too. In some respects, we might understand cricket and sports in general as one of the rewards for having suffered the humility of being a colonial subject. In competing against their colonial masters on the cricket pitch, West Indian cricketers demonstrated that, when the doors to "progress" were open, they could perform admirably, if not exceptionally well. We should also be leery of slipping into an uneasy essentialism that would dismiss James's analysis as not sufficiently "African." James stands as an intellectual giant, and not simply of the Caribbean, as is often suggested. His insights on a range of topics make him one of the true polymaths of the past hundred years, and beyond. But to appreciate *Beyond a Boundary* is also, as Gordon Rohlehr (1998: 158) has suggested, to "move beyond some of its limitations of vision." It is also to appreciate the significance of Nandy's point (which we have seen echoed by Robinson) about what he called cricket's "fatal flaw of character"—namely, that "the Victorian had to see the lower classes as carriers of those 'vulgar' or 'dirty' modern qualities which allowed the upper classes to uphold the traditional virtues and yet enjoy the benefits of modernity" (Nandy 2000: 19). Bondman, as the "dirty" and "vulgar," becomes the inverse reflection of James's heroic figures who averted the tragic social circumstances associated with the underclass, or the so-called lumpen. Clearly, the implication here is that part of Bondman's vulgarity is tied to his Africanity. But there is another way to look at Bondman's relationship to both cricket and society. If it is true that cricket was a "gift" to the colonized, and if we situate it alongside other "gifts," such as Christianity in relation to Rastafari and other Afro-Caribbean religions such as Pocomania and Shango (Nettleford 1998: 83), then we can perhaps gain an appreciation of Bondman not as an anomaly, but as a source of creativity that has found expression in multiple forms throughout the Caribbean and within the black diaspora.

**Bondman without the Bat**

In referring to what he describes as the black fantastic—black creativity, artistry, and popular culture—Iton (2008: 16) highlights what he calls the "minor-key sensibilities generated from the experiences of the underground, the vagabond, and those constituencies marked as deviant—notions of being that are inevitably aligned within, in conversation with, against, and articulated beyond the boundaries of the modern." In other words, the limits of modernity have constrained and contained not only the human potential of black subjects, but also our imaginations and our ability to dream beyond the present by accessing and making use of the creative energies of a particular kind that emanate from outside the eclipsed possibilities of modernity and capitalist fundamentalism. For James, Bondman represented this creativity with the bat in hand. No doubt, this symbolic instrument of progress (not to be confused with the sport itself as a onetime leisure pastime that was the antithesis of modernity) belongs to modernity's dispossessed, too.[7] But can we afford to ignore the cultural, political, and economic destruction that the economic system with which modernity is integrally linked has wrought, and particularly the hyper-modernity of the past hundred years? The untapped potential of the symbolic Bondman perhaps offers us a way to see ourselves out of a cul-de-sac. When Iton speaks of being both aligned with and against the modern, he suggests a place for the subaltern that would be far from unfamiliar to James, but one that James partially neglects in his rendering of the bat-less

Bondman. Without the bat, Bondman represented the subversive "anarchist-inflected" (Iton 2008: 202) presence of the Caribbean's former slaves who, as I have suggested, once produced surplus labor for Europe and the Americas in abundance but since have been rendered superfluous. In the aftermath of slavery, the Bondmans of the world became refuse in a society that could not sufficiently absorb them, or proved unwilling to do so, perpetually consigning them to society's margins and to the marginalia of the dominant narratives of Caribbean and Euro-Western history. The exploration of these so-called lowbrow cultural-aesthetic human possibilities have meaning on their own terms and are laden with political potential. "By bringing into view and into field of play practices and ritual spaces that are often cast as beyond the reasonable and relevant—to the point, indeed, of being unrecognizable as politics," writes Iton (2008: 16–17), "these visions might help us gain normative traction in an era characterized by the dismissal of any possibilities beyond the already existing." The alternative is to reinvest the Caribbean and people of African descent, and the so-called periphery in general, in a notion of modernity and progress that serves to further entrench the master-slave dynamics that James spent so much of his life attempting to overthrow, reducing our sense of what might be humanly possible to the limited conceptions of humanity embedded in modernity's feigned universalisms.

To find these new possibilities in part involves delving into a deep-seated realm of popular culture, the very realm that modernity pushes outside the boundaries of the normal, authentic, and aesthetically pleasing. "If the aesthetic is understood as the science of beauty that forecloses substantive political engagement or challenge," writes Iton (2008: 16), "it must be recognized as a key brick in the wall of modernity and one of the cornerstones of the racialized edifice that has so effectively contained and restricted black life chances." He goes on: we are not looking for "alternative modernities," by which he means a "primary template that might at best allow certain variations on a relatively fixed score," but, rather, the capacity of popular culture, and of course its producers, "to displace modernity as a master signifier within black and global discourse, along with its norms and modal infrastructures" (28). In other words, real possibilities for change lie not in a black or Caribbean version of modernity but in black/Caribbean/African/Third World popular culture, aesthetics, and politics whose existence is appreciated on its own terms, not simply as a counternarrative to modernity and the modern. They are appreciated as an ontological narrative that—while embracing the fact that the legacy of the myth-reality of modernity cannot be effaced—nonetheless attempts to recast the mold of the Caribbean and black diaspora's past and present futures in its own image and likeness. For Iton, this aesthetic-political narrative is to be found within the black fantastic, which includes the creative capacities of Bondman, even without—or, in this instance, especially without—the bat. These narratives already exist, but they have yet to be fully appreciated and sufficiently probed and chronicled. To slightly alter the meaning of James's famous phrase, Caliban has already pioneered into regions that Caesar never truly knew. The world needs new and creative models of what can and might be. As Frantz Fanon reminds, as he beckons us away from mimicry, modernity's longevity and successes hinge on devastation and destruction: "For centuries they [Europeans] have stifled almost the whole of humanity in the name of a so-called spiritual experience. Look at them today swaying between atomic and spiritual disintegration. And yet it may be said that Europe has been successful in as much as everything that she has attempted has succeeded" (Fanon 1968 [1961]: 311).

We might query here the extent to which Europe's successes have been fully conscious and self-determined. But Fanon's point is clear: rather than imitating a failed and failing model, he calls on us to creatively create—that is, to use our imaginations and extend our understanding of human possibilities, to bypass mimicry and think beyond the here and now. "Humanity is waiting for something from us other than such an imitation," he writes, "which would be almost an obscene caricature" (Fanon 1968 [1961]: 315). The figure of Caliban is the product of one of history's most fertile minds. But the Bard's creative imagination is no substitute for a self-portrait with its own lines, contours, and colors. There is a great deal at stake, and perhaps now is the time to abandon the Caliban metaphor and reframe the Caribbean and the black diaspora's reality in new ways that better reflect its past and future possibilities, tapping into the creative (but unromanticized or fetishized) potential that simmers beneath the surface until it finds popular expression, just as the Caribbean and black popular cultures of the Americas have done in the present past.

## Notes

*Epigraphs:* Wynter 1992: 75, 78; Iton 2008: 13; Fanon 1968 [1961]: 311.

1. Based on a speech delivered by Emperor Haile Selassie before the United Nations in 1963, "War" is from Bob Marley and the Wailers, *Rastaman Vibration*, Island/Tuff Gong Records, 1976.
2. In Audre Lorde's (1984: 112) words, "The master's tools will never dismantle the master's house."

**3.** David Scott (2014: 3) argues that, despite being closer to our time than the Haitian Revolution, the Grenada Revolution is perhaps more remote in terms of our memory, consciousness, and political imagination.
**4.** Hereafter, page numbers in parentheses refer to this edition of *Beyond a Boundary*.
**5.** Shango refers to both the god or orisha Shango and the Afro-Caribbean religion in Trinidad, but here I also use it as symbolic of other Afro-Caribbean religious and spiritual forms such as Pocomania in Jamaica, Voudou in Haiti, and Santería in Cuba.
**6.** Selma James made this comment during a session of the C. L. R. James's *Beyond a Boundary*—50th Anniversary Conference, 9–11 May 2013, at the University of Glasgow.
**7.** I am thankful to the editors for pointing out this apparent contradiction and to Eric Laferrière for suggesting that I clarify that I am not discounting the fact that sports historically have been a terrain on which colonial and hegemonic power has been contested.

# PART II.
# THE POLITICS OF REPRESENTATION
# IN *BEYOND A BOUNDARY*
| | | | |

# 6 | "Periodically I Pondered over It": Reading the Absence/Presence of Women in *Beyond a Boundary*

ANIMA ADJEPONG

> Women have always had a special place in the United States, respected as women have been in no other modern country. But the American male has had a passion for human relationships, social and personal, general and intimate, and it is this which above all constitutes the high civilization of the United States. He has not been able to create or establish this relationship with women.
> —C. L. R. James, *American Civilization*

C. L. R. James's writings reveal an ambivalent relationship to the "woman question." This question concerns issues of women's sexual freedom, bodily autonomy, and civic and civil rights among other things. Although recognizing the deeply political implications of answering the question of women's fundamental role in what he terms "the new society," James does not maintain a consistently progressive position on women. Aaron Kamugisha (2011: 77) has argued that James recognized the need for "a radical transformation in gender relations" and, further, that gender was central to James's quest for the new society. However, even when he embraced women as a central part of civil society—"the most advanced manifestation of [the] struggle" (Grimshaw 1991: 41)—James also admitted his failure to engage with women, at least in his personal life, outside a domestic and sexual economy. Whereas his readings of Toni Morrison, Alice Walker, and Ntozake Shange (James 1984: 264–70) engaged with these writers as revolutionary in their own right, for example, James's letters to Constance Webb (James 1996) and his op-ed, "The Women" (James 2003) suggest a less generous acknowledgment of women's place in the world.

In this chapter, I turn to *Beyond a Boundary* to try to understand the roles women played in the social and political world of West Indian cricket. Partially autobiographical, *Beyond a Boundary* offers insight into James's informal and private gender politics in ways that his letters and other published works might not. In the text, James (2013 [1963]: 41) comments that "there is a whole generation of us, and perhaps two generations, who have been formed by [cricket] not only in social attitudes but in our most intimate personal lives, in fact there more than anywhere else."[1] A question arises: who is "us"? This question is necessary, given the almost complete absence of women's voices and perspectives in the world James describes. My main argument in this chapter is that reading the silences about women's role in the world James sees from his bedroom window offers a modest way to recover the contributions women made to social and political life in the West Indies. Through this reading, I think "from the silences and absences" (Mignolo 2011: 206) produced by the normative narrative of revolutionary politics and action in order to make visible women's social and political contributions to challenging colonial authority and norms in the West Indies.

My goal in undertaking such a reading is to make more legible the often erased record of women's labor, contributions, and participation in social and political life and reimagine a world in which women's aspirations are not confined to a domestic and sexual sphere. Furthermore, such a reading illustrates that, although women are rarely mentioned in the text, *Beyond a Boundary*'s theoretical insights can be relevant for thinking more broadly about women's place in sports and politics.

*Beyond a Boundary* is a foundational text in the study of race, sports, and post/colonial studies.[2] Yet the three-day conference organized to mark the fiftieth anniversary of the publication of the text, which led to the present volume, produced only two papers dealing with questions of gender.[3] I make note of this disparity because on some level it mirrors the absence of explicit discussions of gender where *Beyond a Boundary* is concerned. When I make reference to gender, I do not simply mean women, although it is the absence of women that I am most concerned with in this chapter. Instead, I use gender in this context to refer to the production of racialized masculinities and femininities and how they inform the silences about black women in revolutionary texts such as *Beyond a Boundary*.

Throughout the text, James mentions several of his female relatives, albeit briefly: his grandmother; his mother, Bessie; his aunts Judith and Eva; and his sister Olive. Although these women all seem to play a major role in James's life, they are given peripheral positions in *Beyond a Boundary*. Later I consider how women were part of that "whole generation of us" shaped by cricket. Specifically, I examine James's story about his Aunt Judith. But before arriving at Judith's story, I locate this chapter by offering a discussion of how cricket served as a site of resistance against racism and colonialism in the West Indies. I then use Aunt Judith's story as a means of thinking through women's role in the social and political life of the region. I conclude by showing how women's participation in such struggles are neither confined to the home nor designated by men. The historical record does not often represent women's active political presence. Instead, it portrays women's subversive and revolutionary actions as marginal or instrumental to men's efforts, sustaining the idea that *men* make their own history and women just live in it.

**Racialized Gender, Sport, and Cultural Resistance**

In *Beyond a Boundary* cricket is proffered as a politically motivated site for the production of gendered, national, and cultural identities. That a sport of empire should play a substantive role in decolonizing and antiracist struggle is illustrative of the ambiguity of the post/colonial moment, as one "caught in ambivalent tension between, on the one hand, the surpassing of formal colonial governance, and on the other, the continuance of neocolonial relations" (Carrington 2010: 5; see also Carby 1998: 115). The post/colonial here is not simply a temporal marker designating an end to colonial rule followed by a wholly new social and political organizational structure. To talk about postcolonialism is to acknowledge the ambivalence of the end of formal colonial rule and to also note how colonialism changed the world terrain in such a way as to create hybridized identities between colonized and colonizer (see Hall 1996). James makes note of this tension when he describes himself as a "native" who is socialized as British—West Indian but British through and through. I identify the time in which James writes as post/colonial because, although the West Indies were still a British colony, I want to call attention to the anticolonial struggles during that period, which were informed by, and produced out of, contact with British values. Anticolonial struggles push back against the dominance of colonial powers often in a quest for national sovereignty.

Understanding cricket as a sport that simultaneously extended the British empire and challenged it provides a basis for making sense of how James can claim that the sport shaped the social attitudes and intimate personal lives of generations of West Indians. Douglas Hartmann's (2003) two definitions of cricket help us to further understand the role of the sport in the West Indian and other colonial contexts. The first definition remains within the boundaries of the game. It is the cricket that is concerned with bowlers and wicketkeepers. The second definition, which is what James offers in *Beyond a Boundary,* looks beyond the technicalities of playing the game and attempts to understand cricket as a cultural practice integrally related to the identity of a people. Cricket in this sense is not just about bowlers and batsmen; it is about "the players in the game, all those identities and experiences they bring to the game as well as what the game means or represents beyond the usual boundaries of the game" (Hartmann 2003: 454). This definition of cricket illuminates James's point that "cricket had plunged me into politics long before I was aware of it. When I did turn to politics, I did not have too much to learn" (65).

One way in which James examines cricket as a site for antiracist and anticolonial struggle is in his account of how he chose a team to join. Narrating his decision to become a member of the Maple Club instead of Stingo or Shannon, James reveals the ways in which racialized and classed notions of masculinity informed his decision. Although he notes in retrospect that his decision to join Maple instead of Shannon cost him "a great deal [and] delayed my political development for years," joining Maple was a sign of his social position, despite his dark skin. He writes, "So it was that I became one of those dark men whose 'surest sign of... having arrived is the fact that he keeps company with people lighter in complexion than himself'" (53). The racial and class politics involved in choosing a team reveal the dialectical relationship between the playing field and the social structures of the community. The six teams James describes (Queen's Park Club, Shamrock, Constabulary, Stingo, Shannon, and Maple) were, in ways, microcosms of the broader society. That the all-black Constabulary team, for example, had a white captain is telling in this regard. Yet "none of these [racial] lines was absolute" (50), and the racial project that was cricket in Trinidad produced fissures that simultaneously highlighted and undermined the class and gender politics of the society. For James, his upward class mobility led him to a decision that reproduced the racial and class fissures of the society. At the same time, within this space, players challenged the logics of these very hierarchies. Cricket as a tool of anticolonial struggle meant that even though the politics of team formations reproduced certain social norms, it also helped destabilize others.

Through cricket, not only were players forming and maintaining homosocial bonds, but they were also resisting their subordinated class and racial positions. As James writes, "The cricket field was a stage on which [men] played representative roles charged with social significance" (66). In addition to combating racial, colonial, and class oppression, the social significance of taking bat to ball was also gendered. As Ben Carrington (1998: 288) has shown in his study of the Caribbean Cricket Club (CCC) in Leeds, England, the sport "becomes a symbolic and real contestation of masculine and racial pride." Noting the gendered ways in which racism is contested through sport, Carrington (1998: 291) cautions against unqualified claims that equate black men's resistance to racism with black women's emancipatory ambitions, as well. Although such gendered forms of resistance may be mutually beneficial to men and women, it is important to make note of the ways in which sports as a project for resisting racism may also marginalize women.

James does not note the gendered implications of centering cricket as a site where "social and political passions [could] express themselves so fiercely" (72). Instead he described Shannon, the club of the working-class blacks, as playing "as if they knew that their club represented the great mass of black people in the island" (55). This description locates the club and its players as representative of the social and political passions of the whole society. Hazel Carby (1998: 2) calls this notion of collective representation one of the "ideologies of masculinity," which make men's social, cultural, and political productions and strategies of resistance representative of race and nation without noting the gendered way in which these productions occur. Ideologies of masculinity so strongly permeate James's discussion of cricket and politics that, although he is careful to note the clashes of class and caste between Shannon and Maple, as Carby observes, the gendered landscape of James's cricket world reproduces the point of view of the intellectual revolutionary middle classes as decidedly masculine.

Although James's focus is on men's "social and political passions" vis-à-vis cricket, in several instances throughout *Beyond a Boundary* he remarks on the ways in which some of the women in his life engaged with the sport. In the next section I focus on those moments when James comments on women's association with the sport. The majority of the discussion will consider Aunt Judith's story. James spent considerable time discussing his Aunt Judith, in contrast to the few sentences he writes about his grandmother, mother, and sister. The details the reader is presented of Judith's life provide a window through which to consider how and whether cricket stimulated women's political and social passions as it did men's. Paying attention to how women participated in sociopolitical life lends a corrective to their exclusion from historical representations in this arena.

### Black Women's Resistance and the Cult of Domesticity

When discussing the woman question, James begins in the home (see James 1993). For him, women's place is primarily located in a domestic and sexual economy. In an analysis of James's gender politics, W. Chris Johnson (2011: 186) contends that James was a man of his age and time, conforming to normative attitudes of heterosexism that he encountered in the United States, United Kingdom, and Trinidad. Despite James's participation in revolutionary politics that included women, ideologies of masculinity also organized his politics. This patriarchal orientation perhaps tints James's perception of how cricket stimulated shared political and social passions among women. Within this ideological framework, James cannot articulate a more active way in which cricket shaped women's social and political passions. As a result, the political narrative of *Beyond a Boundary* replays "the masculinist character of mainstream ideologies of global Blackness" (Lao-Montes 2007: 315). As Michelle Wright (2004: 133) has noted, accounts of black subjectivity often fail to make room for women, representing them as passive, "especially when one considers how nationalism necessarily relies on a mythic concept of homogeneity, of Others, and of women as passive helpmates to the male subject." This discursive framework interprets men's performances as representative of a homogeneous collective. Carby (1998: 120) similarly argues that cricket provided the basis for James's political consciousness because the masculinity on the playing field shaped his understanding of how colonialism should be opposed—through masculine clashes of political passions played on and beyond the boundary. But women's investment in cricket, although marginally explored in *Beyond a Boundary*, cannot be completely silenced. James notes his aunts' and grandmother's interest in the awful character that was Matthew Bondman—"good for nothing except to play cricket" (5). Although, according to James, his aunt and grandmother were neither "supporters or followers of the game," he also recognizes that the "ability to play cricket [could] atone . . . for Matthew's abominable way in life" (5). If the political and social passions of the island were played out on the cricket pitch, then perhaps James's grandmother's interest in Matthew Bondman signals an investment in the political and social life of Trinidad.

Women's lack of access to the playing field delimited their participation in sports to facilitating and supporting men's games. On the one hand, women's role as spectators can reinforce notions of men's superiority over women (see Hargreaves 1994, 2000). However, women's spectatorship and support for a cricket match that challenges colonial notions of black inferiority can simultaneously reinforce sexism while forming bonds of solidarity between racialized and oppressed subjects. As Angela Davis (1983: 23) reminds us, "[Enslaved] black women were equal to their men in the oppression they suffered . . . and they resisted . . . with a passion equal to their men's." Given the fact that men and women suffered racialized oppression in similar but gendered ways, it becomes important to consider the gendered nature of their resistance. Despite a gendered division of labor and the production of a cult of domesticity among colonialists and slave holders, within the economic sphere colonized and enslaved women and men were not considered too feminine to work in the fields or coal mines, for example (Davis 1983; see also McClintock 1995). At the same time, the colonial mission to control a colonized people by imposing "domesticity rooted in European gender and class roles" (McClintock 1995: 35) must have informed gender relations in Trinidad.

Turning to Aunt Judith's story offers insight into how cricket not only shaped generations of men but also informed and maybe fulfilled women's political and social passions. The story I tell below is pieced together from the two or three sections in *Beyond a Boundary* in which James mentions his aunt. I reconstruct this account of Judith to provide as full a picture as possible of her life as James described it. I contend that Judith's story, like James's grandmother's interest in Bondman's cricket, illustrates gendered moments of resistance to the twin forces of colonialism and conformity to normative heterosexual family life. Especially because Judith did not remarry but instead served as a single-mother matriarch of the family, her story challenges us to think differently about the actual roles that women played in the social, domestic, and political life of the island:

> Judith was a dutiful single mother. She lost her husband early in life and raised her three children, built a modern cottage, and, whenever James visited, fed him with "that sumptuousness which the Trinidad Negroes have inherited from the old extravagant plantation owners." She was also "the English Puritan incarnate." Her training helped James master the principles of cricket and English literature in a way that should have made her proud if she could have understood it. Her face was "often tear-

stained." Later on in life James learned that she "became the matriarch of the neighborhood.... All brought their troubles to her."

She saw Matthew Bondman as "a child of the devil" but would pray for him and nurse him to the end if he were "stricken with a loathsome disease" because "it was her duty." Her son did not play much sport but once a year invited his friends over to play a "festive cricket match." On these occasions, Judith always prepared "a great spread." The cricket match was "merely a preliminary" to the feast that Judith cooked. On the day of her death she "worked as usual from early morning in preparation for the day." After the match, when the men came in to eat, Judith served them, and then suddenly sat down because she wasn't "feeling so well." When they bent over her to find out what was wrong, she was dead. (11–12, 27, 40, 254–55)

Of Aunt Judith's death, James writes, "I thought it appropriate that her death should be so closely associated with a cricket match. Yet she had never taken any particular interest.... Periodically I pondered over it" (12).

I outline Judith's story to make note of several points. First, James's description of Judith as a "puritanical matriarch" highlights a tension between the heterosexual patriarchal colonial cult of domesticity and the disruption that the black matriarch presents to it. The black matriarch is the ghostly matter that haunts the respectable, heterosexual, middle-class black family. The sociologist Avery Gordon (2008: xvi) explains haunting as "one way in which abusive systems of power make themselves known and their impacts felt in everyday life, especially when they are supposedly over and done with (slavery, for instance) or when their oppressive nature is denied (as in free labor or national security)." As ghostly matter, the black matriarch sheds light on the hetero-patriarchal assumptions of respectability. Her persistence is a reminder that the black family may be "heterosexual but never *heteronormative*" (Ferguson 2004: 85) because of the ways in which normative heterosexuality is indexed to logics of white middle-class respectability. Judith as "puritanical matriarch" embodies the contradictions of a cult of domesticity that marginalizes women's participation in civic life and a post-slavery post/colonial inheritance of women's active involvement in shaping the fabric of society. Judith's story further suggests that although the cult of domesticity extends respectability to those who adhere to its requirement, it is also a racialized cult wherein black subjects are only marginally incorporated.

As a post/colonial subject Judith highlights the ambiguities of the post/colonial moment. Simultaneously an embodiment of puritan culture and a black matriarch, Judith, like James, is West Indian but British through and through.

Judith's position as matriarch within the logics of the cult of domesticity serves to efface her participation in the broader economic and civic life of her community (McClintock 1995). Despite being a widow, Judith performed the functions of the respectable middle-class wife: she raised her children under the roof of a "modern cottage"; offered advice to neighbors in efforts to attain reconciliation and peace; and cooked for her relatives and their friends. All of this work contributed to a domestic economy that was not auxiliary to paid economic labor but instead supported it (see Davis 1983).[4] Yet Judith's labor is rendered marginal to the social and political passions of colonial Trinidad. Such a marginal consideration of the work of sustenance that Judith and other "matriarchs" perform in colonized spaces ignores the ways in which such efforts contribute to and shape social and political life. Judith may have been confined to the home, where she raised children, cooked, cleaned, and gave counsel to those who sought it. But her efforts must be understood within a context that simultaneously recognizes the respectability extended to middle classes that adhered to the cult of domesticity, as well as the ways in which the symbol of the matriarch disrupts normative heterosexual family life, with a man as the head.

I also want to suggest a link between Judith's role as matriarch and her occasional interest in the cricket matches that occurred in Tunapuna. According to James, it was not only Judith but also his grandmother and another aunt who "would come in from the street and say, 'Matthew made 55,' or 'Arthur Jones is still batting'" (12). Judith's interest in cricket, as well as the interest that other women expressed in the sport, although only marginally noted in the text, implies an investment in the sociopolitical life of Tunapuna in a way that must be accounted for. If, as James so aptly argues, there was a dialectical relationship between cricket and the tensions of colonization, race, and class, it seems an untenable position to believe that women were outside the ways in which these tensions played out. Yet the dominance of men on the cricket field meant that, within "the early ideological formation of cricket, [women were understood] to be well 'beyond the boundary'" (Beckles 1995a: 224). Beckles has argued that although West Indian women play cricket, even the staunchest (male) cricket fanatics know next to nothing about the women's game, and "women's cricket continues to fight for minimal nonsexist coverage" (Beckles 1995a: 222). The marginalization of women on the playing field informs James's inability to recognize women's role in the ways in which political and social tensions played out. When sport is regarded as part of anticolonial struggles, women's absence from the playing field permits an easy effacement of their contribution to these struggles. Furthermore, active efforts have been made to keep women out of sports in ways that feed the perception that women are uninterested in the symbolic and real struggles that sports establish and incapable of the fortitude required to participate.

In a study of female cricket spectators, Souvik Naha (2012) has shown how women's participation in cricket evolved historically from active participation on the playing field to marginal involvement as spectators who were sometimes ridiculed as ignorant of the sport. Writing about Indian cricket, Naha argues that, despite initial strategies to exclude women from even watching the sport, women still found ways to watch, learn, and read about cricket. Consequently, interested women could be just as knowledgeable about the sport as their male contemporaries. With this in mind, and returning to James's account of Judith's death, "so closely associated with a cricket match," the reader has to wonder why Judith would come in from the street and note what a player made or who was still batting when she apparently took little interest in the sport (12). Judith's, and other women's comments about who was batting or how well, when read along with James's grandmother's verdict that the wayward cricketer Matthew Bondman was "good for nothing except to play cricket," suggests, at the very least, that these women were interested in the sport. In addition, these comments may be indicative of an investment in the local class and race politics played out through cricket, which, as James asserts, in part challenged colonial hierarchies.

Although excluded from the playing field, the women James talks about in *Beyond a Boundary* exemplify different ways in which women supported the practice, as well as the emancipatory politics, associated with cricket. Judith's self-imposed duty to pray for Matthew Bondman should he get sick, her preparation of a post-cricket match feast for her son and his friends, her role as neighborhood matriarch, and her often tear-stained face suggest an emotional and physical support of cricket and her participation in civic life circumscribed by her position as a middle-class woman. But because women were not seen to carry their "bat for the liberation of . . . oppressed people everywhere" (Viv Richards, quoted in Carrington 1998: 281), their participation in the struggle remained marginal. Richards's quote, like James's claim that cricket taught him everything he needed to know about politics, illustrates how the task of political emancipation is believed to be accomplished through masculine and male prowess. Yet I propose that Judith's story is significant in that it portrays the ways in which the unpaid and often unrecognized labor performed by women in support of revolutionary politics is, in the retelling, depicted as marginal or inconsequential. Such a depiction of women's political presence will no doubt leave one pondering over the fact that Judith's death, for example, was so closely associated with a cricket match although she was ostensibly uninterested in it. When Judith's labor in the domestic sphere is rightly recognized as supporting anticolonial efforts and invested in the politics played out within the boundary, she can be acknowledged as a martyr for the cause. Reassessing the different ways women historically have been able to participate in the struggle to change the social order, sometimes in indirect ways, lends a corrective to ideologies of masculinity that silence women's voices and marginalize their political activities and emancipatory needs.

### Women's Presence on and off the Playing Field

Before concluding, I want to take a brief detour to consider representations of women's visible participation in sociopolitical struggles. Although the public record does not tell us much about these women, it would be inaccurate to suggest that the only ways women took part in such struggles was as passive helpmates to male subjects. At the same time, women's marginalization on the sports field and within the national framework reveals how women's participation in political struggles is often refracted through a lens that renders women's actions marginal to the cause.

Revolutionary heroes are not often women, and anticolonial projects and narratives of diaspora are often characterized by discourses that imagine the heterosexual male body as active agent of history and women as objects within that history (Wright 2013). Even when women are incorporated into this discursive frame, the requirements of patriarchy shape popular interpretations of their participation. A prominent account of women's involvement in anticolonial struggle is Frantz Fanon's "Algeria Unveiled," which discusses women's role in the Algerian revolution. Although Fanon (1969 [1965]: 172) does not describe women's involvement in the struggle as decisions they reached themselves—"the decision to involve women as active elements of the Algerian Revolution was not reached lightly"—he is also conscious of how women were wholly active and dedicated to the cause. He writes, "The women had to show as much spirit of sacrifice as the men" (Fanon 1969 [1965]: 172). Yet, unable to grant women's role the same status as that of men, Fanon adds that the Algerian woman learns her "revolutionary mission instinctively," thereby naturalizing women's revolutionary strategies as inherent and happening without conscious thought (Fanon 1969 [1965]: 174). Anne McClintock (1997: 98) describes the contradictory ways in which Fanon constructs women's agency and their participation in the Algerian revolution as "agency by designation." This type of agency "makes its appearance not as a direct political relation to the revolution but as a mediated, domestic relation to a man." Such a representation of women's participation results in the repression of women's involvement in political and revolutionary struggles and reproduces the nation as "identified with the frustrations and aspirations of men" (McClintock 1997: 89; see also Wright 2004). The inability to acknowledge when, where, and how women enter into the national revolution produces what I am calling women's political absence/presence.

Just as women are rendered absent from political discourse, their participation in sports remains marginal.[5] Carrington (2010: 99) suggests that the sporting framework is so characterized by masculinity that, regardless of gender and sporting ability, the black athlete is always coded as male. This coding means that black sportswomen are subsumed by racialized tropes that reproduce stereotypes of black women as outside "true femininity" and sportswomen as mannish. Despite black sportswomen's designation as sporting "space invaders" (Adjepong and Carrington 2014), they have made their presence known on the playing field, challenging their exclusion from national and sporting frameworks.

These examples of women's active participation in sports and politics challenge us to reimagine women's place in the world James creates within and beyond the boundary. Although James's narrative excludes women from the political economy, women certainly participated in these realms of their own accord. Excavating the ways in which women were invested in social and political struggles in *Beyond a Boundary* allows for an expansive reading of the text that is not exclusive to men's frustrations and aspirations. James's theoretical insights about how sports shape political life are not just relevant to men; considering the ways in which these insights inform understandings of women's politics, as well, thus expands the scope of the text. The exercise that this essay undertakes asks us to reconsider the transformative potential of reading the silences in *Beyond a Boundary* as a means to recover women's political participation and look toward a gender-egalitarian future.

## Conclusion

James's (1993: 223) reading of the American male's inability to relate to women on a human level—"the American male has a passion for human relationships . . . he has not been able to create or establish this relationship with women"—provides a window into James's own gender politics. Although he strives for a progressive and egalitarian stance with regard to women in society, this effort is curtailed by an inability to engage with women as equals, undergirded by ideologies of masculinity. I have attempted to counter these ideologies by pondering over the story James tells about his Aunt Judith as a way to uncover women's participation in sociopolitical struggles. Of course, my efforts in this essay are not the only accounts of women's involvement in sociopolitical life. Scholars such as Rhoda Reddock (1994, 1998, 2014) have provided historically grounded examinations of black women's participation in the radical politics of Trinidad in particular, and in the Caribbean more generally. This reevaluation of *Beyond a Boundary* simply exercises a decolonial option by attempting to make more visible women's political presence and participation in the social world of cricket. This world is not invested in maleness or masculinity as a criterion for representation; instead, it multiplies options (Mignolo 2011) for solidarity and representation by rejecting the dominant hierarchies that center masculinity at the expense of women's lives and experiences.

Because James's account of cricket in the West Indies remains foundational to understanding sports and politics, a decolonial feminist reading of this text contributes to reorienting how we think about black women's historical engagement in antiracist and other political struggles. Recognizing that black women are also affected by racism and colonialism means trying to identify the ways in which they have responded to these forms of oppression. To insist on their "agency by designation" marginalizes black women's political activism and their responses to racism and reproduces the sociopolitical sphere as defined by clashes of masculinity. Alternatively, uncovering the silences about women in historical accounts of sociopolitical struggles lends a corrective to the exclusion of women from this field while striving for "a critical and potentially transformative political imagination" (Muñoz 2009: 3).

## Notes

*Epigraph:* James 1993: 223.

1. Hereafter, page numbers in parentheses refer to this edition of *Beyond a Boundary*.
2. I follow Carrington's (2010) use of the virgule in "post/colonial" as a way to highlight the ambivalent tension between the current period of racial formation and the ways in which the post/colonial is experienced differently, depending on geographical location and historical moment.
3. The papers on gender included mine, which forms the foundations for this chapter, and Ben Carrington's presentation, which considered cricket a form of black cultural politics that produces racialized masculinities among West Indian–descended black British men.
4. See also Selma James, *A Woman's Place*, 1952, http://radicaljournal.com/books/selma_james_a_womans_place.
5. Women's resistance to racism is refracted through a sporting lens in ways that render the acts illegible. One final example comes from the film *42—The Jackie Robinson Story* (Helgeland 2013), released in the United States in the fall of 2013. The film is a biopic portrayal of the American baseball star Jackie Robinson and an example of how black liberation, as seen through the lens of sports and politics, relies on the interplay between black and white masculinities. Putting aside the ways in which the film reduces racism to a personal problem, I want to highlight its portrayal of black women. Robinson's wife, Rachel, is one of (at most) five women in the film. In one scene, Rachel Robinson walks into a women's restroom marked "Whites Only." The narrative arc suggests that Rachel has ignored the sign, not as an act of subversion, but because she is ignorant of the rules of Jim Crow South. This intimation downplays the ways in which Rachel had experienced racism directly, and not only through Jackie Robinson's difficulties getting a job. She, too, has a dog in this fight. Yet the inability to see women as implicated in the processes of social and political life undermines the power of Rachel Robinson's subversive act.

# 7 | C. L. R. James, W. G. Grace, and the Representative Claim

NEIL WASHBOURNE

This chapter explores the model (or theory) of the representative hero or figure present in *Beyond a Boundary*, a model that is an important, rich, and suggestive means for exploring individual-collective relationships in real-world contexts. While a great deal of attention has been given to several features of it, the model, to my mind, has not been fully explored in the secondary literature on C. L. R. James.[1] To date, attention has focused on features that include James's account of cricket as an art form, which more broadly develops an understanding and valuation of activities previously undervalued; consideration of the broader question of "what men live for," resolution of which requires moving beyond merely utilitarian or material considerations; and the development and promotion of anticolonial cultural nationalism (Smith 2010: 33–34). James's model possesses further elements, however, yet to receive due attention—most important, James's account of the career and public acclaim of the Gloucestershire, Marylebone Cricket Club (MCC), and England cricketer W. G. Grace (1848–1915). This chapter agrees with James's assessment of the centrality of Grace as a historical figure and symbol of Victorianism and supports his assertion that Grace was the object of intense public enthusiasm and public importance, especially in the summer of 1895. The chapter explores, however, some elements missing in James's account (both of Grace and more generally). It does so to bolster his model, and our understanding, of the public role(s) of representative figures. In doing so, it suggests that the philosophical ideas on which James draws to make this representative claim—particularly Jean-Jacques Rousseau's epistemic notion of democracy and his conception of general will—restrict his ability to focus on the mediations necessary to the existence of representative figures.

First, it helps if we explore further the structure and roles of representative relationships as present, admittedly in a rather dispersed way, in *Beyond a Boundary* to get a sense of the scope of the notion. Second, we need to consider the role of mediations in general (and, in particular, media of communications) in structuring representative relationships. The chapter argues that mediations considerably influence the practice and perception of representativeness and what it is that is being represented. Consideration of such mediation is essential to any viable model of the representative figure. In the case of Grace, we need to consider press and cricketing bodies' idealization of Grace in presenting him as a gentleman-amateur fully in the tradition of Thomas Arnold and Thomas Hughes, and thus able adequately to represent England (and empire). Grace was less than a full gentleman-amateur in many ways, never having attended a public school or Oxbridge. He was also a fake amateur—more highly paid than the best professionals; sometimes, perhaps, a cheat on the field of play; a drinker who became an icon of the temperance movement and so on.

Those idealized representations had a role, unmentioned by James, in privileging middle-class masculinity and its cultural authority in ways that assume that working-class men and non-heteronormative men and women were naturally subordinate. The press coverage of Grace's *annus mirabilis* of 1895 idealized Grace by reproducing his power as an amateur cricket captain; in doing so, it paid no attention to the actually contentious relationship between the very highly paid Grace and the public school ideology that did not represent the largely working-class professional cricketers Grace commanded as captain of Gloucestershire, touring sides, and England. Further, and even more important, Grace was constructed as the hero of 1895 whose clear villain was Oscar Wilde, in relation to whom Grace was presented as a representative of hegemonic, often narrowly philistine, John Bull masculinity. In both cases, Grace as a representative figure is constructed and circulated to uphold restrictive cultural and political models of masculinity. James's own account prefers to consider Grace a presence of the virtues of preindustrial society in industrial Britain (James 2013 [1963]: 177–78),[2] whose celebration in 1895 is spontaneous and unqualified (184), as if Britain is gathered together as an organic community through Grace's actions and their reception. James's account thereby neglects the work of press outlets and cricketing (and other) organizations in circulating carefully edited and constructed accounts of Grace to suit dominant forms of masculine identity.

This chapter, then, considers the implication of the Grace-Wilde contrast in 1895 for the meanings circulating in presentations of Grace as the object of such representative claims. It further suggests that we should draw on

Michael Saward's work to aid us in these concerns and involves an argument for taking mediation into account in the real-world role of these mediated representative claims generally.

### James's Model of the Representative Figure

At the heart of *Beyond a Boundary* is the representative figure whose cultural-political importance to James is as a unifying factor that, in the West Indies, played a role in the struggle for colonial independence and self-worth. In this section, I reconstruct that model, which brings together West Indian cricketers, the clubs for which they play, the recreation grounds on which that play takes place, the culture and art of cricket understood by players and crowds alike, and the broader historical traditions within which the game is played (including the embodied history of particular strokes). James offers us, through this model, a kind of "cultural materialism" in which people play, spectate, and appreciate the skills and identities of the players (and the crowd).[3]

Some of the players considered by James have been written about a great deal. Matthew Bondman has received the greatest consideration; his distinctive combination of personal disreputability and cricketing grace arrests James's attention, and that of many other spectators (3–5; see also Bogues 1997: 27; Bogues 2006: 169; Smith 2010: 84). Somewhat more neglected is Wilton St. Hill, a player of great talent and a skillful exponent of both the cut and the leg glance (6, 83) and thus a product of, and contributor to, the tradition of cricket (82–97). St. Hill is considered a fine example of the type of cricket whose virtues James espouses—one alive to the possibilities of the contest between bat and ball and to the circumstances and moments of the game. St. Hill is "on the go," seeking to shape the game, play strokes, and forge cricketing destinies (86, 95). His cricket, James asserts, embodies the "instinct of an oppressed man" hoping to prove himself at Lords or the Oval in the metropolis of the empire (91). St. Hill is, however, a tragic figure in the end for James, because when he was finally selected for a West Indies tour of England—in 1928—he was an abject failure: "the greatest failure ever to come out of the West Indies" (95). The failure is felt so intensely by James and others because St. Hill's batting "conveyed [to "coloured" Trinidadians] the sensation that here was *one of us* [emphasis added], performing *in excelsis* in a sphere where the competition was open" (93). "Our boy" (94) had fallen and, with him, "all the subterranean aspirations" of West Indies cricket.[4] The tragedy is mitigated later when great West Indian cricketers from the 1930s–1960s, such as Learie Constantine (101–35), George Headley (139–48) and Frank Worrell (257–58), fulfill those aspirations. The case of George John, however, shows that something more than great capacity as a cricketing craftsman is required to create a figure able to represent (stand in for, embody) those aspirations (80).

Island players played for a variety of clubs at various levels of organized cricket in Trinidad and thereby become qualified, should sufficient success ensue, to represent the island and, in the light of great and sustained success, the West Indies. James reports that there were both second-class clubs (60) and first-class clubs, the former including Siparia Cricket Club (11) and, James's home-town club, Tunapuna (6). James gives a sharp analysis of the race and class makeup of the first-class clubs—Queen's Park, Shamrock, Constabulary, Stingo, Maple, and Shannon—and his own, tense biographical relation to them (49–50). Access to these clubs came via selection committees (80) and boards (236–37, 242), involving some players serving as captains and secretaries, as well as committee members (24). It also included trials to test the skills of the best cricketers against one another (69–70). Although the formal selection of cricketers for first-class island and West Indies teams involved being chosen to *represent* the sides in question, in each case James's model recognizes the importance of, but goes far beyond, such formal procedures: he is especially interested in spectators' perceptions that such teams, and the individual players within them, *embody* their aspirations. Further, those formal procedures are often subject to criticism as players appear to spectators to have been selected, or not, for reasons other than cricketing talent (see, e.g., 70, 95, 239–40). So although the structures of clubs and selection committees may be a *necessary* condition of the representative figure, they are not *sufficient* to explain the richness of representation (felt to be) going on. The clubs depend on the creation and upkeep of recreation (3) and sports grounds (56) such as the Queen's Royal College (18) and the Queen's Park Oval (49). The latter is where the great fast bowler George John was head groundsman, where he earned his daily wage—cricket pitches require a lot of upkeep (60). The main ground, the Queen's Park Savannah (54), formed a wide open ground on which most clubs had their pitches. James's close access to such grounds—with his bedroom window directly "behind [the] wicket" (7)—allowed him privileged access to the play, a viewpoint beloved by cricket connoisseurs because from there one can judge the (lateral) movement of the cricket ball. James, therefore, is giving us a rich material analysis of cricket while simultaneously noting the importance of cultural meanings; spectators' perceptions of being represented arise out of informal interpretations of active spectators, not merely or mainly the decisions of selectors.

The Shannon club in particular is explored by James in considering how the informal creation of representation occurs (50–58). Shannon was a club of "the black lower-middle class" and included in its membership both St. Hill and Constantine (50). James attributes to the club an ethos—Shannonism— which was understood by cricketers and spectators alike and was manifest both in the play of the team and of individual players, who represented (were felt or thought to represent) the feelings, values, and aspirations of black Trinidadians (58). Shannonism further "symbolized the dynamic forces of the West Indies" and embodied "cricket's accumulated skills, its historical traditions and its virtues" (58). Constantine avers that Shannon played with "spirit and fire [and] spontaneous self-discipline and cohesion" (57). Although spectators do hear tales of Shannonism, they also, for James's model, are understood as interpreting the embodied symbolism seen in the actions of players (and the team as a whole). The oft-discussed pages on cricket as an art (195–211) provide support and elaboration of the role of such symbolism. Cricket is, after all, a "dramatic spectacle" that requires "some knowledge of the elements" of the game, if not the "finer points" (198).[5]

Binding cricketers and clubs together in a net of formal and informal representative relations are the crowds and spectators of Trinidadian and West Indian cricket (Smith 2010: 86). In *Beyond a Boundary* James provides a rich discussion of spectator and crowd thinking, feeling, and behavior that underpins the informal relation to the representative figure. One aspect of relevance overall to such cricket spectators is James's argument that in the periphery, the sentiment of connection to cricketers is especially strong (92–93). This powerful connection to cricketers means that many spectators went beyond being a member of a crowd and helped run local clubs, as James's brother did for the football association (11). Such crowds also watched practice sessions and not merely matches (89), not only witnessing but also assessing players' styles and form. James's father gave him a bat and a ball, underscoring and supporting the importance of the game to him from an early age (21). In his family, even those who did not follow cricket closely knew others, including C. L. R., for whom it was a passion. This included both James's grandmother and aunt, who passed on cricket news to him (12). James also had access to his cousin Cudjoe's cricket stories (8) and recounts the example of his maternal grandfather, Josh Rudder, who followed cricket assiduously in print although he had not *seen* a game in thirty years (13). Others outside James's family also followed cricket in the press. This even led, on one occasion, to James being mistaken for Wilton St. Hill, since there were those who had read about St. Hill but had never seen him play cricket. (They saw some of the style of St. Hill's batting, about which they had read, in James's play [91].) Fathers of young cricketers swelled with pride as their sons had success against established players (60–61).

Cricket was not just followed closely by spectators and crowds. Such spectators required, and learned, expectations of both the play and the style of play of their teams (49, 55). Rivalries between closely matched teams enhanced those expectations and forms of knowledge (56). Among some of those crowds, a puritanical and public school ideal of cricket held sway (39). Certainly, it was strong in James himself, and it was very common for games to be conducted in an atmosphere of extreme seriousness (60). Such seriousness and interest in the game spread even to those migrants who had no prior experience of the sport. James provides the example of an unnamed Chinese shopkeeper who did not watch matches but whose passion for the game led him to sponsor the local village team (63).[6] Others have discussed the failure to select the Stingo cricketer Telemaque for the Trinidad team. We can get a sense of the significance of the game to popular crowds further through the reaction of family, friends, and neighbors to this disappointment, as reported to James by Hutcheon, Stingo's captain: "[Telemaque's] wife—she weighs 200 pounds—is sitting on a chair out on the pavement, crying because her husband isn't going to Barbados with the Trinidad team, and all the neighbours are standing round consoling her and half of them are crying too" (69).

James's model of the representative figure, therefore, is a materially-based, cultural analysis of the embodied, meaningful action of players and teams within a structure of clubs offering opportunities for players to compete on recreation grounds before spectators who identify with teams and players through both formal and informal frameworks of understanding and passion with the drama on display. In the next section, I explore W. G. Grace as the model for James's idea of the cricketer as representative figure and use that as a starting point for exploring some limitations (and suggestions for improvement) of that model.

## W. G. Grace as Representative Figure in *Beyond a Boundary*

The key focus in this section is how James's fascination with W. G. Grace revealed to him, perhaps even early in his life, the role of a cricketer as representative of the thoughts, ideals, and aspirations of entire populations. First, however, I want to say a few things about how central Grace is to *Beyond a Boundary* tout court. One piece of evidence here is the book's title. James had earlier considered titles for the book that became *Beyond a Boundary* that reveal just how central W. G. was: *W. G., A West Indian Grace* and *West Indian Progeny of W. G.* (see chapter 3 in this volume). Further, the book is dedicated to three people: Learie Constantine, Frank Worrell, and W. G. Grace. To the first- and the last-named, James asserts, "This book hopes to right grave wrongs, and in doing so, extend our too limited conceptions of history and of the fine arts" (v). In Grace's case, this includes the profound neglect, by historians, of cricket as a key part of Victorian life and the historical process more generally (159). Thus, establishing Grace's importance opens the space for establishing and understanding West Indian cricketers as historically, culturally, and politically important figures.

In *Beyond a Boundary*, the whole of part five, "W. G.: Pre-eminent Victorian" (151–94), is given over to understanding Grace and exploring the implications of his life in sport and as a crucially important, if neglected, maker of the Victorian age. Grace is also mentioned on a host of other pages of the book. Although Grace played first-class cricket for more than forty years (1865–1908), James picks out 1895 as the key moment in which Grace took on the most massive symbolic role, making him representative of cricket and other identities. That year, James argues, involved the consummate expression of a more general role Grace had played heretofore; that through him, "Cricket, the most complete expression of popular life in *pre-industrial* England, was incorporated into the life of the nation. As far as any social activity can be the work of any one man, he did it" (171, emphasis added). Grace influenced cricket not only by revolutionizing the playing of the game (178–79) but also by building "the whole imposing structure and of social organization of first-class cricket as we know it today" (173). Among the men who, through cricket, influenced the history of their time, Grace, according to James, is "head and shoulders above *all* others" (101, emphasis added). In 1895—after some years of relative cricketing decline—Grace, age forty-seven, completed his one-hundredth century, scored one thousand runs in May (183–84), and received—to aid those strenuous achievements—"the *spontaneous, unqualified, disinterested* enthusiasm and goodwill of a whole community" (184, emphasis added).

For James, then, Grace embodies the link between hero and people and makes evident that the former provides for the latter some of what they need to live by (151–58; see Bogues 2006: 159). He fulfills a social need (183) present in the "hundreds of thousands of people, high and low, [who] were expecting him to be at his best [or] even to exceed it" (183). He is seen to embody the public school ethic James also explores through the figures of Dr. Arnold of Rugby School and Thomas Hughes of *Tom Brown's Schooldays* fame (161–70). In James's account, Grace is a model of cricket as more than a game—as a central feature of culture and society. He also formed a key part of James's obsessive schoolboy reading, collecting and annotating of Victorian and Edwardian papers and magazines (see, e.g., 16–18). How else could he have known?

It is at this point, in relation to James's access to Grace via print reporting, that our key difficulty with his analysis of Grace and his model of the representative figure comes to light. James never met Grace or saw him play. Grace had completed his first-class career by the time James was seven and died while James was in his early teens. James therefore *depended* on print media for access to stories about Grace and evidence of crowds' enthusiasm for him. It is in relation to questions of mediation broadly considered, and media coverage more narrowly, then, that we need to explore Grace in 1895, supplement James's account of him, and further develop James's model of the representative figure.

### Grace, James, and the Question of Mediation

In this section I argue against the assertion that the public acclaim for Grace as a representative hero in 1895 was the product of "the spontaneous, unqualified, disinterested enthusiasm and goodwill of a whole community." It is both a very significant misreading of Grace and contains the core of a misleading account overall (see Washbourne 2013).[7] The reception of Grace was not as unitary as James suggests (a point I will not develop further here); nor was such unity as did exist simply spontaneous or disinterested. Both mediation more generally (the role of intermediary groups and organizations) and media coverage more specifically played a large role in *what* and how many images and stories of Grace were celebrated in 1895 and *where* those images and attendant stories were distributed and thereby had the potential to influence the attention and understanding of the broader public. In short, press coverage was dominated by a middle-class sensibility and definitions of individual and collective relationships. Further, people depend on media to follow the story of Grace's success in 1895. It is unlikely that even a single person saw all of the twenty-nine first-class and six minor matches Grace played that year. If they had, they would have had to travel among grounds in London (Lords and Oval), England's southeast (Hove and Hastings), the southwest (Bristol, Cheltenham, Gloucester, and Taunton), the Midlands (Birmingham), and the north (Bradford, Manchester, and Nottingham) (Webber 1998: 245–52). The general discussion of Grace in public would have been *highly dependent* on the newspapers and magazines they read. In short, print culture (and media more generally) in part constitutes (mediated) public life (see Washbourne 2010: 18–21). The most important aspect of the public celebration of Grace's success that year was the raising of a shilling national subscription testimonial fund to him by competing organizations: MCC, the ruling club of cricket and its laws at the time, and Gloucestershire County Cricket Club (GCCC, Grace's county side), on one side, and two publications, *The Sportsman* and the *Daily Telegraph*, on the other, dominated by the latter. The testimonial raised nearly £10,000 for Grace. This tied Grace's cricket performances and their meanings into wider issues in public opinion. One key focal issue was the Oscar Wilde scandal. Wilde's second and third criminal trials bookended Grace's one-hundredth first-class century and, in a later match, scores of 257 and 73 "not out" for Gloucestershire versus Kent at Gravesend (with Grace being the first cricketer ever to be on the field for the entire match). That match ended on 25 May 1895—the same evening as Wilde's second criminal trial.

In this context, Grace's image was used as the healthy, masculine, outdoors counterpoint to Wilde's perverse, unwholesome, indoors identity (as revealed by the press accounts of the trials). Ari Adut (2008: 38–72) has argued convincingly that the Wilde scandal was so potentially destabilizing that *active and public* dis-identification with Wilde was necessary. By publishing the names of shilling subscribers to Grace's testimonial, the *Daily Telegraph* in particular provided a dominant space for the public to identify with Grace and publicly and actively dis-identify from what Wilde represented. Subscribers (the Marquess of Queensberry, Wilde's libel trial nemesis, was one) "high and low" did so in the thousands. Representations of Grace provided a public totem for reassurance and the construction and circulation of a philistine, John Bullish version of Englishness/Britishness that provided incentives for public displays of an overt and dominant masculinity (such as the joining of cricket clubs by men anxious to avoid the glare of any, even potential, suspicion).[8] When presenting the results of the shilling testimonial fund to Grace, Sir Edward Lawson, the editor of the *Daily Telegraph*, described the subscriptions as evidence of "a warm appreciation felt throughout the land and the Empire for your own high and worthy qualities as an English cricketer. It comprises, however, above and beyond this . . . a very notable and emphatic expression of the general love for those out-of-doors sports and pursuits, which—free from any element of cruelty, greed or coarseness—most and best develop our British traits of manliness, good temper, fair play, and the healthy training of mind and body" (Rae 1998: 396, emphasis added).

The preamble to the letter has the words, "I permit myself to regard the progress and result of the 'National Shilling Testimonial' as a manifestation by *classes and masses alike* of their abiding preference for *wholesome and honest amusements* in contradistinction to *sickly pleasures* [I suggest, a reference to Oscar Wilde] and *puritanical gloom*" (Powell and Caple 1974: 127–28, emphasis added). Consideration of media coverage and the roles of mediating institutions suggests not only that the reaction to Grace in 1895 was far less *spontaneous, unqualified* and *disinterested* than James claims (there are the commercial interests of the popular press, for example), but that a lacuna is revealed here in James's model of the representative figure. Other features of James's account of Grace are also worth investigating—perhaps most important, the question of class and cricket. James neglects the financial, social, and cultural restrictiveness of English cricket at the time for the (very largely working-class) professional cricketers. In fact, he neglects them in *Beyond a Boundary*, focusing much more on the amateur- and batsman-dominated "Golden Age" (1890–1914) of C. B. Fry, K. S. Ranjitsinhji, Archie MacLaren, and Gilbert Jessop (214–15). It is important to note that Grace himself, also formally an amateur, did not merely go along with an already established divide between amateur and professional—a divide that meant that "players" traveled separately, changed separately, often entered the field from different points, ate separately, and were segregated at or absented from social events. Rather, if anything, Grace used his power to *reinforce, intensify,* and *extend* the divide. As captain of Gloucestershire (and many other teams, including England), the organizer of cricket festivals, and a selector of teams he discriminated in favor of amateur cricketers (he was, for example, the last captain to field an entirely amateur side in the county championship) and upheld, with much energy and both stick and carrot, the distinction. Both aspects of the mediation of Grace (the roles of media coverage *and* mediating institutions) suggest a significant degree of manufacturing of what Grace "meant," and within that, a defense of the distinction between amateur and professional that both expressed and helped maintain broader relations of authority in British society.

## James's Neglect of Mediation

With regard to his account of Grace in 1895—Grace's enthusiastic reception by the public and the public identity created and expressed in the press and more generally in James's model of the representative figure—James neglects the fact of mediation (both the roles of intermediary bodies and of communication media). As we have seen, he insists instead that Grace received "the *spontaneous, unqualified, disinterested* enthusiasm and goodwill of *a whole* community" (emphasis added). In part the account of Grace provided by James licenses him to think that such enthusiasm and goodwill can occur in West Indies cricket. This suggestion is present not only in his accounts of Constantine, Headley, and Worrell as representative figures mentioned earlier but also more generally in his accounts of Trinidadian public life. For instance, elsewhere James found the same spontaneous and disinterested enthusiasm: Trinidad in 1920–32 with Captain Cipriani, and then with Dr. Williams and the People's National Movement (PNM) in 1957–60 (James 2009b: 217–25).[9] I do not find it credible that for such a long period of time such unified enthusiasm is possible (without active suppression of dissent and organized encouragement of assent) even on a small island where more of public life potentially *can* be conducted face to face. Further, this account neglects James's own role in Williams's government and in *promoting* cricketers as representative figures. For example, James cites Williams's encomium of his role in the latter in his address to the Fourth National Convention of his party: "If C. L. R. James took it upon his individual self to wage a campaign for Worrell as captain of the West Indies, and in so doing to give expression not only to the needs of the game but also to the sentiments of the people, we know as well as he that it is *The Nation* and the PNM to whom the people will give the praise" (241). James reports on a key aspect of this campaign: "Soon after I came home I tried to find outstanding sportsmen, who were popular with all classes and could play a *mediating* social role in the acute political tensions" (250, emphasis added). Note the key theoretical issue here is that we are talking not merely about a spontaneous occurrence but, rather, about a carefully thought-through set of actions to which James was actively contributing; an understanding of the proto-representative possibilities of specific sportsmen and further development of such roles via a political organization making use of media of communication (such as *The Nation*) to circulate stories of, and arguments for, particular policies in regard to the West Indies cricket team.

What links this "neglect" of mediation and the notion of (and commitment to) spontaneous sentiment of the people? A key thinker of immense importance to James's development and mature thinking should be explored. Rousseau's work, particularly *The Social Contract*, seems a likely source. James thought, wrote, and lectured quite widely on Rousseau, and Paget Henry has convincingly argued that Rousseau's work was as important as Marx's for James's thinking (see Henry 2014; James 2009b). A major element of what James derives from Rousseau is a systematic theoretical basis in modern thought for deep suspicion of representative government (James 2009b: 111–15). James draws on Rousseau's notion that sovereignty should both be *popular* and (is, necessarily) *unitary* and *unalienable* (Rousseau 1988: 143). Rousseau argues that attempts to slough off decision making from citizens to delegates will destroy popular sovereignty whose existence allows and necessitates the reconciliation of the universal and particular (or community and individual). As James (1973 [1960]: 20) asserts, "The moment you vote and give your power to some other people they begin to represent themselves or other interests, not the interests of the people." For James, this neatly connects with his own, deep commitment to human agency and the capacity of people to run their own lives: "Every cook can govern" (see also Smith 2010: 9–14).

Underpinning James's notion of the possibility of *spontaneous* and *disinterested* political identification is Rousseau's concept of the general will. One commentator on Rousseau very helpfully makes the link to our broader discussion by arguing that Rousseau here asserts that the general will is necessarily manifested "exclusive of any mediation"—meaning by this that it is a concept asserting the abolition of individual differences in consensual decision making or real consent (Bloom 1997: 170).[10] It is worth noting that, although Rousseau is never mentioned by name in *Beyond a Boundary*, his presence is strong. Having read and digested Rousseau's work enables James to assert, unequivocally, from within the authoritative texts of Western modernity that "we should be free to govern ourselves" (115). Further, awareness of Rousseau's conception of the general will helps him make the claim that the cricket hero does "not merely represent his side. For that moment... he *is* his side" (197, emphasis added); it is an *identification* of the individual with the collective. Rousseau's influence is also discernible in a broader, civilizational theme within James (see Schwarz 2006: 131). In his discussion of art, James suggests that even though the aesthetic is an "innate faculty," it is possible that "the progress of civilization can leave it unused, suppress it" (208). He thus expresses a classic Rousseauian theme that the modern spirit often has baneful consequences for the realization of a humane society and community, even if mankind is naturally endowed with many great qualities (Yack 1986: 19–20). What James asserts, therefore, is a creolized and culturalized model of Rousseau's general will. However, the model is not up to dealing with the necessary structures of mediation and media communication that are part of societies of any size and complexity.

### What Is to Be Done? Letting Mediation In

I will very briefly outline some recent work on representation by Saward (2010) that is very useful for suggesting how we might extend and focus James's model of the representative figure and let mediation in. I have discussed some of the issues raised here elsewhere and have room here for only a brief sketch of what is involved (Washbourne 2010: 6–7, 21–25, 85–100). I hope the earlier discussion will flesh out the kinds of account that I have in mind.

Saward moves beyond a focus on elective political representation and argues that contemporary societies are experiencing shifts in our experience of (broadly, political) *representation* whereby elected officials are being supplemented by unelected public figures of all kinds (e.g., popular music stars). Saward (2010: 36) argues, therefore, that we should explore the representative claims that underpin these changing realities. People and institutions make representations, he argues, which establish a subject, which stands for an object, which is related to a referent, and which is offered to an audience. Although it can sound extremely schematic set out in this way, Saward's account is of representation (and claims) as a series of practices, meanings, and events that are thereby open for investigation. (It is also congruent with many aspects of James's model.) It involves representative claimants constructing verbal or visual images for and about their constituencies or countries for instance (2010: 51). It includes, centrally, exploration of the incomplete control claimants have over how their claims are *communicated* (e.g., W. G. Grace and the *Daily Telegraph* in 1895, when Grace actively consented to accept the paper's offer and the money it promised, but he did not, and could not, guide the paper's mode of organizing or advertising the National Shilling Testimonial). Saward's account also suggests that we explore, in detail, how representative claims are *received* by various audiences, who may find such claims unsettling (or comforting), such claims often having a performative character conveyed through aesthetic and cultural frameworks and assumptions (2010: 138). In the example of Grace in 1895, Grace can be regarded as having offered himself up (maker) through his extraordinary cricket to press and magazines, which were even more influential than the cricket institutions such as MCC and GCCC and other interested bodies, such as the established and nonconformist churches and the commercial music hall. The former, then, heavily influenced the offering of "Him" (subject) as the embodiment of manly (not effeminate) national/imperial identity, an identity that had become increasingly hegemonic during the renewed imperial grabs of the United Kingdom (and other Western powers) since the 1880s (object). He was thus known through various ideas of what this object meant (variation of meanings of manliness, such as Christian manliness, martial/imperial manliness, each of which had in common an assumption of men's control over, or responsibility for, the bodies and lives of women, children and [many] other men) (referent) to a number of constituencies. The latter includes, especially, the large-scale, middle-class-identifying public brought into existence by social, political, cultural, and economic transformations of the nineteenth century. All of this was nuanced by the rise of a mass reading public, including many of the working classes, by the century's close (audiences/reading publics).

**Conclusion**

James's model of the representative figure in *Beyond a Boundary* provides a rich material and cultural analysis of cricketers and cricket in the colonial situation, as well as a broader model. In this chapter, I have attempted systematically to summarize and explore the model, which I do not think has yet been done in the secondary literature on James. My task is a scholarly one, although the issues raised are also real-world ones of how these figures become known and how they come to embody wider concerns and identities. I note that W. G. Grace in 1895 provides the locus of James's biographical recognition of the representative figure and of the idea that cricket can form the proper focus of lives and studies. I suggest further that there is reason to think that James has accepted a slanted model of Grace and of the claims that a unitary and spontaneous public gathered around his image. I do not intend to suggest exactly the opposite; rather, I use this point as a way to address the question of the mediations that seem to me to be essential for the making of representative relationships. I argue that James expresses commitment to popular sovereignty through a cultural reworking (creolization) of Rousseau's notion of the general will applied to the situation in the Trinidad in the first five or six decades of the twentieth century and that this forms much of the ground for the appeal—to him—of this conception of the representative figure. I also explore the notion that Rousseau's account bypasses consideration of intermediary processes and figures. I argue, contra to Rousseau, that it is incumbent on us, both in scholarly productions and politically, to recognize the complex mediating work (mediation and media communications) that intervenes between representative claims and the complex cultural-material reception of those claims.

## Notes

1. Andrew Smith (2010: 122) neatly defines the issues involved, yet at each point this opens up a range of questions of conceptualization and application: "If such a performer becomes representative this is because the way in which they do what they do makes recognizable the shaping effect of particular social and historical circumstances."
2. Hereafter, page numbers in parentheses refer to this edition of *Beyond a Boundary*.
3. Smith (2010: 46) neatly summarizes James and points out that the formal possibilities of cricket and the individual encounters fostered by it make it especially pregnant for inculcating representative figures. Without mentioning James, Steve Connor (2011) works in the Jamesian spirit of analyzing sports—and cricket in particular—in terms of their formal possibilities. It has not, to my knowledge, been used by James scholars to extend the range of Jamesian reflection on these concerns.
4. Smith (2010: 119) argues something of great interest here. He asserts that St. Hill took on board the condescending judgment of the London press, which thereby contributed to his failure. I am not sure that this interpretation is present in *Beyond a Boundary*, however insightful it may be.
5. Accounts of James's theory of cricket as art can be found in *Beyond a Boundary* (195–211) and are widely commented on in the secondary literature. For example, Smith (2010: 21, 55–65, 142) explores and summarizes James's approach and cites

much of the secondary literature. James's assertion that what matters with cricket and all of the arts is "not the finer points but what everyone with some knowledge of the elements can see and feel" (198) expresses his commitment to democracy and the knowledgeability of people, but this, to my mind, is in some tension with the amount and types of knowledge "of the elements" that are required and with James's own drawing on, use of, and celebration of his own cricket expertise gained from playing, watching, and reading about the game as recounted in stories across *Beyond a Boundary*.

6. King (2001: 125–26) uses this example of creolization, whereby cricket functions "as a mechanism of synthesis that both cements a sense of cultural community and mends rifts of class antagonism in the post-slavery Trinidadian community." It may be worth exploring the power relations, too, that sustain such cultural community. One might think of sponsorship of the local cricket team functioning as a kind of "insurance policy" for a local businessman.

7. In addition to my research here, I draw on published biographies (Low 2010; Rae 1998), as well as scholarly work on Grace's career (Webber 1998). *A Social History of England* (Briggs 1987: 281) contains the best (though extremely short) published account of Grace and Wilde as the hero and villain, respectively, of 1895.

8. This suggests, contra Smith (2010: 141)—who argues that "the bodily quality of sport" puts it beyond the reach of the "forces of social authority"—that the sportive body can be *mediated* (narrated and pictured [cartoon, illustrations and photographs]) and *edited* for the benefit of such social authorities. Ed Cohen (1993: 126–72) argues that Wilde was typed through word and images in the press as perverse, unmanly, and deviant. Asa Briggs (1987) asserts that the representation of Grace as a strong, manly, and vital figure in word and image was used to defend political and cultural reaction against the challenges to gender and identity associated with Wilde's literary and cultural modernity.

9. Note that I am aware of the influence, also, on James's thought of Hegel and Marx, from whom the desire for, and analysis of, the reconciliation of universal and particular, and individual and community, also comes, let alone his own political organizing throughout his life (see Høgsbjerg 2014: 38–125).

10. Janusz Grygiénć argues that Rousseau's idea of general will has been read in two main ways: with either a politico-legal or an ethical emphasis. James's "reading is closer to the ethical position in which ideal members of the community conscientiously fulfil their duties 'desiring nothing beyond the good of the common self'" (Grygiénć 2013: 181), leading to an undivided society obeying its own will *in* articulating the general will.

# 8 | Shannonism: Learie Constantine and the Origins of C. L. R. James's Worrell Captaincy Campaign of 1959–60: A Preliminary Assessment

CLEM SEECHARAN

In my cricket I was brought up the hard way. Sporting to the *n*th degree but I asked no favours and I gave none.
—Learie Constantine, *The Changing Face of Cricket*

This chapter is a preliminary inquiry into the foundations of C. L. R. James's campaign, in early 1960, to pressure the West Indies Cricket Board of Control to appoint Frank Worrell as the first captain of African ancestry for the West Indies tour of Australia in 1960–61. It is plausible that Learie Constantine was the moral and intellectual force whence James's campaign emanated. It is a coincidence that they were both working in Trinidad at the time—James as editor of the governing party's organ, *The Nation*, and Constantine as a minister in Eric Williams's government. Arguably, James's single-handed championing of Worrell for the captaincy constituted a timely site that facilitated his endeavor to repay debts he felt he owed Constantine from the 1920s–1930s. It is no coincidence, therefore, that James's great book, *Beyond a Boundary*, is permeated by Shannonism—engendered by the indomitable resolve of Constantine's old club in Trinidad (Shannon)—and concludes with the success of the captaincy campaign and Worrell's vindication of that trust in Australia: the quintessence of Shannonism. Thus, it is comprehensible why it should be that Constantine is one of the people who receives high recognition, virtual adulation, in the book and one to whom it is dedicated in James's desire "to right grave wrongs."

Constantine and James were both born in 1901 in Trinidad. The comparative brevity of the Trinidadian experience of plantation slavery (four or five decades) bred a more confident persona—a discernible bravura. After emancipation, sparsely populated Trinidad quickly attracted landless freed Africans from Barbados. Colonized in the 1620s, Barbados was always British, with a white creole population of planters and merchants secure in their credentials of belonging to the island while treating "their negroes" with a degree of paternalism. By the late nineteenth century, many black Barbadians were educated at least to the primary level. Some had self-belief fed by their technical skills honed on the sugar plantations. Many were proud of their exposure to, if not mastery of, key idioms of the English colonial mission: education and cricket. Therefore, James's family, mainly Protestant migrants from Barbados, with origins in the stratum of skilled artisans, knew they had a lot of which to be proud.

James would memorialize this legacy in his magisterial book of 1963, *Beyond a Boundary*. He reveals much about his black lower-middle-class family, secure in their cultural inheritance. It made them fastidious with respect to their status above plebeian blacks and obsessed by fear of regressing into the morass of the unrefined. This latter category is epitomized by Matthew Bondman in James's book, a name evocative of a crude type bereft of status. James's family would not have found much to celebrate in their African antecedence, even if they were so inclined. As James recalls of his paternal grandfather, a skilled migrant to Trinidad, "My grandfather went to church every Sunday morning at eleven o'clock wearing in the broiling sun a frock-coat, striped trousers and top-hat, with his walking-stick in hand, surrounded by his family, the underwear of the women crackling with starch.... He fell grievously ill, the family fortunes declined and the children grew up in unending struggle not to sink below the level of the Sunday-morning top-hat and frock-coat" (James 2013 [1963]: 7–8).[1]

James became a formidable radical intellectual, yet he remained an Anglophile. Moreover, he placed great store by his learning within the European tradition: "I want to make it clear that the origins of my work and my thoughts are to be found in Western European literature, Western European history and Western European thought.... I didn't learn literature from the mango-tree, or bathing on the shore and getting the sun of the colonial countries; I set out to master the literature, philosophy and ideas of Western civilization. That is where I come from, and I would not pretend to be anything else" (James 1970: 54).

James took pride in his intellectual frame of reference, with its rigid moral code. In his youth he challenged his colonial milieu with continual little revolts, going "against the current," as he titled a chapter in *Beyond a Boundary*, yet he was profoundly shaped by it. It implanted instincts that never left him. It gave him a peculiar kind of ambition—what he would later identify as

Shannonism, derived from the local cricket tradition and exemplified in the indefatigable play of Constantine's club. But this colonial enculturation had some negative consequences for many of the most educated lower-middle-class black men immersed in its definitive imperial ethos, as James discovered in retrospect:

> It was only long years after that I understood the limitations on spirit, vision and self-respect, which was imposed on us by the fact that our masters, our curriculum, our code of morals, *everything* began from the basis that Britain was the source of all light and leading, and our business was to admire, wonder, imitate, learn; our criterion of success was to have succeeded in approaching that distant ideal—to attain it was, of course, impossible. Both masters and boys accepted it as in the very nature of things. . . . As for me, it was the beacon that beckoned me on. (29–30)

Although James is not explicit, that "beacon" was accompanied by an instinct for self-deprecation—a partiality for whiteness or lightness of skin. It was internalized by many of the black or dark beneficiaries of the system, even those who were oppressed by it. It is arguable, therefore, that James's predominant "cause" from the 1930s—the class struggle as the principal instrument for change (the theorizing and refining of which consumed many decades of James's life), his Pan-Africanism, and the unremitting rage against imperialism—was a reaction against the internalized Eurocentric assumptions of his colonial education, in spite of its bountiful credits, of which he was always proud. James never seemed uncertain about his cause; neither did he reflect on his apparent predilection for whiteness or lightness with respect to women, for instance. Most of his known intimate relationships were with white or light women. This arguably had its origins in his colonial upbringing in Trinidad, where lightness was prized by all.

James's first wife, Juanita Young, whom he married in Trinidad in 1929, was a light woman of Spanish Chinese ancestry; Constance Webb (1918–2005), his second, was a white American, as was his last, Selma Weinstein (1930– ), who was of Jewish American extraction. Webb was seventeen years his junior; Weinstein, twenty-nine. James had the intellectual and oratorical gifts, charisma, and handsomeness to attract several young light or white women into the small Marxist groups in which he was one of the principal thinkers (see Cripps 1997). After 1932, in England and America, it was much easier for him to meet and impress light or white women than it was in Trinidad. By then he was fortified in his Marxist ideological and theoretical formulations and habituated to militant intervention on behalf of black people, wherever they were located. Providing he was satisfied that he was not remiss in championing the most urgent black causes, he felt vindicated, despite his apparently Eurocentric conceptualization of feminine beauty. But, as James relates, this colonial-bred penchant for lightness was severely tested earlier, around 1919, soon after he left Queen's Royal College, as he agonized over which first-division cricket club he should join. That decision, possibly the most portentous he ever made, and at a crucial time (age eighteen), would have a profound impact on his life. It was "my first serious personal problem" (53), he recalled.

James states in *Beyond a Boundary* that subtle distinctions in color, framed within an imperial articulation of power, had deep roots in the colonial environment that shaped him. Therefore, it is admirable that, in retrospect, he recognized he had unconsciously internalized many of the assumptions that tended to privilege lightness: the basis of his decision to join a light or brown cricket club, an option available to him because of his learning and acquired class status. Gordon K. Lewis (1968: 191) observes that "shade" prejudice meant that "specific degrees of discriminatory treatment were frequently prescribed with reference to even marginal differences in pigmentation... something people were driven into, frequently without knowing why, by the system."

Thus, in *Beyond a Boundary* James observes that in colonial Trinidad of the 1920s, all the main cricket clubs were constituted on the basis of race, color, or class. Queen's Park, the oldest, was the most prestigious; its members were primarily white Anglo-Saxon Protestants, with a sprinkling of very light Coloureds (of mixed ancestry) who could often pass as white. Shamrock was the club of the Catholics, mainly the French creoles, with a few Madeiran Portuguese (fellow Catholics) who had arrived by way of success in commerce. Both of these clubs were out of bounds for James. So, too, was Constabulary, the club of the predominantly black policemen. Technically, James could have joined Stingo, the club of the black plebeians, but he admitted there was no way a young man of his standing and aspirations could have contemplated joining lowly Stingo. It was "totally black and [had] no social status whatsoever.... Queen's Park and Shamrock were too high and Stingo was too low. I accepted this as easily in the one case as I did in the other" (50). That left James with two options: Maple or Shannon. He should have gone naturally to Shannon because it was the club of the black lower middle class, of the Constantines (the patriarch Lebrun, and his sons, Learie and

Elias), Victor Pascall (Learie's mother's brother), and the gifted batsman, Wilton St. Hill, and his brothers, Edwin and Cyril, as well as Ben Sealey and Cyril Fraser. They were prepared to welcome James because of his promising cricketing credentials, and he was one of them: dark enough and of the lower middle class. However, James went light, to Maple, the club of the Coloured middle class: brown-skinned men who would have repudiated any emphasis on their partial African antecedence.

But James was emphatic that in the 1920s the darker Shannon Club played the highest standard of cricket in Trinidad, especially against lighter Maple. Their pursuit of excellence is encapsulated in James's notion of Shannonism and was embodied in the cricket of Constantine and the other Shannon men:

> The Shannon Club played with a spirit and relentlessness, [and] they were supported by the crowd with a jealous enthusiasm which even then showed the social passions which were using cricket as a medium of expression.... It was not mere skill. They played as if they knew that their club represented the great mass of black people in the island. The crowd did not look at Stingo in the same way. Stingo did not have status enough. Stingo did not show that pride and impersonal ambition which distinguished Shannon. As clearly as if it was written across the sky, their play said: Here on the cricket field if nowhere else, all men in the island are equal, and we are the best men on the island.... No Australian team could teach them anything in relentless concentration. They missed few catches and looked upon one of their number who committed such a crime as a potential Fifth Columnist. (54–55)

In a decade of fierce contest, Shannon defeated James's club, Maple, in nine of ten encounters. When Trinidad won the prestigious Inter-Colonial Cup, the symbol of cricket supremacy in the region, in February 1929, defeating Barbados by an innings at the Queen's Park Oval in Trinidad, the team comprised six Shannon men: Constantine, Wilton St. Hill, Edwin St. Hill, Cyril St. Hill, Ben Sealey, and Cyril Fraser. There was only one Maple man: Clifford Roach. The others were Joe Small and the wicket keeper, Errol Hunt of Stingo, and Nelson Betancourt (captain), G. Liddelow, and C. A. Wiles of Queen's Park. The latter three were the only whites on the victorious team. Constantine made 133 and took 7 for 71 in the match.

James observes that, to get anywhere, one had to be white or light or enjoy the patronage of such people: "The social milieu in which I had been brought up was working on me. I was teaching, I was known as a man cultivated in literature, I was giving lectures to literary societies on Wordsworth and Longfellow. Already I was writing. I moved easily in any society in which I found myself. So it was that I became one of those dark men whose *'surest sign of... having arrived is the fact that he keeps company with people lighter in complexion than himself'*" (53, emphasis added).

This last reference is taken from James's first book, *The Life of Captain Cipriani: An Account of British Government in the West Indies*, completed shortly before he left for England in February 1932. The book was published in Nelson, Lancashire, that same year (paid for by Constantine). James first reproduced the quote in his ghost-written autobiography of Constantine, *Cricket and I* (1933), and he did so again in *Beyond a Boundary* thirty years later. Therefore, it may be considered a belated and conscious atonement by James, designed to conciliate Constantine for his rejection of Shannon—for going light to Maple:

> Between the brown-skinned middle class and the black [lower middle class] there is a continual rivalry, distrust and ill-feeling, which, skilfully played upon by the European people, poisons the life of the community.... There are the browns, intermediates, who cannot by any stretch of the imagination pass as white but who will not go one inch towards mixing with people darker than themselves.... Clubs are formed of brown people who will not admit into their number those too much darker than themselves, and there have been warm arguments in committee, the whole question being whether such and such a person's skin was fair enough to allow him or her to be admitted into a club without lowering the tone of the institution. (James 2014 [1932]: 55–56)

James was dark, yet he was accepted by brown-skinned Maple, and he played cricket and football for them for more than ten years. He had "arrived." His intellectual gifts had elevated him above the Constantines and the St. Hills. In his agonizing decision to join lighter Maple and in marrying Juanita Young, James arguably did what many black professional men of lower-middle-class origin were inclined to do: marry light or seek to father a child with a lighter woman while cultivating the company of lighter people with higher status. The mulatto/mixed or Coloured woman has always drawn inordinate physical attraction in the West Indies, so there was probably a potent erotic foundation to this predilection for lightness among many successful black men. But there was also a pragmatic prompting: wide recognition that lighter offspring naturally had better credentials for mobility in colonial society.

It is not known when James realized that his joining Maple had severely undermined his relationship with many lower-middle-class black Trinidadians, particularly Learie Constantine. As he observed in *Beyond a Boundary*, "My decision cost me a great deal. For one thing it prevented me from ever becoming really intimate with Wilton St Hill, and kept Learie Constantine and myself apart for a long time. Faced with the fundamental divisions in the island, I had gone to the right and, by cutting myself off from the popular side, delayed my political development for years. But no one could see that then, least of all me" (53).

James noted that when he left Trinidad for England in 1932, "I didn't know [Constantine] very well. He had a point of view which seemed to me unduly coloured by national and racial considerations" (111). His ten-month sojourn in Nelson (Lancashire) in 1932–33 probably aggravated the rupture that dated from his rejection of Shannon around 1919. James recalled his self-possessed intellectual pursuits while he stayed in Constantine's home: "I was reading hard. Night after night I would be up till three or four. I must have seriously discommoded that orderly household. Often I was abstracted and withdrawn [and] I committed the unpardonable ingratitude and ill-manners of taking or leaving Learie's cricket as the mood suited me, a violent contrast from my attitude at home. It must have hurt him deeply" (121).

It may not be a coincidence that in the summer of 1932, Constantine recorded his lowest scores in the nine years that he was the highly paid professional with Nelson in the Lancashire League. From June to September he made only two half-centuries; his other innings were abbreviated, with scores of 1, 14, 16, 22, 3, 7, 26, 24, 13, 0, and 22. James suggests that Constantine's rare failure could have been occasioned by "the disruptive presence of a strange personality in the house" (122).

In an interview with Darcus Howe for the BBC in 2006, Constantine's daughter, Gloria Valere, recalled a memorable instance of James's pronounced abstraction at their home in Nelson: "My mother and I were in the living room and his bedroom was directly above the living room and my mother said to me: 'Do you smell something burning?' And so I said: 'I think so.' She said: 'Oh my goodness!' And so she went up the stairs. There is Nello [James] very busy writing or doing something or reading or doing something, sitting in a cardigan near an electric fire and his cardigan is on fire. And when my mother pointed out to him: 'Nello, you on fire!' he said: 'Oh my goodness! Oh my goodness!' but the thing is he hadn't a clue.'"

Howe asked Gloria whether she was aware that a man "of great importance" was staying in their home. She answered forthrightly: "No. Just remember that in our house in Nelson, my father was the man of great importance." Gloria was not yet five (she was born in April 1928), so the fact that she remembered the incident with such precision, however amusing in retrospect, suggests that it had become lodged in family lore, possibly an enduring marker of a time of some stress (quoted in Høgsbjerg 2014: 49).

It is reasonable to surmise, therefore, that Constantine must have harbored some suspicion of James's motives. Peter Mason, Constantine's biographer, feels that the rift between Constantine and James was never really bridged and that even before James left England for America in 1938, the relationship had petered out: "James was a handsome and charming womaniser whose often caddish extra-curricular activities and embrace of Trotskyism would eventually rub up uncomfortably against Constantine's strong moral views [as a devout Catholic] and dislike of dogma" (Mason 2008: 49).

Strangely, apart from *Cricket and I* (ghostwritten, as noted earlier, by James), Constantine never wrote a word about James in his nine or ten books, so one may never know how he really felt about him. Even when *Beyond a Boundary* appeared in the spring of 1963, with its ample recognition of Constantine, it evoked no public response from him. However, James made the magnanimous statement that the fundamental prompting of his book was the indomitable will and racial pride of the dark men of the Shannon Cricket Club of Trinidad in the 1920s: "*The old Shannon Club of those days is a foundation pillar of this book. A man's unstated assumptions, those he is often not aware of, are usually the mainspring of his thought. All of Constantine's fierce and sustained attacks against the way West Indies cricket is managed stem from his Shannon experience. He believes that the real West Indies team should be a team that would play with the spirit and fire, the spontaneous self-discipline and cohesion, of Shannon*" (57, emphasis added).

From at least the early 1930s, James arguably was remorseful at his rejection of Shannon and very mindful of its repercussions for him. He recalls that it was a brown man, Mr. Roach (Clifford Roach's father), on whose mature counsel he finally opted for brown Maple: "These are the people whom you are going to meet in life. Join them; it will be better in the end." But joining Maple, "with our insolent rejection of black men," cut James off from the "popular side" and arrested his political development. Consequently, he sought later to celebrate the virtues embedded in Shannonism wherever he encountered them among black people. This permeates several of his articles in the radical Trinidadian journal *Beacon* before he left for England in 1932. This may be seen as an aspect of James's atonement to Constantine, for whom he harbored very deep respect as cricketer and man. However, it was not until after he returned to England from America in 1953, released now from the theoretical and political imperatives of his group, that he had the intellectual space and freedom to explore the tormenting weight of Shannonism and his enormous debt to Constantine in *Beyond a Boundary*.

The ethos of the Shannon team—the aspirational beacon of the black masses—was built from much toil, discipline, and self-pride. Constantine (1933: 4) got to the core of the matter in paying tribute to his father, Lebrun Constantine, a disciplinarian who abhorred half-measures:

> You were not allowed to miss anything. If one ball got away from you and then another, it was as well if you were far from him [Lebrun], for if you were near he would give you a rap on the head. "Sheer carelessness!" . . . which to him was the unforgivable sin. Often he put us to stand just a few feet behind his back and hit the catches over his shoulders while we caught them behind. With his strong wrists and forearms he could hit fairly hard in any direction. They were awkward to judge, but that was not accepted as an excuse for missing, my father's theory being simplicity itself: if you were paying attention you did not miss. "Pay attention!" "Pay attention!" and again "Pay attention!" To this day I pay attention, and when I don't my side suffers.

Constantine, imbued with self-belief bred by Shannonism, argued in the early 1930s that after the 1923 tour of England, under H. B. G. Austin, the captain should have been a black man capable of comprehending the temper of black cricketers (already in the majority). Such a leader could have done what very few white captains seemed able to: forge them into a unit with the determination to win.

Constantine was perturbed because racial prejudice was gnawing at the fabric inherited from pioneers such as his father, Lebrun, as well as H. G. B. Austin and Bertie Harragin, a white Trinidadian captain of great repute. Why did the West Indies teams in which Constantine played lack the formidable spirit of his own Shannon Club? By scrutinizing the matter with James in the early 1930s, Constantine was, in fact, sensitizing him to an appreciation of what Shannonism meant to the black Trinidadian masses in the 1920s. Besides, Constantine was unconsciously prompting James toward a radical politics that he would soon pursue passionately. In turn, James would seek to atone for his assumptions of superiority over lowly black people such as Matthew Bondman, as well as Constantine's Shannon:

> Test cricket today [1932–33] is no sort of game. It is a battle. And to win you need not only the strenuous effort of individual players: the work of each player must be backed by a sense of solidarity, of all the others supporting him, not only actually, but so to speak, in the spirit. The lack of this is the chief weakness of the West Indies team in big cricket. We have not been able to get together in the sort of spirit which says: "Look here, we are going out today against those fellows and it is war to the knife!" . . . Until all members of a West Indies side realise that every consideration must give way before the necessity of uniting in spirit and in truth to win through a series of Test matches, the West Indians will not play the cricket I know they can play. Much depends on the players, much more depends on the leadership, which must itself be above pettiness, sympathetic, and yet be strong and command respect from all in the team. (172)

As James remarked in *Beyond a Boundary*, "[Constantine] was a cricketer of concentrated passion, irked all his big cricket life by the absence of what he found only when he played with Shannon" (58). After World War II, Shannonism still illuminated Constantine's perspective on race in West Indies cricket and particularly what he considered the ruse of amateurism. This mantra originated in the Marylebone Cricket Club's class prejudices, the notion that captaincy must be the prerogative of men of independent means (the higher orders). Ostensibly it suggested a nobility of purpose: not profaning the honor of leadership with financial gain. In the West Indies, this policy was rooted in the belief that dispassionate European rule must continue indefinitely to safeguard the native's welfare. But this was no longer tenable for black West Indians after the regional labor agitations of the late 1930s—the rise of trade unions and the emergence of political parties espousing liberal democracy and Fabian socialism; the coming of adult suffrage in Jamaica in 1944 and in Trinidad in 1946—all permeated by the resonant Garveyite redefinition of blackness as intrinsically deserving of pride.

Within the boundary, the victory of the West Indies against England at Bourda, in Georgetown, British Guiana, in 1930 had enhanced belief in the West Indian capacity for self-rule. Victory by West Indies in the series against England in 1935 (2–1) in Jamaica, effectively under the captaincy of Constantine (Jack Grant was injured on the first day and took no further part in the match), probably deepened nationalist promptings. Conversely, after the war, the emergence of nationalist leaders such as Norman Manley and Alexander Bustamante in Jamaica and Grantley Adams in Barbados accelerated the demand for change within the boundary.

Therefore, in his books after the war Constantine was ventilating a popular sentiment that black cricketers were deliberately denied the captaincy of the West Indies cricket team on racial grounds to sustain the myth that whites were naturally endowed with the gift of leadership. No Test matches were played by West Indies between 18 March 1935 and 24 June 1939. But Constantine, having led the West Indies in their last Test to their first victory in a series in 1935, was denied the captaincy for the West Indies tour of England in 1939. Another white novice, Rolf Grant of Cambridge University, younger brother of Jack (both of whom were taught by James at Queen's Royal College), captained a team that included Constantine and the great Jamaican batsman George Headley.

Constantine was the cricketer with the greatest experience and authority to call time on the machinations of the West Indies Cricket Board. In *Cricket in the Sun* (1946), he argued that the appointment of incompetent white captains constituted an act of racism. This bigotry not only undermined the quality of the captaincy. It also facilitated the selection of several mediocre players purely because they were white or light. This is what Constantine thought of Grant, a white Trinidadian graduate of Cambridge and the captain on the West Indies tour of England in 1933:

> Once more the old, old story—some of our best men left behind, not nearly enough play together prior to the tour to weld us into a *team* (we were more like a *mob*!), and insufficient confidence in captaincy. Grant did his best but he did not know us well enough. How could he? He might not even have known the game well enough; but that is a personal opinion.... It would have been altogether wiser to explore the field and find someone who had a deeper experience of West Indies players and possibilities [presumably Constantine or Headley]. Some knowledge, too, of the strength and weakness of our opponents was really essential. (Constantine 1946: 63)

He was no less censorious of his captain in his last series in Test cricket, on the tour of England in 1939, or of several of the other men chosen: "Rolf Grant took charge despite obvious inexperience, on the ground that a white leader was better than any black man, and certainly not on any test of ability that I could see. Modern Test cricket is hard enough, and a bitter struggle enough.

A side that does not rely confidently on its captain is doomed before a ball is bowled ... how much more so ... when half our talent is left at home!" (63).

Constantine was just as forthright on the partiality for lightness in West Indian society as a whole. The prejudices of James's Maple probably still rankled:

> To be brown-skinned, that is to say to have any trace of white blood in one, always gives a man an advantage in the West Indies. To put it plainly, if two men went for a job or were considered for a Test team, and one was black and the other brown-skinned, superior ability in the black man would not get him the job or the place—no, not once in a thousand times. The fact is, West Indies captains, and as far as possible, West Indies players, have always been selected from among the same coterie.... The time has come when I have become nationalist enough to plead openly, knowing what will be said of me, that all this nonsense should come to an end. Until players and captains are considered on their merits by a justice blind to the colour of their skins, the West Indies will never take a place in Test match cricket commensurate with the skill of individual West Indian exponents. (64–65)

In 1948, Constantine was prophetic in recognizing that blatant discrimination against black cricketers with regard to the captaincy had so antagonized the black masses in the region that he could foresee their frustration being vented through acts of violence:

> Cricket ... is a drug in their poverty-stricken and toiling lives which may inflame them to follies big enough to hit the headlines one day soon ... and there may be some rowdy Tests played in the West Indies in the next few years, unless this colour bar business is brought out in the open and wiped out in the game there once and for all; and it must be done soon.... Cricket is the most obvious—some would say glaring!—example of the black man being kept in "his place," and this is the first thing that is going to be changed. (Constantine 1948: 171–72)

James did not return to England from America until 1953, but he would witness how, between 1955 and 1958, the white-/light-controlled West Indies Cricket Board of Control contrived to preclude a black man from becoming captain of the West Indies. The popular view was that any one of the Three Ws (Everton Weekes, Frank Worrell, or Clyde Walcott, all now around thirty and black Barbadians) was eligible for the post on merit. Worrell was the vice-captain in 1954 against England in the West Indies, but he was inexplicably replaced in 1955, against the touring Australians, by a transparently less accomplished white Barbadian, Denis Atkinson. Moreover, strangely, even before the start of the series against Australia, the captain for the tour of New Zealand in 1956 (nearly a year away) was announced: Denis Atkinson. The board was making it clear that, despite robust popular sentiment, none of the three Ws would be considered for leader. The treatment of Worrell was ostensibly a reflection of the board's policy of amateurism. But black West Indians, immersed in the cricket culture and politicized by the nationalist temper of the time, rejected the policy as an artifice to deprive black men of the captaincy. It rankled throughout the second half of the 1950s.

When the incumbent captain, Jeff Stollmeyer (a white Trinidadian), was injured before the first Test in Jamaica in 1955, Atkinson took his place. Stollmeyer returned to captain the second and third Tests but was injured again, so Atkinson deputized for him in the fourth and fifth Tests. Walcott made five centuries in the series, but Australia's victory was emphatic: 3–0, by huge margins. Disgusted by the machinations over the captaincy, Worrell and Walcott decided not to tour New Zealand in early 1956. By then, Worrell had concluded that he had no future in West Indies cricket; so, too, had Walcott, having accepted a permanent post as sports organizer in British Guiana. In the autumn of 1956, Worrell entered the University of Manchester for a degree in anthropology and administration. John Goddard, the former captain, who had not played Test cricket since 1952, emerged to tour New Zealand in 1956, under Atkinson. Strangely, Goddard (a white Barbadian) was reinstated as captain for the tour of England in 1957, with Clyde Walcott as vice-captain. Weekes and Worrell, who was completing his first year at the university, were also in this side. It was a disastrous tour (they lost 0–3): factionalism was rife, and players were demoralized. Goddard retired from cricket after the tour, yet instead of appointing Walcott (the vice-captain in England) as captain against Pakistan in the West Indies in 1958, the board offered the captaincy to Worrell, fully aware that he was in the second year of university. As expected, he refused. Gerry Alexander, who had played only three Tests, was then offered the captaincy. He was a nearly white Jamaican and a graduate of Cambridge University. Weekes and Walcott played against Pakistan under this novice. It came as no surprise, therefore, that at the end of the series both Walcott and Weekes retired from Test cricket, at thirty-one and thirty-three, respectively. Bizarrely, Worrell was offered the captaincy again for the tour of India and Pakistan in 1958–59. But he was completing his final year at the university and turned it down for the second time. Alexander retained the captaincy and led the West Indies to a 3–0 victory in India.

Alexander rose to the responsibilities thrust upon him. His leadership qualities blossomed; his batting improved; and his wicket keeping became world-class. However, he could not dissipate the popular perception that he had been maneuvered into the captaincy, which more gifted and experienced black players such as Walcott and Weekes deserved on merit. Alexander's stature as captain took a severe blow when he and the manager, Berkeley Gaskin (a black Guyanese), made the decision to ban their fastest bowler, Roy Gilchrist, a Jamaican from the lower class (like Matthew Bondman in *Beyond a Boundary*), on the eve of their tour of Pakistan in 1959. Gilchrist was a devastating bowler who had intimidated and humiliated the Indians with his bouncers and beamers (to the head), taking twenty-four wickets at 16.11 in four Tests. He and Wes Hall (thirty wickets at 17.11 in five Tests), constituted a formidable pair of opening bowlers—the fastest in the world. But Gilchrist had many chips on his shoulders, and his behavior, on and off the field, contravened the ethos that Alexander was seeking to build to eliminate the indiscipline of previous years. As Garry Sobers (2002: 161–62) recalls, "[Gilchrist] had bowled beamers and told the captain that he chucked them with intent to hurt. Alexander told him never to bowl them in any match he was in charge of. His warning fell on deaf ears." However, popular West Indian sympathies were with the black underdog, Gilchrist, in his collision with the white (in fact, very light-colored) Alexander. Against a backdrop of nationalist fervor, toward the end of empire, nothing could appease the masses other than the lifting of the ban on their demon fast bowler.

Worrell returned to the West Indies team after the completion of his degree in 1959. In fact, the West Indies selectors had requested this following the death in a road accident in England of the brilliant young all-rounder Collie Smith in September 1959. Worrell played under Alexander's captaincy against England in the West Indies in early 1960. This was the context in which James launched his "Alexander Must Go" campaign, aimed at making Worrell the captain. He had returned to Trinidad in 1958, after twenty-six years, to edit the *Nation*, the organ of Eric Williams's ruling People's National Movement. James in essence was responding to Constantine's agenda, which had been first articulated nearly three decades before and consistently after the war. Moreover, it is arguable that he was invoking Shannonism in the process, having completed most of the manuscript of *Beyond a Boundary*, in which the concept is formulated. One of the ministers in Williams's government was Constantine. So while the campaign was valid in its own right, we may think of it as essentially James's way to repay Constantine—as he puts it in his partial dedication of *Beyond a Boundary* to him, "To right grave wrongs." James's brief, passionate campaign and its successful conclusion in March 1960 was the culmination of what Constantine had proposed in *Cricket and I* in 1933 and reiterated with greater ardor in *Cricket in the Sun* (1946) and *Cricket Crackers* (1948): the need to have a black man, selected on merit, captain the West Indies team. But it was also significant for James in a specific sense: it probably represented the exorcising of the gnawing guilt of going fair or light—because of his rejecting dark Shannon for light Maple—as elaborated in the chapter titled "The Light and the Dark" in *Beyond a Boundary*.

James launched his "Alexander Must Go" campaign in the *Nation* on 5 February 1960, and in the issue of 12 February, he spoke of the public conviction that the captaincy "has been manipulated ... deliberately to exclude black men": racism (for James's open letter to the Queen's Park Club, see 242–49). It was a deft intervention following the West Indies' defeat at the hands of England in Trinidad, by 256 runs, a few days before. On 30 January 1960, as West Indies capitulated to England in their first innings, the crowd started a riot, hurling bottles and other objects to the ground, when Charran Singh of Trinidad was incontestably run out, with the score at 98 for 8 (all out for 112). Constantine was at the ground, and he tried to pacify the crowd, to no effect. He must have reflected on his own prediction in 1948 that if black players were blatantly excluded from the captaincy, the people would express their frustration through violence.

James had, in fact, kindled the campaign against Alexander before the English team arrived in the region. He linked the captaincy of Alexander, in the public imagination, to the banning of Roy Gilchrist. "He is not only a splendid cricketer; he is a symbol," James wrote of Gilchrist in the *Nation* of 20 November 1959. He predicted, "I believe the Board of Control is playing with fire, because if the Englishmen in an early match make 400 for 2, a tremendous cry would arise from tens of thousands of throats: 'We want Gilchrist.'" The defeat by England in Trinidad was difficult to absorb. It was attributed largely to the banning of Gilchrist, for which Alexander and the board (considered white or light and of the old order) were indicted. As James wrote in *Beyond a Boundary*, "Gilchrist was not merely another West Indian cricketer. He was one of the plebs and to them a hero—he was their boy. They would not judge him by ordinary standards" (234).

In a region dogged by insularity, the West Indies team was the highest manifestation of the idea of regional integration. The main plank of James's campaign was the claim that on the threshold of independence, and in line with popular sentiments, it was right for a black man to be made captain. Worrell was that man. He had become a folk hero because of his elegance and prolific record as a batsman, in addition to the widely held belief in his capacity for leadership and potential as a statesman. The perception that, even though he was the vice-captain in 1954, the board had blatantly contrived to deprive him of the captaincy (between 1955 and 1957) struck a chord with the people. In addition, the fact that Worrell was offered the position in 1958–69, when the board knew he was at the university and highly unlikely to be available, was perceived as a pernicious ploy to prevent the appointment of a black captain. This was confirmed by the appointment of Alexander over Walcott and Weekes.

I am suggesting that James saw Worrell's belated elevation to captain as an exemplification of Shannonism; personally, his successful campaign also represented atonement for his Maple error—going light four decades before. But was his seminal partiality for lightness inexpiable? Could his independent Marxism, the Pan-Africanism, and his celebration of black achievement universally (the core of Shannonism) also be interpreted as manifestations of a search for atonement that lasted to the end of his life? Given Constantine's silence, did James feel he had not done enough in his overtures to Constantine in *Beyond a Boundary*? The answer is probably discernible in Anna Grimshaw's (1996: 4) sagacious reading of James's vast correspondence with his second wife, Constance Webb: "The Webb correspondence lays bare both the scope and limitations of an individual personality. Its tragedy lies in James's final recognition that, although he believes the individual is able to transcend the limitations of society and history, he cannot in fact defeat the demons inside himself. At times James imagined himself striding the stage of world history as universal man; but the heroic bravado is ultimately shattered by the tremendous flaws in his restricted and divided personality."

Worrell's achievement as captain of the West Indies team was impressive: in fifteen Tests between 1960 and 1963, nine were won; three, lost; two, drawn; and one, tied (his first as captain). Worrell died on 13 March 1967, at forty-two. Constantine wrote in his obituary, "Though he made his name as a great player, [Worrell's] greatest contribution was to destroy forever the myth that a coloured cricketer was not fit to lead a team. Once appointed, he ended the cliques and rivalries between the players of various islands to weld together a team which in the space of five years became the champions of the world. He was a man of true political sense and feeling, a federalist."[2]

James conceded that he was unfair to Alexander in his campaign. Alexander toured Australia in 1960–61 under Worrell, as vice-captain, and topped the batting averages, apart from keeping wicket brilliantly. Moreover, he was solidly behind his captain. The team owed much to Gerry Alexander. Roy Gilchrist (1934–2001) never played again for the West Indies, but in the absence of official board documents, the truth about his treatment may never be known. Alexander, who died in 2011, never said a word on the matter.

Australia won the series 2–1. Yet in February 1961, a quarter-million people took to the streets of Melbourne to say goodbye to the West Indies team. James inquired of Worrell after the tour why things had gone so well: "If something was wrong I told them what was right and left it to them" (258). James concluded, "West Indians can often tell you what is wrong and some even what will make it right, but they don't leave it to you. Worrell did. It is the ultimate expression of a most finished personality, who knows his business, theory and practice, and knows modern man. . . . He expanded my conception of West Indian personality" (258, 260).

Shannonism!

## Notes

*Epigraph:* Constantine and Batchelor 1966: 135.

1. Hereafter, page numbers in parentheses refer to this edition of *Beyond a Boundary*.
2. Learie Constantine, "Sir Frank Worrell: Hero of Barbados," 1968, in *Wisden Almanack 1968*, www.espncricinfo.com/wisdenalmanack/content/story/152383.html.

# PART III.
# ART, HISTORY, AND CULTURE IN C. L. R. JAMES

9 | C. L. R. James and the Arts of *Beyond a Boundary*:
Literary Lessons, Cricketing Aesthetics, and
World-Historical Heroes

CLAIRE WESTALL

Bold, subtle, humane, and full of revolutionary intent, *Beyond a Boundary* is a book of heroic proportions and of world-historical figures read through their cricketing art—that is, their "style" (James 2013 [1963]: 202).[1] Its publication in 1963 gave, as V. S. Naipaul (1974 [1963]: 106) wrote, "solidity to West Indian literary endeavor." Notably, the text bespeaks the literary lessons of C. L. R. James's imperial boyhood, his early barrack-yard fictions, including *Minty Alley* (1936), and his writing for *The Beacon* across the 1930s. Depicting James's lifelong intellectual and ethical development, as well as his effort to grapple with his own, imperially derived code of conduct, this "cricketing classic" supports the rise of Frank Worrell as the first recognized black captain of the West Indies and pushes for Caribbean self-actualization. Helen Tiffin (1995: 364) conceives of the book, though, as a fundamentally divided work that staves off a "head-on confrontation" with the imperial British culture of James's colonial education in Trinidad. In contrast, for Bill Schwarz (2006: 128) it is a "strange book," carrying "a devastating critique of England and its civilization" within its "old fashioned," memoir-like tone. And quite famously, Grant Farred (1996a: 176) sees it as "a text of last resort," a creative but strained effort to bind together James's cricketing and Marxist allegiances—both gained "against the current"—in a new literary genre made out of the multiplicity of forms it mobilizes.

However strongly autobiographical and notably interventionist, *Beyond a Boundary* should primarily be thought of as James's greatest effort at intellectual integration, at using his desire to "absorb everything" (Walcott 1995: 36) to articulate an expansive and emancipatory universalism via a materialist "sociopoetics of cricket" (Lazarus 1999: 147)—specifically, its dramatic and visual aesthetics of movement and action as performed by its heroic practitioners. Cricket, in James's analysis, is not a "metaphor," as some have claimed. Rather, it is a sociopolitical "field" of representational force akin to Pierre Bourdieu's notion of a "field" (see Smith 2006b). It is a kind of monadological realm with its own—intriguingly complicated—formal, structural, and aesthetic qualities that make the game "an art." As evidence of James's most mature thinking, the text relies on the theoretical work on Hegelian Marxism he undertook in the United States in the 1940s (Schwarz 2006: 129), especially on the dialectic as method, for its dealing with history, world-historical figures, and the ongoing journey toward freedom. As Andrew Smith (2006b: 95) has written, James expresses the relationship between cricketing technique and "a wider zeitgeist of history." Moreover, with Hegel and Marx behind him, James blows apart colonial claims to universality without abandoning universal ambition itself.

This chapter examines two interlinked dimensions of *Beyond a Boundary*'s investment in heroes. First, it analyzes the literary lessons built into the text and their connection to James's portrayal of cricket and cricketing heroics, paying particular attention to the traditions of the realist novel, the *bildungsroman*, and the repeated use of dramatic theory and the tragic hero. Second, it reads the importance of world-historical figures as expressed through James's highly nuanced theorization of performative aesthetics and his concern with the relationship between an individual and the community. The chapter assesses what is at stake in James's aesthetics of heroic endeavor and how his commitment to masculine heroics makes it difficult to determine whether the revolutionary weight of a world-historical figure is to be desired, admired, or passed by on the way to a new world order. Ultimately, critical responses to James's world-historical approach are telling and say much about how far we have come in our thinking about his work, but they should not occlude the notable and revolution-oriented push forward he makes in conceiving of a popularly readable sporting aesthetics of world-historical import.

### Literary Lessons: Realism, the Bildungsroman, and Tragic Heroes

In James's narration of his early childhood, he describes how the educational "trinity" of "English Puritanism, English Literature and cricket," as set against "the realism of West Indian life," established "the powder for a war" that raged throughout his adolescence (20–21)—and, we might add, across the breadth of his writing. This was initially a domestic war with familial and colonial authority, but it became one that took on many of the cultural domains that constitute First World capitalism and its indoctrinatory exports. James's explanation of himself as a "British intellectual long before [he] was ten" (18) is largely premised on his voracious appetite for reading—the combination of his mother's "indiscriminate" love of books and his father's canonical filtering (16)—and on his absorption of the public school code offered by Thomas Hughes's popular remolding of Rugby's Thomas Arnold in *Tom Brown's School Days* (1857) (24–28, 161–62). Indeed, *Beyond a Boundary* is littered with references to the literary vista of James's youth with the "four Williams" (Shakespeare, Hazlitt, Wordsworth, and Thackeray) featuring strongly and standing alongside seemingly everything from the Bible, *The Odyssey*, and the Greek tragedies, through the poetry of Coleridge, Shelley, and Keats, to the prose of Dickens, Eliot, and "the whole bunch of English novelists" (28). It also includes G. A. Henty; P. G. Wodehouse; a plethora of cricketing or schoolboy stories; a good run of pamphlets, periodicals, magazines, and biographies; and much more besides.

We should note here that James's youthful reading maps the canon of English Literature, even as it still functions today, but takes place as this canon is solidifying—that is, as the discipline of English Literature is taking root in England, particularly via the Leavises at Cambridge University (see Hill 2013). In this way, James's career as a young "British intellectual" is an example of the colonial grounding of English Literature's cultural dominance and testament to the importance of imperial superiority that is built into the "sweetness and light" of the discipline's British self-aggrandizement (see Westall 2013). When describing how his cultural education and school curriculum functioned, James states: "*Everything* began from the basis that Britain was the source of all light and leading, and our business was to admire, wonder, imitate, learn; our criterion of success was to have succeeded in approaching that distant ideal—to attain it was, of course, impossible. Both masters and boys accepted it as in the very nature of things" (30). From his early literary intellectualism James acquired "the basic rhythm of English prose" (17) that is so clearly evident in *Beyond a Boundary* and a grounding in English Literature's burgeoning disciplinary logic, with its prioritization of authorial "genius" and character studies. James gained a love of Thackeray, especially *Vanity Fair* (1848), a clear conception of the "genius" as a singular creative force and a whole host of genre expectations and protagonist-based assumptions that were then being built into English Literature.

As with English Literature, James's Romantic version of Victorianism contains a forceful sense of the spirit or soul, the depths of thinking that constitute human possibility, and the importance of the exceptional individual or hero. In *Conscripts of Modernity* (2004), David Scott explains that like "a swathe of mid-Victorian intellectuals," James was preoccupied by hero worship and that even before his own encounter with Hegel's "moral-aesthetic of the man of action," he would have intellectually journeyed through the traditions of German Romanticism (that stood behind Marxism) as reframed by Britain's imperial literary culture (75–76). Scott (2004: 75) writes, "One link between the German Romantic sources of Hegel's hero worship and Victorian Romanticism is, of course, to be found in Thomas Carlyle, whose work James certainly knew, in all likelihood, thoroughly," and Carlyle himself "was influenced in a profound but complicated way by Goethe, Fichte, and Novalis. It is through them, at least in part, that his reverence for the man of genius takes the messianic shape it does."

For all their obvious differences, there are a number of striking similarities between Carlyle's *On Heroes, Hero Worship and the Heroic in History* (1840) and *Beyond a Boundary*, not least their shared insistence on the hero being recognized by their people and in their historical moment. Carlyle (1840: 51–52) writes that "the most significant feature in the history of an epoch is the manner it has of welcoming a Great Man." In *Beyond a Boundary*, James repeatedly indicates the collective recognition granted to cricketing heroes—the crowd's response to their performances and the way that their skills somehow seem to atone, or compensate, for other aspects of their lives, as with Matthew Bondman. He also presents cricket's world-historical figures as being received as epoch-defining men, with examples that include W. G. Grace in the Victorian period, George Challenor and Learie Constantine between the two world wars, and Donald Bradman under "the welfare state of mind" (212). James emphasizes the aesthetic dimensions and political significance of this recognition, but he also states that "if the West Indies cannot afford to keep their great cricketers at home they don't deserve to have them" (110). Here James adapts the conception of historical recognition to mark the conditions of capitalist modernity: the need to live, work, and earn, as well as play cricket.

A crucial part of the German Romantic tradition as it influences James's writing is that of the bildungsroman—the coming-of-age narrative, typically a realist novel, telling of the youthful sensibilities that, after a set of worldly trials and uncertainties, burgeon into bourgeois individualism and corresponding authorial or poetic possibility. (Goethe's *Wilhelm Meister's Apprenticeship* [1796] is sometimes taken as an early example and was first translated into English by Carlyle.) *Beyond a Boundary*'s semiautobiographical content takes from this genre, tracking James's journey from seeming political and racial innocence, through domestic and international conflicts, into full-blown anticolonial cricketing and Marxist maturity. Throughout, James is unpacking the politicized content of his past. This, though, is not the first text in which James has placed a version of himself within the "bildungsroman conventions" he also disrupts (King 2001: 52). *Minty Alley*, James's only novel, exhibits the pivotal tension between individual and community that underpins the bildungsroman. Brian Alleyne (2006: 177) sees James as staying close to the characteristic realist device of positioning the protagonist to be "just like the reader: this reader [being] the new bourgeois individual who, from the eighteenth-century onwards, began to express an aesthetic sensibility more concerned with individual life and sentiment than the classically oriented outlook of the European aristocracy." According to Aldon Nielsen (1997: 23), James was "one of the first authors to apply the aesthetic techniques of realism to ... Trinidad's barrack-yards." Moreover, Nielsen (1997: 24) notes, James's literary realism "redoubled" the initial "shock" of European realism as a literary style by unpacking "the political and social realities of race and colonialism." While working to expose the "inexperienced" Haynes as the bourgeois intruder in the barrack-yard in need of initiation and education (King 2001: 57), the novel also allows its protagonist to behave much like one of his nineteenth-century precursors, remaining, in Farred's (2003: 102) analysis, totally unaware of how the women he encounters "usher him into maturity" and unconcerned by "the fact that the woman who cleans his shoes is also his lover." Following similar lines of argument, Nicole King (2001: 53) questions the limitations of genre emulation, seeing "the reader [as] left to contemplate what kind of radical messages can be derived from within the conservative ideological boundaries set up by the bildungsroman form." She contends that, for all his efforts to vernacularize and creolize the bildungsroman, James's novel "falters" when it attempts to give voice to the masses. Farred's assessment of James's "desire for interpellation into subaltern life" (2003: 109) catches hold of the paradox of his class-determined position and James's ongoing efforts to position the intellectual in relation to the knowing masses. Juxtaposing *Minty Alley* and *Beyond a Boundary*, Farred (2003: 103) sees the first as James's "alienation expresses itself most poignantly" and the latter as the work where his "marginality is ... dramatically overcome."

The importance of the protagonist hero underpinned much of Victorian realist fiction—both "highbrow" and "lowbrow." James's early consumption of such novels, as he "studied and practiced assiduously the art of fiction" (64), clearly rubbed off on his writing. In *Beyond a Boundary*, each of James's narrative episodes has its own heroic figure, whether a family member or local cricketing actor, and each of these narratives proceeds as a politicized character study, written through James's appreciation of the exceptional achievements of the "great" cricketer. This is made explicit in his portrayal of Cousin Cudjoe, the blacksmith who "shook" his bat in defiance of a "famous fast bowler" shaking his own weapon—the ball—until Cudjoe hit his first delivery "out of the world" (8). Another familial example is James's rendering of his "physical and spiritual grandfather" (15), Josh Rudder, the engineer whose refusal to explain "how" he fixed the standing sugarcane factory engines expresses the knowing dissent of future independence and foreshadows Learie Constantine's "they are no better than we" sentiment (112–13). In addition, there are numerous examples of narrative episodes that bring into focus a specific and exceptional local protagonist—as with the portraits of Matthew Bondman, Arthur Jones, George John, and Piggott, "one of the world's greatest wicketkeepers" (66). This leads King (2001: 122) to consider *Beyond a Boundary* one of James's "most contradictory" texts when it comes to the relationship between an individual and the community, because it moves between offering James as the protagonist to presenting "a local cricketer, a historical figure, or an anonymous community member" as equally significant but held within James's autobiographical frame. However, this movement—to and fro, toward heroic acts and actors who remain held within an autobiographical narrative of development—is exactly how James is working through the significance of his own political conscience and giving weight to what he understands as the creative, even revolutionary, energy of Caribbean self-expression. Hence, he cannot relinquish his own position as a kind of exceptional intellectual; nor can he underplay the importance of the lessons he has gained from watching his cricketing heroes and their followers. It is his struggle to conceptualize the relation among different forms of aesthetic heroic endeavor that provides the core of *Beyond a Boundary*'s originality.

We also know of James's early identification with the realist tradition of the protagonist hero because of his "violent shock" at discovering that, in Thackeray's *Vanity Fair*, "George Osborne was the hero" yet was "killed [when] the book . . . had still much more than half to go" (39). In his sustained analysis of James's lifelong interest in *Vanity Fair*, Smith follows Paul Buhle in suggesting that the novel's satire gave "James his first glimpse of a British empire that was fallible within and vulnerable without" (Smith 2011a: 14). In this way, the text exerts a kind of anticolonial impetus, or at least a preempting of the long decline James and Constantine help push forward. This is emphasized by Smith's unpacking of the position of Sambo at the start of the novel. In addition, and as Smith points out (2011a: 14), both Kent Worcester and Caryl Phillips have described how the "novel's simultaneous subversion of and preoccupation with manners and subtleties of convention would have found some resonance in the equally status-conscious and manner-bound world of the black middle class in Trinidad." Such preoccupations were, of course, discernible in James's anxiety about choosing Maple as his island club. Smith (2011a: 13) deals specifically with James's approach to reading and readerships and argues that, "for James, clearly, the reading of a text is inextricable from the effort to read the world in which readers find themselves." For Smith (2011a: 22), "James' approach to the crowds and readers of popular culture is underwritten by the faith he had in the ability of the oppressed to read accurately, and to respond appropriately, to the text of their own lives." Much of their reading, though, James pins to the dramatic action and tragic heroes of West Indian cricket.

Appreciating that, from the ancient Greek and Roman masses onward, crowds are able to read physical and artistic texts, James parallels cricket and drama. Scott (2004: 147) neatly summarizes the case: "If tragic drama was the institutional form that enabled the integration of the individual and the community in democratic Athens, then in the Caribbean (the Anglo-Creole Caribbean, at any rate) a similar role fell to the institution of cricket." Writing under the Shakespearian formulation of "All the World's a Stage," in *Beyond a Boundary* James presents himself as "an actor on the stage in which the parts were set in advance" (40) by his imperial enculturation. He goes on to present cricket in terms of drama: "Cricket is first and foremost a dramatic spectacle. It belongs with the theatre, ballet, opera and the dance. . . . Its quality as drama is more specific. It is so organized that at all times it is compelled to reproduce the central action which characterizes all good drama from the days of the Greeks to our own: two individuals are pitted against each other in a conflict that is strictly personal but not less strictly representative of a social group" (196).

Insisting on the representative function of the players, especially the batsman and bowler, James regards these roles as "charged with social significance" (66). He is determined, with his text, to "place on record some of the characters and as much . . . of the social conflict" as possible (66). This is befitting of James's understanding of drama and of cricket. In "Notes on *Hamlet*," he explains how "all the great tragedies deal with precisely [the] question of the confrontation of two ideas of society and they deal with it according to the innermost essence of drama—the two societies confront one another within the mind of a single person" (James 1992 [1953]: 243). He positions Shakespeare as working this out from *Henry V* onward and as capturing it in his four "great" tragedies. James goes on to describe how "Aristotle placed thought in its proper place—in a dramatic character. It gives the motives for action; but it is subordinate to the action itself. But for Hamlet the process of thought is his conception of action" (245). James is clearly concerned with character, particularly the tragic hero, and, as Scott (2004: 152) records, in 1953 James wrote that "what is most important" in dramatic theory "is the idea that the great tragic writer has to work out an adequate conception of the character in its perfection." While this seems to downplay "action" in the Hegelian sense, it actually seeks to position action as bound to character, as emerging from character, and as evidence of the historical importance of specific characters. As with Hegel, for James (1992 [1953]: 156–57) "the best tragedies center less on the question of the flaw that disfigures and finally destroys the hero or heroine than on tragic conflict." In this context, it seems appropriate to pinpoint the opposition between white masters and black slaves as the intrinsic "tragic conflict" within which James is working and to flag Susan Buck-Morss's (2000) revelatory rereading of Hegel's master-slave dialectic as emerging from Hegel's awareness of slavery and, specifically, of the slave revolts of the late eighteenth century, including those led by Toussaint Louverture. Thanks to Buck-Morss, we can understand James's Hegelian dialectic as, at source, a method of analysis bound to slavery and the figures at the heart of its disruption.

James's study of Toussaint and the San Domingo/Haitian slave revolution of 1791–1804 in *The Black Jacobins* (1938) creates a "dramatic figure out of a historical one" (Rabbit 1995: 120). It also mobilizes some of the literary impetus found in his earlier play-text on the same subject matter and, as Kara Rabbit has established, deploys the tragic hero model in its portrayal of Toussaint. (As an aside, there is a parallel between how Toussaint was sometimes described as "the Black Napoleon" and how George Headley was labeled the "Black Bradman." In both cases, James recognizes what is at stake in the aggrandizing/belittling comparative and pushes to assess each of the men on his own world-historical merits.) Rabbit (1995: 120) homes in on the blending of fictional and historical narrative styles in *The Black*

*Jacobins* and James's attempt to manage the tensions between his "materialist analysis of history and [his] portraiture of a powerful individual" whose heroic failure is "neglect" of his people. James marks this neglect as Toussaint's tragic flaw. It was not a "moral weakness," as one might expect, but, rather, "a specific error," a fundamental failure to communicate with his people, to take their side and lead them into further revolt. In an Aristotelian fashion, Toussaint falls from grace while the primacy of action and of future revolutionary ambition—held within the creative potentiality of the people—remains. Rabbit (1995: 130) writes that the "lesson" of *The Black Jacobins* becomes about the "rising up of a creative capacity of the people, overlooked by, yet epitomized in, the figure of Toussaint-Louverture." To James, Toussaint's "mistake" was inevitable, a condition of circumstance and history. His famous Hegelian lines capture this exactly: "Great men make history, but only such history as it is possible for them to make. Their freedom of achievement is limited by the necessities of their environment" (James 2001 [1938]: xix). Toussaint, then, was as transformative as he could be at that moment, in that place, and with his striking, and strikingly exceptional, personal history. His shortcomings were the markers laid down for future action in the ongoing conflict of history—as both Toussaint and James seemed to comprehend. What is especially useful for reading *Beyond a Boundary*, though, is to compare James's configuration of Toussaint as a tragic hero with his portraits of Wilton St. Hill and George John in the later text.

Playing in the 1920s as a "great" West Indian batsman, St. Hill became the performative body within which "all the subterranean aspirations of West Indies cricket met and crashed" (71). For the West Indian cricket crowds watching him and, more often, reading about him, St. Hill was their "boy" (93). Yet when he went to play in England in 1928, he was, according to James, "a horrible, a disastrous, an incredible, failure, the greatest failure to come out of the West Indies" (95). Neil Lazarus (1999: 165) explains that in James's analysis, "The role played by St. Hill . . . was a tragic one. It was tragic because, as a batsman, St. Hill carried all before him except for one season; but that one season . . . was historic." His domestic heroism collapsed on the international stage in a spectacular but perhaps inevitable fashion. "St. Hill failed," Lazarus (1999: 166) writes, "because no one person could have succeeded, at that time, in what he was asked to do. . . . His failure was therefore a failure to perform uncolonizability." Like Toussaint, St. Hill was historically significant and yet premature; his batting achievements helped develop the West Indian self-awareness that came to fruition in the world-historical presence of Learie Constantine, but they were limited within and by his place in history.

To James, George John was also a "tragic hero." John was the "knight-errant of fast bowling" (73), even "the fast bowlers' bowler" (81). He was "not hostile, he was hostility itself" (75). He "incarnated the plebs of his time" and "their complete independence from the values and aspirations that competed in the spheres above" (73). John's career was interrupted by World War I, but he toured England in 1924, when he was at least thirty-nine; his bowling and that of Learie Constantine and George Francis made them all heroes and helped the West Indies gain Test status in 1928. Playing their part on a mixed-raced regional team, these men planted the seeds of what Hilary Beckles, in his book of the same name, calls *A Nation Imagined* (2003). It is this moment in 1928—this historic and collective entrance onto the world stage as potential sporting equals to England, still the colonial and cricketing Massa—from which John was excluded. This exclusion forms part of the background for his son Errol's play about a fallen cricketer entitled *Moon on a Rainbow Shawl* (1958 and 1962), to which James alludes (80). However, as a member of the "generation of black men bowling fast [that] was more sure of itself" (79), it was John who offered James an example of a perfect tragic hero: "In his complete dedication and disregard of all consequences I saw something of the quality which made the tragic hero, except that in John there was no flaw. He was flawlessly intent on getting the batsman out and when anything went wrong he was flawlessly angry" (76).

This effort to create a perfect hero, to construct and offer up for reading the exceptional and pristine figure of heroism, provides a foundation for James's theorization of cricketing aesthetics. James insists on using bowling to convey the aesthetic and intellectual dimensions of the game because batting traditionally has been thought of as artistic. James's effort to comprehend the perfect hero also cuts across his encounters with prose, as well as drama. This is seen in his approach to Herman Melville in *Mariners, Renegades and Castaways* (James 1985 [1953]). According to Alleyne (2006: 189), James "pursued his thesis of American exceptionalism because of his belief that societies were characterized in different historical epochs by typical personalities—that is, Hegelian world-historical individuals." This view is supported by James's description of Melville's literary, specifically character-based effort. In "Fiction and Reality," he writes about Melville as moving steadily toward the rarest of achievements: the creation of a character that will sum up a whole epoch of human history (see James 1977 [1953]). Such heroes are at the very heart of *Beyond a Boundary*.

### Cricketing Aesthetics and World-Historical Cricketers

Across his work, James repeatedly portrays "great men" as making and transforming history. Unsurprisingly, then, across the range of critical responses to James's writing runs a repeated concern with his concentration on male heroes and masculine leadership, as well as his effort to connect these figures to their people. Paul Miller (2001: 1087) characterizes James as relying on the Enlightenment-based separation of the leader from the "anonymous" or "pliant" masses, but this is explicitly challenged in James's cricket writing (see also Smith 2010: 90). A number of related gender-based critiques of James's work have also emerged. Following on from Kenneth Surin's (1995: 318) early salvo in this direction, Hazel Carby (1998: 114) analyzes James's favoring of political biographies from his studies in the 1930s of Cipriani and Toussaint onward. She sees James as constructing those men who act against their own class in the interests of the people, or the masses, as heroic, while on the flip side the masses become "feminized"—as, for example, in *Minty Alley*. Carby (1998: 128) goes as far as to suggest that in James's heroic mode, there is a "sexual union between men and history." There are some important merits to this reading, but with *Beyond a Boundary* specifically, the relationship between heroism and history needs further probing. James's use of Hegel's world-historical figure has been mentioned regularly in critical discussions of the text but rarely linked to his account of cricketing aesthetics—the core of his mode of dialectical analysis.

While many cite E. P. Thompson's (1981) correct assessment of James as unthinkable without cricket, this observation should stand alongside Santiago Colás's (1996: 137) contention that James's "understudied" *Notes on Dialectics* (1980 [1948]) is the key to his developing method and approach in later works—including *Beyond a Boundary*. For James, Hegel's dialectic is the crucial thinking tool for forward movement, for an open but future-oriented approach to the struggles of the present (James 1980 [1948]: 9). James makes clear in that text that he is keen to take from Hegel's dialectic "a new way of organizing thought. Not of thinking. But of knowing what you do when you think" (James 1980 [1948]: 13). Brian Stoddart's (2006: 925) response to *Beyond a Boundary* insists that James did not "handle" change well, and that his analysis is not suited to contemporary cricketing developments. Yet Stoddart fails to deal with the very warning that James carried from Hegel—namely, that "one of the chief errors of thought is to continue to think in one set of forms, categories, ideas, etc., when the object, the content, has moved on" (James 1980 [1948]: 15). As James states, "In true dialectical fashion, we establish a category only to break it up" (1980 [1948]: 47). This warning may also be used in relation to the critique of James's approach to gender. That James concentrates on the male hero is a noted limitation, but the gender categories in play can be rethought, undone, even moved beyond without the dialectic itself being rescinded—that is, without the revolutionary ambition of his dialectical method being abandoned. A world-historical woman is not beyond a Jamesian-inspired mode of thinking.

In Hegelian thought, the "world-historical is that which partakes in actualizing the meaning of the world" wherein the unity of history is the long unfolding of freedom, of *Geist* (Berry 1981: 157). Although James amusingly dismissed "world-spirit" (*Weltgeist*) out of hand (see Douglas 2008: 427; James 1980 [1948]: 56), he maintained the "troublesome" conception of the world-historical individual (Berry 1981: 155). According to Hegel's *The Philosophy of History* (2001: 44), "great historical men," rather than laboring for "private gain," have aims that are the "will of World-Spirit." Their lives are wholly "labour and trouble," and "when their object is attained they fall off like empty hulls from the kernel. They die early, like Alexander; they are murdered, like Caesar; transported to St Helena, like Napoleon" (Hegel 2001: 45). Hegel's fullest explanation of the world-historical figure is that

> they may be called Heroes, inasmuch as they have derived their purpose ... from a concealed fount.... They are men, therefore, who appear to draw the impulse of their life from themselves; and whose deeds have produced a condition of things and a complex of historical relations which appear to be only *their* interest, and *their* work. Such individuals had no consciousness of the general Idea they were unfolding, while prosecuting those aims of theirs; on the contrary, they were practical, political men. But at the same time there were thinking men, who had an insight into the requirements of the time—*what was ripe for development*. This was the very Truth for their age, for their world.... World-historical men—Heroes of an epoch—must, therefore, be recognized as its clear-sighted ones; *their* deeds, *their* words are the best of that time. (Hegel 2001: 44–45)

Hegel (2001: 62–63) goes on to specify that, while "World-Historical peoples" reach a culmination that is specific to them and their time, and therefore "do not present a generally applicable political base," this does not mean that nothing can be learned from the past. In fact, there is a "continuous development from the same structures" in science and art, and it is in these domains that learning from the past is possible. James positions the people of the Caribbean as world-historical; as a critical community bound to the Enlightenment and responsible for vast quantities of Europe's acquired wealth; and as a kind of contrapuntal community ripe for exposing the hypocrisies and hidden potentialities of much that Europe, and Britain especially, has claimed for itself. In his writing on cricket heroes, James is working within this conception of the Caribbean and within the world-historical terms Hegel articulates, seeking to integrate cricket into what he calls, in *Beyond a Boundary*, the "movement of the times" (195) as the Caribbean moves toward independence. But as with so much in his theoretical resource kit, James is adapting his sources as he goes, and his world-historical adaptations are best seen in his presentation of cricketing technique and in the chapter titled "What Is Art?"

In positioning cricket as "an art," a dramatic and visual art that stands as a "full member" of the "community" of arts, James establishes the sport as having "a technical foundation," which means that analysis of the game and its actors requires close reading of technique (179). This is at the critical core of James's approach to cricket, and *Beyond a Boundary* is an eloquent exemplification of reading for and through the technique or style of individual players—in terms of batting, bowling, and fielding. James not only opposes the division of "high" art from "low" sporting culture, of music from cricket, as in Neville Cardus's work (195). He goes further, seeking to pinpoint the detrimental omission of "popular sports and games" from the work of "aestheticians" (199) and simultaneously challenges the "antiquated instruments which the historians still cling to" when approaching the history of sports and its heroes (182). He does this with his reassessment of W. G. Grace as the "greatest of popular heroes" for the Victorians and a living expression of the "passions and forces" (182) that characterized that age and were appreciated by thousands of fans across the decades of Grace's career. Here, in the recognition of form and movement, in the popular and individualized appreciation of aesthetic action, is the heart of James's case for cricket as art. In "What Is Art?" James unifies his two central arguments: that cricket is a dramatic art that (re)enacts the sociopolitical dynamics and history of the Caribbean, and that it is a "visual art" recognized as such by the knowledgeable masses who "see and feel" this quality, particularly as repeated in the "style" of great players (196–204). In short, he contends that cricketing performances are physical gestures of independence for the individual and the community. Rereading Bernhard Berenson's conceptions of "tactile values" and "movement" as the two key characteristics of "significant form," James tracks how the batting of George Challenor, Wilton St. Hill, Learie Constantine, and the Three Ws (Worrell, Everton Weekes, and Clyde Walcott) is the manifestation of their personality and a very particular articulation of the sociopolitical and historical circumstances that bring them to the wicket. Their movements; back and forward play; management of angles, strength, and space-creation; and invention all express the manner in which the West Indian condition has come into being and is being transformed. Their actions, their very physical movements, are political acts, often "the best of their time" and recognized as defining an epoch. (And we could push this into a gender-neutral space if we were responding to the technique of all sporting figures.)

In addition, throughout *Beyond a Boundary* singular moments of action stand as significant aesthetic acts and are read, felt, and absorbed by those that observe—whether James alone or a full West Indian crowd. This is clear when the "long low 'Ah!'" comes from the spectators as Matthew Bondman executes his "slash through the covers" (4); when Arthur Jones brings his "bat down across the ball as a woodsman puts his axe to a tree" in his signature cut shot that brings the crowd to "burst out in another shout" (5); or when Learie Constantine, as the "finest fieldsman yet known" (106), "national hero, and the pride of the populace" (207), creates a new shot to survive the late break in a delivery: "Doubling himself almost in two, to give himself space, he cut the ball a little to the left of point," James writes, surprising his audience by showing them an entirely new stroke, necessary for the moment, that "remain[ed] in the mind, as a single gesture" of artistic expression (138). What is important is "what everyone with some knowledge . . . can see and feel" (198), because humans "respond to physical action" (208) and have within "civilized life for countless centuries" (209). As James says, "The spontaneous outburst of thousands at a fierce hook or a dazzling slip-catch, the ripple of recognition at a long-awaited leg-glance, are as genuine and deeply felt expressions of artistic emotion as any" (207).

James concludes his crucial "What Is Art?" chapter by writing, "We may someday be able to answer Tolstoy's exasperated question: What is art?—but only when we learn to integrate our vision of Walcott on the back foot through the covers with the outstretched arm of the Olympic Apollo" (211). We may be critical of James's recourse to seemingly elitist/imperialist classical mythology, but we should first appreciate the appropriateness of his comparison. On one side, Apollo stands for classical art, and the image of him with an "outstretched arm" is the visual recollection of the Colossus of Rhodes, one of the Seven Wonders of the World. The powerful figure of Apollo combines music and poetry with athletics and archery—high art with popular culture. He is also the God of the Sun, colonization, and medicine/healing. On the other side, Walcott stands as the embodiment of powerful batting, famous for his back-foot cover drive and ferocious ball-striking strength. Walcott was a notably large figure of sporting strength, and yet his imposing presence in front of the stumps as a batsman was matched by his athletic agility behind the stumps as a wicket keeper. James's response to the question of art inscribes Walcott's powerful "style" with beauty and elegance, with the political aesthetics of self- and communal expression. He claims that the fullest and most meaningful understanding of art must come through the integration of classical Apollo with popular, physical forms of aesthetic expression embodied by the massive figure of Walcott as a modern Apollo, a cricketing colossus who may also be a Caribbean God of the Sun, (de)colonization, and healing. It is the cricketing crowd that knows all this through their keen observations, and it is the aestheticians that need to adapt.

Throughout *Beyond a Boundary*, James repeatedly alludes to the historical significance and skills of Sir Garfield Sobers: one of those "singular players[s] who stamps all he does with the hallmark of individual style" (205); whose 365 "not out," captured as a "painted sign," helped fill the "gap in the historical consciousness of the people" (233); and who stood as "the greatest living batsmen" during his career (257). However, it was in his essay on the Barbadian legend that James extended his reading of Sobers's style. As with Learie Constantine, Collie Smith, and Rohan Kanhai—all of whom he describes as expressing their "West Indian heritage" through their play and playing styles—Sobers's batting, bowling, and fielding, for James, "are a living embodiment of centuries of a tortured history," changing history and tradition as they are performed against the backdrop of Caribbean cricketing imperialism and nationalist, anti-imperial protest (James 1980 [1969]: 225). Although James identifies and writes about Sobers's "individual style"— indeed, he places immense value on interpreting all cricketers through their aesthetic performances—he rejects an English journalist's view of Sobers as a singular talent distinct from his sociopolitical milieu. Instead, he asserts that Sobers brought together immense talent, dedicated training, and the unique history of the region to make him "the fine fruit of a great tradition" (213). Surin (1995: 318) positions himself against James's reading of Sobers in world-historical terms, arguing that no one—not even as great a player as Sobers—can contain or express a fraction of the Caribbean's "impulses and disposition." This, though, is too prompt a rejection of the Hegelian method and a failure to recognize, as James does, that the philosopher identifies the historical manifestation of change, of the dialectic force of forward movement, carried by the world-historical individual. In James's reading, Sobers does not "contain or express" every variant of experience and communication lived in the Caribbean. Instead, the aesthetics of his performance are recognized as the culmination of all that has passed within a specific "tortured history." Sobers is not offering the observer an identity-based political claim to representativeness or historical comprehensiveness and should not be thought of within such a frame. He is enacting a mode of beautiful, recognizable, and perfected attack that connects him to the long history of Caribbean rebellion and positions him as fundamentally arising from, and connected to, his community. When Anthony Bateman (2009: 501) responds to the same reading of Sobers, he recognizes the "world-historical" categorization that is being made and briefly explains that, for James, this is because "historical content . . . provides the basis for formal achievement." The reverse is also true. Formal achievements, as specific aesthetics acts, provide the basis for a reading of history, of the historical significance and force at issue—as conveyed through the world-historical hero. In this way, James is advancing the Hegelian movement forward into freedom through technical and aesthetic physical performances while also positioning these acts as part of a wider world revolution of social and political relations.

In fact, James's interpretation of Sobers is very much like his view of Lenin, especially his description of the Russian revolutionary in a scathing attack on Sidney Hook's *The Hero in History* (James 1980 [1943]). James attacks Hook's work on the grounds that it fundamentally fails to understand that "the interpretation of history is a class question" and decries Hook for "snigger[ing]" at Marxism even as he fails to come to grips with a class-based reading of history. James then stands against Hook's reading of "the Russian Revolution [as] due to the character of Lenin," arguing that, "far from being a gifted individual who took advantage of a national calamity, Lenin was the most representative Russian of modern Russia, embodying in his life and work nearly two centuries of Russian history. Yet this individual is and will always be the greatest practical leader and teacher of international socialism. To understand this is to understand not only the relation of party and leader but the whole problem of our time" (1943: n.p.).

This assertion—of the importance of one man as expressing "the whole problem of our time"—stands behind James's cricketing writing and his investment in specific cricketing heroes. However, in James this is filtered through a reading of cricketing aesthetics that reemphasizes the terms of the dialectic, especially conflict and movement, as aspects of world-historical sporting play. Beckles and Walcott follow James's lead in writing, "Only the following of cricket heroes transcends national, ideological and generation boundaries" (Beckles and Walcott 1995: 373). Like James, they see recognition of the world-historical importance of specific players, and their styles, as providing "a unique terrain for artists and intellectuals to speak to the region as one about itself as a unified cultural space" (Beckles and Walcott 1995: 373). Beckles also takes up James's methods and applies them to postindependence cricket, including the prominent place afforded to Brian Lara. However, there is a loud note of caution about heroes to be found in the sentiment of another leading Third World liberationist. *The Wretched of the Earth* (1968 [1961]), Frantz Fanon's examination of national consciousness and national culture—areas of analysis in which he shares much with James—insists that "the people" are the social and political force that stands beyond the exaltation of any single individual, including within sports, and that they should not be forgotten in the pursuit of heroic exceptionalism. According to Fanon:

> The capitalist conception of sport is fundamentally different from that which should exist in an under-developed country. . . . If games are not integrated into the national life, that is to say in the building of the nation, and if you turn out national sportsmen and not fully conscious men, you will very quickly see sport rotted by professionalism and commercialism. Sport should not be a pastime or a distraction for the bourgeoisie of the towns. The greatest task is to understand at each moment what is happening in our country. We ought not to cultivate the exceptional or seek for a hero, who is another form of leader. We ought to uplift the people; we must develop their brains, fill them with ideas, change them and make them human beings. (Fanon 1968 [1961]: 158–59)

James's writing stands with Fanon's in its insistence on the history of capitalism being the spur to analytical probity, on the fundamental opposition between the bourgeoisie and the claims of the people, and on the dangers of sporting commercialism. While I cannot open a full comparative study of Fanonian and Jamesian thinking on heroics here—a task well worth completing—it is important to suggest that a key difference between them is that James positions the people as being the "uplift" that brings life to, and is expressed in, exceptional action, cricketing and revolutionary. It is with the crowd, through the crowd, and via the crowd's recognition, or reading, of the world-historical cricketer in aesthetic action that James sees the Caribbean asserting itself and setting the pattern for the perpetual pursuit of freedom—historical, domestic, and international. Hence, *Beyond a Boundary* is crucial to his understanding of world history, of the world-historical as manifest in specific people and communities and as expressed in singular, specific, and aesthetic moments of revolutionary sporting action.

**Note**

1. Hereafter, page numbers in parentheses refer to this edition of *Beyond a Boundary*.

# 10 | The Very Stuff of Human Life: C. L. R. James on Cricket, History, and Human Nature

ANDREW SMITH

Near the beginning of *Beyond a Boundary* there is a passage in which C. L. R. James describes the way in which he and his young teammates, playing in the second eleven for Queen's Royal College, on treacherous dirt pitches, developed a particular technique to deal with "the problem of the dead shooter" (James 2013 [1963]: 35).[1] James is referring here to a ball that, instead of bouncing up as one would expect, shoots straight along the ground. Faced with this particular "problem," he recalls, he and his teammates learned or improvised a specific response: rather than moving their back foot across the stumps, as was—and remains—the orthodox practice for batsmen in the game, they stayed still so that if they needed to, they could, without their feet getting in the way, jam the bat straight down and dig the ball out.

In itself, this insight into local cricketing technique must appear to be of interest only to very serious aficionados of the game. Yet James's entire approach in *Beyond a Boundary*—an approach in keeping with his thinking more widely—was to seek out the "connected pattern" that linked together and rendered meaningful "merely isolated memories" (7) of this kind. In this instance, James has a particular reason for offering us his recollection, because he goes on to contrast this practice with the response of his older self, playing with the same teammates a few years later, after they had graduated to the school's first eleven, on more carefully prepared and thus more reliable matting wickets. In that context, of course, the "shooter" was a much less frequent "problem," and when it did occur, James and his teammates found that they no longer had an appropriate technique to deal with it. They had, in other words, reverted to orthodoxy, moving their feet back and across in front of the stumps, with the result that the ball cannoned into their pads, and they were out. When that happened, James says, "We felt that the gods had conspired against us" (36).

James tells us very explicitly that he introduces this recollection to suggest something about how we might approach cricket "critically." By critically, of course, he means in historical terms: "I was reading cricket and looking at it critically so early that casual experiences which would have passed unnoticed stayed with me and I worked at them as if on some historical problem" (35). What this particular "casual experience" reveals is that changes in cultural or creative practices are shaped by the specific demands of local situations and by the responses of those involved to those situations. That includes, in the case of cricket, the material conditions of the game in the most literal sense: where it is played and on what kind of surfaces. No cricketer, one might suggest, can afford not to be a materialist in that immediate regard. Changes in technique—these moments of improvisation that come to form new styles of play—however tiny and inconsequential they may appear in their own right are thus, for James, evidence of the historicity of the game. They demonstrate precisely why it is necessary to think of popular culture as a theater of "historical problems," as something that we can understand adequately only when we understand the ways in which it is born in, and is thus expressive of, particular social and historical contexts.

Hence, James ends his story by saying, "Much of the answer to the perpetual comparison between great players of different periods is contained in that experience" (36). In other words, even this small, comparative example reveals the fallacy of any attempt to ask questions about the game that are not rigorously historical. As he said more bluntly elsewhere, attempts to determine who is the greatest player of all time—enjoyable as these may be as debating exercises—betray a profound miscomprehension. Such a question is conceivable only on the assumption that the game exists in some timeless, magical space of its own. The "orthodoxy" in cricketing technique that ended up constituting a trap for James and his classmates is thus the echo—or, we might say, the objective correlate—of a wider intellectual orthodoxy that presumes there are eternal or ahistorical standards against which sporting practice can be judged.

James's thinking about politics and culture was always interrelated. We should recall that a rejection of blind adherence to orthodoxy defined his approach to struggles beyond the sporting boundary, as well. He continually insisted, in this respect, on the need not to be encaged by pre-given interpretations and strategies or by the reified categories of established "understanding," as he described it in his famous study of Hegel (James 1980 [1948]).[2] Put more positively, what James insisted on was the need to continually reevaluate both the means and the ends of political struggle in light of the demands that were given voice by emergent forms of popular insurgency. James's effort to reconceptualize socialism in relation to black antiracism in the United States is one significant example of his own concerted effort to avoid being trapped in orthodoxy. In the more specific context of *Beyond a Boundary*, in any case, James's concern is to underscore the fact that one can understand or assess individual players or teams only by recognizing how they respond to the particular historical problems with which they are faced. It is by virtue of the historical specificity of sporting practice that it can be said that even sportsmen and women express something of their social world in the styles and postures of their play.

These arguments are, of course, well known and already well discussed (see, among others, Baucom 1999: chap. 4; Hamilton 1992; Kingwell 2002: chap. 4; Lazarus 1999: chap. 3; Wynter 1992). James's great achievement in *Beyond a Boundary*, the achievement that has made the text such an enduring reference point, is precisely his success in thinking historically about a popular cultural practice such as cricket; his detailed working through of the ways in which sporting play gives evidence of its particular social context while also offering a space in which that social context—or aspects of it—might be contested or thrown into critical relief. This historical meaningfulness encompasses, for James, of course, far more than just the question of pitches and how they shape batting technique. Quite intentionally, it seems to me, it is in the paragraph immediately following this anecdote that he goes on to state explicitly, for the first time, the central thesis of the book—that is, that cricketing play is part of a historical zeitgeist, that it is bound up with and gives expression to the sociological order in which that play occurs. He says here what he also repeats toward the end of his study: "A particular generation of cricketers thinks in a certain way and only a change in society . . . will change the prevailing style" (36).

So far, then, so familiar. In reading through *Beyond a Boundary*, we are provided by James with lesson after object lesson in the historical analysis of sporting play. Yet then we arrive, toward the end of the book, at that chapter in which James seeks to defend his other central thesis, which is that cricket should be considered a form of art—not, as he famously says, "a bastard or a poor relation, but a full member of the [artistic] community" (196). In the course of this chapter, James makes a series of claims that seem to sit in open opposition to his otherwise consistent emphasis on a historical approach to understanding the game. Indeed, James himself gives the impression, in the sentences that open the chapter, that he wishes to signal that the discussion that follows represents a kind of caesura with regard to his wider argument: "I have integrated [cricket] in the historical movement of the times. The question remains: What is it?" (195).

James goes on to defend the idea that cricket is a form of art in two broad respects. First, he argues that the sport has many of the qualities of *dramatic* art. He identifies two particular characteristics of the game in this regard. It is, on the one hand, a game structured around a continuously repeated confrontation between individuals who stand, in their play, as representatives of the wider team of which they are part. In this sense, James argues, the sport contains, "in itself," much of that "fundamental relation of the One and the Many" (197) on which great drama also rests. On the other hand, it is also a game in which each individual passage of play has the potential to radically alter the ultimate outcome of the match. In this respect, James points out, cricket, like other dramatic arts, is founded on a fundamental relationship between pattern and contingency, "episode and continuity . . . the part and the whole" (197). The game has, as a consequence, a "glorious uncertainty" at its heart, but it is an uncertainty that does not dissipate into mere randomness, because each discrete event is rendered significant through the wider structure of meaning provided by the game. Here again, and as elsewhere in James's cricket writings, one can sense how much his love of the sport inflected, and was inflected by, his thinking about history and social change more widely. In this case he deliberately emphasizes—as have other commentators (Nandy 2000)—what might be called the "anti-determinist" quality of cricket's dramatic structure, in which a seemingly foregone conclusion can be undone by a moment of spontaneous brilliance or by a period of sustained counterattack. Cricket thus contained a lesson that James treasured in other contexts of his life: the ability of human activity to unsettle and throw into doubt what appeared to be the inevitable conclusion of "history hitherto."

Second, James argues that the sport shares crucial qualities with *visual* art. In developing this argument, he follows the lead of the art critic Bernhard Berenson, taking from him, in particular, the concept of "significant form." This, as James uses it, refers to the capacity of visual art to create joy by virtue not of its powers of representation but through its appeal to the "tactile consciousness" of the viewer—that is to say, a heightened recognition, felt as much as thought, of the human capacity for intentional movement. "Without the intervention of any artist the spectator at cricket extracts the significance of movement and tactile values," says James. He or she "experiences the heightened sense of capacity" (202). What the spectator seeks and sees in such a moment is something with the undeniable ring of artistic truth but that has its own, less grandiloquent name in the cricketing vernacular: "style."

From the point of view of James's wider argument in *Beyond a Boundary*, what is so striking about both of these claims is that they appear to rest on presumptions about what is of significance to human beings *as such*. In seeking to defend his claim that cricket is an art, James seems to suspend his interest in understanding the sport's contingent, historical expressivity. Thus, for example, when he argues that cricket can be considered a dramatic art because it encapsulates the relationship between the one and the many, he is talking specifically about a symbolic relationship built into the sport "in itself." In other words, he is *not* referring back here to the sociological analysis that he provides earlier in the book, in famous chapters such as "The Light and the Dark," about the ways in which specific teams or individuals came to play representative roles vis-à-vis particular communities within colonial Trinidad or elsewhere. He quite explicitly puts such concerns to one side, describing cricket's capacity for dramatizing social conflict as "superficial" or commonplace: something it shares with all other games "in a greater or lesser degree" (196). This seems astonishing because it has been exactly the extent to which sport dramatizes social conflicts that has been central to James's account thus far. Yet he is unequivocal here: his explanation as to why cricket's dramatic qualities matter to its audience deliberately leaves to one side any such question of a particular historical or political investment in the sport. Rather, he says, the dramatic qualities of the game—"attack, defence, courage, gallantry, steadfastness, grandeur, ruse" (198)—are expressions of "elemental sensations. We never grow out of them, of the need to renew them. Any art which by accident or design gets too far from them finds that it has to return or wither. They are the very stuff of human life. It is of this stuff that the drama of cricket is composed" (198).

James has already explained that for Berenson, the achievement of the greatest visual art has nothing to do with the question of a painting's or sculpture's representative qualities, its "lifelikeness" vis-à-vis a specific object. It is born, rather, of its capacity to generate a sense of recognition that exceeds or surpasses straightforward mimesis and gives to the viewer something more enduring and profound: a purified or renewed sense of what it is to be alive and embodied as a human being as such. In precisely the same way, then, in seeking to make the case for cricket as art, James puts aside his foregoing claim about cricket's historical and political meaningfulness, its ability to "represent" particular communities or movements, and emphasizes something that, he implies, exceeds or surpasses such concerns: the opportunity to witness, in the game's great players, a life-enhancing visual enactment of the body in motion.

It is no surprise, then, that when, toward the end of the chapter, James moves on to ask why "significant form" should matter to the crowds who come to watch cricket matches, he insists that these instances of movement have a resonance that goes beyond their meaning in terms of the game itself or the question of who wins and who loses. Wally Hammond's cover drive or Ray Lindwall's approach to the crease—such moments speak directly to something that is part of our "human endowment." The "basic motions of cricket," he says, "represent physical action which has been the basis not only of primitive but of civilized life for countless centuries. In work and in play they were the motions by which men lived and without which they would perish. The Industrial Revolution transformed our existence. [But] our fundamental characteristics as human beings it did not and could not alter" (209).

What, then, are we to make of this? We have the C. L. R. James who pioneers the historical analysis of sporting practices, who teaches us so much about how sports, and other forms of human creativity, express particular political meanings for particular audiences; who teaches us to recognize popular culture as a context in which social struggles are refracted. Yet we also have the C. L. R. James who defends cricket's artistic credentials on account of the sport's ability to reproduce dramatic forms that are said to be "elemental" and "universally recognizable," or visual expressions that are said to appeal to the "fundamental characteristics" of all human beings. In other words, James the critical and political thinker or the historical materialist, on the one hand, and the James who appeals to the idea of a settled human nature, on the other. Is there not an inconsistency here in James's argument—one that, indeed, comes close to self-contradiction?

Predictably, I want to argue that there is no such contradiction. Indeed, I want to go further and claim that there is a necessary relationship between these seemingly opposed claims that James makes. Before saying anything else, we should be clear that James himself is more than aware of the danger that his comments will be misinterpreted as a kind of mysticism or as an appeal to an essentially romantic idea of an indwelling feel for the beautiful that is ineffable or mysterious. Indeed, he parts company with Berenson, whose work he has drawn on so extensively during the chapter, at precisely this point: "Mr. Berenson calls the physical process of response [to significant form] mystical. There I refuse to go along any further, not even for the purpose of discussion. The mystical is the last refuge, if refuge it is" (207).

Of course, one of the reasons that the term "essentialism" has become a dirty word in the contemporary social sciences and humanities—and this is largely why James's willingness to use this language is likely to seem surprising to academic readers today—is that claims about the essential nature of particular groups of human beings were a prominent part of racist discourse throughout the colonial period and gained a particularly tragic authority in the era of so-called scientific racism (see, e.g., Appiah 1996; Fredrickson 2003; Hannaford 1996). Assertions that colonized peoples were constitutionally incapable of cultural development or inherently unable to manage their own affairs politically, economically, or, for that matter, on the cricket field, were, as James knew only too well, standard components of the ideology of empire. Indeed, on more than one occasion he contested such views explicitly: one can think, for example, of his early refutation of a white colonial scientist's racism in his essay "The Intelligence of the Negro" (see Bogues 1997: 20–21), published in *The Beacon* while he was still in Trinidad. Or we might recall his equally scathing response to what he saw as a failure to do justice to Frederick Douglass's political awareness on the part of the communist historian Herbert Aptheker (James 1949a, 1949b; see also Smith 2010: 61–62). Or, most famously perhaps, we can remember his central involvement in the campaign to have Frank Worrell instated as the first permanent black captain of the West Indies (see chapter 8 in this volume).

James's appeal to the idea of "the human" in general, and to the idea of a common human capacity to respond to art more specifically, has to be understood, at least in part, as a response to this ideology of essential racial difference. There are earlier examples of such arguments in his work. In his excellent study of James's years in Britain in the 1930s, Christian Høgsbjerg (2014: 71–74) recovers a significant exchange of letters between James and Stanley Casson, Fellow of New College, Oxford, from the pages of *The Listener* in 1933. James had written initially in response to Casson's reflections on a recent exhibition of African art at the Lefevre Galleries in London. Casson's predictable argument was that the simplicity of African sculpture reveals nothing more than an underlying childishness in "primitive" mentality. James's retort refers to the work of Franz Boas and others to challenge the basis of claims about innate racial inequalities but also, and more tellingly, insists on his own interpretation of these sculptures, which finds in their stripped-down vividness a "freshness of outlook" (74) characteristic of all great art. In other words, against a reading of artistic forms that finds in those forms evidence of insuperable human difference, James discerns an artistic achievement that, he implies, is capable of making an aesthetic claim on all of us.

In just the same way, then, James insists in *Beyond a Boundary* that the capacity to respond to the artistically heightened representation of human form belongs to human beings as such. In this respect, he deliberately compares the response to "the line, the curve, the movement" that we encounter on the cricket pitch or in high Renaissance art, with the imagery to be found in prehistoric cave art. James draws this comparison precisely to make the point that the capacity for aesthetic response is *not* "the gift of high civilization, the last achievement of noble minds" (208). In that regard, then, his assertion of a common longing for significant form is an assertion *against* claims of fixed racial differences or against reified understandings of ethnic or cultural potentiality, just as it is also, of course, a claim against the elitist assumptions of critics such as Berenson and Cardus that working-class men and women have no "feel" for these things; that they are merely lumpen in the face of true art.

James spends little time seeking to demonstrate the fallacy of such views on philosophical grounds. Instead, he appeals to much more straightforward and compelling empirical evidence. Just listen, he says. Listen properly, as he, of course, so often did, to the responses of the crowd that has gathered to watch "the line, the curve, the movement"; listen to the "long low 'Ah'" that follows a particularly anticipated shot by Matthew Bondman; listen to the "spontaneous outburst of thousands at a fierce hook or a dazzling slip-catch." These are, he says, "as genuine and deeply felt expressions of artistic emotion as any I know" (207). Indeed, James insists, until this is understood, not only will the critics fail to understand popular sporting practices, but they will fail no less to understand even that sphere of creativity for which they reserve the word "art." In an address delivered in the same year that *Beyond a Boundary* was published, he makes this explicitly clear: "[Until] these gentlemen ... understand that what 35,000 people come to see [at a Test match] is also definitely an art form and an artistic expression, that is felt by many people in an artistic manner, you will never be able to write properly about the art criticism of Michelangelo and Raphael. That's my belief" (James 1986 [1963]: 144).

James thus uses the capacity for artistic response as one indication of a common humanity to be defended against the invidiousness of colonial racism and against the no less invidious effects of class prejudice. Nevertheless, if we are to understand the full resonance of James's argument here, we need to recognize the extent to which these claims in *Beyond a Boundary* are informed also by his concerted reconsideration of the Marxist tradition, a reconsideration that, especially in the writings he produced during his time in America, had sought to place the idea of "the human" at the very heart of its historical analysis and that did not accept that there was any contradiction in so doing. In common with his fellow sojourner in America, Erich Fromm (2013 [1961]), for example, and in ways that intersect with the broadly contemporaneous work of thinkers such as Henri Lefebvre (2014 [1958]) and Agnes Heller (1984 [1970]) on the other side of the Atlantic, James sought to develop an account of Marxism that was centered above all on the active, creative human being. Crucially, then, he—along with his comrades at the time, especially Raya Dunayevskaya and Grace Lee—sought to make the question of "concrete" human longing central to their account of *why* political struggle occurs (an argument, in this context, made against a view in which social change is seen to be determined by, or a mere effect of, technological change). At the same time, this account treated the idea or ideal of the "human" as ethically central to any understanding of the "ends" or purposes of political struggle (an argument made against an understanding of socialism as some kind of destination defined only in terms of a formal or bureaucratic alteration in the ownership or distribution of material goods).

One example will need to suffice here, given the limitations of space. In a typically sweeping essay titled "Dialectical Materialism and the Fate of Humanity," James (1980 [1947]: 80) insisted that thinking dialectically presumes and requires "a theory of the nature of man." But this theory, he goes on to make clear, is not based on a religiously inspired presupposition about the God-given character of human beings; nor does it derive from a biological or psychological fatalism. Rather, it emerges from the close examination of what, historically, human beings have struggled to achieve and defend in their lives. In other words, it arises through an insistence on asking the questions, "What is man? What is the *truth* about him? Where has he come from and where is he going?" (80). James did, indeed, routinely ask such questions of the ordinary men and women that he met. In this particular essay, however, his focus is historical, and he provides a panoramic account of the emergence of Christianity and of some of the pivotal political confrontations of the modern era—the Reformation; the English, French, and Russian revolutions—each of which he reads as entailing a dialectical struggle. Each is a struggle, in other words, between those classes that wanted to reserve for themselves, or to render merely abstract, the very freedoms that wider popular forces were fighting to make real in their daily lives. This leads James to the conclusion that the idea of "the human" emerges as something that is fought for or postulated in and through the history of popular struggle. Such struggle is defined, he says, by a "quest for universality in the need for the free and full development of all the inherent and acquired characteristics of the individual" (95). Or, as he puts it elsewhere in the essay, "The history of man is his effort to make the abstract universal concrete. He constantly seeks to destroy, to move aside, that is to say, to negate what impedes his movement towards freedom" (84).

It is clear, in other words, that for James, as for Marx (see Geras 1983), the idea of human nature was necessary to any adequate historical understanding for both explanatory *and* normative reasons. His account of historical causality, on the one hand, treats human nature—defined in terms of this "search for completeness"—as the cause of social struggle: men and women consistently seek to overcome the cribbed, limited and destructive reality of their day-to-day lives. Hence, James (1980 [1947]: 83) says, "To be a socialist is an expression of the need for concrete universality which is not so much *in* as *of* the very nature of man." Correspondingly—and the two points are inextricable—a conception of what is in "the very nature of man" becomes a key normative measure by which we are able to critique the world as it is. It is by virtue of our having some sense of what is in the best interests of human beings that we can respond critically to the absence of conditions appropriate to those interests in the world in which we find ourselves. Hence James's own claim that "it is the crime of capitalism that it uses men only partially" (104).

In saying this, James echoes the Marx of *Capital* who recognized that one of the many crimes of capitalist production processes was the way in which they confined and orchestrated the bodies of workers, denying them recourse to at least one fundamental human need: "the many-sided play of the muscles" (Marx 1976: 548). For James, moreover, it was precisely for this reason that the broadly contemporaneous emergence of industrial production and modern forms of organized sport could be understood as something more than a mere coincidence. The popular audience is drawn to sports precisely because it finds there something that is denied to it in its working life. This, too, is evidence of the "search for completeness," something that cannot be conceived or understood without our attention being drawn to the fundamental human needs that are expressed in and by such a search.

None of this, therefore, should lead us to assume that "human nature" is fixed eternally. Rather, as will be clear, James understands human nature as something that we read out of, and through, history. Human beings have needs that they find unfulfilled in the world as it is, and it is in recognition and awareness of those needs that people seek to overcome the negations they face. Men and women struggle against the confinements of their historical lives insofar as those lives prevent them from being the kinds of human being it is in them to be. However, because those struggles are as yet unresolved, the human remains a historically open category: it is what people struggle toward, but it remains, as it were, a "postulate" of those struggles. As Lefebvre (2014 [1958]: 191–92) puts it, in words that postdate James's thinking on these questions but with which I think he would have agreed, "The realm of freedom is established progressively by 'the development of human powers as an end in itself.' . . . Freedom must be won; it is arrived at through a process of becoming."

All of this, I hope, helps us to understand more clearly what is at stake when James seeks to discuss cricket's appeal to "fundamental" human characteristics in *Beyond a Boundary*. What he does here, in a way that it absolutely congruent with the broader theoretical arguments I outlined earlier, is to historicize the conception of the human. Human being, he suggests, emerges as the unfinished historical outcome of a process of evolutionary change: "We respond to physical action or vivid representation of it, dead or alive, because we are made that way. For unknown centuries survival for us, like all other animals, depended upon competent and effective physical activity. . . . The use of the hand, the extension of its powers by the tool, the propulsion of a missile at some objective and the accompanying refinements of the mechanics of judgements, these marked us off from the animals" (208).

Thus, to talk about the "innate faculties" of the human does not have to be mysticism, because it can refer to qualities that make human beings, *historically*, what they are and not something else. That means that these qualities are not unchanging or fixed once and for all, although, as is clear from this quote, James did believe that the response to the vivid representation of movement is very deeply rooted within us. Nevertheless, these "endowments," as he calls them—these "needs"—are the endowments *of history*: they spring from the historical process of human emergence. Thus, they are, on James's account, products of the historical struggle for survival but are also, of course, born of the distinctively human ability to reflect on and represent those struggles to themselves—to master them in consciousness, as Marx puts it. In this regard they are precisely evidence of "the process by which we have become and remain human" (208). The word "process" is crucial here, it seems to me, because it underscores James's assumption that these responses or instincts are not passive or fixed once and for all. Rather, they are part of the long run of our "becoming," continually re-created in and through our engagement with the world, in and through an undeterred struggle for freedom.

This is also why the term "movement" has such a crucial double meaning for James. On the one hand, it is in and through the wonderful movements of its great players that cricket's claim as art stands or falls. James, of course, dismisses the idea that because such movements are transitory, they are somehow artistically disqualified. There are some strokes that "the writer has carried in his consciousness for over forty years" (205), he says. On the other hand, such movement is of interest to James, not because it provides a mere exhibition of physical prowess, but for what is revealed in the flash of lightning of "significant form." What is cast into light by the "existential vividness" (James 1986 [1967]: 201) of the great players is the human ability to act in a way that changes the world as it is encountered. As Hans-Georg Gadamer (1986: 124) points out, "The playfulness of human games is constituted by the imposition of rules and regulations that only count as such within the closed world of play." Yet for Gadamer, as for James, this does not make the play of freedom and constraint in games a mere "show." The freedom that the best players of human games reveal is their ability to turn the more-or-less arbitrary constraints of the game into a mode of self-expression. That freedom points us toward the possibility of human freedom in its wider, political sense: the capacity of human beings to make and remake themselves and their world. Gadamer (1986: 128), with wonderful disdain, talks about those who cannot see beyond the game itself, who disregard the freedom toward which it points us as being "like the dog that looks at the pointing hand." James says just the same, in terms more famous and no less pithy: What do they know of cricket who only cricket know? It is in just this sense, then, that James insists that the response to "the perfect flow of motion," as he puts it, is not a mechanical or bodily reflex. It is, instead, evidence of a distinctively human ability to take joy in our shared capacity to turn conditions of constraint into conditions of expression. It is, in other words, a glimpse of historical movement happening.

So although it may appear at first glance that James's discussion of the essential qualities to which art appeals is at odds with his concern to think historically about such things, it seems to me that he is in fact saying that the former leads us precisely to the latter. What is essential in us and what explains the popular response to sports is the struggle for movement, and cricket, in common with other art forms, can, within its own small, symbolic world, provide us with a glimpse of a much greater historical lesson. What is significant in the forms of cricketing play is not what they reveal about the constitutional makeup of players ("not what you are or what you have"). It is what they reveal about our common capacity to change things as we encounter then ("where you have come from, where you are going, and the rate at which you are getting there" [113]).

At the end of the chapter in which James reflects on the depressed state of cricket in the 1950s, with its uninspiring, safety-first approach, he imagines the emergence of a new figure who will break the shackles of the game as it is currently being played. We will, he says, extol this person's eyesight, their wristwork, their footwork. "Nationalist fanatics" will put their talent down to "ancestry" or "climate" (222). (In other words, they will pack it back into a claim about essential human differences.) But what that person will be doing, James says, and what the great players of the game always do, is "reshap[e] the medium [so] that it can give new satisfactions to new people" (222). What draws us to the best of sporting creativity, thus, is precisely the demonstration it provides of the human ability to "reshape" the contexts in which we find ourselves; it puts us within intellectual reach of an idea of "newness." Through their own vivid physical movement, and through the way in which those movements "reshape the medium" in which they are playing, those players bring us within sight of the movement of history.

## Notes

1. Hereafter, page numbers in parentheses refer to this edition of *Beyond a Boundary*.
2. Relatedly, Christian Høgsbjerg draws our attention to the early influence of Henri Bergson on James and, in particular, his interest in Bergson's attack on abstract or Mechanical "understanding" (2014: 84–85).

## 11 | C. L. R. James: Beyond the Boundaries of Culture
PAGET HENRY

The primary aim of this chapter is to provide a comprehensive account of C. L. R. James's theory of culture and the place of *Beyond a Boundary* within it. Like his writings on economics, James's writings on culture are widely dispersed and exist in a variety of texts. Nevertheless, it is still possible to see the clear outlines of a dialectical approach to culture, which made it the sum total of the material and immaterial creations of art and science—of the creative upsurges by which they were advanced and the education by which they were cultivated and transmitted, as well as the norms, values, manners, and practices accumulated by a people through their struggles for self-realization. Culture is therefore simultaneously the creative expression and the institutionalized results of our ever changing relationships with nature and society and with one another. This is the larger vision that is quite often visible in James's writings. James scholars such as Paul Buhle (1993) and Andrew Smith (2010) have examined these aspects of his approach to culture. My goal here is to make James's crossing of these internal and external boundaries of culture more explicit, to link them to the Caribbean ontology of creative realism and to James's civilizational sociology.

Within James's broader vision of culture, we can distinguish three crucial moments, which came together in changing syntheses to constitute the dynamism of the larger dialectical whole. Further, within this larger whole we can recognize three distinct ways in which James formulated and integrated the cultural, political, and economic aspects of his thought. I argue that these three different syntheses of economics, politics, and culture were themselves creative expressions of an expanding process of integration taking place within James as a subject in formation.

## Three Moments in the Life of Culture

The first constitutive moment of James's larger view of culture is culture's expressive aspect. This moment in the larger being of culture discloses the processes by which its various forms or modes of appearing come into being as creative eruptions released by the self-formation of human subjects. Particularly in the early Trinidadian phase of his career, James made use of a poeticist approach that treated culture as the artworks that resulted from the symbolic, discursive, ludic, or performative activities inherent in our self-formative processes. In short, from this expressive perspective culture was the creative activity through which the self narrated and visualized the existential challenges confronting its growth and future formation.

Supplementing these expressive aspects of culture in James are its more objectified modes of being. These more institutionalized aspects of culture include such forms as established beliefs, ideals, norms, rituals, and values. In these more fixed forms, culture becomes a shaper of human subjectivity, and sometimes an oppressor, and thus less a creative expression of that subjectivity. James used the term "culture" in both of these senses.

The third moment in James's dialectical discourse on culture is its civilizational dimension. James developed a complex civilizational sociology as an integral part of his discourse on culture, attempting to understand the rise and fall of these complex social formations. We will have to examine closely James's civilizational sociology, as it is vital for our understanding of the crowning place of *Beyond a Boundary* in his theory of culture.

There is a fourth important dimension of James's writing on culture: the practice of cultural criticism. His engagement with this practice was extensive—particularly, literary and cricket criticism. Although very important for a comprehensive account of James's theory and practice of culture, space will not allow us to address this area of James's work on culture. Fortunately, for the goal of grasping those three important syntheses with politics and economics, the first three aspects noted earlier are the most crucial.

## The Three Syntheses

The first major synthesis through which James linked the cultural, economic, and political aspects of this thought was a poeticist one, which centered literature and cricket. This synthesis was the creative reflection of the specific process of inner integration that the young James was experiencing at the time. His short stories; his novel *Minty Alley* (1997 [1936]); and his first political text, *The Life of Captain Cipriani* (2014 [1932]) were all products of this first synthesis. As *The Life of Captain Cipriani* makes clear, politics was barely visible within the spaces of this poeticist synthesis.

The second of James's great syntheses of culture, politics, and economics was the larger creative eruption that accompanied the emergence of the political theorist in James to a position of dominance. Roles were exchanged between the literary artist and the political theorist. As a result, politics, culture, and economics came together within the framework not of a literary/ludic poetics but that of a socio-historical poetics. This was the synthesis that informed the writing of works such as *World Revolution* (1993 [1937]) and *The Black Jacobins* (2001 [1938]).

The originality and distinctness of *Beyond a Boundary* derive from its being the creative expression of yet another Jamesian process of inner integration. In this new subjective formation, a mature and supremely confident literary artist again trades places with the political theorist. It was as though this trade was the special condition, the only womb out of which *Beyond a Boundary* could have come. We can call this third synthesis James's poetic socio-historicism. These, in brief, are the three distinct strategies by which James linked culture, politics, and economics. Together with the three dynamic moments in the life of culture noted earlier, they will enable us to grasp fully the significant changes in James's dialectical theory of culture.

**Culture and Creative Self-Projection**

James's first, or poeticist, approach to culture was the creative companion of the self-formative process that established him as a literary and cricketing subject. In the opening chapters of *Beyond a Boundary*, James describes the birth and formation of this literary/ludic self and how hard he had to fight to preserve it from the professional plans of his parents and teachers. He founds this self-formative process on his early identifications with the cricketers Matthew Bondman, Arthur Jones, and Wilton St. Hill. Along with these identifications, James describes his early identifications not only with the language of the Bible and the world of English literature but, most famously, with Thackeray's *Vanity Fair*. As James notes, *Vanity Fair* "was not to me an ordinary book. It was a refuge into which I withdrew. By the time I was fourteen I must have read the book over twenty times" (James 2013 [1963]: 18).[1] These widely differing identifications were subsequently pulled together by the creative powers of James's ego genetic process. He writes, "Somehow from around me, I had selected and fastened on to the things that made a whole" (18).

This whole was the literary/cricketing identity that would clash so violently with the plans of parents and teachers. In chapter 2, "Against the Current," James describes the strength and determination of this boyish self to play cricket and pursue literature in spite of all the pressures from his parents and teachers at the prestigious Queen's Royal College. Earlier, in chapter 1, James wrote, "To that little boy I owe a debt of gratitude" (18). He established quite securely the identity of James the writer and cricketer, as he will be the author of short stories, *Minty Alley*, and essays on cricket.

This account of James's early self-formation provides us with important clues to his approach to the expressive moment of culture. First, it assumes but leaves implicit the deep or originary structures of subjectivity and intersubjectivity that make self-formation possible. In James's account, we see the importance of founding identifications and the assumption of a spontaneous ability to exclude factors and make a whole out of those that were included. In other words, the core of the ego genetic process is the self-organizing activities by which human beings establish the sense of "I."

Second, although not discussed in *Beyond a Boundary*, human beings form collective identities or the sense of a "We." Vital to the formation of this We-self are the structures of intersubjectivity, such as language, that make possible the joining of individual egos in various forms of collective solidarity. The ontological status of this We-self is of course a highly contested issue, but for James it was very real and the major source of the sociogenic creativity by which societies and civilizations advance. James's poeticism associated high degrees of creative or world-making activity with the formation of both the I-self and the We-self. These society-forming types of creativity are encoded in the self-organizing capabilities of these two important dimensions of our subjectivity.

This central assumption of the inherent creativity of the human self is one that James shared with a number of other Caribbean writers, such as Wilson Harris, George Lamming, V. S. Naipaul, and Orlando Patterson. Because of the peculiar nature of the cultural environment of the region, this Caribbean poeticist tradition has taken the position that the inherent creativity of the self is the only viable starting point for the Caribbean writer. For Harris (1973: 13), the cultural environment of writers in the region is one in which inherited African and Indian symbolic worlds imploded under the colonizing impact of European imperialism. He describes this cultural terrain as "bare." For Patterson (1967), the terrain is marked by "an absence of ruins." To these characterizations, we can add James's (2014 [1932]: 49) hyperbolic statement that Caribbean people "have no other religion except Christianity, in fact, their whole outlook is that of Western Civilization modified and adapted to their particular circumstances." This unusually high degree of cultural disabling and denuding has left equally exposed and accessible the inherent creativity of the self. The embracing of this exposed creativity as the most relevant starting point for Caribbean writers I have called "creative realism." Rather than catching the self shaped and identified by established traditions, it reveals the creativity through which the self projects constructions that may later become parts of an established tradition. James's poeticism was informed by this ontology of creative realism, which stayed with him as he fashioned his other two syntheses.

*Minty Alley* is clearly the major work that accompanied and reflected James's formation as a writer. It was the major creative work released by the processes of fusion and fission that were taking place within him. As with the opening chapters of *Beyond a Boundary*, the deep or originary structures of subjectivity and intersubjectivity through which James creates the different characters of this novel remain implicit. His narrative strategy is one that takes an open-ended, incomplete, and implicit approach to the expressive structures of human subjectivity.

### The Culture of Self-Projection in *Minty Alley*

James's protagonist, Haynes, is a shy, solitary boy who grew up under the shelter of his mother. She wanted him to be an independent professional young man. But subjectively, Haynes is too inhibited and lacks the assertiveness required for such an independent life. Unlike the case of James himself, this resistance to a professional life does not lead to assertiveness in other areas, such as sports or literature. Haynes's mother gets him a job in a bookshop, which he keeps throughout the course of the novel.

We meet Haynes not long after his mother's death and therefore in the process of deciding how to reorganize his life now that she is no longer there to guide and protect him. Haynes is strikingly unable to work out these practical details and is rescued by the maid, Ella. Indeed, it is Ella who makes the arrangements that bring Haynes to the working-class neighborhood of No. 2 Minty Alley. She will continue to prepare Haynes's meals while he works at the bookshop and spends a lot of his time in his room reading.

Haynes wanted to make a break with his past and his dependence on his mother but was too inhibited to formulate and put into action such a project of personal independence. James (1997 [1936]: 23) describes Haynes this way: "His life was empty. He did not think these things out clearly, but he knew them as people are aware of things without putting them into words. The sea of life was beating at the walls which enclosed him. Nervously and full of self-distrust, he had been fighting against taking the plunge, but he would have to sometime." Living at No. 2 Minty Alley, Haynes will not take the plunge. Instead, we will feel the intentional aspects of his subjectivity moving inward rather than out toward the existential challenges of his life. Without making explicit the specific configuration of psycho-existential factors at work, James very artfully portrays Haynes as one whose ego genetic process remains prematurely interrupted, thus blocking the emergence of capacities for empathy, inner strength, good judgment, and autonomy.

The residents of No. 2 Minty Alley are also individuals with severely blocked processes of self-formation. They have all fallen short of reaching the heights of their human potential. However, again leaving implicit the psychosocial details, James links narratively these interruptions of inner growth to their racialized working-class situation. This social location is responsible for the fact that, unlike Haynes, they have not been able to develop their capacities for ideas. As a result, they are individuals who live primarily by their emotions. In contrast to Haynes, who is unable to launch his project of independence, the other residents of No. 2 are capable of launching emotionally driven but morally compromised projects of selfhood that often get them into trouble. The turbulence in the lives of these residents derives from the clashing of these emotionally driven projects.

Thus, Mrs. Rouse's project of being a landlady in partnership with her lover, Mr. Benoit, clashes violently with Nurse's project of being a professional woman and married to Mr. Benoit. For James, this is more than a love triangle. It is also very much about self-creative projects for overcoming working-class conditions of material poverty. In other words, these are cases of self-projective creativity in the interest of economic survival. At the same time, James is also showing us the negating and warping of human subjectivity that often occurs in these social settings. Although not developed in this text, the cultural or world-making activities that have given the world steel bands, calypso, Carnival, and cricketers such as Matthew Bondman, constitute the more aesthetic creations of these interrupted processes of working-class subject formation. As such creations, they could be compared to James's writing of *Minty Alley*. This is the difficult context for the treatment of the expressive moment of culture in the novel.

**Culture as Objectified Forms and Practices**

So far I have been arguing that, from the expressive standpoint, the emergence and arrival of a human self brings into being a world of cultural significance. In other words, cultural worlds are correlated with the birth of specific subjectivities. Correspondingly, cultural worlds weaken and decline when their correlated subjectivities change or are forced into retreat. From the perspective of the more objectified moment in the being of culture, before an individual can reach this level of world-making maturity, he or she must have gone through a youthful period during which individual development was driven primarily by socialization into a particular culture. This is the period in which the individual acquires a language; learns a variety of social roles inside and out of the family; and adopts beliefs, ideals, and practices that will shape his or her identity and future. In this period of youthful socialization, culture takes on a more objectified form and is experienced as an established set of rules, prescriptions, expectations, and information that we internalize, rather than visions of existence that we externalize. Further, from this perspective, the particular world established by such a mature individual may or may not become part of an established tradition. Jesus, Buddha, and Marx are classic cases in which the worlds associated with their self-formation were institutionalized and made exemplary to the point of shaping and even displacing the worlds spontaneously arising out of the ego genesis of millions of people.

James examines and makes extensive use of this more objectified moment in the life of culture in both his early works, such as *The Life of Captain Cipriani*, and later ones, such as *Beyond a Boundary*. *The Life of Captain Cipriani* is not a typical biography. It was for James the best way he could think of, at the time, to make the case for West Indian self-government from Britain. Cipriani was a leader of this movement in Trinidad, and the artist in James, who saw social change through personal relationships, pushed him to look at this political movement through the life and relations of Cipriani. Further, James thought that it was important for his readers to know the major social players in this movement—the British, the British creoles, and the West

Indians—if they were to understand his case. He therefore described the cultural world of these three groups using this more objectified form. Let us look, for example, at his account of the British.

James describes the British in the following way, starting with their virtues. They are bold, energetic, and enterprising while at the same time highly prejudiced. The British are further distinguished by their genius for politics, which they owe to their "common sense, their capacity for tolerance and their instinct for compromise" (James 2014 [1932]: 40). They are an honest people, even though they are quite sharp in business. They are also an aristocratic people and thus very snobbish. This snobbery makes them "bow and scrape before their superiors" (James 2014 [1932]: 40). They are a patriotic people with great respect for law and order, and their genius for politics has enabled them to combine aristocracy with substantive democracy.

Like other people, the British have their faults. James notes three significant ones. First, they are "not an intellectual people" (James 2014 [1932]: 41). He acknowledges their share of genius and talent, but for the most part they are "concerned with culture only as a means of personal advancement" (James 2014 [1932]: 41). Second, James points out that the British are not very social. They are stiff in social intercourse and thus not very friendly. The third and final flaw that James finds in British subjectivity is that it thinks too highly of itself. This for James is one factor that explains their level of racial prejudice.

With this listing of the virtues and faults of the British "We," James is not yet done. He goes on to describe some of the changes that were observed in British subjects when they arrived in the Caribbean colonies. In general, this arrival exaggerates many of the faults listed here. First, it inflates the tendency to think too well of themselves. This inflation leads to a "powerful conviction of his own importance in the scheme of things" (James 2014 [1932]: 43), and to the assumption that West Indians cannot do the work that the British do. As they encounter West Indian men and women who are as talented as, or more capable than, they are, they fall back on cultural clichés such as "the ability of the Anglo-Saxons to govern" (James 2014 [1932]: 45). These and other exaggerations mark British colonials in the Caribbean.

After making similar sketches of the British creoles and the West Indians, James turns a critical eye on this objectified approach to the culture of these populations. In *Beyond a Boundary*, he retracted his characterization of the British as not being intellectual (164). In the case of the West Indians, he showed how their internalization of British notions of whiteness led to deep divisions within their ranks along shades of whiteness. This distorting of Afro-Caribbean subjectivity clearly required the critique of these objectified forms of cultural whiteness that James consistently practiced. However, in *The Life of Captain Cipriani* we do not get many glimpses of the expressive moment in the life of culture.

### James's Socio-Historical Poetics

Although it was James's first political text, *The Life of Captain Cipriani* was clearly a work of his literary phase. The political theorist in James had not yet fully emerged. However, James describes very clearly his emergence in *Beyond a Boundary*: "Fiction-writing drained out of me and was replaced by politics. I became a Marxist, a Trotskyist" (151). This dramatic shift was the surface manifestation of a major reordering of James's subjectivity— one that brought the political theorist to a position of dominance. This rise of the political theorist also reflected James's centering of the American experience with liberal democracy, capitalist industrialization, and the resistance of workers. The discursive world associated with this shift, James's socio-historical poetics, was very different from the more literary one that produced *Minty Alley* and *The Life of Captain Cipriani*. This second phase saw the development of what Sylvia Wynter (1992: 76) has called James's "theoretics," with his poetics in the background. With the political theorist in charge, the link with culture was mediated primarily through philosophy and popular culture rather than literature. It was James's novel treatment of popular culture that influenced Stuart Hall and, later, the field of cultural studies. This shift is particularly evident in works such as *State Capitalism and World Revolution* (1986 [1950]) and *American Civilization* (1993). We cannot here examine the Trotskyist and direct democratic phases that James's theoretics went through before they were forced to make more room for the return of a stronger and more mature literary and cricketing poeticist concern. However, the works of this period, some of which were indicated earlier, are very well known.

### James's Poetic Socio-Historicism

*Beyond a Boundary* is the product of a third synthesis, James's poetic sociohistoricism, that reflected the return of an empowered literary/cricketing subjectivity. It was also associated with a shift away from the United States and a temporary recentering of his concerns on the imperial nexus between Britain and the Caribbean. In this case, too, James describes the inner transition that made it possible: "I was increasingly aware of large areas of human existence that my history and my politics did not seem to cover" (151). James is now less certain that even his direct democratic politics has given him the best answers to questions such as "What do men live by?" (151)—what fires their souls in the way that literature and cricket had set his ablaze?

This break with his socio-historical poetics was not quite the draining out that marked the decline of the youthful poeticist. Rather, it was a gentler and friendlier break, closer to the shifts between instruments in some jazz compositions. As a rising trend, this third synthesis could be seen in works such as *American Civilization* and *Mariners, Renegades and Castaways* (1985 [1953]), in which James wrestled seriously with the question, What do people live by? In addition to producing *Beyond a Boundary*, this third synthesis allowed James to bring together the world-making activities associated with the genesis of both the I-self and the We-self within the framework of an expanded civilizational sociology. It is in terms of its place in the new synthesis that produced *Beyond a Boundary* that I will now focus on James's civilizational sociology.

By a civilizational sociology, I am referring to a theoretical account of those eruptions of collective and sociogenic creativity from deep changes within the We-self of a people, which are able to move their societies onto paths of ascent or descent. James's civilizational sociology had been in formation for a long time and had been fed by writers such as Thackeray, Herman Melville, T. S. Eliot, Matthew Arnold, Oswald Spengler, and his fellow poeticist Wilson Harris. Its expansion and incorporation into the third synthesis was motived by James's need to answer the question posed earlier, "What do men live by?" He needed new answers, as he was no longer satisfied with the ones supplied by his politics.

Drawing more on his poetics, James responds to the question with the claim that human beings live by the projects, practices, and ideals that fulfill their maturing subjectivity and their material needs. Thus, the significant shift in emphasis is toward a revaluing of the importance of expressive subjectivity. It is in the context of this new answer that James raises once again the question of who are the people, and which institutions are the major carriers, of these projects and ideals by which men and women live and by which civilizations are changed. Are these individuals the great political leaders? Are these carrier institutions the church, the arts, or the academy?

After acknowledging the contributions of these institutions, James proceeds to add individuals and institutions that have been overlooked, that have been hiding in plain sight: athletes and organized games. Sports, he argues—like literature, religion, or music—could be the carriers of projects and ideals that are capable of lifting the souls of men and women to higher levels of social and subjective existence. In the case of cricket, James makes the now famous argument that the game is a dramatic art. Further, because of their collective nature—involving both players and the audience—organized games are capable of cultivating not only processes of individual ego genesis but also the genesis of a highly creative We-self. The ability of sports to advance this humanizing process James links to larger sociogenic and civilizing projects that can arise when the contributions of the arts and other carriers are added to those of organized games. It is this systematic inclusion of sports among the great sociogenic forces of human history that distinguishes James's civilizational sociology and makes *Beyond a Boundary* such a special work.

In articulating the civilizing contributions of sports, James examines in a highly original way the place of organized games in the rise of Greek and British civilizations. For him, "The first recorded date in European history is 776 BC, the date of the first Olympic Games" (154). The Greeks "who laid the intellectual foundations of the Western world were the most fanatical players and organizers of games that the world has ever known" (154). In addition to describing the organization and scope of these games, James points to two factors that are important for his question, What do people live by?

First, he notes that Olympic athletes embodied ideals of excellence, courage, dedication, and high achievement. As such, they were objects of hero worship. The Greeks believed that "an athlete who had represented his community at a national competition, and won, had thereby conferred a notable distinction on his city. His victory was a testament to the quality of the citizens" (156). In short, it is the ideals that the Olympic athletes embodied and realized in their victories that reveal to us what Greek men and women live by, and thus the inner life of Greek civilization. As carriers of these ideals by which Greek civilization thrived, Greek athletes were advancing the humanizing of the population in much the same way that Greek arts, religion, or philosophy were doing.

The second factor about the games to which James draws our attention is that they attracted the great scholars and poets of Greece: Socrates, Plato, Pythagoras, Pindar, Herodotus, and others were all there. In addition to attending, they organized conferences and did readings during the period of the games. Thus, sports and the arts were together performing and legitimating the ideals by which people lived and civilizations advanced.

James turns next to the place of sports in the revival of British civilization in the second half of the nineteenth century. He points to an association, similar to the Greek one, between the rise of organized sports in Britain, particularly cricket, and the rise of the modern phase of British civilization. James begins by noting the first golf tournament in 1860; the founding of the Football Association in 1863; the first organized athletics championship in 1866; and the departure in 1862 of the first English cricket team for Australia. For him there is a definite connection between these outbursts of organized sporting activity and the new industrial and democratic civilization that was emerging in Britain. In support of this claim, James (1986: 189) then sketches with delicate and well-placed strokes the contributions of cricket and, in particular, W. G. Grace to the phase of British civilization that emerged between 1860 and 1930. In particular, James uses this correlation between the rise of organized games and the industrial phase of British civilization to explain what he calls "a great period of cricket from 1895 [to] 1914," and the phase of decline that followed.

Having examined the cases of Greek and British civilizations, James expands the reach of his civilizational sociology even further to include the rise of West Indian cricket between the 1940s and the 1960s and the correlation of this rise with projected ideals of racial equality, regionalism, industrialization, and political independence—in other words, the ideals of a new phase in West Indian civilization. As James was familiar with the history of cricket and other organized games in England, he was equally knowledgeable about the game in the West Indies, where he also saw it as a dramatic art. In pieces that preceded the writing of *Beyond a Boundary*, James traced the origins of West Indian cricket in the 1840s, with its white captains, to the rise of Test Match cricket in the early decades of the twentieth century, with black captains. He also identified the period 1900–39 as one defined by the emergence of a clear correlation between cricket and West Indian nationalism (James 1986: 120). Also emerging at this time was another feature of West Indian cricket that was important for the game and also for James's civilizational sociology: individual players achieved very high standards but often failed to reproduce such performances consistently. James saw in this lack of consistency a reflection of the level of social organization or disorganization of West Indian society (1986: 22).

James approached the sociogenic creativity of West Indian cricket in much the same way that he approached the creativity evident in the region's literature. He rooted it in the thesis of the unusually barren cultural terrain with which colonization left West Indian societies (1986: 118–19). In other words, as Caribbean poeticists took a creative realist approach to the literature produced by the I-self of regional writers, James took a similar creative realist approach to the cricket produced by the West Indian We-self. Thus, he saw the rising performances of West Indian cricket teams as surface manifestations of deeper subterranean shifts and formations taking place in the English-speaking Caribbean We-self.

From the 1950s to the 1990s, the dramatic art of West Indian cricket had become a major carrier not of bourgeois Victorian values, as in the case of England, but of values of, and hopes for, racial equality, regional integration, industrialization, and political independence—in short, the values and ideals of a postcolonial civilization. As a dramatic formation, the game became a major medium in which the West Indian We-self was able to act out and represent to itself the hidden changes and new postcolonial aspirations that were unfolding within it. Cricket was therefore a site of national consolidation, "a field where the social passions of the colonials, suppressed politically, found vigorous if diluted expression" (James 1986: 121). For James, the great all-rounder Garfield Sobers was the quintessential embodiment of this rising period in the history of West Indian cricket, which would be followed by a phase of world dominance from around 1977 to 1995.

James did not get the opportunity to write about the "1914" of West Indian cricket, its fall from the heights of this golden period. However, he was fully aware that this period of West Indian ascendency would not last forever. He knew that the powerful combination of social forces behind these outstanding performances could collapse for internal reasons or be countered by external forces. It was in this spirit that James asked, rhetorically, in an article first published in 1966, "When will it stop, when and how we will meet our 1914, I don't know" (1986: 189). But in spite of the fact that he was not able to write about the decline of West Indian cricket, his civilizational sociology is evident in the works of other cricket scholars, such as Tim Hector, Hilary Beckles, and Neil Lazarus. Here we can take only a quick look at Hector's extension of James's civilizational sociology.

Hector extended James's civilizational sociology in two important ways. First, he expanded James's account of the period of ascent; and second, he applied it to the period of decline. Hector noted that within the ascendant phase analyzed by James, there was the internal problem of the exclusion from West Indian teams of cricketers from the smaller islands, with the exception of Barbados. Hector linked the successful fight against this exclusion to major changes in the social life of these smaller islands. He did this by telling the story of "the largest demonstration held in Antigua in the 1950s."[2] The Marylebone Cricket Club was coming, and popular sentiment was that Hubert Anthonyson should have been playing for the West Indies as the opening fast bowler. But he was not selected, which resulted in this massive demonstration, which included a steel band. The success of this organized resistance brought many outstanding players, such as Vivian Richards and Andy Roberts, to West Indian teams, which certainly contributed to the subsequent period of dominance.

Although there were earlier warning signs, for Hector it was the defeat in Australia in 1995, followed by the defeat in Pakistan in 1997, that announced the arrival of the "1914" of West Indian cricket. As Hector wrote, "The mighty have fallen at long last."[3] The shock was both deep and wide. Hector captured this impact when he wrote, "Now since C. L. R. James's magnificent book, *Beyond a Boundary*, not a few—mostly those who have read on excerpts—have come to the view that cricket is the centre-piece of Caribbean civilization. And whenever, as now, the West Indies cricket team is not doing well such people feel that Armageddon is approaching and that our civilization is at an end."[4] While acknowledging that something was seriously wrong, Hector resisted this rising tide of panic. Instead, he made some modest suggestions, one of which was: "The factors that produced the great West Indies teams between 1977 and 1995 have changed dramatically."[5] Among these factors, he emphasized two. First, he noted that integral to the production of these great teams was the rigorous training they got, not from regional play, but from playing in English county cricket. Indeed, this training was responsible for the clearing up of the consistency problems of the formative years, which James had noted. When West Indian cricketers were excluded from English county cricket, the old consistency problem returned, because they had to rely solely on less rigorous regional competitions for their training.

The second important factor that had changed for Hector was the now unsatisfactory state of the earlier projected postcolonial civilization, which was encoded into the ethos of the cricket of the 1950s. Its major projects were no longer in a state of ascendance; they were in a state of stasis, decline, and crisis. Profound changes had taken place in the postcolonial hopes and aspirations of the West Indian We-self. As a result, the subjective foundations of West Indian cricket in the late 1990s were very different from what they were between 1977 and 1995. However, it was Hector's belief that appropriate changes in these two factors would greatly improve the performances of West Indian cricket teams. This use of James's civilizational sociology by Hector is just one example of its lasting influence and of the larger synthesis of which it is a part.

### After *Beyond a Boundary*: Culture, Politics, and Economics

James's third synthesis, his poetic socio-historicism, which was the womb of his mature civilizational sociology and *Beyond a Boundary*, was by no means a final synthesis that permanently replaced the second. Rather, what followed the writing of *Beyond a Boundary* was a complex pattern of back-and-forth movements that James made between his poetic socio-historicism and his socio-historical poeticism. The mutually decentering pattern of these movements took James's thinking outside the categorical frameworks of both classical Hegelian and Marxian dialectics. Further, they went beyond the binary contradictions of analytic thinking to include crossing disciplinary boundaries, multiplying the centers of revolutionary discourse to embrace race, gender, culture, and sports and much more open relations in which the multiple centers can temporarily displace one another.

Underlying this new dialectic was what Wynter (1992: 63) has called James's "pluri-conceptual framework"—that is, a framework in which "such factors as gender, color, class and education are non-dogmatically integrated." It is this mode of nondogmatic integration of analytic discourses whose centers can shift with changing contexts and objects of knowing that is really important here. This more complex dialectic is marked by three crucial characteristics. First, there can be no fixing or closing of these syntheses into a final system. Crossing an increased number of analytic boundaries, as well as the poetic requirement of threading social movements and orders through personal relations, blocks such tendencies to closure. Second, we can see the same resistance to closure in James's representation of subjectivity, in the way he crosses the boundaries between "moments" in the being of culture, as well as in his rejection of disciplinary confinement. Third, as Wynter notes, in the years just before and after he wrote *Beyond a Boundary*, James as a thinking subject was profoundly pluri-centered but, at the same time, more subtly integrated, thus making earlier models of subjective and dialectical integration obsolete.

The key to this new dialectic is the stance James takes toward epistemic practices, such as leaving something implicit, shifting relations between the centers of his analytic discourses, and crossing the boundaries among disciplines or those among his three moments in the life of culture. The quickest way to characterize the epistemic move that James makes at these and other junctures is to liken it to what we can call the Du Boisian hesitation. In his essay "Sociology Hesitant" (2000 [1904]), W. E. B. Du Bois took up the following question: How is it possible for sociologists to apply causally deterministic models to the study of humans, who, they insisted, were free beings? His answer was that sociologists operated with two incommensurate paradigms—one of freedom and one of determinism—and quite unknowingly performed an epistemic hesitation as they quietly shifted from one paradigm to the other. In the course of this unacknowledged hesitation, sociologists were in fact stealthily carrying out the transcendental moves of shedding the conceptual categories of one paradigm and putting on those of the other. This response to categorical incommensurability was the way Du Bois crossed the boundary between quantitative and qualitative approaches in sociology and integrated them in a work such as *The Philadelphia Negro*. Throughout his corpus, we can see Du Bois using this hesitation as he crosses disciplinary boundaries and shifts the centers of his larger discourse from poetics to sociology to history and back.

I think the new dialectic that James developed just before and after *Beyond a Boundary* can be effectively grasped with the aid of this Du Boisian hesitation. It helps us to understand the many transversal or epistemic boundary crossings that became integral parts of this new and subtler dialectic, as well as the new relations between James the political theorist and James the literary/cricketing poeticist. Thus, it is important to note that while he was writing *Beyond a Boundary*, James was also working on *Facing Reality* (1958), *Modern Politics* (1973 [1960]), and *Party Politics in the West Indies* (1962)—all works of the political theorist of the second synthesis. Further, more than a decade after *Beyond a Boundary*, James published *Nkrumah and the Ghana Revolution* (1977) and *Notes on Dialectics* (1980 [1948]), although *Notes on Dialectics* was written earlier.

In sum, one of the major challenges of the period after *Beyond a Boundary* is the clear grasping of the nature of a new dialectic within which James had come to link the complex dynamics among culture, politics, and economics. In the wake of the financial crisis which radiated across the globe from the heart of Wall Street after 2008, it is easy to see James the political theorist picking up and revising the America-centered discourse of the second synthesis and using it as a lens through which to grasp our post-socialist and post-neoliberal present. The cultural element in this revision of his political thinking would have focused on the creative upsurges needed to move beyond it. This he would have done without having to reject or drain the life from the literary/cricketing persona that gave us *Beyond a Boundary*.

**Notes**

1. Hereafter, page numbers in parentheses refer to this edition of *Beyond a Boundary*.
2. Tim Hector, "Cricket and Decolonization," *Outlet*, 7 December 1990, 10.
3. Tim Hector, "It Is the West Indies That Is in Peril, not West Indies Cricket," *Outlet*, 12 December 1997, 10.
4. Tim Hector, "Lara, the Captaincy and West Indies Cricket," *Outlet*, 16 January 1998, 10.
5. Hector, "Lara, the Captaincy and West Indies Cricket," 10.

# PART IV.
# REFLECTIONS
| | | | |

## 12 | Socrates and C. L. R. James

MICHAEL BREARLEY

In *Beyond a Boundary*, C. L. R. James puts this challenge to us: "What do they know of cricket who only cricket know?" The sentence, which he had originally suggested as a title for the book, is in effect a subtitle. The question can be generalized: what does one know of $x$ if one only knows $x$? The phrase echoes, of course, interestingly, Rudyard Kipling's question, "What do they know of England who only England know?"

In this chapter, I will try to spell out some implications of James's question and his explicit and implicit answer to it. I will link it with questions Socrates asked, considering, in turn, how James's question applies (perhaps differently) to players, to coaches, and to social historians such as James himself. I will then return to the book and give a more extensive account of how the author demonstrates that understanding cricket as he does is enhanced by an understanding of social history and of the psychology of groups. For instance, cricket could be both the locus of a deep prejudice and a field in which such prejudice can be mitigated—even possibly overcome and reconciled.

James also proves his own point in a broader sense: it is only by ambivalently going beyond boundaries that one can deepen one's knowledge. (As a colonial, James was beyond the boundary of the British and admired the pride of the darker-skinned Shannon players, but at the same time, deeply imbued in British culture, James affiliated himself with the paler Maple.) James was inherently, Socratically, subversive, not only with regard to the British, but with regard to aspects of the anticolonial movement.

The book is, among other things, a celebration of the appointment in 1960 of the first black man as captain of West Indies for a whole series: Frank Worrell. (George Headley—"the so-called black Bradman"—had captained the team, but only for a single Test in 1948.) As editor of the Trinidad newspaper the *Nation* (the mouthpiece of Eric Williams's People's National Movement), James had campaigned for this selection for two years. But *Beyond a Boundary* is far wider and more embracing than this.

One way to characterize the book is by saying that it offers an account of the significance of cricket for a whole society. James describes W. G. Grace as the best known of all Englishmen of the Victorian age (James 2013 [1963]: 180),[1] unifying the country in a way that nothing and no one else could. Through him, "Cricket, the most complete expression of popular life in pre-industrial England, was incorporated into the life of the nation" (171). In parallel to this, James showed how important the game was in the variedly colored strata of Trinidad; how vital it was for the pride of the black man. Success on the field for unprivileged black individuals represented a victory over the colonial and class-ridden upper ranks; such successes enabled the man and woman in the street to walk taller, to conceive that they had a right to regard themselves as the equals of those who set themselves up as their social and cultural superiors. "They are no better than we," Learie Constantine (1901–71), the great Trinidadian all-rounder and, later, the first black man in the House of Lords, said to James in the early 1920s (112). And James himself wrote, "The cricket field was a stage on which selected individuals played representative roles charged with social significance" (66). Shannon, the team of the black lower middle class, best exemplified the unrelenting pursuit of excellence that the more or less level cricketing playing field made possible.

James showed how British values included the idea of fair play and (to greater or lesser degrees) embodied it on the cricket field. He linked this value to the qualities of the English literature he studied at school and read at home in books sold by the itinerant bookseller (whose impact on his life I will return to later). One might, therefore, sum up the thesis of *Beyond a Boundary* in terms James himself used in an interview with the filmmaker Mike Dibb: "Something is required and someone steps in. This someone thereby breaks new ground."[2] The arrival of this someone is not a matter of pure chance. As James said, "You wouldn't call Shakespeare or Michelangelo an accident." This last point is true: of Grace, of Worrell, *and* of James himself.

An aside: I suggest that James's implication that there has to be only a requirement, and then someone steps in, is an overstatement—one that underplays the creativity of the person stepping in. On the one hand, it is true that the person who became Shakespeare arrived at a specific cultural situation and could not but emerge out of and address himself to that. When a breakthrough comes in science, the new thrust arrives as a response to certain scientific conundrums, perhaps even to a crisis in the science, where (as Thomas Kuhn [1962] put it) the paradigms were breaking down, requiring too many special exemptions or complex arrangements to accommodate new discoveries and ideas. However, it would be wrong to think that there was only one route possible for, say, Einstein or Darwin or Freud—or for Shakespeare. This is also true of Grace, Worrell, and James himself. That *Beyond a Boundary* could not have been written at any other point in history does not imply that it had to be written or that only it could have been written.

To return to my line of thought, the book is far richer than any simple summary could propose. The main point I want to make is that the book itself is an example of its own epigraph or subtitle. James knows a lot more of cricket than only cricket, and it is his wider historical and social understanding that gives depth and force to his arguments about Worrell, as to the book itself. This is why *Beyond a Boundary* tells us so much about cricket. It could not have been written at other stages of history, or in other contexts, but it is a radically new child of its time. On this occasion, it was true that "cometh the hour, cometh the man."

**Knowledge of Cricket?**

James's question prompts the further question: What *is* "knowledge of cricket"? James's is a Socratic question, inspired by Socratic irony (see Lear 2011), for the implication of the question is that the person most devoted and experienced in cricket, as player or coach or commentator, does not, without other knowledge, know what cricket is. Such questioning was Socrates's mode of approach. He persuaded generals to admit their ignorance of what courage is (*Laches*); priests, their ignorance about piety (*Euthyphro*); rulers and judges, their ignorance about justice (*Republic*). At the end of each discussion or dialogue, the experts, reduced to perplexity (*aporia*) by the Socratic examination (*elenchos*), agree with his conclusion that no one knows what courage, piety, or justice is.

Partly, this was an outcome arrived at by means of Socrates's logical sleight of hand (the fact that no *definition* of these complex concepts covers all cases does not entail that no one knows what these things are; also, the fact that people cannot put into words what something is does not mean they do not know what it is—as Ludwig Wittgenstein [1953: sec. 78] said, knowing what a clarinet sounds like does not involve being able to say so in words). But Socrates goes beyond this, forcing his interlocutors (and us) to realize how hard it is to be courageous, pious, just, or virtuous. Like Søren Kierkegaard (1970), who says that in all Christianity there is no (real) Christian, Socrates challenges all ordinary claims to excellence or virtue.[3] He raises questions that are more radical than the ordinary ones about our practical identities and roles. James does not go quite so far, but if we take his question seriously, we, like Socrates's generals and priests, have to interrogate our assumptions about knowledge of cricket and about what it takes to achieve excellence as a cricketer.

There are different kinds of "knowledge of cricket," a range of possible forms or levels of knowledge. There is, first, practical knowledge, know-how: how to play; how to be a batsman, bowler, fielder. Second, there is the critical knowledge of a coach or commentator (including the making of discriminations and judgments and the spotting of talent). And third, James has in mind a more reflective knowledge (being able to say what cricket's importance is, socially and psychologically; being able to relate cricket to other matters, as he does in *Beyond a Boundary*). Are the first two kinds of knowledge not really knowledge or, at any rate, knowledge of cricket? Are they somehow too limited to count as knowledge? What does being practically knowledgeable, or critically knowledgeable, call for? In what follows, I will consider each of these categories in turn.

**The Player's Knowledge**

Let us first consider, then, those in my first category: the players, who may be said to know cricket neither in the philosophical or comparative way evinced by James himself nor in the overall way of the coach or commentator. Yet surely, we might protest, they understand it in a way no one else does. Can anyone who has not been on the front line know what war is really like?

I would say that even here James has a point. To be a complete player, the player needs to understand more than his own particular niche or skill within the game. One thing I liked about the old pre- and postwar Yorkshire tradition in cricket was that players were brought up to think about the game as a whole. A typical Yorkshire team exemplified the old Latin saying "Quot homines tot sententiae," which can be translated as "However many people, so many opinions."

By contrast, I heard recently a story that shocked me about an international bowler who was part of the fielding side in a recent One Day International. At a drinks break, it turned out that he had no idea of the situation of the game; he seemed not to know how many overs were left or with what sort of run rate the opposition was faced. All he could think of was whether his wrist was at exactly the correct angle in delivery.

Thus, professionalism in sport may atrophy into a narrow focus on one's own task, so that each player is imbued with guidelines about his own performance based, perhaps, on computerized printouts telling him how to bowl against each opposition batsman. Such narrow knowledge is gained at the expense of an appreciation of and emotional involvement in the tactics of the game and the problems and skills of one's teammates. The player becomes a cog in a machine, a worker bee in a hive, rather than a thinking member of a team.

In American football, teams change entire sections of their personnel when a defensive play is replaced by an offensive one, or vice versa. The division of labor is extreme. The role of the defensive lineman, say, can become so specialized and limited that the person fulfilling it need know nothing at all about the play or overall strategy of the team. Such developments rob sportsmen of their full humanity. No longer having to consider the process as a whole makes it impossible for them to understand how their own world makes sense. Like Charlie Chaplin in *Modern Times*, the defensive lineman becomes a conveyor belt attendant, whose task is reduced to a small range of repeatable, automated, physical skills. On the broad sociopolitical level, James was vehemently opposed to what he saw as the encroaching alienation in modern capitalistic ways of living.

My own aim as captain of a cricket team, by contrast, was to turn players into a team of potential captains, of thinkers about the game. Individuals' responsibilities did not cease when they were not involved in their individual first-order skills of bowling or batting. I wanted them to be thinking about the whole situation, about one another's strengths, weaknesses, vulnerabilities, and opportunities, as well as about those of the opposition. They might then be able to offer ideas or advice to others or to the captain or to the team as a whole. No one (in any organization) knows where the next good idea will come from. I believe, too, that the effort to see things from other people's points of view helps in the development of the individual's own skill: as a batsman, he can see the anxieties and doubts to which even the best bowlers are subject; as a bowler, he can appreciate the nervousness behind the strut even of the great batsman.

Nor is batting or any other practical skill simply a matter of mastery of a technique in the abstract. A person who knows batting, say, in the sense of having an excellent technique may not be a good batsman. He may not be good at turning technique into scores, or he may do so only when the pressure is off. A batsman, however skillful and correct, is not fully a batsman unless he can build an innings, turn promising starts to big scores, fight his way through unpromising starts, and pace a run chase; unless he can perform when the chips are down, against the best bowlers or in conditions that suit the bowler; unless he can assess early on, and convey to the team, what a good score on a particular pitch might be; unless he has a reliable sense of when to risk his wicket in the interests of the team and when, by contrast, to conserve his wicket, even if his performance then risks being misinterpreted in some quarters as selfishness. The excellent bowler also has to do more than bowl good balls. He can make the best of difficult circumstances—a pitch that does not suit him or being put on at the wrong end (from his own selfish point of view)—or, alternatively, he can make the worst of a bad job. He is not intimidated by bowling to a destructive batsman. He will stick at his task even when the going is hard. Specialists of all kinds become more creative as craftsmen if they are open to developing a broader range of options. And all cricketers, like all sportsmen, have to deal with "those twin impostors": success and failure (Kipling 1910). Some manage this difficult task better than others.

So at this first level, what does a performer have to know to function well enough on the field? The ideal player is capable of understanding more than how to hit a cover drive or bowl a fast out-swinger. He who (in a narrow sense) only cricket (only cricketing technique) knows is not going to be as good a player as he might be. He needs to be more broadly understanding (though not necessarily able to articulate) and capable of a greater range of assessments; he needs to have strengths of character that go beyond flamboyant or exceptional technical ability. He needs a gear of flamboyance or freedom beyond the merely pedestrian and correct.

I think it is considerations such as these that make sense of a striking attitude of those who were running Australian cricket a few years ago, when they were undoubtedly the best team in the world. John Buchanan and Steve Waugh, coach and captain, were convinced that improving the team's performance went hand in hand with helping players to mature as people, so they adopted various ploys and approaches with this in view. En route to England for one tour, the team visited the scene of the loss of many Australian (and other) young lives in World War I: the Dardanelles. Growing up as a cricketer includes realizing (they believed) that potential failings or losses in cricket pale into insignificance compared with losses of young life on the battlefield. Moreover, on these tours players were encouraged to phone home to make contact with people whom they might have ignored; they were invited to read out to the rest of the team passages from books or from their own diaries that meant a lot to them. (I cannot resist making a couple of other comments. First, such broadening seems a far cry from sacking four players, as the Australian management did in India in 2013 for not sending in a written homework assignment. And second, Steve Waugh's approach to leadership did surprise me. I had obviously had a limited understanding of the poetic and emotionally attuned world of the Australian dressing room. It was not how they used to talk to me.)

These leaders recognized the truth in James's assertion: that those who know nothing of life cannot learn what they need to know and have inside them if they are to reach their full potential as cricketers, however talented and committed. Clearly, such a lesson applies to activities beyond cricket or sport.

### The Knowledge of the Expert—Coaches and Commentators

What, then, about those in my second category: people experienced in the game at various stages, now perhaps using their expertise in working as coaches, umpires, or commentators or in other ways?

A person may, as K. S. Ranjitsinhji (1897: 230) put it, "grow grey in the service of the game," yet remain "astonishingly ignorant about it." But I am not talking about such people—the narrow or bigoted or unimaginative. I am talking about people who themselves excelled as players and who are rooted in the game's techniques, lore, values, and character and the characters of those playing it. I do not mean to imply that only people with top-level experience and expertise can become good coaches, pundits, and so on, but some of the most perceptive in these categories are former players who have devoted a lifetime to the game. Once they retire, in their mid-thirties or early forties, they go into coaching or commentary or umpiring. People such as Ian and Greg Chappell, Ray Illingworth, Keith Fletcher, Sunil Gavaskar, Michael Holding, Michael Atherton, Geoffrey Boycott, Graham Gooch, and

Peter Willey are steeped in the practice and observation of the game and its players.

In what sense might one say that these people know only cricket (and therefore do not know cricket)? An expert of this kind can know cricket through and through without understanding its actual and potential social role (they may not have much to say about Grace's role in English social history, for example, or even about Worrell and his place in colonial and postcolonial West Indian history).

However, such men understand a lot that goes beyond cricket simply conceived. They know about character, about relaxation and concentration, about pressure and responses to it. These experts know the game tactically and psychologically, as well as technically; they are shrewd in their assessment of whom to pick, of who (for example) can be relied on in a crisis. In their day-to-day coaching, they would constantly be switching between, on the one hand, talking to the players at a technical level and, on the other, making suggestions or opening up discussion about matters of character and personality. Noticing how tense I was, the elderly former Warwickshire player and coach Tiger Smith asked me once why I frowned when I played imaginary shots in the pavilion with his walking stick, which he had suggested I hold and use as a bat. Did I think I would hit the ball harder? He was questioning my unacknowledged assumption that doing well is based on trying harder, which itself seemed to imply (to me at that moment, at least) a sort of rigidly tense effort of concentration. In fact, one cannot hit a ball well when one's body is tense. The coach understood all this. He might have approached my problem from a more purely technical point of view, but he did not. He got me to think about what my underlying and largely unconscious belief was so that, having seen how wrong-headed (and wrong-bodied) it was, I could orient myself differently.

Graham Gooch, England's former batting coach, says that what he coaches is not batting but run scoring, by which I think he means it is not so much technique as the whole approach to batting, so that the batsman gets used to making big scores or recovering from bad patches. Gooch is coaching more than batting per se. With experienced Test players, he has a relatively small amount of work to do on technique alone, but there may be much that can be tweaked psychologically, in terms of attitude and approach, with regard to motivation and passion. (There was a lot to be learned, James reminds us, from Shannon.)

Gooch and others understand risk and safety in both teams and individuals. The true coach or leader understands people, knows what makes them tick. He recognizes the importance of personal qualities and draws on intangible and hard-to-describe sources of ambition and dedication in members of the team, including proper pride, which motivated West Indian teams during their glory days and to some degree lay behind their utter determination to be the best. The coach or journalist may not be able to express such knowledge in James's fluent prose, but it would be there in their attitudes. Like a good parent or teacher, they know something about the balance between telling and consulting, about the need for respect for others' opinions while holding on to one's own.

James has a good point. Knowing cricket and cricketers does call for knowledge of more than cricket's technicalities (though one might say all this is involved in knowing cricket). Knowledge in a practical activity such as cricket involves levels of understanding that go beyond the acquisition of, or the capacity to convey or sum up, technical skills. Such understanding involves a sense of self and of others. It includes a capacity to grasp or sum up a game as a whole.

This general point has application far beyond cricket, beyond sports. In most roles and jobs other skills and understandings are required beyond the narrowly technical ones. We have a good idea, but can we get it across? We have particular skills, but can others tolerate us being part of their team? Can we mesh with others in a cooperative way? On the Radio 3 program *Private Passions*, Rowan Williams, until recently Archbishop of Canterbury, spoke about what was called for in being a chorister. He said (I paraphrase) that it involves not only technical improvements in singing and following the score, but also learning how to listen and respond to other voices, to be in conversation with others, holding on to one's own line of music or point of view but also hearing and responding to the voices of others.[4] On the cricket field, in choirs, in other teams or groups, if we put others off too much or too radically, they will not want to hear what we have to say. James quotes Worrell: "If something was wrong I told them what was right and left it to them" (258). One element in leadership, in transmitting understanding or even knowledge, is "leaving it to them."

The psychoanalyst and psychiatrist Tom Main, who led the Cassell Hospital in West London during the 1950s and '60s, was once asked by a frantic young psychiatrist what he should do with a particularly difficult and demanding patient. Main listened to the doctor, was silent for a while, and then said, "Don't just do something; stand there."[5]

**Focus and Scale: Tactics and Strategy**

One skill that we need as players and as leaders is the capacity to move between a narrow and a wide focus. In the Middlesex team, which I captained for twelve years, the person I usually went to for advice about what to do next, or right now, was Clive Radley. He was perceptive, down to earth, pragmatic. Moreover, if I did not follow his suggestion and things went wrong, he would still be open to my request for help an hour or a day later. He was the perfect person to check out immediate plans with. Mike Smith, another senior player, was a very different kind of person. He was less direct, more vague or indecisive when it came to what to do now, but he often had helpful suggestions on wider issues, such as which younger players had class, what the balance of the team should be, the longer-term prospects of the side. He was more reflective—almost, one might say, more philosophical. He was a strategist, while Radley was a tactician. A third player, Roland Butcher, was even more wide ranging in what he was capable of noticing. He was more like a psychoanalyst to the team. I remember two comments he made. One was when I called a team meeting after we had lost four games on the trot (immediately after winning the first eleven completed matches in the season). In the meeting, many people, including me, voiced their opinions, and several of these opinions were to the point. Late in the discussion, Butcher added something like this: "I think we have started to count the trophies that we assume we'll have on our mantelpieces at home at the end of the season. We are speaking as if we only have to turn up to win. Our attitude has become complacent, totally different from what it was early in the season. We have to stop thinking about the distant future and once again concentrate on each ball, each over, each hour, each session."

On another occasion, when I was unhappy about the tendency of some players to sulk when they had been dropped or felt they were not being given the prominence that was their due, Butcher came in with, "Yes, but do you appreciate what it feels like to be left out of this side? One minute, you're part of the set-up; the next minute, you're changing in a side room down the corridor, and no one really talks to you in the same way." No wonder, he might have added, one or two are prone to sulk. They have something to be aggrieved about.

Here are three valuable contributions, none more or less useful than any of the others. For a full understanding of a team at work, one would need each kind of intelligence, each kind of contribution: pragmatic, strategic, psychological. Socrates (and Plato), with their elevation of abstract intellect, might have placed the three in a hierarchy, with Butcher or Smith on top, then Radley. A modern professional player or coach might reverse the order. I see them as having equivalent weight. Sometimes one needs more of one than the other, but all are needed.

It is rather as if one were to ask which kind of scale is of most value in a map. The answer is, It depends what you need at the moment. The closer the map is to a replica of the environment, the less it becomes a map, but also the more detail one can see. The smaller the scale, the more one sees one's route in relation to other places, other journeys, but the less detail one can pick up. Sometimes one needs one kind of scale, sometimes another. The microscope and the telescope—minute particulars and a panoptic vision— each complements the other.

Perhaps there is an analogy here to the traditional values of professionalism and amateurism. The typical professional knows the game close to. He has to. His living depends on it. He has to put in time at the technicalities; he practices and trains assiduously. The old pro can read a pitch, since he has seen similar and different pitches over many years. He knows cricket from having played in and watched games played in a wide variety of conditions of pitch and atmosphere. He has ideas about how to combat a wide range of opponents. The amateur may be less closely acquainted with the detail, but at best he plays with a spontaneity that comes from love of the activity. He can, we hope, take risks; he can try new methods and be more independent; his livelihood does not depend on it. He can relax. He has other things in life, so that cricket can be seen as not the be-all and end-all of life. Failure is not perhaps so devastating.

James himself is keen to emphasize the need for new vision, for attitudes that transcend the conventions of the day, whether in sport, art, politics, or life. He quotes Franz Stampfl, the trainer of athletes such as Roger Bannister, Christopher Chataway, Chris Brasher, and others: "By far the most important part of a great performance is played by the mind. Once the athlete is convinced that the prevailing standards are not high, and that improving upon them is a not very difficult task, he will crack them. Long hours of training are not in the least necessary.... The record-breaker of the future will be a man of intelligence with an imaginative approach. The greatest performances will be produced by 'the poet, the artist, the philosopher'" (220–21).

This seems to me to be willfully one-sided. I would say that both sets of qualities (professional and amateur, philosophical and pragmatic) are invaluable and need to be held in balance. In fact, the point should really be made in terms of attitudes and temperaments rather than differences related to whether or not one is paid to play. There are plenty of people who did not and did not need to get paid to play cricket whose approach was of the former kind, and vice versa. Think of the batting of Trevor Bailey, the amateur who batted like a caricature of a professional, and Colin Milburn, the professional who batted like the proverbial amateur. Think of the two professionals, Gooch (who emphasized work, training, practice, and dedication and became a top Test opening batsman) and David Gower (elegant, lazy, hating training, not much time for practice, with an ironic attitude that at times could veer into the lackadaisical, but whose batting was a delight of timing and touch).

An analogy. I am considering cricket, but the lessons may apply in other fields. I read recently of Mozart's support for democracy, not in politics itself, but in the music of his operas. How so? Mozart gave his minor parts complex characters, with complex music. They are not simply pawns, either in the plot (content) or in the music they are given to sing (their form). He shifted music away from a hierarchical tradition; his music gave each instrument and voice a unique line of its own rather than relying on a totally dominant top line, with others in unison beneath it, supplementing, harmonizing, fitting in—in short, serving the dominant tune. As in psychoanalysis, there is a democracy of potential significance finders: free association gives a potentially equal place to all productions of the mind.

### What Else Do They Who Know Cricket Know?

James asks, "What do they know of cricket who only cricket know?" So what were these areas of other knowledge that deepened and broadened James's own knowledge of cricket? What embedded *his* kind of knowledge of cricket?

In what follows I focus mainly on the first chapter of his book, where he seeks out his own roots, which were clearly planted and bearing fruit in the first decade of his life. Of prime importance is the place of cricket in the life of the society. On *Beyond a Boundary*'s very first page, we see the six-year-old boy staying with his grandmother and two aunts in Tunapuna, a small town eight miles outside Port of Spain. "Like all towns and villages on the island, it possessed a recreation ground," James writes. "Recreation meant cricket, for in those days, except for occasional athletic sports meetings, cricket was the only game" (3).

Cricket was the only game, and the ground was at the center of the community. Later, James describes the death of his older aunt, Judith. She had prepared as usual a feast for the annual match organized by her son when she "sat down, and said, 'I am not feeling so well.' She leant her head on the table. When they bent over her to find out what was wrong she was dead." James writes, "I thought it appropriate that her death should be so closely associated with a cricket match. Yet she had never taken any particular interest [in cricket]. She or my grandmother or my other aunt would come in from the street and say, 'Matthew [Bondman] made 55' or 'Arthur Jones is still batting' but that was all" (12). My point is, even for women who were "not particularly interested," cricket was central to the culture of the time and place, and this is what made it "appropriate" for her to die when and where she did.

Standing on a chair in the bedroom of this house of his grandmother's, the young boy could watch practices and matches on the Tunapuna recreation ground from behind the bowler's arm. Here was "shaped one of my strongest early impressions of personality in society." There follows a famous if brief description of a neighbor, Matthew Bondman, discussed in other chapters in this volume: a ne'er-do-well, an "awful character... generally dirty... would not work... an almost perpetual snarl. He would often without shame walk up the main street barefooted 'with his planks on the ground,' as my grandmother would report.... But Matthew had one saving grace—Matthew could bat. More than that, Matthew, so crude and vulgar in every aspect of his life, with a bat in his hand was all grace and style." And his grandmother's "oft-repeated verdict" on Matthew—"good for nothing except to play cricket"—puzzled James. How could a person's ability at cricket make up for his "abominable way of life" (3–4)?

James goes on to quote an eighteenth-century account of the great cricketer William Beldham: "It was a study for Phidias to see Beldham rise to strike.... Men's hearts throbbed within them, their cheeks turned pale and red. Michelangelo should have painted him" (5). Thus, James's childhood passion for cricket touches quickly not only on sociology (the center of the town, the universal interest shown even in his aunt's casual knowledge), but also on aesthetics, especially as revealed in classical Greece and in the Renaissance (he refers to the impact of Bondman's batting—"a long low 'Ah' came from many a spectator and my own little soul thrilled with recognition and delight" [4]; Phidias and Michelangelo should have sculptured Beldham's cut shot, which the eighteenth-century cricket writer lyricizes). Thus, understanding cricket at James's level includes seeing both its place in society and knowing on one's pulses its aesthetic appeal.

From the same bedroom chair, the young James "could mount on to the window-sill and so stretch a groping hand for the books on top of the wardrobe" (3). This, too, we learn on the first page, and his interest in books, and especially in English literature, is described soon after. His mother "was a reader, one of the most tireless I have ever known. Usually it was novels, any novel.... My mother's taste in novels was indiscriminate, but I learned discrimination from my father" (16). And there was an itinerant bookseller who "came once a fortnight carrying a huge pack on his shoulders." Side by side with the child's growing obsession with cricket books and articles was "another—Thackeray's *Vanity Fair*. My mother had an old copy with a red cover. I had read it when I was about eight, and of all the books that passed through that house this one became my Homer and my bible. I read it through from the first page to the last, then started again, read to the end and started again" (17). James had read *Vanity Fair* twenty times by the time he was fourteen (18). Along with this novel were biblical influences, pamphlets found on the top of the wardrobe, their themes or references later explored more thoroughly in the "many bibles that lay about the house, including the large one with the family births and deaths.... Somewhere along the way I must have caught the basic rhythms of English prose. My reading was chiefly in the Old Testament and I may have caught, too, some of the stern attitude to life which was all around me, tempered, but only tempered, by family kindness. Certainly I must have found the same rhythms and the same moralism when I came to *Vanity Fair*" (17–18).

So along with social significance and aesthetic appeal, we find here the third and fourth pillars of James's upbringing, the aspects of the culture that he internalized and that became significant in his personal understanding of cricket: literature and Puritan values as found and expressed in the Bible and in his family influences. Rhythms and grace of expression and a serious morality and attitude to life—he found both exemplified in the cricket and cricketers he admired.

Finally, the last root: pride. I recall James's story of his maternal grandfather, Joshua Rudder, being called in when retired to repair the cane-crushing engine that had broken down at the crucial crop-cutting time. His grandfather asked to go in alone. Within two minutes he was out, and the big wheels started to revolve again. All wanted to know how he had done it. James writes, "The always exuberant Josh grew silent for once and refused to say. He never told them. He never told anybody. The obstinate old man wouldn't even tell me. But when I asked him that day, 'Why did you do it?' he said, 'They were white men with all their big degrees, and it was their business to fix it. I had to fix it for them. Why should I tell them?'" (14–15).

This brings me back to the cricket pride of Shannon, the team of the lower middle classes in Trinidad, the team of the Constantines (the great Learie and his father, Lebrun) and the St. Hills. How much integrity was needed, how much maturity and confidence, to find this route to self-respect in so deeply prejudiced and unjust a world. The achievement included (I would say) a principled refusal either to kowtow or to rebel with a violence or stupidity that could have set back the cause of the very fair play so admired on the cricket field itself. Indeed, this fair play was not only admired but also constitutive of cricket's being the locus par excellence for such a demonstration of equality. Without that code of play, the field could not have served as the site for a symbolic demonstration of black success in the way that it did. What happened within the boundary would profoundly shape what happened beyond the boundary, but by the same token, what was learned in life was carried over the boundary onto the cricket field.

Cricket is a social phenomenon. At times, it involves the expression of racial superiority, but also, and at other times, it involves the expression of racial pride and renewal. In its range and variety of skills it evinces an aesthetic power; it can be an arena for the exercise of values of truth and honesty, as implied by the old dictum, "It's not cricket," however much these values are and have always been under threat. James's own national campaign for the appointment of Worrell, a black man, as captain of the national team, especially for the series against Australia and England, was based on these underlying themes and understandings and was given its power and its intellectual underpinning by them. Cricket is understood in its deeper currents only if one can bring in art, politics, sociology, and psychology. Religion, too, may play its part.

It is remarkable, to my mind, how much West Indian cricketers have achieved over the decades, thanks partly to the legacy of the likes of James, in one sphere, and the Constantines and Worrell, in another. The Constantines and Worrell took this quaint British game that has so much that is good in it and made it their own, playing it in their own inimitable style (or, rather, styles). As James famously has it, at the opening of *Beyond a Boundary*, "To establish his own identity, Caliban, after three centuries, must himself pioneer into regions Caesar never knew" (n.p.).

I mention here five roots of James's knowledge of cricket, five other areas that enabled him to surpass knowing "only" cricket: his appreciation of its social place; its aesthetics; its links to art and literature and their values; its moral place; and its roles (both as repressive symbol and as symbol of potential freedom) in politics. James himself reduces these to three categories— "social relations, politics and art" (7). He suggests that they had earlier come together under the aegis of Thomas Arnold and his then revolutionary idea of education, as initiated at Rugby School in the nineteenth century. These ideals were still current and practiced in James's own schooling at Queen's Royal College, Port of Spain. I will quote this passage more fully: "It is only within very recent years that Matthew Bondman and the cutting of Arthur Jones ceased to be merely isolated memories and fell into place as starting points of a connected pattern. They only appear as starting points. In reality they were the end, the last stones put into place, of a pyramid whose base constantly widened, until it embraced those aspects of social relations, politics and art laid bare when the veil of the temple has been rent in twain as ours has been" (7).

As James suggests, most accounts of social history ignore sports and its place in people's lives. He does indeed link sports into the rest of our lives, both socially and individually. Sport can be, as it has been in the Caribbean, a key locus for social pride, for cohesion. (Since independence, the only entities that embrace the entire collection of islands and countries that make up the West Indies have been the University of the West Indies and the West Indies cricket team.) Morally, aesthetically, and personally, James has shown us how sport (in particular, cricket) is an expression of deep human capacities and beliefs. In doing so, he challenges a long-standing form of intellectual snobbery. Often enough in the history of Western culture there has been a split, with mutual contempt, between the physicality of sport and the intellectual emphasis of the literati. Although Plato did at least design to write about sports (in *Republic*), famously placing the spectators at the top of his hierarchy of participants at the Olympic Games (reasonable, reflective souls), followed by the athletes (emotional souls), followed (in last position) by the vendors and others whose appetitive souls use these festivals to conduct business, he has left his legacy. Neville Cardus, a forerunner of James in recognizing the aesthetic qualities of cricket, placed it in relation to music, but even Cardus never introduced cricket into his writings on music while frequently using music to throw light on cricket. "He is," James continues, "a victim of that categorisation and specialisation, that division of the human personality, which is the greatest curse of our time" (195). James, as I suggested earlier, admirably opposes such alienation.

## Conclusion

*Beyond a Boundary* is one of the best books written on a sport—cricket—an activity and a tradition that has been rich enough to inspire some of the best of sports writing. Its author both describes and shows through his own thinking how broader ideas can enrich one's understanding and appreciation of something as apparently constricted as sports, or one particular sport. James shows how a whole universe of culture lies behind and sustains the evolution of cricket in the West Indies and elsewhere and how, in its turn, the game is able to bear myriad responsibilities with which it has been saddled historically, both in England and in the old empire. James manifests brilliantly his own conception of the richness and fluidity of knowledge. One has to go beyond a boundary to understand cricket and its complex place in society and in the mind.

## Notes

I thank Clem Seecharan. In 1986 I wrote a foreword to one edition of *Beyond a Boundary*. In 2008, at his invitation, I gave the fourth Sir Frank Worrell Lecture at the Caribbean Studies Centre, London Metropolitan University. Since then, Clem has been instrumental in getting me to read more about cricket in the Caribbean and was generous in his advice and comments with regard to this chapter.

1. Hereafter, page numbers in parentheses refer to this edition of *Beyond a Boundary*.
2. Both this and the following quotation are taken from an interview with James in the film *Beyond a Boundary*, directed by Mike Dibb and originally broadcast as part of the *Omnibus* series in 1975 [from 44:35 onwards].
3. For this discussion I am indebted to Jonathan Lear's study *A Case for Irony* (2011).
4. Rowan Williams, *Private Passions*, radio broadcast, BBC Radio 3, 22 June 2008.
5. Jennifer Johns, personal communication.

# 13 | My Journey to James: Cricket, Caribbean Identity, and Cricket Writing

HILARY MCD. BECKLES

**Barbados, Bombay, and Barnsley**

I took him at face value—that he was from India and a Sikh. He wore brightly colored turbans and exuded in his manner a matured dignity. We never exchanged names. He addressed me with the moniker "Barbados Beckles." To him I appeared an unlikely Barnsley Town recruit. The Yorkshire Cricket League was generally rough and tough, cultivated as humor-taunting racist expression, and was therefore no place for a black West Indian youth.

It was late in the '70s, and I, in my early twenties, was a doctoral student in historical science at the University of Hull on the coastal side of the rugged county. My Sikh interlocutor seemed an insensitive man, made of a material far from silky. He fit in, I thought, with the harsh physical landscape of the Barnsley region. His eyes were focused—fierce, in fact—and he was fanatical in support of the club he could not join. I was impressed by his persistence, sitting at a measured distance from the clubhouse—invariably alone but very vocal.

My mandate was to bowl fast and hit sixes. I was expected to win matches, entertain my home crowd, and be a good Caribbean sport. I felt at home, as I do in any cricketing place. But I understood that politically I was a good distance from home. As a student of Africa's deep historical past I knew how to discern the sound of a distant domestic drum. My identity was secured.

Once I saved a difficult match for "our" team. My Sikh comrade chased me across the carpark as I was leaving. He stuffed mixed notes totaling £10 into my pocket. My resistance was ignored. During the tea interval of the next match the following weekend, I learned that he had sent ten times the amount to the clubhouse for Martyn Moxon, my talented junior partner in the victory and a future Test cricketer. He was prone to such displays of belonging, mostly not subtle. He was a kind of native. I was just a commuting weekend cricketer.

On one occasion, he presented me with a clipping from an Indian newspaper. It was a story on Frank Worrell, written by C. L. R. James. Worrell, he said, was a messiah. His father, he proudly said, had patted him on the back during a match in Bombay. I was touched by the humanity of the narrative and thanked him with a promise to read and report on our next encounter.

I do not recall that the piece was possessed of any original thought. By then I was familiar with the literature, and more intrigued with the visitor. His mind seemed mangled as he sought to build a narrative in which his icon and guest could be linked. He needed, it seemed, a framework within which his presence and postures could make sense. We were outsiders within Geoff Boycott's Barnsley Cricket Club. Bombay and Barbados were playing a game deep in the coal mines of Yorkshire, beyond the boundary.

We are all judge and jury of our journeys. I had arrived in Britain's Birmingham from Britain's Barbados in 1969, a keen teen ready to join any team to continue with my obsession. I did not know why, but I could swing a ball, old or new, both ways and could clobber it farther than I could throw. The Atlantic crossing to the "West Midlands" was miserable in every sense. The truth is that I was deported by my grandparents to my parents who had been in "Brum" long enough to feel a sense of belonging—Enoch Powell's terrorism notwithstanding.

My test scores in school were weak. Week after week it became clearer to teachers and villagers that I cared more for bat and ball than books. Only my father, they said, could rein me in, cure the kid of his cricket craze. He was expected to reverse my priorities. My principal had failed. The hidden hope of the agenda, I unearthed, was that my dad would be aided by the cold, gray, grim world into which I was sent.

It was, for my grandmother, a divisive decision. She had to see, she said, the bigger picture. I had let the side down with small textbook scores. Recreation was no substitute for education. The poverty that imprisoned us in the small rural community was no joking matter. There was no escape other than through the portal of an airplane. It was good to be good at cricket, she said, but we could not eat it, and neither could it feed us.

Worrell was her hero, a personal prophet she had never seen but spoke about with a reverence otherwise reserved only for Jesus of Nazareth. She read James—not C. L. R. but King James, who branded her Bible. Reading was no prerequisite to comprehension. Her understanding of the game preceded James's and in some ways was more profound and present.

Worrell she loved because he had taken her team and our community up the lonely colonial mountain and shown them the Promised Land. Garry Sobers was her Joshua. James would not have known, but she was his village advocate in the campaign to secure Worrell's captaincy. From the sermons of their local preacher, the community came to understand the seriousness of cricket matters.

**A Tale of Two Deaths**

The Lord giveth and He taketh. How many times had I heard these words as she spoke during ceremonies of celebration for the life of a departed church member? But Frank Worrell was just forty-two. I was a mere twelve. For many members, it just did not add up. The burial was not massively attended but was a deeply moving ceremony. He passed while at the Mona Campus of the University of the West Indies (UWI) in Jamaica. The Jamaicans had rescued him from the neocolonial powers of his native Barbados after his retirement from cricket. There he served as director of sports and student services.

It was 1967. His body was flown to Barbados. Prime Minister Errol Barrow, his friend, would have it no other way. Jamaica loved and embraced him and had made a just claim. His homeland was a mere one-year-old as an independent nation-state. The site chosen for his interment was the newly created Cave Hill Campus of the university.

Campus and country were in their infancy. The plane carrying his body flew over Kensington Oval. A game was being played; Barbados versus Rest of the World XI—part of the national independence celebration. Worrell had publicly opposed the concept of the game. It was, he said, an expression of the desire of the part to be larger than the whole. The West Indies team, he insisted, should have been on the field.

I was there, in attendance at his funeral. James may have been. I do not know. I cannot ascertain. Granny, who sold fruit and vegetables in a Bridgetown market two miles away, had made special arrangements. She was determined to bid "her" man farewell. It was as official an event as can be imagined. The elite of the cricket world—and beyond—gathered around the grave. We were not invited; we had no ticket. We ignored their formality and found our way. We had nothing to say. He was "ours."

The politics of the proceedings were neither here nor there. Granny had business to attend. We crashed! A clearing was carved in the shrubbery beyond the barricades. From there we pierced the perimeter and gazed on priests and politicians, cricket legends and commercial titans, as the giant returned to the ground from whence he came.

There were floods of tears under the umbrellas on the inside. Bewilderment, confusion, and the feeling of being lost in space were the sentiments that filled faces within the fence. We, on the outside, scattered among the bushes, buried our fears and shed no tears. There was serenity and a sense of settlement. Granny's view was that folks inside the fence lacked faith. It led them to question the choice made above for the chosen. When one door is closed, another is opened.

I harbored, during many conversations, a fear of knowing the facts. Many moments came and went, and I could not ask James about his relationship to that moment. I had seen no record of his presence. Had we shared the moment? Maybe I feared most a possible refrain: "Let the dead bury the dead." I was uneasy with his cutting, sometimes acerbic wit and wisdom. It was born of an inability to grasp the range of his relations to things and people.

The "shrubbery stand" is no longer there. It is now the site of the Sir Frank Worrell student dormitory that surrounds his memorial. There he rests with Lady Worrell and their only child, Lana. To his west, a wicket's length away, rests Sir Clyde Walcott. Sir Everton, who turned ninety this year (2015), is aware of the precise location of his place—twenty-two yards to the north of Sir Clyde, and half the distance from the boundary of the Three Ws Oval. There, once again, they will form a holy trinity, restoring an unbroken partnership, forever.

Granny's innings came to an end in 1992. She "took a turn for the worst," the physician said. But not mentioned in prognosis was her contemplation of the expected loss of the Sir Frank Worrell Trophy. It was a constant in our last conversations. When it finally came in 1995, at Sabina Park, in the exact week of the third anniversary of her passing, the matter was settled in my mind.

James had died four years earlier. As I prepared Granny's eulogy, I realized how deeply affected I was by the departure of two souls who had shaped my senses. I spoke from the pulpit of her love of cricket and her awareness of the politics of social justice and moral outrage it had spawned across the Caribbean. I asked, How was it that a barely literate, barefooted peasant woman could read so complex a cultural practice with precision and stand up for the principles that produced cricketers who represented the game's finest values?

I took time to explain how she would respond with small, telling facial expressions to the word of John Arlott and Alan McGilvray. The crackling radio was her line to heaven. She wallowed in their descriptions and knew intuitively the script so well explored by James. The cathedral of the Pentecost was filled with well-wishers and cricket narratives. It had taken three deaths and two funerals to give me the needed focus. There and then I made the decision to honor my pledge to James; to begin my journey.

**Timing Is Everything!**

It was a bitterly cold, snowy, dark February night in Brixton, 1983, and C. L. R. was due to speak at 6 PM. It was expected that the audience would comprise West Indians, Africans, and a sprinkle of local leftists and Laborites. He was invited to speak on the mayhem that had befallen the people of Grenada as their revolution imploded into calypso carnage. Young boys with guns, and grown men without sense, had gutted their leader, Maurice Bishop, and his supporters.

Selfishly, I hoped that he would locate the Grenada content within the historical context of the Haitian and Cuban revolutions and speak to the tendency among extremists, within the heat of conflict, to abandon reason and resort to mindless destruction. He spoke instead about the democratizing impulse of cricket and the role of West Indians in raising that pulse. Grenada was a metaphor for foul play and the abandonment of rules: that was not cricket.

At moments to 6, we were fewer than six in the hall. Sixty at least were expected. A family member pleaded with the speaker, who was immaculately dressed, hat and scarf matching and jacket and trousers reminiscent of Sherlock Holmes. The request I thought was reasonable under the circumstances. "Uncle Cyril," could you please delay your presentation by thirty minutes to allow snow-trapped folks to gather in greater numbers?

The rejected plea was as predictable as the winter snow. Weather was no excuse in the clicking cogs of James's mind. Lack of respect for time by farmers and peasant folk, he said, was the root cause of the carnage in Grenada. They were in a horrid hurry to complete a revolution in a week. Here, in London, in the heart of industrial time, he said, audiences should be more respectful of the chime of time. He wanted no part of any pardoning.

He began precisely as he had intended. He spoke with passion to his few loyalists for forty minutes. At first he was indifferent to the arrival of a hundred folks who rushed from the subway into the hall, removing coats, scarves, and gloves. But irritated by the metallic rattling of chairs, he paused for two minutes to allow them to settle. Then, he calmly said, "In summary, therefore...." He stood erect after taking his hat from his crossed knee and, placing it on his head, prepared to leave.

I was part of the party that escorted him to the train. On the way, he spoke about the popes of Rome who had blessed slave ships and cursed the enslaved's quest for freedom. We did not discuss cricket. There was no need. The West Indies were doing what he had predicted and expected. They were sweeping all before them.

By this time, there was a global surge of interest in *Beyond a Boundary* and his other writings. Universities the world over were engaged in a discourse called "Jamesian studies." He was centrally invoked and celebrated in postmodern, postcommunist, postcolonial, postfeminist, and post–Black Power literary and academic circles. He was the giant guru of "post-studies," the man in the middle, batting like Worrell, fielding like Constantine, and bowling like Sonny Ramadhin and Alf Valentine. He wrote, he said, to illuminate, and he spoke to mobilize.

His mind was made up. Predictably, his opening strokes on politics in the Caribbean began with an exposition on Cicero. In Brixton, he moved quickly on to Jean-Paul Sartre on the Cuban experiment. I once asked him whether he was aware that young black audiences felt uncomfortable with his apparent obsession with Europe's philosophical traditions. "If they cannot appreciate this tradition," he said, "never will they know their own."

It was dismissive but intellectually instructive. He quibbled about the Soviets' copyright claim to the first workers' revolution. They were literate and yet refused to read his book on Toussaint Louverture's Haiti. For this, he said, they could not be excused. The enslaved of the Caribbean, he proclaimed, were the first workers of the world to seize power and create a state of the people. The West Indies cricket team, he said, had followed suit, overthrowing colonialism and living in a free state. Blacks in Brixton were exposed to neither Rome's rhetoric nor Haitian history and could be forgiven.

We met again in the same year at the University of Hull. He was there to receive an honorary degree. We were on common ground. An academic conference on slavery and abolition was organized around his visit. I watched in admiration as he filed in procession. I anticipated the opportunity during cocktails to discuss Viv Richards's dominance in comparative perspective.

Typically, the Hull event was skillfully historicized and placed within contexts that eluded all but the most historically savvy. The city had in its annals of parliamentary representatives one William Wilberforce, who, in two decades before and after 1800, had fought for the ending of his nation's transatlantic trade in enchained, enslaved African bodies. But he was no progressive and certainly in no way a radical.

But Hull for James was a site of memory in the monumental movement to end the crime against humanity. The university had sought to live up to aspects of this legacy. His invitation to speak and his honoring were expressions of this commitment. A few years earlier the university had invited another distinguished West Indian to be its vice-chancellor. Sir Roy Marshall, a white Barbadian, had distinguished himself as a professor of law at the University of Sheffield and was recognized as a race relations lawyer without equal.

James paid brief tribute to Sir Roy and proceeded to speak about the traditions of Yorkshire cricket and their similarities with those of the Caribbean. They were bred in the same stable. The "whites rule" of Barbados, before the age of Worrell, found its family in Yorkshire's refusal to embrace its own black folks. I told him I had shared the new ball with Neil Mallender for Hull City and guided Moxon at Barnsley, and that the respect they enjoyed in the county as young players was for me a source of pride.

James was a keen listener. His interest was not in my story but in the deductions I had made from the experience. Approvingly he said, "Well, here it is young man. You are Barbadian; you play the game; and you are a student of history. Write! It's your duty to write!" He could do that kind of thing to a person.

I was not the only one. He had instructed Michael Manley many years before to take a sabbatical, put aside party politics, and write about cricket. When I met Michael, and we became good friends, I discovered he was still trapped in admiration for James. For ten years, poor chap, he labored on his *A History of West Indies Cricket* (1988) and feared publishing it while James was alive.

In 1984, I transferred from the Mona (Jamaica) Campus of the UWI to the Cave Hill (Barbados) Campus. I rejoiced in the reconnection to Granny's stories from the inner world of cricket. By this time, she seemed agitated by the concept of "class" as it relates to players. Those without grace and grit, technique and tenacity—that is, "class"—were dismissed; those with, she celebrated. Kanhai, whom she loved for his elegance, was removed from the category. Far too often, she said, he had surrendered his "hand" in the 90s. Hunte, whom she knew as a village boy, was too flashy to fit. She was looking for tenacity and stamina—hence, her celebration of Wes Hall, Sonny Ramadhin, Garry Sobers, and Lance Gibbs.

It seemed so classically Jamesian. A few years later, I would hear him apply Granny's thesis to Gordon Greenidge and Desmond Haynes and Vivian Richards and Andy Roberts. Endurance through adaptation was his proof of class, a characteristic born to a player that defined and determined his destiny.

I had gone home to Granny and, critically, to the Cave Hill Campus, where a generation ago she had taken me to say goodbye. Be true to your soul, says the African sage. Within a short time, I took the first step and established within the History Department an annual Frank Worrell Memorial Lecture. Manley, now with the office of prime minister behind him, presented the inaugural to an audience of six hundred—ten times the number that had eluded C. L. R. in London two decades earlier. He opened with C. L. R.'s description of Worrell's 261 against England at Trent Bridge in 1950 and ended with this classic paragraph from *Beyond a Boundary*:

> What do they know of cricket who only cricket know? West Indians crowding to Tests bring with them the whole past history and future hopes of the islands. English people, for example, have a conception of themselves breathed from birth. Drake and mighty Nelson, Shakespeare, Waterloo, the Charge of the Light Brigade, the few who did so much for so many, the success of parliamentary democracy, those and such as those constitute a national tradition.... We of the West Indies have none at all, none that we know of. To such people the three Ws, Ram and Val, wrecking English batting, helped to fill a huge gap in their consciousness and in their needs. (James 2013 [1963]: 233)[1]

The house came down when he was done.

Manley's performance was more than magisterial. It was lyrical and poetic. Inspired by his brilliant treatment of James, I moved to the second initiative: the establishment of the C. L. R. James Cricket Research Centre. This facility now has the finest library dedicated to cricket in the West Indies, comprising an archive of manuscripts and audiovisual materials. It is the cornerstone of what serves as a source to sustain the Jamesian legacy.

The time had come to bring cricket studies fully into the faculty's curriculum. A final year undergraduate course, "The History of West Indies Cricket since 1800," came into being to provide an exciting intellectual focus for students with a discursive capacity and conceptual imagination. Special presentations from legends such as Sir Everton Weekes, Sir Garry Sobers, Wes Hall, Allan Rae, Michael Holding, and a dozen others provided students with a little piece of heaven in "History."

We pressed on and offered a master's degree in cricket studies whose pedagogy was based on the literary archive of James and his critics. It was the first university program of its kind anywhere in the world. We could think of no better way to scientifically scrutinize James's work and to expose students and community to his "text." Each year, hundreds of people visit the James Centre—cricketers, journalists, students, and pundits in search of statistical certainty to reinforce their quarrels in rum shops.

**The Jewel in the Crown**

The telephone rang, annoyingly. It was not yet 10 in the morning. I had arrived in London at dawn from Barbados. Every fiber in my shattered frame called out to ignore the madness and to return to the dream disturbed. The year 2006 was fast approaching; Christmas and flashing lights were penetrating the curtains. Twice I reached out and retreated. Persistence won the contest. George Lamming, the brilliant Barbadian novelist, friend, and mentee of C. L. R., was on the line.

I sat up, involuntarily. He spoke in his well-known authoritarian tone. Admiration had morphed into respect. "Listen here, Hilary," he said, "the original manuscript of C. L. R.'s *Beyond a Boundary* goes on auction in the city this morning at 10. You ought to go there and secure the manuscript for the University of the West Indies and the people of the Caribbean. Let me know how you get on." I took the details, made a few phone calls.

The starting bid was expected to be deep into the thousands of pounds. I was taken out of the market before I got out of bed. This is not cricket, I thought. I could hear the skeptics: "Where on earth did the UWI get that kind of money for this kind of thing!" I made contact with the "owner" of the object. He seemed a very gentle, kind, and cultured man. South African, I surmised; Jewish, I later gathered. I pleaded for a special dispensation, beyond the market.

The manuscript had been in his possession, as a comrade of James, for decades. It worked as a fundraiser in the service of the Anti-Apartheid Movement and the African National Congress. What an extraordinary Caribbean contribution, I thought, serving sweetly in tandem with Cuban soldiers, Marley's music, and Manley's leadership of the sports boycott movement. How romantic, it seemed, that its time had come to be decommissioned; to be put out to archive, there to engage and agitate generations of students and teachers, writers, researchers, and raconteurs.

I spoke; he listened:

> Sir, for over two decades the University of the West Indies at Cave Hill has done all within its power to sustain the work and legacies of C. L. R., and Sir Frank, the hero he had re-created. Not only was the last draft of the manuscript prepared in Barbados, but it's the manifesto of the movement for Worrell whose mortal remains reside on my campus. We have a C. L. R. James Cricket Research Centre, which hosts the annual Sir Frank Lecture and makes available to students of cricket studies, and the public, all his published materials. We are the professional custodians of West Indies cricket materials, and the official record keepers of West Indies cricket organization. This manuscript, Sir, is the crown within the jewels and properly belongs with us, the librarians of C. L. R.'s legacy. Sir, we urge your support!

Within three weeks the prized manuscripts were lodged at the university. George Lamming was pleased. So, too, I believe, were C. L. R. and Sir Frank.

**A Cricket Writer Is Manufactured**

I did not readily succumb to C. L. R.'s challenge. Such things take time. Many circumstances have to align as the moment is manufactured. Timing is everything. Manley, while writing his magisterial *A History of West Indies Cricket*, tried to trigger my finger. I had told him about my discussion with C. L. R. With dry, demure humor he uttered the aside that it would take a brave soul to deny C. L. R. a request. He was right. I had been haunted, and so was he.

"Beyond James" would be my theme. I would imagine his conceptual trajectory and bring his work into the twenty-first century. I would answer two questions: what of the representation of cricket culture in the post-nationalist era of West Indian society, and how has the growing political and social disillusionment with the nation-building agenda, by the majority working-class communities, affected their commitment and communion with cricket? Effectively my project was to creative a discursive device to enable the propulsion of James's work into an even greater future relevance—into the age of globalization.

From the colonial to the nationalist era, and into this global time, West Indians have made their largest single political and economic investment in cricket. Elite and grassroots communities continue to expect high returns. Society expects, in addition to performance excellence, a cultural engagement that enhances the social popularity of the game, as well as its iconic status within popular culture.

James had predicted and witnessed the rise of the magnificent edifice of performance and personification that was the West Indies cricket team in the decade before his death in 1988. In the decade after, it came crashing down as the doors to the twenty-first century opened. The West Indian Test team is now ranked as the weakest traditional team in the international arena. The players have no recognizable attachment to any political or philosophical set of ideas or movement. They are heckled rather than hailed around the world as amateurish professionals, unable to attract a commercially viable gate and without a social agenda beyond the market.

For media experts and academics alike, this descent from awesomeness to awfulness is considered one of the most dramatic dislocations in the modern history of sports. Brian Lara, fellow Trinidadian, had been captain of the team for three terms between 1998 and 2006. Critics and supporters alike were quick in drawing the compelling conclusion that his leadership and legacy negatively affected the fortunes of West Indies cricket and laid the volcanic foundations for the invention of Christopher Gayle as his inevitable ideological successor.

No generation of West Indian cricket stars since James started his campaign for Worrell's leadership in 1957 has had as divisive an impact on the loyalty and imagination of West Indians as that of Lara and Gayle. The failure of their teams to compensate for the spreading sense of despair in socioeconomic development led to an intensely critical perception of both as politically unfit for the role of captain.

The hard core of Caribbean cricket support insists that the team has an important political role "beyond the boundary," although the social majority believes it has been hijacked by a seemingly uncaring cohort of professionals, players without social concerns, who have stripped the legacy of its high cultural meaning. Fans and fraternity are not prepared to renegotiate cricket's role along the rocky road the nation-building project has to travel.

How would James have theorized, for example, Gayle's challenges with the West Indies Cricket Board and the clash with public opinion that insist cricket stars must play in their hearts for country rather than cash? Undoubtedly, he would have seen this development as indicative of the general youth revolt against the oppressiveness of post-nationalist Caribbean society. Relationships between "star" and state have soured, are unhealthy, and are not believed to be mutually supportive.

Would James have seen independent Caribbean islands as failed states? Lara is considered the "father" of the post-nationalist approach to leadership that is in galloping globalization and expressed in Michael Jackson's style-street culture of youth in revolt and the glitter in "Thriller." If Lara is hailed the circus master, Gayle in this tale represents the logical consequence and ultimate fulfilment of "Prince" Lara's leadership style. He commanded discipline from his boys and set for them a standard of mental application consistent with the image of the "supercool" dude who feels no pain and sheds no tears for the Test game his predecessors had mastered and improved on for the glory of the sporting world.

The ability of Gayle to command the loyalty of players from across the region attests to the proliferation and regional acceptance of Jamaican-style street culture—its music, dance, macho mentality, and gender-relationship structure. While there are still positive values for youth development in aspects of this popular culture, its inability to promote the learning systems necessary for international competitive standards suggests its inadequacy as a pillar on which West Indian cricket can rise. The on-field performance records of Lara and Gayle constitute undoubted monuments to greatness in West Indies cricket. But the selection of Darren Sammy as captain, a player with relatively modest performance achievements and an enormous West Indian heart, was the official declaration of a conceptual break with the Lara-Gayle leadership and its legacy. The Caribbean world heard the West Indies Cricket Board loud and clear that a leader within and beyond the boundary was required, not just a captain.

Related to cricketers' rejection of traditional political idealism is their overt, aggressive embrace of the global market economy of cricket. "Show me the green" became the mantra of the team. Stars consider the concept of the cricket hero as a moral and political standard-bearer outdated and, quite frankly, inimical to their interests. The idea of playing for one's country as an ultimate status that drives players' motivation became obsolete in the mass mentality that sees the nation as an obstacle.

Players drawn from poor families and communities that know no other experience but full unemployment, police brutality, drug trading, and endemic violence have asked the question, "What has my country done for me"? In so doing, they speak to the political concept of "failed nations" that dominates social-science discourse on postcolonial developing countries. For them, the benefits of nationhood did not pour in, or trickle down, to their households. Fiscal and monetary policies have left them ravished by unfettered market forces. Corporate elites defined them as "unemployable," and middle class–led political parties consider them a "social problem."

How, then, would James have seen these developments? Remember how he described the relations between the anticolonial events of the 1950s and the rise of West Indian cricket as a democratizing force. He wrote in *Beyond a Boundary*, "Once in a blue moon, that is, once in a lifetime, a writer is handed on a plate a gift from heaven. I was handed mine in 1958" (225). It was his defining moment as a scribe of Caribbean civilization.

The issue to which James referred was the relations between West Indies cricket and the rise of the West Indies Federation. "The intimate connections between cricket and West Indian social and political life," he insisted, "were established so that all except the wilfully perverse could see" (225). For him, the campaign for Worrell as captain was a metaphor for the rise of democracy in a dying colonialism. *Beyond a Boundary*, then, was the political manifesto of an ascendant nationalism that would launch West Indians on the world stage as equal citizens.

### Sequel from a Student

The issues before the post–Jamesian West Indian world were crying out for articulation—the sequel. Systemic cricket decline and long-term socioeconomic recession are obviously linked in an umbilical fashion. The region continues to experience the externally driven and designed structural adjustment of economies, widespread youth disillusionment, weakening of functional regionalism, and growing political insularity. Citizens with reduced economic gains and a cricket team reeling in pain would have presented James with a second gift from heaven.

My intervention dealt with these issues. It took the form of a two-volume work: *The Development of West Indies Cricket, Volume One: The Age of Nationalism* (1999a) and *The Development of West Indies Cricket, Volume Two: The Age of Globalization* (1999b). It was the fulfillment of a promise made to both

C. L. R. and Michael Manley. It was written to bring closure to a conversation and intended to extend the reach of their thoughts beyond their years. It was an ambitious project, imagined in part in the spiritual realm. It was at once a tribute and a thanksgiving. C. L. R., from far beyond, still shapes the debate of cricket, culture, consciousness, and character beyond the boundary.

Finally, in 2013 the Cave Hill Campus hosted an international conference of cricket writers and academics under the theme "Beyond C. L. R. James." I was honored to have been invited by John Nauright and Alan Cobley, conference organizers, to give opening remarks and to speak specifically to my social and academic relations to James (see Nauright, Cobley, and Wiggins 2014). This is a part of the story told. After C. L. R. James, then what? I asked. There remains much to be said and written.

**Note**

1. Hereafter, page numbers in parentheses refer to this edition of *Beyond a Boundary*.

# 14 | Confronting Imperial Boundaries
SELMA JAMES

*Beyond a Boundary* was published as the 1963 cricket season opened. Reviews, though not unfavorable, gave no hint that the book was in any way special. We had to wait until January 1964 and *Wisden Cricketers' Almanac* for a deeper appreciation. John Arlott (1964: 993), cricket's most distinguished (and antiracist) broadcaster and commentator, wrote that

> 1963 has been marked by the publication of a cricket book so outstanding as to compel any reviewer to check his adjectives several times before he describes it and, since he is likely to be dealing in superlatives, to measure them carefully to avoid over-praise—which this book does not need. It is *Beyond a Boundary*.... [I]n the opinion of this reviewer, it is the finest book written about the game of cricket.... There may be a better book about any sport ... if so, the present reviewer has not seen it.

Years later, in *A Century of Wisden*, a compilation made up of "An Extract from Every Edition 1900–1999," Arlott's review, with its extraordinary claims, was the extract chosen from 1964, confirming the book's classic status.

It is hard to know from Arlott's review that *Beyond a Boundary* could not at first find a publisher. Those who published books on sports rejected it for sports fans; other publishers doubted that the general reading public would buy a book on cricket. How much these rejections had to do with refusal to consider a book by a West Indian who had the audacity to redefine cricket and its boundaries we will never know. We wondered at the time. It is worth recalling that cricket more than half a century ago was far more elitist on grounds of race as well as class (as we will see).

In desperation, C. L. R. asked our friend George Lamming for help. Hutchinson had not long before published Lamming's *In the Castle of My*

*Skin* (1953), a great novel. Lamming used its *succès d'estime* to introduce this other Caribbean manuscript to Robert Lusty, Hutchinson's chair and managing director. To our relief, they accepted the manuscript. The title on the contract: *Who Only Cricket Know*.

Years later, we learned that it was also Lamming who had renamed the book—almost. Hutchinson announced it was to be *Beyond the Boundary*, and we rejoiced. But then they changed "the" to "a" for no reason we could agree with. "The" challenges boundaries generally, not only those belonging to cricket.

It was a book C. L. R. had to write. Devoted to the game since a child, he had studied over the decades the batting and bowling statistics, as well as cricket's literature. He was convinced he understood the game in ways many other commentators did not. He thought commentators often did not give a precise enough account of the play, favoring instead impressionistic flights of linguistic fancy. This aggravated him. He complained that similar imprecision had invaded literary criticism and much else.[1]

C. L. R. had the contradictory advantage of being an outsider—a colonial—who was educated inside. He saw the game not only as it was played but also as it was lived. In his first period in England, he lived with Learie and Norma Constantine in "Red Nelson" in the north of England. Learie was playing in the Lancashire League, and this life and the cricket it produced are described in the book. (For an account of this period of James's life, see Høgsbjerg 2014.)

But the field of play that shaped him was the West Indies—a colonial society stratified by class and race. It offered few routes out of poverty and even fewer out of obscurity, even for the most talented in any direction. His unblinking description of the shades of status among the cricket clubs of his youth is reminiscent of the race hierarchy in prerevolutionary Haiti, described in *The Black Jacobins* (1938), and it cuts like glass here, too.

Because he was clever and was known early as a journalist and sportsman, C. L. R. was invited to join the clubs of both the lighter- and the darker-skinned cricketers.[2] He confesses to regret having chosen the former: "So it was that I became one of those dark men whose 'surest sign of . . . having arrived is the fact that he keeps company with people lighter in complexion than himself.' My decision cost me a great deal . . . by cutting myself off from the popular side, [I] delayed my political development for years" (James 2013 [1963]: 53).[3] It was the "popular side" in society generally with whom he was to spend most of the rest of his life.

Establishing the interconnection between cricket and divisions of race and class through his personal history, he paved the way for drawing out other connections. He could not claim cricket as an art without defining art, just as the social history of sports must lead to the ancient Greeks, who invented and organized the first Olympic Games. Three chapters that are devoted to reevaluating the towering figure of W. G. Grace challenge, among much else, the respected liberal historians who never mention Grace, although the public had chosen this enormously talented cricketer as their hero.[4]

James's pursuit of the implications of each subject is far from academia's fragmentation of reality, which is pervasive nowadays and results in or from gross inaccuracy, prejudice, and worse. How much can be hidden by fragmentation? How much is misunderstood? What do we know of cricket, or anything, if it is severed from every other aspect of our life and struggle? What, indeed.

| | | | |

*Beyond a Boundary* was a long time coming. It had originally been planned much earlier and was nearly completed in 1958 before being finished in 1962. It was, all the same, right on time for the 1960s. This was the decade when massive movements challenged almost every authority, prejudice, and relationship and broke through cordons, fences, and barriers of many kinds. It was a decade that saw the assertion of many previously ignored rights and needs, even transforming musical taste—that same year the Beatles rose to international stardom. People had greater expectations and more open minds and were more ready to be active on their own behalf than they had been for years.

Since the 1940s, C. L. R., a Marxist who saw history as a process involving everyone from the bottom up had been trying to figure out how to address the power relation between working-class people and intellectuals, especially within the anticapitalist movement to which he was committed. He was convinced that those of us who were considered politically backward were better equipped to change the world than the formally educated. They knew far more than they were credited with and were at least as capable of understanding anything once it was made accessible. For him, appreciating this and acting on it was what being a Marxist was all about. (*Notes on Dialectics* [1980 (1948)] was C. L. R.'s attempt to make the dialectical materialism of Hegel available to those who had no training in philosophy. It is soon to be republished after years of out of print. C. L. R. considered it his finest work.)

Living in the United States, he initiated a bold experiment: creating a political organization that was based on the experience, insights, and instincts of grassroots members and their networks rather than on those of formally educated people who invariably assume leadership.[5] Members were invited to write and speak publicly. They were also asked to read and comment on the political writing of intellectuals, including C. L. R. himself. Working to understand the implications of people's comments and questions was political training for both intellectuals *and* workers, and the final edit was much more likely to be accessible to a wider audience and likely to be a better and more effective piece. *Mariners, Renegades and Castaways* (1985 [1953]), C. L. R.'s analysis of Herman Melville's *Moby-Dick*, was rewritten through this process.[6]

Thus, the man who wrote *Beyond a Boundary*, a great teacher, had the habit of making information and sophisticated concepts accessible to a non-academic audience. No wonder the book's unfamiliar subjects and connections have proved themselves to be accessible to a remarkably wide variety of readers.

Addressing the non-specialist, often "uneducated" but interested audience was a practice that was being adopted by others in that same period. One commentator, for example, has noted that the literary critic Frank Kermode (1919–2010) "wrote in the introduction to [his book *Continuities*, published in 1968] that any literary journalism that was able to satisfy non-specialist interests 'without loss of intellectual integrity' was 'more demanding than most of what passes for scholarship.' He was to continue to think this, and to write wonderfully well in this form."[7] Here, too, the implication is that assuming the nonspecialist as part of the audience increases the quality of the work.

Motown, the famous 1960s music label from Detroit, worked out a musical form that would sell Black music to a White audience. They called this "crossover" and thus named the social process of moving beyond the boundaries that confine us to our own sector. Motown music had its own validity, although some of the original quality was bypassed. Can the "crossover" process happen for a mass audience maintaining or even raising rather than lowering the quality of the work?

Again in 1963, as we waited for the arrival of *Beyond a Boundary* from the printer, the following massive class crossover was reported in the press. On 20 January, *The Sunday Times* announced that "the new young gladiators of BBC Television [had just] made their entry... to take over key positions." They were trained and led by Grace Wyndham Goldie, who spelled out a new job description for the producers of TV programs: "I have a great belief in the intelligence of the audience. When a producer fails with a programme and says it was because it was over the heads of the audience, I tell him it is he who has failed.... There is a confusion that the informed are mature and the uninformed are immature. Often it is quite the opposite. I like to think our audiences are mature people who want to be informed."[8]

This anti-elitism that gainfully employs the educated to make accessible what they know to the rest of us—never leveling down or talking down and certainly not dumbing down—produced the most remarkable television. The most memorable was the brilliant and irreverent *That Was the Week That Was*, still talked about, although most of the tapes have been mysteriously wiped. A satirical look at the week's news, it was enormously popular with everyone but the government.

| | | | |

When the manuscript was nearly complete, C. L. R. was invited to return to Trinidad after twenty-six years away. He worked with others for four years to bring the English-speaking Caribbean together in a federation so that the coming independence would be stronger and based on popular power. Independence of a sort came, but the federation failed. What stayed federated was the cricket team. No one dared suggest otherwise.

But this great cricketing nation, with a primarily Afro- and Indo-Caribbean population, had always been captained by a white man, and many seethed with resentment. This had to change. Moreover, there was a cricket precedent for moving such elitism aside.

In England in the 1950s, the game was still divided by class, between professionals (the players) and amateurs (the gentlemen). "Gentlemen v. Players" was an annual fixture. As late as 1958, the Marylebone Cricket Club (MCC), cricket's international governing body, affirmed its "wish to preserve in first-class cricket the leadership [read, captaincy] and general approach to the game internationally associated with the Amateur player."

Len Hutton, a professional whom many believed to be the finest batsman in England and maybe in the world at that time, was part of the England team of 1953 that toured Australia. He was called to substitute as captain and did so well that he brought home the Ashes.[9] There was no avoiding it: Hutton had to be made the first professional to captain England. (Nevertheless, the distinction between gentlemen and players was not abolished until 1962.)

C. L. R. told this story (among many others) to my son (Sam Weinstein, referred to in *Beyond a Boundary* as "the son of the house"), who became his cricket mate from when he was six. They would relish the way MCC, once it had been well and truly beaten, had gone to meet Hutton on his return at Southampton dock with an MCC tie—his passport to membership of the "Kremlin of cricket," as one West Indian was heard to call it. The overthrow of elite captaincy had happened in England. It could happen again, in the West Indies.

Everyone knew who the captain of the West Indies team should be. Frank Worrell was a great batsman, a great cricketing mind, an extraordinary human being, a natural leader. But Worrell, though middle-class, was Black. C. L. R. seized the time. He set out to lift the lower orders to their rightful place, at least within the boundary of Caribbean cricket. He opened the campaign to make Worrell captain. Now editor of *The Nation*, the newspaper of Trinidad's nationalist party, he had the support of a mass anticolonial movement. Every issue had articles, front-page editorials, cricket facts. The penultimate chapter of *Beyond a Boundary* describes something of the campaign. It also analyzes the cause of a bottle-throwing incident during the Test series of 1960; this was provoked by "local anti-nationalist people [who] were doing their best to help the Englishmen defeat and disgrace the local players" (227). The crowd's furious response strengthened the Worrell campaign. Some of these "anti-nationalist people" thought challenging the racism that had always dominated cricket would lead to "communism."

We won, of course, and the day after Worrell was declared captain, Prime Minister Eric Williams opened his party's annual conference with an address that aimed to placate the "anticommunists" who were attacking C. L. R. He said, "If C. L. R. James took it upon his individual self to wage a campaign for Worrell as Captain of the West Indies team . . ." That was all I heard. Williams's words were drowned in a roar of applause and jubilation; a small but significant piece of the imperial past had crumbled. C. L. R. saw and heard the approbation as we sat at the back of the hall. But he was not invited to the front.[10]

Like Sir Len Hutton, Worrell (who was also knighted) captained in Australia. The West Indies played such cricket and were such a team in a remarkable series, which included the famous "tied Test," that when they left for home, many thousands of Aussies came into the streets to wish them a genuinely fond farewell.

| | | | |

Soon after *Beyond a Boundary* appeared, despite calls to "keep politics out of sports," the antiapartheid boycott of South Africa swept across every sport and every continent. In 1967, Muhammad Ali refused to be drafted into the US Army for the Vietnam War, although the price was giving up his brilliant boxing career, widely acknowledged as "the greatest." Ali had demanded an answer to the question, "Why should they ask me to put on a uniform and go ten thousand miles from home and drop bombs and bullets on brown people in Vietnam while so-called Negro people in Louisville are treated like dogs and denied simple human rights?" (Marqusee 2005: 214). A year later, in 1968, a Black Power salute from the Olympic podium in Mexico City shook the world. Nowadays, political campaigns in sports (including against sexism) hardly startle. Alas, what sportspeople of color have to contend with on the playing field is still often disconnected from injustice a few steps beyond sporting boundaries—from stop and search and racial profiling to benefit cuts to disabled people camouflaged with hard-won Paralympics praise. The Palestinians, as part of their resistance to Israeli occupation and to defend their footballers who "have been shot, beaten, bombed, and incarcerated along with their fellow citizens," have been pressing FIFA to expel Israel from international soccer.[11]

*Beyond a Boundary* has opened the way for more wide-ranging sports journalism. It also inspired Joseph O'Neill to write the best-selling novel *Netherland*, dissecting American society after 9/11 using the cricket community brought by Caribbean immigrants to New York. The Indian film *Lagaan* (2001), about a cricket match, is a wonderful example of the beauty and truth that can emanate from a judicious and artistic mix of cricket, class struggle, and anti-imperialism. Eduardo Galeano's splendid book on football, *Soccer in Sun and Shadow*, also places every World Cup in its contemporary political and historical context.

My favorite chapter of *Beyond a Boundary* (part of which I typed many times—no computers then to input corrections in successive drafts) has always been "The Most Unkindest Cut." It reminds us that C. L. R. was also a novelist. It is the tragic story of Wilton St. Hill, who deserved to be chosen for a side that toured England but was left out; a story, told with great compassion, of one of many lives shattered by transparent but inescapable injustice.

As one would expect, Caribbean people were delighted that one of theirs had told the English about the game that used to be exclusively theirs but that others—once called "lesser breeds without the Law" (Kipling 1897: 13)—had adopted and adapted as their own. But the book goes well beyond that boundary as all kinds of people love it—in particular, grassroots people, who are gratified to see their passions and preoccupations respected, explored, and celebrated.

—Selma James, Georgetown, Guyana, 19 May 2016

**Notes**

1. It was F. R. Leavis's critical focus on the text that C. L. R. admired and trusted, despite Leavis's snobbish narrow-mindedness.
2. The East Indian population of Trinidad was not visible in the cricket hierarchy of race and class at that time. The first East Indian cricketer who was part of the West Indies team was the Trinidadian Sonny Ramadhin, who, together with the Jamaican Alf Valentine, demolished the English batting on the tour of England of 1950. The first indigenous player we know of, the Dominican Adam Sanford, emerged with the West Indies team in 2002.
3. Hereafter, page numbers in parentheses refer to this edition of *Beyond a Boundary*.
4. A recent book by Richard Tomlinson, *Amazing Grace: The Man Who Was W. G.* (2015), shows how the establishment had to pay Grace because he was so popular but used this imperative to retain the class division in cricket. *Beyond a Boundary* may well have helped inspire such recent reexaminations of Grace.
5. For a description of this aspect of the Johnson-Forest Tendency, as this organization was called, see Selma James 2012.
6. *Moby-Dick* had particular relevance to a working-class audience. It deals with the relation between the crew and their "monomaniac commander" who leads them to the bottom of the ocean. *Mariners, Renegades and Castaways* aimed to reach readers who may never have read *Moby-Dick*, let alone a critique of it; *Mariners, Renegades and Castaways* was sold in factories for $1 as part of C. L. R.'s campaign to prevent his deportation from the United States during the McCarthy period.
7. John Mullan, "Frank Kermode," *The Guardian*, 18 August 2010, 32.
8. I was told by one of her producers on the flagship daily *Today* program that Grace Wyndham Goldie was a Tory. Irrelevant. More to the point, she had worked for the Workers Education Association giving classes to miners on the medium of television. This must have helped shape her respect for the popular audience.
9. The Ashes is a Test cricket series played between England and Australia, usually biennially. Following Australia's defeat of England in 1882, a mock obituary in *The Sporting Times* announced the death and subsequent cremation of English cricket. Subsequent meetings between the teams have thus been represented as a battle for ownership of these original "ashes."
10. The full passage reads, "If C. L. R. James took it upon his individual self to wage a campaign for Worrell as captain of the West Indies team and in so doing to give expression not only to the needs of the game but also to the sentiments of the people,

we know as well as he that it is the *Nation* and the [People's National Movement] to whom the people will give the praise" (241; see also James 1962). Here Williams tried to undermine C. L. R. while taking credit for what he had achieved. This was the first salvo of a political attack aimed at distancing himself from C. L. R., his once close ally. The defining issue was the US base at Chaguaramas, which the independence movement wanted back. Unknown to C. L. R., Williams had made a deal with the United States, details of which began to emerge later that same day.

11. "We Call on FIFA to Suspend the Israel Football Association," *The Guardian*, 15 May 2015.

APPENDIX | What Do They Know of England?

C. L. R. JAMES

*This appendix provides the text of the concluding chapter of* Beyond a Boundary *as it appears in the first version of the manuscript, from 1958, written before James moved to Trinidad in April of that year. It was identified among the C. L. R. James* Beyond a Boundary *papers by Christian Høgsbjerg and was transcribed by him. It is reproduced here with the kind permission of the C. L. R. James Estate. The dedication of this version of the manuscript was, "For W. G. Grace / Still confined to the footnotes of history / And Learie Constantine / More fortunate in his place and time." The original draft typescripts of* Beyond a Boundary *were donated by James to an appeal to raise money for the Anti-Apartheid Movement (Anne Darnborough, Manuscript Exhibition Appeal Committee, C. L. R. James, letter, 18 September 1968, C. L. R. James Collection, Alma Jordan Library, University of the West Indies, St. Augustine, Trinidad, box 10, folder 241). Others who contributed to the appeal included George Lamming (who donated the typescript of* Pleasures of Exile*), Basil Davidson (who donated the typescript of* Black Mother*), Chinua Achebe, Ilya Ehrenburg, David Mercer, Iris Murdoch, Conor Cruise O'Brien, Bertrand Russell, Jean-Paul Sartre, and Wole Soyinka. The* Beyond a Boundary *typescript was ultimately purchased for the University of the West Indies (see the account of this event in chapter 13 in this volume), where it is anticipated that it will be made available for consultation by scholars and researchers.*

In Trinidad in 1955 [Learie] Constantine was doing his job as a welfare officer. There was a political upheaval in the island, with incredible rapidity a new party, the People's National Movement, nationalist and progressive, was organised. Constantine had never been a practising politician. But the political organisation of the party did not have to think twice. They called on him to be the chairman of the new party and he agreed. In the 1956 elections, the party swept to power and Constantine is now a Minister. That is not all. Nationalist parties in colonial countries, and particularly the leaders are almost all coloured—the whites have, as a general rule, opposed the movement for self-government and independence too long to find a place among those who have fought and are fighting for it. Trinidad has broken new ground. Victor Stollmeyer (brother of Jeffrey) who had 96 at the Oval Test in 1939, joined the P.N.M. and declared his adherence in the first number of the party paper. The party nominated as an additional member of the Legislative Council Cyril Merry, the 1933 Test player. When he is away Victor serves in his place. They have their qualities. Victor is a successful lawyer. Cyril is a member of one of the biggest firms in the island. Yet if they have learnt confidence in the people and the people have learnt confidence in them, both learnt it not least on the cricket field. The conjunction is an event of far-reaching importance for these islands. Another former warrior, Clifford Roach, has been elected on the party ticket as a councillor for the municipality of Port of Spain. In addition to its other virtues, the P.N.M. can challenge and defeat any other political party in the world in a match of ex-Test cricketers. The political leader, Dr. Eric Williams, a Corinthian, who if he had been at Oxford in 1956 instead of 1936, would certainly have got his blue. I doubt if in any other part of the world where cricket is played Test cricketers have ever played so striking a role in politics. If this is seen as an accident, then I have written in vain.

The West Indian team in England in 1957 did not fulfil the hoped-for role. Nevertheless, it achieved far more than that. The thousands of West Indians who have come to England since 1950 brought to Lord's, the Oval, to Edgbaston new, disturbing emotions. The English people for years have been subjected to a constant barrage of colonial requests, demands, defiances, conciliations, reconciliations, new demands unending. The emigrant West Indian brought all this out of newspapers, radio and television into life. March had seen the highly publicised independence of Ghana. In July the first African Prime Minister attended for the first time a Prime Ministers conference. The West Indians in the crowd wanted badly to win, even more than when they were at home. Victory now would get many things right. The English crowd also wanted to win, more than ever before. England had been overwhelmed in 1950 and had fought its way to international supremacy. Defeat by the West Indians now would be painful.

In dress, in voice, in demeanour, the West Indians remained completely West Indian. Many English people did not know what to make of them in their thousands. You could see in the Press and at public and private gatherings a nervous anxiety that the West Indian ebullience should not be misunderstood or be taken awry. The old relations with coloured colonials were going: what should the new ones be? They were being established there around the ropes. The men on the field were the focus of those who were watching and those who were not. All the English people I meet in the normal course of living, cricketers or not, make it their business to talk to me about the West Indian cricketers in a way they had not talked about any other. They wanted England to win, but did not wish the West Indians to experience the chagrin of defeat.

I followed the West Indian team from ground to ground and sat in the crowd and talked to people. All asked about Constantine. I made a point of saying that he was now Chairman of the political party in power and a minister. They shook their heads reflectively. Some asked point-blank what many were thinking: where did I think it would all end? Would the West Indians want to break away from the Old Country? Where the answer would help and not hurt, my reply was more or less this: most West Indians I know wish to govern themselves. I don't know nor have I ever heard of any who want to break away; that in any case depended upon political considerations which are quite unpredictable in the world we live in. But whatever happens we are different from any other coloured colonials. Language, religion, outlook, aims are cast in the British mould. I could not imagine any future in which we would not revere Milton and Shakespeare, Hazlitt and Shelley, W. G. Grace and Sidney Barnes, Jack Hobbs and Denis Compton.

One day at Lord's I saw behind the ropes a West Indian, a man of about thirty, a working man. He and a dozen Englishmen, most of them staid middle-class, sat together, bound by enthusiasm: they had queued many hours before the gates opened so as to get the precious vantage-ground near the sight screen. On the West Indian's head was perched a cap of unique shape. He wore a blinding shirt, composed of more colours than all those around him added together. They spoke little and softly, he much and loud. That did not last. He was confident and provocative. As the game went against him, his companions could not resist the opportunity and chaffed him steadily. He was a man of wit and gave as good as he got. They were the liveliest bunch in sight.

Late in the afternoon came the West Indian innings. Kanhai was out for 0 in the first over. But almost at once Statham bowled a shortish ball to [Clyde] Walcott, who stepped back and hooked it square to the boundary, the stroke of the day. There was a burst of applause, the umpire made a routine signal. The ball was returned to Statham, who started his long walk back. The match settled down for the next ball. Then it was with a true dramatic instinct, our friend rose to his feet, cap, shirt and all. Without a word, he signalled the boundary all over again. Like an umpire he solemnly waved his arm from side to side. It was a superb gesture and it brought down the house. I am sure that all who saw it will remember it long after the tour is forgotten. From his far island he had come to headquarters, bringing his sheaves with him.

# REFERENCES

Adelman, Paul. 1989. *Gladstone, Disraeli and Later Victorian Politics*. Harlow: Longman.
Adjepong, Anima and Ben Carrington. 2014. "Black Female Athletes as Space Invaders." In *Routledge Handbook of Sport, Gender and Sexuality*, ed. Jennifer Hargreaves and Eric Anderson, 169–78. London: Routledge.
Adut, Ari. 2008. *On Scandal: Moral Disturbances in Society, Politics and Art*. Cambridge: Cambridge University Press.
Alleyne, Brian. 2006. "C. L. R. James, Critical Humanist." In *Beyond Boundaries: C. L. R. James and Postnational Studies*, ed. Christopher Gair, 175–96. London: Pluto.
Antoni, Robert. 2015. *As Flies to Whatless Boys: A Novel*. Leeds: Peepal Tree.
Appadurai, Arjun. 1996. "Playing with Modernity: The Decolonization of Indian Cricket." In *Modernity at Large: Cultural Dimensions of Globalization*, 89–113. Minneapolis: University of Minnesota Press.
Appiah, Kwame Anthony. 1996. "Analysis: Against Races." In *Color Conscious: The Political Morality of Race*, 30–74. Princeton, NJ: Princeton University Press.
Arlott, John. 1964. "Cricket Books, 1963." In *Wisden Cricketers' Almanac 1964*, 993–94. London: Wisden.
Austin, David. 2009a. "Introduction: In Search of a Caribbean Identity: C. L. R. James and the Promise of the Caribbean." In *You Don't Play with Revolution: The Montreal Lectures of C. L. R. James*, ed. David Austin, 1–26. Oakland, CA: AK Press.
———, ed. 2009b. *You Don't Play with Revolution: The Montreal Lectures of C. L. R. James*. Oakland, CA: AK Press.
———. 2010. "Inside-Outside: Edward Said's Caribbean and the Dilemmas in Contrapuntalism." In *Counterpoints: Edward Said's Legacy*, ed. May Telmissany and Stephanie Tara Schwartz, 123–46. Newcastle upon Tyne, UK: Cambridge Scholars.
———. 2013a. "Cabral, Rodney and the Complexities of Culture in Africa." In *Claim No Easy Victories: The Legacy of Amilcar Cabral*, ed. Firoze Manji and Bill Fletcher Jr., 315–26. Dakar, Senegal: CODESRIA and Dajara Press.

———. 2013b. *Fear of a Black Nation: Race, Sex, and Security in Sixties Montreal*. Toronto: Between the Lines.

Barnes, Natasha. 2006. *Cultural Conundrums: Gender, Race, Nation and the Making of Caribbean Cultural Politics*. Ann Arbor: University of Michigan Press.

Bateman, Anthony. 2009. "'From Far It Looks like Politics': C. L. R. James and the Canon of English Cricket Literature." *Sport and Society* 12, nos. 4–5: 496–508.

Baucom, Ian. 1999. *Out of Place: Englishness, Empire and the Locations of Identity*. Princeton, NJ: Princeton University Press.

Beckles, Hilary McD. 1995a. "A Purely Natural Extension: Women's Cricket in West Indies Cricket Culture." In *Liberation Cricket*, ed. Hilary McD. Beckles and Brian Stoddart, 222–35. Manchester: Manchester University Press.

———. 1995b. "The Origins and Development of West Indies Cricket Culture in the Nineteenth Century: Jamaica and Barbados." In *Liberation Cricket*, ed. Hilary McD. Beckles and Brian Stoddart, 33–43. Manchester: Manchester University Press.

———. 1999a. *The Development of West Indies Cricket, Volume 1: The Age of Nationalism*. London: Pluto.

———. 1999b. *The Development of West Indies Cricket, Volume 2: The Age of Globalization*. London: Pluto.

———. 2003. *A Nation Imagined: First West Indies Test Team*. Kingston, Jamaica: Ian Randle.

Beckles, Hilary McD., and Brian Stoddart, eds. 1995. *Liberation Cricket: West Indies Cricket Culture*. Manchester: Manchester University Press.

Beckles, Hilary McD., and Harclyde Walcott. 1995. "Redemption Sounds: Music, Literature and the Popular Ideology of West Indian Cricket Crowds." in *Liberation Cricket*, ed. Hilary McD. Beckles and Brian Stoddart, 370–83. Manchester: Manchester University Press.

Belcham, John. 1991. *Class, Party and the Political System in Britain, 1867–1914*. Oxford: Basil Blackwell.

Berry, Christopher. 1981. "Hegel on the World-Historical Individual." *History of European Ideas* 2, no. 2: 155–62.

Besson, Jean, ed. 1989. *Caribbean Reflections: The Life and Times of a Trinidad Scholar, 1901–1986*. London: Karia.

Birley, Derek. 1999. *A Social History of English Cricket*. London: Aurum.

Blackburn, Robin. 1988. *The Overthrow of Colonial Slavery, 1776–1848*. London: Verso.

Blackledge, Paul. 2014. "Sport: Capitalism at Play." *Socialist Review* (April): 390.

Bloom, Allan. 1997. "Rousseau's Critique of Liberal Constitutionalism." In *The Legacy of Rousseau*, ed. Clifford Orwin and Nathan Tarcov, 143–67. Chicago: University of Chicago Press.

Bogues, Anthony. 1997. *Caliban's Freedom: The Early Political Thought of C. L. R. James*. London: Pluto.

———. 2003. *Black Heretics, Black Prophets: Radical Political Intellectuals*. New York: Routledge.

———. 2006. "C. L. R. James and the Politics of the Subject, Culture and Desire." In *Beyond Boundaries: C. L. R. James and Postnational Studies*, ed. Christopher Gair, 157–74. London: Pluto.

———. 2010. *Empire of Liberty*. Lebanon, NH: Dartmouth College Press.

Bourdieu, Pierre. 1993. "How Can One Be a Sportsman?" In *Sociology in Question*, 117–31. London: Sage.

Briggs, Asa. 1987. *A Social History of England*. London: Penguin.

Buck-Morss, Susan. 2000. "Hegel and Haiti." *Critical Inquiry* 26, no. 4: 821–65.

Buhle, Paul. 1993. *C. L. R. James: The Artist as Revolutionary*. London: Verso.

Bunce, Robin, and Paul Field. 2014. *Darcus Howe: A Political Biography*. London: Bloomsbury.

Carby, Hazel V. 1998. *Race Men*. Cambridge, MA: Harvard University Press.

Cardus, Neville. 1949 [1930]. "The Champion." In *The Essential Neville Cardus*, 24–31. London: Jonathan Cape.

———. 1963. "What is Cricket?" *The Guardian*, 17 May: 7.

———. 1987. "William Gilbert Grace." In *The Faber Book of Cricket*, ed. Michael Davie and Simon Davie, 91–97. London: Faber and Faber.

Carew, Dudley. 1963. "Not Out." *Times Literary Supplement*, 21 June: 459.

Carlyle, Thomas. 1840. *On Heroes, Hero Worship and the Heroic in History*. London: Chapman and Hall.

Carrington, Ben. 1998. "Sport, Masculinity, and Black Cultural Resistance." *Journal of Sport and Social Issues* 22, no. 3: 275–98.

———. 2010. *Race, Sport and Politics: The Sporting Black Diaspora*. London: Sage.

———. 2013. "The Critical Sociology of Race and Sport: The First Fifty Years." *Annual Review of Sociology* 39: 379–98.

Chase, Malcolm. 2011. "Exporting the Owenite Utopia: Thomas Powell and the Tropical Emigration Society." In *Robert Owen and His Legacy*, ed. Noel Thompson and Chris Williams, 197–217. Cardiff: University of Wales Press.

Chawansky, Megan. 2010. "Letters to a Young Baller: Exploring Epistolary Criticism." *Qualitative Enquiry* 16, no. 9: 721–27.

Cohen, Ed. 1993. *Talk on the Wilde Side*. London: Routledge.

Colás, Santiago. 1996. "Silence and Dialectics: Speculations on C. L. R. James and Latin America." In *Rethinking C. L. R. James*, ed. Grant Farred, 131–63. Oxford: Blackwell.

Cole, G. D. H. and Raymond Postgate. 1949. *The Common People, 1746–1946*. London: Methuen.

Collins, Tony. 2013. *Sport in Capitalist Society: A Short History*. Abingdon, UK: Routledge.

Connor, Steve. 2011. *A Philosophy of Sport*. London: Reaktion.

Constantine, Learie. 1933. *Cricket and I*. London: Philip Allan.

———. 1946. *Cricket in the Sun*. London: Stanley Paul.

———. 1948. *Cricket Crackers*. London: Stanley Paul.

Constantine, Learie, and Denzil Batchelor. 1966. *The Changing Face of Cricket.* London: Eyre and Spottiswoode.

Cowley, John. 1996. *Carnival, Canboulay and Calypso: Traditions in the Making,* Cambridge: Cambridge University Press.

Cripps, Louise. 1997. *C. L. R. James: Memories and Commentaries.* New York: Cornwall.

Cudjoe, Selwyn R. 1983. *Movement of the People: Essays on Independence.* Ithaca, NY: Calaloux.

———. 1992a. "The Audacity of It All: C. L. R. James's Trinidadian Background." In *C. L. R. James's Caribbean,* ed. Paget Henry and Paul Buhle, 39–55. Durham, NC: Duke University Press.

———. 1992b. "C. L. R. James Misbound." *Transition* 58: 124–36.

———. 2003. *Beyond Boundaries: The Intellectual Tradition of Trinidad and Tobago in the Nineteenth Century.* Amherst: University of Massachusetts Press.

Cudjoe, Selwyn R., and William E. Cain, eds. 1995. *C. L. R. James: His Intellectual Legacies.* Amherst: University of Massachusetts Press.

Davis, Angela Y. 1983. *Women, Race and Class.* New York: Vintage.

Denzin, Norman. 2012. "A Box of Books." *Qualitative Enquiry* 18, no. 2: 191–92.

Denzin, Norman, and Yvonne S. Lincoln, eds. 1994. *Handbook of Qualitative Research.* London: Sage.

Diawara, Manthia. 1990. "Englishness and Blackness: Cricket as a Discourse on Colonialism." *Callaloo* 13, no. 4: 830–44.

Douglas, Andrew J. 2008. "Democratizing Dialectics with C. L. R. James." *Review of Politics* 70, no. 3: 420–41.

Du Bois, W. E. B. 2000 [1904]. "Sociology Hesitant." *Boundary 2* 27, no. 3: 37–44.

Eagleton, Terry. 1976. "Criticism and Politics: The Work of Raymond Williams." *New Left Review I* 95 (January–February): 3–23.

Edmondson, Belinda. 1994. "Race, Tradition and the Construction of a Caribbean Aesthetic." *New Literary History* 25, no. 1: 109–21.

Elias, Norbert. 1978. *What Is Sociology?* London: Hutchinson.

———. 1994 [1939]. *The Civilizing Process: Sociogenetic and Psychogenetic Investigations.* London: Blackwell.

Eliot, T. S. 1948. *Notes towards the Definition of Culture.* New York: Harcourt, Brace.

Epstein, James. 2012. *Scandal of Colonial Rule: Power and Subversion in the British Atlantic during the Age of Revolution.* Cambridge: Cambridge University Press.

Escobar, Arturo. 2007. "Worlds and Knowledges Otherwise." *Cultural Studies* 21, nos. 2–3: 179–210.

Fanon, Frantz. 1968 [1961]. *The Wretched of the Earth,* trans. Constance Farrington. New York: Grove.

———. 1969 [1965]. "Algeria Unveiled." In *The New Left Reader,* ed. Carl Oglesby, 161–85. New York: Grove.

Farred, Grant. 1996a. "The Maple Man: How Cricket Made a Postcolonial Intellectual." In *Rethinking C. L. R. James,* ed. Grant Farred, 165–86. Oxford: Blackwell.

———, ed. 1996b. *Rethinking C. L. R. James*. Oxford: Blackwell.
———. 2003. *What's My Name?: Black Vernacular Intellectuals*. Minneapolis: University of Minnesota Press.
Ferguson, Roderick A. 2004. *Aberrations in Black: Toward a Queer of Color Critique*. Minneapolis: University of Minnesota Press.
Flett, Keith. 2013. "Cricket: Gentlemen and Players." In *Capitalism and Sport: Politics, Protest, People and Play*, ed. Michael Lavalette, 119–24. London: Bookmarks.
Fredrickson, George M.. 2003. *Racism: A Short History*. Princeton, NJ: Princeton University Press.
Fromm, Erich. 2013 [1961]. "Marx's Concept of Man." In *Marx's Concept of Man*, 1–71. London: Bloomsbury.
Froude, James Anthony. 1888. *The English in the West Indies; or, The Bow of Ulysses*. London: Longmans, Green.
Gadamer, Hans-Georg. 1986. *The Relevance of the Beautiful and Other Essays*, ed. Robert Bernasconi. Cambridge: Cambridge University Press.
Galeano, Eduardo. 2013. *Soccer in Sun and Shadow*. London: Avalon.
Geras, Norman. 1983. *Marx and Human Nature: Refutation of a Legend*. London: Verso.
Gikandi, Simon. 2000. "The Embarrassment of Victorianism: Colonial Subjects and the Lure of Englishness." In *Victorian Afterlife: Postmodern Culture Rewrites the Nineteenth Century*, ed. John Kucich and Dianne F. Sadoff, 157–85. Minneapolis: University of Minnesota Press.
Gilroy, Paul. 2004. *After Empire: Melancholia or Convivial Culture?* Abingdon, UK: Routledge.
Girard, Philippe, ed. 2014. *The Memoir of General Toussaint Louverture*. Oxford: Oxford University Press.
Glaberman, Martin, ed. 1999. *Marxism for Our Times: C. L. R. James on Revolutionary Organization*. Jackson: University Press of Mississippi.
Gordon, Avery. 2008. *Ghostly Matters: Haunting and the Sociological Imagination*. Minneapolis: University of Minnesota Press.
Gregg, Robert. 2000. *Inside Out, Outside In: Essays in Contemporary History*. Houndsmill, UK: Macmillan.
Grimshaw, Anna. 1991. *C. L. R. James: A Revolutionary Vision for the 20th Century*. New York: Smyrna.
———. 1996. "Introduction." In *Special Delivery: The Letters of C. L. R. James to Constance Webb, 1939–48*, ed. Anna Grimshaw, 1–35. Oxford: Blackwell.
Grygiénć, Janusz. 2013. *General Will in Political Philosophy*. Exeter: Imprint Academic.
Guha, Ramachandra. 2002. *A Corner of a Foreign Field: The Indian History of a British Sport*. London: Picador.
Hall, Stuart. 1992. "C. L. R. James: A Portrait." In *C. L. R. James's Caribbean*, ed. Paget Henry and Paul Buhle, 3–16. Durham, NC: Duke University Press.

———. 1996. "When Was 'the Post-Colonial'? Thinking at the Limit." In *The Postcolonial Question: Common Skies, Divided Horizons*, ed. Ian Chambers and Lidia Curti, 242–60. London: Routledge.

Hamilton, Cynthia. 1992. "A Way of Seeing: Culture as Political Expression in the Works of C. L. R. James." *Journal of Black Studies* 22, no. 3: 429–43.

Hannaford, Ivan. 1996. *Race: The History of an Idea in the West*. Baltimore: Johns Hopkins University Press.

Hargreaves, Jennifer. 1994. *Sporting Females: Critical Issues in the History and Sociology of Women's Sport*. London: Routledge.

———. 2000. *Heroines of Sport: The Politics of Difference and Identity*. London: Routledge.

Hargreaves, Jennifer, and Ian McDonald. 2000. "Cultural Studies and the Sociology of Sport." In *Handbook of Sport Studies*, ed. Jay Coakley and Eric Dunning, 48–60. London: Sage.

Harris, Wilson. 1973. *Tradition, the Writer and Society*. London: New Beacon.

———. 2008. "History, Fable and Myth in the Caribbean and Guianas." *Caribbean Quarterly* 54, nos. 1–2: 5–38.

Hartmann, Douglas. 2003. "What Can We Learn from Sport if We Take Sport Seriously as a Racial Force? Lessons from C. L. R. James's *Beyond a Boundary*." *Ethnic and Racial Studies* 26, no. 3: 451–83.

Hegel, Georg Wilhelm Friedrich. 2001. *The Philosophy of History*, trans. J. Sibree. Ontario: Batoche.

Heller, Agnes. 1984 [1970]. *Everyday Life*. London: Routledge and Kegan Paul.

Henry, Frances. 2001. "Reclaiming African Religions in Trinidad: The Orisha and Spiritual Baptist Faiths Today." Centre for Research on Latin America and the Caribbean (York University) Working Paper Series, June.

Henry, Paget. 2000. *Caliban's Reason: Introducing Afro-Caribbean Philosophy*. New York: Routledge.

———. 2014. "C. L. R. James, Political Philosophy and the Creolizing of Rousseau and Marx." In *Creolizing Rousseau*, ed. Jane Anna Gordon and Neil Roberts, 143–70. London: Rowman and Littlefield.

Herskovits, Melville, and Frances Herskovits. 1947. *Trinidad Village*. New York: Alfred A. Knopf.

Hill, Robert A. 1999. "C. L. R. James: The Myth of Western Civilisation." In *Enterprise of the Indies*, ed. George Lamming, 255–59. Port of Spain: Trinidad and Tobago Institute of the West Indies.

———. 2013. "C. L. R. James and the Moment of *Beyond a Boundary*." Keynote address presented at *Beyond a Boundary*: 50 Years On, University of Glasgow. http://www.clrjames.uk/video/beyond-a-boundary-conference/c-l-r-james-and-the-moment-of-beyond-a-boundary.

Hobsbawm, Eric. 1997. *On History*. London: Abacus.

Høgsbjerg, Christian. 2006. "Beyond the Boundary of Leninism? C. L. R. James and 1956." *Revolutionary History* 9, no. 3: 144–59.

———. 2007. "Facing Post-Colonial Reality? C. L. R. James, the Black Atlantic and 1956." In *1956 and All That*, ed. Keith Flett, 181–201. Newcastle: Cambridge Scholars.

———. 2014. *C. L. R. James in Imperial Britain*. Durham, NC: Duke University Press.

———. 2016. "'What Would an Athenian Have Thought of the Day's Play?' C. L. R. James's Early Cricket Writings for *The Manchester Guardian*." *Journal of Postcolonial Writing*, 52, no. 3: 249–61.

Hooker, J. R. 1975. *Henry Sylvester Williams: Imperial Pan-Africanist*. London: Rex Collins.

Howe, Stephen. 2003. "C. L. R. James: Visions of History, Visions of Britain." In *West Indian Intellectuals in Britain*, ed. Bill Schwarz, 153–74. Manchester: Manchester University Press.

Hughes, Langston. 1931. "People without Shoes." *New Masses* 7, no. 5 (October): 12.

———. 1932. "White Shadows in a Black Land." *The Crisis* 39 (May): 157.

Hurbert, Philip. 2007. "Winifred Atwell." In *The Oxford Companion to Black British History*, ed. David Dabydeen, John Gilmore, and Cecily Jones, 33–34. Oxford: Oxford University Press.

Iton, Richard. 2008. *In Search of the Black Fantastic: Politics and Popular Culture in the Post–Civil Rights Era*. Oxford: Oxford University Press.

James, C. L. R. 1938. *The Black Jacobins: Toussaint Louverture and the San Domingo Revolution*. London: Secker and Warburg.

———. 1943. "The Philosophy of History and Necessity: A Few Words with Prof. Hook." *The New International* 9, no. 7: 210–13; and 9, no. 9: 273–77. https://www.marxists.org/archive/james-clr/works/1943/07/hook.htm.

———. 1949a. "Herbert Aptheker's Distortions." *Fourth International* 10, no. 11: 337–41.

———. 1949b. "Stalinism and Negro History." *Fourth International* 10, no. 10: 309–14.

———. 1958. *Facing Reality*. Detroit: Correspondence.

———. 1962. *Party Politics in the West Indies*. San Juan, Trinidad: Vedic Enterprises.

———. 1964. "Rastafari at Home and Abroad." *New Left Review I* 25 (May–June): 74–76.

———. 1969. "The West Indian Intellectual." In John Jacob Thomas, *Froudacity: West Indian Fables Explained*, 24–49. London: New Beacon.

———. 1970. "Discovering Literature in Trinidad: The Nineteen Thirties." *Savacou* 2 (September): 54–55.

———. 1973 [1960]. *Modern Politics*. Detroit: Bewick.

———. 1977. *Nkrumah and the Ghana Revolution*. London: Allison and Busby.

———. 1977 [1953]. "Fiction and Reality." In *The Future in the Present: Selected Writings*, 142–59. Westport, CT: Lawrence Hill.

———. 1978 [1931]. "Michel Maxwell Philip: 1829–1888." In *From Trinidad: An Anthology of Early West Indian Writing*, ed. Reinhard Sander, 253–69. New York: Africana Publishing.

———. 1980. "Marxism and the Intellectuals." In *Spheres of Existence: Selected Writings*, 113–30. London: Allison and Busby.

———. 1980 [1938]. *The Black Jacobins: Toussaint L'Ouverture and the San Domingo Revolution*, London: Allison and Busby.

———. 1980 [1943]. "The Philosophy of History and Necessity." In *Spheres of Existence: Selected Writings*, 49–58. London: Allison and Busby.

———. 1980 [1947]. "Dialectical Materialism and the Fate of Humanity." In *Spheres of Existence: Selected Writings*, 70–105. London: Allison and Busby.

———. 1980 [1948]. *Notes on Dialectics: Hegel, Marx, Lenin*. Westport, CT: Lawrence Hill.

———. 1980 [1959]. "The Artist in the Caribbean." In *The Future in the Present*, 183–90. Westport, CT: Lawrence Hill.

———. 1980 [1969]. "Garfield Sobers." In *The Future in the Present*, 213–25. Westport, CT: Lawrence Hill.

———. 1984. *At the Rendezvous of Victory: Selected Writings*. London: Allison and Busby.

———. 1985 [1953]. *Mariners, Renegades and Castaways: The Story of Herman Melville and the World We Live In*. London: Allison and Busby.

———. 1986. *Cricket*, ed. Anna Grimshaw. London: Allison and Busby.

———. 1986 [1950]. *State Capitalism and World Revolution*. Chicago: Charles Kerr.

———. 1986 [1963]. "The 1963 West Indians: Address to the *Cricket Society*." In *Cricket*, ed. Anna Grimshaw, 134–47. London: Allison and Busby.

———. 1986 [1967]. "George Headley." In *Cricket*, ed. Anna Grimshaw, 190–202. London: Allison and Busby.

———. 1986 [1970]. "'Introduction' to *Cricket: A History of its Growth and Development throughout the World* by Rowland Bowen." In *Cricket*, ed. Anna Grimshaw, 270–76. London: Allison and Busby.

———. 1992. "Black Studies and the Contemporary Student." In *The C. L. R. James Reader*, ed. Anna Grimshaw, 390–404. Oxford: Blackwell.

———. 1992 [1953]. "Notes on *Hamlet*." In *The C. L. R. James Reader*, ed. Anna Grimshaw, 243–46. Oxford: Blackwell.

———. 1992 [1963]. "From Toussaint L'Ouverture to Fidel Castro." In *The C. L. R. James Reader*, ed. Anna Grimshaw, 296–314. Oxford: Blackwell.

———. 1993. *American Civilization*, ed. Anna Grimshaw and Keith Hart. Oxford: Blackwell.

———. 1993 [1937]. *World Revolution*, Atlantic Highlands, NJ: Humanities.

———. 1996. *Special Delivery: The Letters of C. L. R. James to Constance Webb, 1939–48*, ed. Anna Grimshaw. Oxford: Blackwell.

———. 1997 [1936]. *Minty Alley*. Oxford: University of Mississippi Press.

———. 2000. "Lectures on *The Black Jacobins*." *Small Axe* 8: 99–100.

———. 2001 [1938]. *The Black Jacobins: Toussaint L'Ouverture and the San Domingo Revolution*. London: Penguin.

———. 2003. "The Women." In *Letters from London: Seven Essays by C. L. R. James*, ed. Nicholas Laughlin, 91–107. Port of Spain: Prospect.

———. 2006. *A Majestic Innings: Writings on Cricket*. London: Aurum.

———. 2009a. "The Haitian Revolution in the Making of the Modern World." In *You Don't Play with Revolution: The Montreal Lectures of C. L. R. James*, ed. David Austin, 51–70. Oakland, CA: AK Press:.

———. 2009b. "Rousseau and the Idea of General Will." In *You Don't Play with Revolution: The Montreal Lectures of C. L. R. James*, ed. David Austin, 217–25. Oakland, CA: AK Press.

———. 2009c. "Shakespeare's *King Lear*." In *You Don't Play with Revolution: The Montreal Lectures of C. L. R. James*, ed. David Austin, 79–81. Oakland, CA: AK Press.

———. 2012. *A History of Pan-African Revolt*. Oakland, CA: PM Press.

———. 2013 [1963]. *Beyond a Boundary*. Durham, NC: Duke University Press.

———. 2014 [1932]. *The Life of Captain Cipriani*. Durham, NC: Duke University Press.

James, Selma. 2012. "Striving for Clarity and Influence: The Political Legacy of C. L. R. James." In *Sex, Race and Class: The Perspective of Winning, A Selection of Writings, 1952–2011*, 283–96. Oakland, CA: PM Press.

Johnson, W. Chris. 2011. "Sex and the Subversive Alien: The Moral Life of C. L. R. James." *International Journal of Francophone Studies* 14, nos. 1–2: 185–203.

Kamugisha, Aaron. 2006. "Reading Said and Wynter on Liberation." In *Caribbean Reasonings: After Man, towards the Human*, ed. Anthony Bogues, 131–56. Kingston, Jamaica: Ian Randle.

———. 2011. "The Hearts of Men? Gender in the Late C. L. R. James." *Small Axe* 34: 76–94.

———. 2013. "On the Idea of a Caribbean Cultural Studies." *Small Axe* 41: 43–57.

Kierkegaard, Søren. 1970. *Journals and Papers, Volume 2*, ed. Howard V. Hong and Edna H. Hong. Bloomington: Indiana University Press.

King, Nicole. 2001. *C. L. R. James and Creolization: Circles of Influence*. Jackson: University Press of Mississippi.

Kingwell, Mark. 2002. "Keeping a Straight Bat: Cricket, Civility and Post-Colonialism." In *Practical Judgements: Essays in Culture, Politics and Interpretation*, 116–52. Toronto: University of Toronto Press.

Kipling, Rudyard. 1897. "Recessional," *The Times*, July 17: 13.

———. 1910. "If . . ." In *Rewards and Fairies*, 181–82. New York: Doubleday, Page.

Kuhn, Thomas S. 1962. *The Structure of Scientific Revolutions*. Chicago: University of Chicago Press.

Lamming, George. 1953. *In the Castle of My Skin*. London: Michael Joseph.

———. 1989. "C. L. R. James, Evangelist." In *The George Lamming Reader: The Aesthetics of Decolonisation*, ed. Anthony Bogues, 95–100. Kingston, Jamaica: Ian Randle.

Lao-Montes, Agustin. 2007. "Decolonial Moves: Trans-Locating African Diaspora Spaces." *Cultural Studies* 21, nos. 2–3: 309–38.

Larkin, Philip. 1988. *Collected Poems*. London: Faber and Faber.

Larsen, Neil. 1996. "Negativities of the Popular: C. L. R. James and the Limits of 'Cultural Studies.'" In *Rethinking C. L. R. James*, ed. Grant Farred, 85–102. Oxford: Blackwell.

Lazarus, Neil. 1995. "Cricket and National Culture in the Writings of C. L. R. James." In *Liberation Cricket*, ed. Hilary McD. Beckles and Brian Stoddart, 342–55. Manchester: Manchester University Press.

———. 1999. *Nationalism and Cultural Practice in the Postcolonial World*. Cambridge: Cambridge University Press.

Lear, Jonathan. 2011. *A Case for Irony*. Cambridge, MA: Harvard University Press.

Lefebvre, Henri. 2014 [1958]. *Critique of Everyday Life: The One Volume Edition*. London: Verso.

Lewis, Gordon K. 1968. *The Growth of the Modern West Indies*. London: MacGibbon and Kee.

Lloyd, Clive. 1998. "Introduction." In Michael Manley, *A History of West Indies Cricket*, v. London: Andre Deutsch.

Lorde, Audre. 1984. *Sister Outsider: Essays and Speeches*. Trumansburg, NY: Crossing Press Feminist Series.

Low, Robert. 2010. *W. G. Grace: An Intimate Biography*. London: Metro.

MacLean, Malcolm. 2010. "Ambiguity within the Boundary: Rereading C. L. R. James's *Beyond a Boundary*." *Journal of Sport History* 37, no. 1: 99–117.

Macherey, Pierre. 1978. *A Theory of Literary Production*, trans. Geoffrey Wall. London: Routledge and Kegan Paul.

Maguire, Joseph. 1999. *Global Sport: Identities, Societies, Civilizations*. Oxford: Polity.

Major, John. 2008. *More than a Game: The Story of Cricket's Early Years*. London: Harper Perennial.

Majumdar, Boria. 2002. "Cricket in Colonial India: The Bombay Pentangular, 1892–1946." *International Journal of the History of Sport* 19, nos. 2–3: 157–88.

Makalani, Minkah. 2011. *In the Cause of Freedom: Radical Black Internationalism from Harlem to London, 1917–1938*. Chapel Hill: University of North Carolina Press.

Maldonado-Torres, Nelson. 2008. *Against War: Views from the Underside of Modernity*. Durham, NC: Duke University Press.

Manley, Michael. 1988. *A History of West Indies Cricket*. London: Andre Deutsch.

Marable, Manning. 1985. "Review of *Beyond a Boundary*." *Journal of Sport and Social Issues* 9, no. 1: 38.

Marqusee, Mike. 2005. *Redemption Song: Muhammad Ali and the Spirit of the Sixties*. London: Verso.

Marx, Karl. 1926 [1852]. *The Eighteenth Brumaire of Louis Napoleon*, trans. Eden and Cedar Paul. London: George Allen and Unwin.

———. 1976. *Capital: A Critique of Political Economy, Volume 1*, trans. Ben Fowkes. Harmondsworth, UK: Penguin.

Mason, Peter. 2008. *Learie Constantine*. Oxford: Macmillan Caribbean.

Mathurin, Owen Charles. 1976. *Henry Sylvester Williams and the Origins of the Pan-African Movement*. Westport, CT: Greenwood.

Matthews, Dom Basil. 1953. *Crisis of the West Indian Family*. Port of Spain: Extra Mural Department, University of the West Indies.

Mbembe, Achille. 2001. *On the Postcolony*. Berkeley: University of California Press.

McClintock, Anne. 1995. *Imperial Leather: Race, Gender and Sexuality in the Colonial Contest*. London: Routledge.

———. 1997. "'No Longer in a Future Heaven': Gender, Race, and Nationalism." In *Dangerous Liaisons: Gender, Nation, and Postcolonial Perspectives*, ed. Anne McClintock, Aamir Rashid Mufti, and Ella Shohat, 89–112. Minneapolis: University of Minnesota Press.

McKibbin, Ross. 1998. *Classes and Cultures: England, 1918–1951*. Oxford: Oxford University Press.

Mignolo, Walter. 2007. "Introduction: Coloniality of Power and De-colonial Thinking." *Cultural Studies* 21, nos. 2–3: 155–67.

———. 2011. *The Darker Side of Western Modernity: Global Futures, Decolonial Options*. Durham, NC: Duke University Press.

Miller, Paul B. 2001. "Enlightened Hesitations: Black Masses and Tragic Heroes in C. L. R. James' *The Black Jacobins*." *MLN* 116: 1069–90.

Moore-Gilbert, Bart. 2009. *Postcolonial Life-Writing: Culture, Politics and Self-Representation*. Abingdon, UK: Routledge.

Morton, A. L. 1938. *A People's History of England*. London: Gollancz.

Muñoz, José Esteban. 2009. *Cruising Utopia: The Then and There of Queer Futurity*. New York: New York University Press.

Naha, Souvik. 2012. "Adams and Eves at the Eden Gardens: Women Cricket Spectators and the Conflict of Feminine Subjectivity in Calcutta, 1920–1970." *International Journal of the History of Sport* 29, no. 5: 711–29.

Naipaul, V. S. 1972. *The Overcrowded Baracoon and Other Articles*. Harmondsworth, UK: Penguin.

———. 1974. "Cricket." *New Community* 3: 1–2.

———. 1974 [1963]. "Cricket." *Journal of Ethnic and Migration Studies* 3, nos. 1–2: 104–6.

Nandy, Ashis. 2000. *The Tao of Cricket: On Games of Destiny and the Destiny of Games*. Oxford: Oxford University Press.

Nauright, John, Alan Cobley, and David Wiggins, eds. 2014. *Beyond C. L. R. James: Shifting Boundaries of Race and Ethnicity in Sport*. Fayetteville: University of Arkansas Press.

Nettleford, Rex. 1998. "Cricket and the Artistic Tradition: West Indian Cricket as a Performing Art." In *The Spirit of Dominance: Cricket and Nationalism in the West Indies*, ed. Hilary McD. Beckles, 73–88. Kingston, Jamaica: Canoe Press and University of the West Indies.

Nielsen, Aldon Lynn. 1997. *C. L. R. James: A Critical Introduction*. Jackson: University Press of Mississippi.

Oborne, Peter. 2004. *Basil D'Oliveira. Cricket and Conspiracy: The Untold Story*. London: Little, Brown.

———. 2014. *Wounded Tiger: A History of Cricket in Pakistan*. London: Simon and Schuster.

O'Shaughnessy, Andrew Jackson. 2000. *An Empire Divided: The American Revolution and the British Caribbean*. Philadelphia: University of Pennsylvania Press.

Padmore, George. 1972. *Africa and World Peace*. London: Frank Cass.

Patterson, Orlando. 1967. *An Absence of Ruins*. London: Hutchinson.

———. 1995 [1969]. "The Ritual of Cricket." In *Liberation Cricket*, ed. Hilary McD. Beckles and Brian Stoddart, 141–47. Manchester: Manchester University Press.

Phillips, Caryl. 2001. "C. L. R. James: Mariner, Renegade and Castaway." In *A New World Order*, 152–71. New York: Vintage.

Plato. 1997. *Complete Works*, ed. John Cooper. Indianapolis: Hackett.

Powell, A. G., and S. Canynge Caple. 1974. *The Graces. E. M., W. G. and G. F.* Bath, UK: Cedric Chivers.

Rabbit, Kara M. 1995. "C. L. R. James's Figure of Touissaint-Louverture: *The Black Jacobins* and the Literary Hero." In *C. L. R. James: His Intellectual Legacies*, ed. Selwyn R. Cudjoe and William E. Cain, 118–35. Amherst: University of Massachusetts Press.

Rae, Simon. 1998. *W. G. Grace*. London: Faber and Faber.

Ranjitsinhji, K. S. 1897. *The Jubilee Book of Cricket*. Edinburgh: Blackwood.

Reddock, Rhoda. 1994. *Women, Labour and Politics in Trinidad and Tobago: A History*. London: Zed.

———. 1998. "Women's Organizations and Movements in the Commonwealth Caribbean: The Response to Global Economic Crisis in the 1980s." *Feminist Review* 59 (Summer): 57–73.

———. 2014. "Radical Caribbean Social Thought: Race, Class Identity and the Postcolonial Nation." *Current Sociology* 62, no. 4: 493–511.

Reiss, Tom. 2013. *The Black Count: Glory, Revolution, Betrayal and the Real Count of Monte Cristo*. London: Vintage.

Rice, Jo, Tim Rice, Paul Gambaccini, and Mike Read, eds. 1982. *The Guinness Book of 500 Number One Hits*. Enfield, UK: Guinness Superlatives.

Richardson, Joanna. 1962. *The Pre-eminent Victorian: A Study of Tennyson*. London: Jonathan Cape.

Robinson, Cedric. 1995. "C. L. R. James and the World System." In *C. L. R. James: His Intellectual Legacies*, ed. Selwyn R. Cudjoe and William E. Cain, 244–59. Amherst: University of Massachusetts Press.

———. 2000 [1983]. *Black Marxism: The Making of the Black Radical Tradition*. Chapel Hill: University of North Carolina Press.

Rodney, Walter. 1990. *Walter Rodney Speaks: The Making of an African Intellectual*. Trenton, NJ: Africa World Press.

Rohlehr, Gordon. 1998. "C. L. R. James and the Legacy of *Beyond a Boundary*." In *The Spirit of Dominance: Cricket and Nationalism in the West Indies*, ed. Hilary McD. Beckles, 124–46. Kingston, Jamaica: Canoe Press and University of the West Indies.

Rosengarten, Frank. 2008. *Urbane Revolutionary: C. L. R. James and the Struggle for a New Society*. Jackson: University Press of Mississippi.

Rousseau, Jean-Jacques. 1988. *Rousseau's Political Writings*, ed. Julia Conaway Bondanella. New York: W. W. Norton.

Rush, Anne Spry. 2011. *Bonds of Empire: West Indians and Britishness from Victoria to Decolonization*. Oxford: Oxford University Press.

Said, Edward. 2000. "The Politics of Knowledge." In *Reflections on Exile and Other Literary and Cultural Essays*, 372–85. London: Granta.

Saward, Michael. 2010. *The Representative Claim*. Oxford: Oxford University Press.

Schwarz, Bill. 1996. "'The Only White Man in There': The Re-racialisation of England, 1956–1968." *Race and Class* 38, no. 1: 65–78.

———. 2002. "Unspeakable Histories: Diasporic Lives in Old England." In *Philosophies of Race and Ethnicity*, ed. Peter Osbourne and Stella Sandford, 81–96. London: Continuum.

———. 2003a. "Claudia Jones and the *West Indian Gazette*: Reflections on the Emergence of Post-Colonial Britain." *Twentieth Century British History* 14, no. 3: 264–85.

———. 2003b. "Crossing the Seas." In *West Indian Intellectuals in Britain*, ed. Bill Schwarz, 1–30. Manchester: Manchester University Press.

———. 2003c. "George Padmore." In *West Indian Intellectuals in Britain*, ed. Bill Schwarz, 135–52. Manchester: Manchester University Press.

———. 2006. "C. L. R. James's *American Civilization*." In *Beyond Boundaries: C. L. R. James and Postnational Studies*, ed. Christopher Gair, 128–56. London: Pluto.

———. 2007. "Locating Lamming." In *The Locations of George Lamming*, ed. Bill Schwarz, 1–25. Oxford: Macmillan.

Scott, David. 2004. *Conscripts of Modernity: The Tragedy of Colonial Enlightenment*. Durham, NC: Duke University Press.

———. 2014. *Omens of Adversity: Tragedy, Time, Memory, and Justice*. Durham, NC: Duke University Press.

Silverman, David. 1993. *Interpreting Qualitative Data: Methods of Analysing Talk, Text and Interaction*. London: Sage.

———, ed. 2004. *Qualitative Research: Theory, Method and Practice*. London: Sage.

Smith, Andrew. 2006a. "'A Conception of the Beautiful': C. L. R. James's *Glasgow Herald* Cricket Articles, 1937–1938." *International Journal of the History of Sport* 23, no. 1: 46–66.

———. 2006b. "'Beyond a Boundary' of a 'Field of Cultural Production': Reading C. L. R. James with Bourdieu." *Theory, Culture and Society* 23, no. 4: 95–112.

———. 2010. *C. L. R. James and the Study of Culture*. London: Palgrave Macmillan.

———. 2011a. "C. L. R. James, *Vanity Fair* and the Audience." *New Formations* 73: 11–25.

———. 2011b. "'Concrete Freedom': C. L. R. James on Culture and Black Politics." *Cultural Sociology* 5, no. 4: 479–99.

Smith, Ed. 2008. *What Sport Tells Us about Life*. London: Penguin.

Sobers, Garfield. 2002. *Garry Sobers: My Autobiography*. London: Headline.

Springfield, Lopez Consuelo. 1989. "'What Do Men Live By?' Autobiography and Intention in C. L. R. James's *Beyond a Boundary*." *Caribbean Quarterly* 35, no. 4: 85–97.

St. Louis, Brett. 2007. *Rethinking Race, Politics and Poetics: C. L. R. James's Critique of Modernity*. Oxford: Routledge.

Stoddart, Brian. 1990. "C. L. R. James: A Remembrance." *Sociology of Sport Journal* 7, no. 1: 103–6.

———. 1995. "Cricket, Social Formation and Cultural Continuity in Barbados: A Preliminary Ethnohistory." In *Liberation Cricket*, ed. Hilary McD. Beckles and Brian Stoddart, 61–85. Manchester: Manchester University Press.

———. 2006. "Sport, Colonialism and Struggle: C. L. R. James and Cricket." *Sport in Society* 9, no. 5: 914–30.

Strauther, John. 1963. "Calypso and the Mass Party." *International Socialism* (Autumn): 40.

Surin, Kenneth. 1995. "C. L. R. James's Materialist Aesthetic of Cricket." In *Liberation Cricket*, ed. Hilary McD. Beckles and Brian Stoddart, 313–41. Manchester: Manchester University Press.

———. 1996. "'The Future Anterior': C. L. R. James and Going *Beyond a Boundary*." In *Rethinking C. L. R. James*, ed. Grant Farred, 187–204. Oxford: Blackwell.

Thomas, Eudora. 1988. *History of the Shouter Baptists in Trinidad and Tobago*. Ithaca, NY: Calaloux.

Thomas, John Jacob. 1869. *The Theory and Practice of Creole Grammar*. Port of Spain: Chronicle.

Thompson, E. P. 1961. "The Long Revolution. Part I." *New Left Review I* 9 (May–June): 24–33.

———. 1981. "C. L. R. James at 80." In *C. L. R. James: His Life and Work*, ed. Paul Buhle, 249. London: Allison and Busby.

Thornton, A. P. 1959. *The Imperial Idea and Its Enemies: A Study in British Power*. London: Macmillan.

Tiffin, Helen. 1995. "Cricket, Literature and the Politics of Decolonization: The Case of C. L. R. James." In *Liberation Cricket*, ed. Hilary McD. Beckles and Brian Stoddart, 356–69. Manchester: Manchester University Press.

Todd, Cain. 2007. "Cover Driving Gracefully: On the Aesthetic Appreciation of Cricket." *Sport in Society* 10, no. 5: 856–77.

Tomlinson, Richard. 2015. *Amazing Grace: The Man Who Was W. G.* London: Little Brown.

Tronchin, L. B. 1888a. "A Lecture: On the Political and Literary State of the Colony During the Administration of Lord Harris." *Public Opinion* (31 January): n.p.

———. 1888b. "Charles Wm. Warner and His Article," *Public Opinion* (28 January): n.p.

Trotsky, Leon. 1930. *My Life: An Attempt at an Autobiography.* New York: Charles Schribner's Sons.

———. 1937. *The Stalin School of Falsification.* New York: Pioneer.

———. 1973. *On Britain.* New York: Monad.

Trouillot, Michel-Rolph. 1995. *Silencing the Past: Power and the Production of History.* Boston: Beacon.

———. 2003. *Global Transformations: Anthropology and the Modern World,* New York: Palgrave Macmillan.

Turim, Maureen. 2001. "High Angle on Her Shoes: How Cinema Views Footwear." In *Footnotes: On Shoes,* ed. Shari Benstock and Suzanne Ferris, 58–90. New Brunswick, NJ: Rutgers University Press.

Vickers, Sir Geoffrey. 1952. "The Siege Economy and the Welfare State of Mind." *The Lancet,* 27 December, 1265–68.

Walcott, Derek. 1995. "A Tribute to C. L. R. James." In *C. L. R. James: His Intellectual Legacies,* ed. Selwyn R. Cudjoe and William E. Cain, 34–48. Amherst: University of Massachusetts Press.

Washbourne, Neil. 2010. *Mediating Politics: Newspapers, Radio, Television and the Internet.* New York: Open University Press and McGraw-Hill.

———. 2013. "Celebrating (Dis)Grace: Oscar, W. G. and Troubles with Masculine Social Status in 1895." Paper presented at the Social History Society Conference, University of Leeds, 23–25 March.

Webb, Constance. 2003. *Not without Love: Memoirs.* Hanover, NH: Dartmouth College.

Webber, J. R. 1998. *The Chronicle of W. G.* West Bridgford, UK: Association of Cricket Statisticians.

Welsch, Wolfgang. 2005. "Sport Viewed Aesthetically, and Even as Art?" In *The Aesthetics of Everyday Life,* ed. Andrew Light and Jonathan M. Smith, 135–55. New York: Columbia University Press.

Westall, Claire. 2010. "What They Knew of Nation and Empire: The Interwoven Questioning of Rudyard Kipling and C. L. R. James." In *Kipling and Beyond: Patriotism, Globalisation and Postcolonialism,* ed. Kaori Nagai and Caroline Rooney, 165–84. Basingstoke, UK: Palgrave Macmillan.

———. 2013. "The New Rise and Fall of English Literature." In *Literature of an Independent England: Revisions of England, Englishness and English Literature,* ed. Claire Westall and Michael Gardiner, 218–33. Basingstoke, UK: Palgrave MacMillan.

Wheen, Francis. 1998. "Foreword." In Mike Marqusee, *Anyone but England: Cricket, Race and Class*, 9–11. London: Two Heads.

Williams, Raymond. 1958. *Culture and Society: Coleridge to Orwell*. London: Chatto and Windus.

——. 1973 [1961]. *The Long Revolution*. Harmondsworth, UK: Penguin.

Wittgenstein, Ludwig. 1953. *Philosophical Investigations*. Oxford: Blackwell.

Wright, Michelle M. 2004. *Becoming Black: Creating Identity in the African Diaspora*. Durham, NC: Duke University Press.

——. 2013. "'Can I Call You Black?' The Limits of Authentic Heteronormativity in African Diasporic Discourse." *African and Black Diaspora* 6, no. 1: 3–16.

Wynter, Sylvia. 1986. "In Quest of Matthew Bondman: Some Cultural Notes on the Jamesian Journey." In *C. L. R. James: His Life and Work*, ed. Paul Buhle, 131–45. London: Allison and Busby.

——. 1992. "'Beyond the Categories of the Master Conception': The Counterdoctrine of the Jamesian Poiesis." In *C. L. R. James's Caribbean*, ed. Paget Henry and Paul Buhle, 63–91. Durham, NC: Duke University Press.

Yack, Bernard. 1986. *The Longing for Total Revolution: Philosophic Sources of Social Discontent from Rousseau to Marx and Nietzsche*. Berkeley: University of California Press.

Young, James D. 1999. *The World of C. L. R. James: His Unfragmented Vision*. Glasgow: Clydeside.

## CONTRIBUTORS

**ANIMA ADJEPONG** is Assistant Professor of Sociology at Simmons College whose research examines the relationship between cultural practices and the ideologies of race and ethnicity, gender, class, and sexuality. Adjepong has pursued these questions by studying sports and black immigrant communities. Adjepong's published work can be found in edited books and journals, including *Ethnic and Racial Studies* and *Sport in Society*.

**DAVID AUSTIN** teaches in the Department of Humanities, Philosophy and Religion at John Abbott College, Montreal. He is the editor of *You Don't Play with Revolution: The Montreal Lectures of C. L. R. James* and the author of *Fear of a Black Nation: Race, Sex and Security in Sixties Montreal*, as well as numerous articles on black, Caribbean, and African radical and anticolonial politics and thought.

**HILARY MCD. BECKLES** is Professor and Vice-Chancellor at the University of the West Indies. He is the author of *The Development of West Indies Cricket*, a two-volume history of West Indian cricket, and of numerous other studies of the social history of the Caribbean and the histories of slavery and resistance to slavery.

**MICHAEL BREARLEY** was one of the most widely respected England Test captains. Subsequently, he has served as president of the British Psychoanalytic Society and president of the Marylebone Cricket Club. He is a frequent columnist in *The Guardian*, *The Observer*, and *The Times* and the author of another classic cricketing text, *The Art of Captaincy*.

**SELWYN R. CUDJOE** is Professor of Africana Studies at Wellesley College. He is (with William E. Cain) the editor of *C. L. R. James: His Intellectual Legacies* and the author of numerous studies of Caribbean intellectual and cultural history.

**DAVID FEATHERSTONE** is Senior Lecturer in the School of Geographical and Earth Sciences, University of Glasgow. He is the author of *Solidarity: Hidden Histories and Geographies of Internationalism* and of many other studies of black radicalism and subaltern networks of resistance.

**CHRISTOPHER GAIR** is Senior Lecturer in the School of Critical Studies, University of Glasgow. He is the editor of *Beyond Boundaries: C. L. R. James and Postnational Studies*, coeditor of the journal *Symbiosis*, and author of many articles on literature and popular culture in the twentieth century.

**PAGET HENRY** is Professor of Africana Studies and Sociology at Brown University. He is the editor of the *C. L. R. James Journal* and coeditor (with Paul Buhle) of *C. L. R. James's Caribbean* (Duke University Press, 1992). He is the author of numerous other studies of critical theory, political sociology, and the Caribbean intellectual tradition.

**CHRISTIAN HØGSBJERG** is Lecturer in Critical History and Politics at the University of Brighton. He is the author of *C. L. R. James in Imperial Britain*, the editor of *C. L. R. James's Toussaint Louverture: The Story of the Only Successful Slave Revolt in History* and *World Revolution, 1917–1936: The Rise and Fall of the Communist International*, and the coeditor (with Charles Forsdick) of *The Black Jacobins Reader*. All of these titles are part of the Duke University Press C. L. R. James Archives series.

**SELMA JAMES** is an activist and writer. She is the author of, among other pioneering texts, *The Power of Women and the Subversion of the Community* and *Sex, Race and Class*. She was married to C. L. R. James during the period in which *Beyond a Boundary* was written and was responsible for the much of the labor involved in the production of its drafts and redrafts.

**MINKAH MAKALANI** is Associate Professor of African and African Diaspora Studies at the University of Texas, Austin. He is the author of *In the Cause of Freedom: Radical Black Internationalism from Harlem to London* and coeditor (with Davarian Baldwin) of *Escape from New York! The New Negro Movement Reconsidered*.

**ROY MCCREE** is Senior Fellow at the Sir Arthur Lewis Institute of Social and Economic Studies, University of the West Indies, St. Augustine. His research focuses on sports, and he has published several articles on the subject in relation to the media, gender, identity formation, and sports policy.

**CLEM SEECHARAN** is Emeritus Professor of History at London Metropolitan University and the author of numerous books on Caribbean history, including *Muscular Learning; Cricket and Education in the Making of the British West Indies at the End of the 19th Century* and *Hand-in-Hand History of Cricket in Guyana, 1865–97, Volume 1*.

**ANDREW SMITH** is Reader in Sociology at the University of Glasgow. His research focuses on the politics of culture in the context and aftermath of empire. He is the author of *C. L. R. James and the Study of Culture* and *Racism and Everyday Life*.

**NEIL WASHBOURNE** is Senior Lecturer and course leader for the Master of Arts in Media in the School of Cultural Studies and Humanities, Leeds Beckett University. He is the author of *Mediating Politics* and of numerous articles on politics, media, and culture.

**CLAIRE WESTALL** is Senior Lecturer in the Department of English and Related Literature at the University of York. She is author of articles on cricket and literature in *The Cambridge Companion to Cricket* and *The Making of English Popular Culture* and of the forthcoming monograph *The Rites of Cricket and Caribbean Literature*.

# INDEX

Achebe, Chinua, 18, 263
Adams, Sir Grantley, 88, 91
Adelman, Paul, 70n13
Adorno, Theodor, 17
Adut, Ari, 145
African National Congress (ANC), 249
Alexander, Franz Copeland Murray ("Gerry"), 6, 24, 165–69
Alexander, Robert (James's father), 39–40, 141
Ali, Muhammad (Cassius Marcellus Clay), 260
Allen, David, 2
Alleyne, Brian, 177, 182
*American Civilisation* (James), 3, 54, 123, 135, 212–13
Aptheker, Herbert, 197
Arlott, John, 18–19, 75, 85–86
Arnold, Matthew, 46–47, 50n11, 57
Arnold, Thomas, 56–57, 64–65, 100, 138, 144, 175, 238
Atkinson, Denis, 165
Atherton, Michael, 229
Atwell, Winifred, 40, 50n6
Aunt Judith, 124–25, 127, 129–33, 135, 235
Austin, Cyril, 39–40
Austin, Sir H. B. G., 161

Bailey, Trevor, 234
Bannister, Sir Roger, 233
*Barbados Advocate*, 75
Barnsley Cricket Club, 240–42
Bateman, Anthony, 188
Barnes, Natasha, 105, 110
Barnes, Sidney Francis, 52, 265
*Beacon, The*, 161, 173, 197
Beacon Group, 40–41, 71n15
Beckles, Sir Hilary McD., 132, 182, 189, 216
Beldham, William ("Silver Billy"), 235–36
Berenson, Bernhard, 186, 194–96, 198
Berger, John, 21
Bergson, Henri-Louis, 203n2
Besson, Jean, 39, 44
Betancourt, Nelson, 157
*Beyond a Boundary* (James): as autobiography, 4–6, 10–12, 125–27, 140–41, 156–69, 174–78, 206–8, 234–37; process of drafting and naming, 1–2, 23, 51–55, 72–87, 254–61; purchasing of original manuscript by the University of the West Indies, 248–49, 263; use of the conventions of tragedy, 180–83
Birley, Sir Derek, 19
Bishop, Maurice, 244

*Black Jacobins, The* (James), 18, 35, 41–44, 53, 90, 97, 100, 106, 115, 180–81, 206, 255
Blackledge, Paul, 68
Boas, Franz, 197
Bogues, B. Anthony, 91
Bonaparte, Napoleon, 10, 45, 180
Bondman, Matthew, 5–6, 17, 93–98, 100, 106–19, 128, 130–32, 139, 154, 162, 166, 176, 178, 186, 198, 206, 209, 235, 238
Bourdieu, Pierre, 17, 174
Boycott, Geoffrey, 229, 241
Bradman, Sir Donald, 69, 113–14, 176, 180
Brasher, Chris, 233
Brearley, Mike, 29, 101n7
Briggs, Asa, 152n7, 152n8
Brooke, Rupert, 55
Buchanan, John, 228
Buck-Morss, Susan, 180
Buhle, Paul, 178, 204
Burgin, Andrew, 69, 70n3
Bustamante, Sir Alexander, 163
Butcher, Roland, 232–33

calypso, 98–100, 114, 209
*Capital: A Critique of Political Economy* (Marx), 54, 63, 68, 71n9, 200
Carby, Hazel, 125, 127–28, 183
Cardus, Sir Neville, 8, 13, 57–61, 65, 70n11, 75, 185, 198, 238–39
Carlyle, Thomas, 57, 176–77
Carnival, 98–99, 209
Carrington, Ben, 9, 125, 127, 133–34, 136n2, 136n3
Casson, Stanley, 197
*Case for West Indian Self-Government, The* (James), 42
Castoriadis, Cornelius, 71n18
Castro, Fidel, 97
Césaire, Aimé, 46
Challenor, George, 176, 186

Chaplin, Sir Charles ("Charlie"), 227
Chappell, Ian, 229
Chappell, Greg, 229
Chataway, Sir Christopher, 233
Chen, Eugene, 35
Chesterton, G. K., 57
*Children of Sisyphus, The* (Patterson), 112
Cicero, 245
Cipriani, Captain Arthur Andrew, 41–42, 147, 158, 183
Cliffe, Lionel, viii
Close, Brian, 2
Cobley, Alan, 253
Colás, Santiago, 183
Cole, G. D. H., 57, 70n10
Collins, Tony, 63–65, 67–68
Compton, Denis, 52, 265
Connor, Steve, 151n3
*Conscripts of Modernity: The Tragedy of Colonial Enlightenment* (Scott), 70n5, 176
Constabulary Cricket Club, 126, 156
Constantine, Elias, 157
Constantine, Learie (Baron Constantine), 3, 5, 7, 14, 25, 55, 69, 81, 110, 140–41, 143, 147, 153, 156–69, 176, 178–79, 182, 186–87, 224, 237, 245, 255, 263–65
Constantine, Lebrun, 156, 161, 237
"Cousin" Cudjoe, 6, 107, 142, 178
Cowdrey, Colin (Baron Cowdrey of Tonbridge), 2
Cox, Oliver Cromwell, 35
*Cricket and I* (Constantine), 158, 160, 167
*Cricket Crackers* (Constantine), 167
*Cricket in the Sun* (Constantine), 163, 167
Cudjoe, Selwyn, 107

*Daily Gleaner, The*, 75
*Daily Telegraph, The*, 145–46, 150
Darwin, Charles, 57, 225

*David Copperfield* (Dickens), 4
Davidson, Basil, 263
Davis, Angela, 129
Dessalines, Jean-Jacques, 106
*Development of West Indies Cricket, Volumes 1 and 2, The* (Beckles), 253
"Dialectical Materialism and the Fate of Humanity" (James), 199–201
Dibb, Mike, 224, 239n2
Dickens, Charles, 3–4, 47, 57, 94, 175
Dockworker's Strike (Trinidad, 1919), 7
D'Oliveira, Basil, 29, 31n14
Douglass, Frederick, 197
Douglin, Canon Philip, 42–43
Du Bois, W. E. B., 18, 219
Dumas, Alexandre, 45–46
Dunayevskaya, Raya, 199
Dussel, Enrique, 92

Eagleton, Terry, 66
Ehrenburg, Ilya, 263
1895 (W. G. Grace's *annus mirabilis*), 61, 137–38, 143–47, 150–51
Einstein, Albert, 225
Elias, Norbert, 73–74
Eliot, George (pseud. for Mary Anne Evans), 57
Eliot, T. S., 66, 100, 175, 213
Escobar, Arturo, 100

*Facing Reality* (James), 219
Factory Act (1847), 63
Fanon, Frantz, 18, 46–47, 103, 118, 133–35, 189–90
Farred, Grant, 95, 173, 177
Fingleton, J. H. ("Jack"), 74, 78
Fletcher, Keith, 229
*42: The Jackie Robinson Story* (film), 136n5
Francis, George, 182
Frankfurt School, 14, 17

Fraser, Cyril, 157
Fraser, George MacDonald, 13
Freud, Sigmund, 225
Fromm, Erich, 199
Froude, J. A., 10, 46–48
*Froudacity* (Thomas), 42
Fry, C. B., 146

Gadamer, Hans-Georg, 202
Galeano, Eduardo, 260
Garvey, Marcus, 46–47, 162
Gaskin, Berkeley, 166
Gavaskar, Sunil ("Sunny"), 229
Gayle, Chris, 250–51
Gibbs, Lance, 247
Gikandi, Simon, 88
Gilchrist, Roy, 166–67, 169
Gilroy, Paul, 16, 17
*Glasgow Herald, The*, 8, 12, 52
Glaberman, Martin, 55–56, 67
Gloucestershire County Cricket Club, 145–46, 150
Goddard, John, 165
Goethe, Johann Wolfgang von, 176
Golden Age (of cricket), 3, 8, 146
Goldie, Grace Wyndham, 258, 261n8
Gooch, Graham, 229–31, 234
Gordon, Avery, 130
Gower, David, 234
Grace, W. G., 3–5, 9, 11, 15, 24, 52, 56–61, 64–65, 68–69, 70n10, 80–81, 94, 100, 137, 142–47, 150–51, 176, 185, 215, 224–25, 230, 256, 261n4, 263, 265
Grant, Jack, 162
Grant, Rolf, 163
Gray, Thomas, 55
Greenidge, Gordon, 247
Gregg, Robert, 13
Grenadian Revolution, 106, 119n3, 244
Griffith, Sir Charles Christopher ("Charlie"), 2

Grimshaw, Anna, 168
Grygiénć, Janusz, 152n10
Guha, Ramachandra, 19

Haitian Revolution, 37, 53, 90, 97, 106, 119n3, 180, 244–45
Hall, Stuart, vii–viii, 8, 19, 125, 212
Hall, Sir Wesley Winfield ("Wes"), 2, 166, 247–48
*Hamlet* (Shakespeare), 180
Hammond, J. L., 57
Hammond, Wally, 196
*Hard Times* (Dickens), 3
Hardy, Thomas, 55
Harrington, Bertie, 161
Harris, Sir Theodore Wilson, 207, 213
Hartmann, Douglass, 125–26
Haynes, Desmond, 247
Hazlitt, William, 7, 47, 50n11, 52, 59–60, 175, 265
Headley, George, 5, 140, 147, 163, 180, 223
Hector, Tim, 216–18
Hegel, G. W. F., 174, 176, 180–81, 183, 256
Heller, Agnes, 199
Henry, Paget, 148
*Henry V* (Shakespeare), 180
*Hero in History, The* (Hook), 188
Herodotus, 214
Hill, Robert A., viii, 67
*History of Negro Revolt, A* (James), 18
*History of West Indies Cricket, A* (Manley), 246, 249
Hobbs, Sir John Berry ("Jack"), 52, 57, 265
Hobsbawm, Eric, 35
Høgsbjerg, Christian, 50n11, 197, 203n2, 255, 263
Holding, Michael, 229, 248
Hook, Sidney, 188
hooks, bell (pseud. for Gloria Jean Watkins), 20

Howe, Darcus, viii, 159–60
Howe, Stephen, 54
Hughes, Langston, 94
Hughes, Thomas, 56, 62, 64–65, 100, 138, 144, 175
*Humming Bird*, 98
Hungarian Revolution, 24, 67
Hutchinson (publisher), 73, 76–87, 101n9, 254–55
Hutton, Sir Leonard ("Len"), 258–59

Illingworth, Raymond ("Ray"), 229
*In the Castle of My Skin* (Lamming), 76, 254–55
Iton, Richard, 102n13, 103, 111, 116–18

Jackson, Michael, 251
James, C. L. R.: and Africa, 43–44, 90, 92, 95, 96–99, 107–8, 112–19, 154, 157; and anti-colonialism, 6–9, 12–13, 17–18, 20, 52, 79, 83–84, 88–91, 98, 125–27, 139, 147–48, 155, 173, 180–81, 188–90, 210–12, 216, 223, 252, 265; and the campaign for Worrell's captaincy, 5–6, 24, 147–48, 153, 164–69, 173, 197, 223–24, 237, 242, 252, 258–60, 261n10; and Caribbean intellectual history, 35–49, 83, 85, 87–102, 153–54, 173, 185, 207–8, 215–16; and civilizational theory, 9–10, 51–69, 149, 182–83, 213–20; and classical civilizations, 62, 100, 108, 175, 179–80, 187, 214–15, 245, 256; and cricket's artistic qualities, 8, 21, 24, 89–90, 94, 100, 109–10, 149, 173, 179, 182–83, 185–90, 193–203, 214, 256; and cricket's representative role, 15–17, 57–69, 125–27, 137–52, 173–90, 194–96, 214–20, 256; and English culture, 2–4, 7, 9, 41, 43, 45–48, 51–69, 81, 85, 87–102, 106–9, 143–44, 154–55, 207–8, 214–16, 223–24, 236, 265; and

290 | Index

gender politics, 15, 123–36, 138, 177, 183–84, 186; and Marxism, 8, 10–13, 17, 20, 24, 54, 62–64, 66–68, 90–92, 97, 100, 111, 113, 148, 155, 168, 173–74, 176, 188–89, 199–203, 212, 218, 245, 256–57; on the "welfare state of mind," 66–67, 176, 203; on "world historical figures," 174–90

James, Elizabeth (James's mother), 40, 44, 108, 124

James, Selma, 83, 97, 114, 136n4, 155

Jameson, Fredric, 19

John, Errol, 182

John, George, 95–96, 98, 140, 178, 181–82

Johnson, W. Chris, 128

Johnson-Forest Tendency, 261n5

Jones, Arthur, 5–6, 96, 131, 178, 186, 206, 235, 238

Jones, Claudia, 52

Kamugisha, Aaron, 123

Kanhai, Rohan, 187, 247, 265

Kermode, Sir Frank, 257

Kierkegaard, Søren, 226

*King Lear* (Shakespeare), 114

King, Nicole, 152n6, 177–78

Kipling, Rudyard, 9, 55, 81, 98, 223, 228, 260

Kuhn, Thomas, 225

*Lagaan* (film), 260

Lambert, David, 69n1

Lamming, George, 76, 82–83, 86, 89, 98, 207, 248–49, 254–55, 263

Lara, Brian, 189, 250–51

Larkin, Philip, 1–2

Laski, H. J., 57

Lawson, Sir Edward, 146

Lazarus, Neil, 67, 181–82, 216

Leavis, F. R., 175, 261n1

Lee, Grace, 199

Lefebvre, Henri, 199, 201

Lewis, Gordon K., 156

Lenin, V. I., 188–89

Liddelow, G., 157

*Life and Adventures of Martin Chuzzlewit* (Dickens), 4

*Life of Captain Cipriani, The* (James), 41–42, 158, 206, 210–12

Lindwall, Ray, 196

*Listener, The* (Oxford), 197

de Loppinot, Charles Joseph, 37

Lorca, Federico García, 100

Lorde, Audre, 104, 118n2

Louverture, Toussaint, 10, 12, 90, 97, 106, 180–81, 183, 245

Lukács, Georg, 67

Lusty, Sir Robert, 76–84, 86, 245

Macaulay, Lord Thomas Babington, 57

Macheray, Pierre, 36

MacLaren, Archibald Campbell ("Archie"), 146

Main, Thomas Forrest ("Tom"), 231

Maldonado-Torres, Nelson, 92

Mallendar, Neil, 246

*Manchester Guardian, The* 8

Manley, Michael, 24, 105, 246–47, 249, 253

Manley, Norman, 89, 163

Maple Cricket Club, 7, 94–95, 126–27, 140, 150, 156–60, 168, 179, 223

Marable, Manning, 10, 12, 52, 57

Maran, René, 46

*Mariners, Renegades, and Castaways* (James), 3, 182, 213, 257, 216n6

Marqusee, Mike, viii

Marley, Robert Nesta ("Bob"), 104, 118n1, 249

Marshall, Sir, Roy, 246

Marx, Karl, 63, 65, 68, 100, 114, 148, 174, 200, 203, 210

Marylebone Cricket Club, 24, 29, 137, 145, 162, 217, 258–59
Mason, Peter, 160
Mbembe, Achille, 99
McClintock, Anne, 134
McGilvray, Alan, 244
Melville, Herman, 4, 114, 182, 213
Mercer, David, 263
Merry, Cyril, 264
Michelangelo, di Lodovico Buonarroti Simoni, 224, 235–36
Mighty Sparrow (pseud. for Slinger Francisco), 98–99, 114
Mignolo, Walter, 92, 124
Milburn, Colin, 234
Miller, Paul, 183
Milton, John, 52, 55, 265
*Minty Alley* (James), 35, 41, 53, 114, 173, 177, 183, 206–10
*Mirror, The* (Trinidad), 40
*Moby Dick* (Melville), 4; 216n6
*Modern Politics* (James), 219
*Modern Times* (film), 227
Montalembert, Baron de (Jean Charles), 37
*Moon on a Rainbow Shawl* (John), 182
Morrison, Toni, 123
Morton, A. L., 70n10
Motohashi, Ted, vii
Moxon, Martin, 240, 246
Mozart, W. A., 234
Murdoch, Iris, 263
Murray, J. Middleton, 57
*My Life: An Attempt at an Autobiography* (Trotsky), 10–11

Naha, Souvik, 132
Naipaul, Sir Vidiadhar Surajprasad ("Vidia"), 12, 21–22, 35, 51, 56, 61, 99–100, 173, 207
Nandy, Ashis, 103–4, 115

*Nation*, 23–24, 44, 147–48, 153, 166–67, 224, 259
Nauright, John, 253
Nelson Cricket Club, 7, 159, 255
*Netherland* (O'Neill), 260
Nettleford, Ralston Milton ("Rex"), 105
Ngũgĩ wa Thiong'o, 18
Nielsen, Aldon Lynn, 177
*Nkrumah and the Ghana Revolution* (James), 219
Nkrumah, Kwame, 44, 264
*Notes on Dialectics* (James), 183–84, 192, 219, 256
*Notes Towards the Definition of Culture* (Eliot), 66
Nyren, John, 67

Oborne, Peter, 19
O'Brien, John, 45
O'Brien, Conor Cruise, 263
O'Neill, Joseph, 260
*On Heroes, Hero Worship, and the Heroic in History* (Carlyle), 176

Padmore, George (pseud. for Malcolm Nurse), 9, 35, 46–47, 49
*Party Politics in the West Indies* (James), 24, 44, 219
Pascall, Victor, 157
Patterson, Orlando, 14, 112, 207
People's National Movement (PNM), 40, 44, 88, 98, 147–48, 166, 224, 262n10, 263
*Philadelphia Negro, The* (Du Bois), 219
Philip, Michel Maxwell, 41–43, 45, 47–48
Phillips, Caryl, 22, 179
*Philosophy of History, The* (Hegel), 184–85
Picton, Sir Thomas, 37
Piggott (Stingo Cricket Club wicket-keeper), 178
Pindar, 214

Plato, 214, 233, 238
*Port of Spain Gazette*, 40
Postgate, Raymond, 57, 70n10
Powell, Enoch, 241
Pythagoras, 214

Queensbury, 9th Marquess of (John Douglas), 145
Queen's Park Cricket Club, 6–7, 126, 140, 156–57, 167
Queen's Royal College, 4–5, 41, 64, 107, 140, 156, 163, 191, 207, 238

Rabbit, Kara, 180–81
Radley, Clive, 232–33
Rae, Alan, 248
Ramadhin, Sonny, 245, 247
Ranjitsinhji, K. S., 146
Rastafari, 100, 112, 114, 116
Read, Sir Herbert, 57
Reform Act (1867), 62, 70n13
reggae, 104, 112, 114, 249
Reddock, Rhoda, 135
*Republic* (Plato), 238
Rhodes, Cecil, 57
Richards, Sir Isaac Vivian Alexander ("Viv"), 133, 217, 245, 247
Richardson, Joanna, 70n7
Roach, Clifford, 7, 157, 160, 264
Roberts, Sir Anderson Montgomery Everton ("Andy"), 217, 247
Robinson, Cedric, 13, 111
Robinson, Jack Roosevelt ("Jackie"), 136n5
Robinson, Rachel, 136n5
Rodney, Walter, 102n12
Rohlehr, Gordon, 115
Rosengarten, Frank, viii, 12, 54, 66
Ross, Alan, 13
Rousseau, Jean-Jacques, 114, 137, 148–49, 151

Rudder, Josh, 37, 39, 142, 178, 236–37
Russell, Bertrand Arthur William (3rd Earl Russell), 263

Said, Edward, 19
Sackville-West, Vita (Lady Nicolson), 57
St. Hill, Cyril, 157
St. Hill, Edwin, 157
St. Hill, Wilton, 7, 69, 95, 139, 141–42, 151n4, 157–59, 181, 186, 206, 260
Sammy, Darren, 251
Sanford, Adam, 261n2
Sartre, Jean-Paul, 245, 263
Saward, Michael, 139, 149–50
Schwarz, Bill, 52, 54–55, 173
Scott, David, 9, 70n5, 119n3, 176, 179–80
Sealey, Ben, 157
Seecharan, Clem, 239
Selassie, Emperor Haile, 118n1
Shakespeare, William, 47, 52, 55, 100, 114, 118, 175, 179–80, 224, 265
Shange, Ntozake, 123
Shango, 43, 108, 116, 119n5
Shannon Cricket Club, 7, 94–95, 126–27, 140–41, 153–69, 223–24, 230, 237
Shelley, Percy Bysshe, 52, 175, 265
Sheppard, David (Baron Sheppard of Liverpool), 29
Shamrock Cricket Club, 126, 140, 156
Singh, Charran, 167
Siparia Cricket Club, 140
Small, Joe, 157
Smith, Andrew, 151n1, 151n3, 151n4, 151n5, 152n8, 174, 178–79, 204
Smith, O'Neil Gordon ("Collie"), 166, 187
Smith, Ed, 13
Smith, Ernest James ("Tiger"), 230
Smith, Mike, 232–33
Sobers, Sir Garfield St. Aubrun ("Garry"), 15, 89, 92–93, 95, 97–98, 101n7, 166, 187–88, 216, 242, 248

*Soccer in Sun and Shadow* (Galeano), 260
*Social Contract, The* (Rousseau), 148
Socrates, 214, 223–26, 233
Soyinka, Wole, 263
Spengler, Oswald, 66, 70
*Sportsman, The*, 145
Springfield, Consuelo Lopez, 10, 50n11
Stampfl, Franz, 233–34
*State Capitalism and World Revolution* (James), 212
Stingo Cricket Club, 6, 95, 126, 140, 156–57
Stoddart, Brian, 183–84
Stollmeyer, Conrad, 70n15
Stollmeyer, Jeffrey Baxter ("Jeff"), 71n15, 165, 264
Stollmeyer, Victor, 71n15, 264
Stowe, Harriet Beecher, 3–4
Strachey, Lytton, 57
Suez Crisis, The, 23, 67
*Sunday Times, The*, 257
Surin, Kenneth, 15–17, 54, 65, 67–68, 183, 188

Tacarigua-Arouca area (Trinidad), 36–40, 43, 50n7
Telemaque (Stingo cricketer), 7, 142
Tennyson, Lord Alfred, 57
Thackeray, W. M., 3, 11, 57, 94, 100, 175, 178, 206
*Theory and Practice of Creole Grammar, The* (Thomas), 42
Thomas, J. J., 37, 42–43, 46–47
Thompson, E. P., 4, 66, 183
Tiffin, Helen, 13, 53, 173
*Times Literary Supplement*, 61–62
Tolstoy, Count Lyov ("Leo"), 56, 186
Tomlinson, Richard, 26n4
*Tom Brown's Schooldays* (Hughes), 62, 64, 175
Trevelyan, G. M., 57, 67

*Trinidad Chronicle*, 40
*Trinidad Guardian*, 40
Tronchin, L. B., 47–48
Trouillot, Michel-Rolph, 91–92, 103, 106
Trotsky, Leon, 2, 8, 10–12, 62, 68–69
Tunapuna Cricket Club, 131, 140, 235
Turim, Maureen, 94
Twenty 20 Cricket, 2–3, 16–18, 20, 251–52

*Uncle Tom's Cabin* (Stowe), 3–4
uneven and combined development, 10–11, 68, 91–92, 99
University of Hull, 240, 245–46
University of the West Indies, 70n3, 73, 89, 238, 242–43, 246–53

Valentine, Alfred Louis ("Alf"), 245, 261n2
Valere, Gloria, 159–60
*Vanity Fair* (Thackeray), 3, 175, 178–79, 206, 236
Vickers, Sir Geoffrey, 67

Walcott, Sir Clyde Leopold, 8, 164–65, 168, 186–87, 243, 265
Walcott, C. M. Harclyde, 189
Walcott, Sir Derek Alton, 20, 110
Walker, Alice, 123
Warner, Robert Stewart Aucher, 95
Warner, Charles, 47–48
Waugh, Steve, 228–29
Webb, Constance, 52, 12, 155, 168
Weekes, Sir Everton DeCourcy, 8, 110, 164–65, 168, 186, 243, 248
Weinstein, Sam, 258–59
Welsch, Wolfgang, 21
West, Cornel, 19–20
West Indian Tour of Australia, 1961, 153, 168–69, 259
West Indian Tour of England, 1957, 165, 168, 205, 264–65

West Indian Tour of England, 1963, 79–80
West, Dame Rebecca, 57
Wheen, Francis, 64
Wilberforce, William, 246
Wilde, Oscar, 138, 145–6
Wiles, C. A., 157
Williams, Eric, 24–25, 35, 40, 44, 88, 98–99, 147, 153, 166, 224, 259, 262n10, 264
Williams, Henry Sylvester, 35, 42–43
Williams, Raymond, 19, 66
Williams, Rowan (Baron Williams of Oystermouth), 231
Willey, Peter, 230
Wittgenstein, Ludwig, 225–26

Wodehouse, Sir Pelham Grenville ("P. G."), 175
Woods, Joseph ("Float"), 95
Worcester, Kent, 179
Wordsworth, William, 67, 158, 175
*World Revolution* (James), 206
Worrell, Sir Frank Mortimer Maglinne, 1, 3, 5, 6, 8–9, 17, 24, 81, 95, 110, 140, 143, 147, 153–69, 173, 186, 197, 223–25, 230–31, 237, 241–42, 245, 249, 252, 259
*Wretched of the Earth, The* (Fanon), 189
Wright, Michelle, 128
Wynter, Sylvia, 90–91, 95–96, 103, 107, 112–15, 212, 218

Young, Juanita, 155

CPSIA information can be obtained
at www.ICGtesting.com
Printed in the USA
JSHW032204020520
5459JS00004B/168